Women Faculty of Color
in the White Classroom

Higher Ed

Questions about the Purpose(s) of Colleges & Universities

Norm Denzin, Josef Progler, Joe L. Kincheloe, Shirley R. Steinberg
General Editors

Vol. 7

PETER LANG
New York • Washington, D.C./Baltimore • Bern
Frankfurt am Main • Berlin • Brussels • Vienna • Oxford

Women Faculty of Color
in the White Classroom

Narratives on the Pedagogical
Implications of Teacher Diversity

EDITED BY
Lucila Vargas

PETER LANG
New York • Washington, D.C./Baltimore • Bern
Frankfurt am Main • Berlin • Brussels • Vienna • Oxford

Library of Congress Cataloging-in-Publication Data

Women faculty of color in the white classroom: narratives on
the pedagogical implications of teacher diversity / edited by Lucila Vargas.
p. cm. — (Higher ed; vol. 7)
Includes bibliographical references and index.
1. Afro-American women college teachers. 2. Discrimination in higher
education—United States. 3. Sex discrimination in higher education—United
States. 4. Multicultural education—United States. I. Vargas, Lucila. II. Series.
LB2332.32. W66   378.1′2′08996073—dc21   2001029036
ISBN 0-8204-4994-6
ISSN 1523-9551

Die Deutsche Bibliothek-CIP-Einheitsaufnahme

Women faculty of color in the white classroom: narratives on
the pedagogical implications of teacher diversity / ed. by: Lucila Vargas.
–New York; Washington, D.C./Baltimore; Bern;
Frankfurt am Main; Berlin; Brussels; Vienna; Oxford: Lang.
(Higher ed; Vol. 7)
ISBN 0-8204-4994-6

Cover watercolor by Alpha Elena Escobedo
Cover design by Lisa Dillon

The paper in this book meets the guidelines for permanence and durability
of the Committee on Production Guidelines for Book Longevity
of the Council of Library Resources.

Printed in the United States of America

Para ti Maye

CONTENTS

❧ ACKNOWLEDGMENTS

EDITING THIS BOOK was a rewarding experience because of the intellectual and emotional support I received from many people. I learned a great deal about pedagogy and also about myself as both a teacher and a person from the stimulating dialogue with the contributors to the anthology and with the faculty who participated in my earlier research on the topic. I also gained much insight from students and colleagues at Chapel Hill, who helped me think through difficult issues. To each and every one of them, thank you very much. I especially would like to express my gratitude to Kristina Casto, my bright and dutiful research assistant; to Ryuko Kubota, my supportive colleague; and to Jennifer Drolet, my copyeditor. Finally, thanks to the institutions that provided material support for the project: the School of Journalism and Mass Communication and the University Research Council of the University of North Carolina at Chapel Hill.

Thanks to *The Urban Review* for kindly granting permission to reproduce parts of the essay, "When the 'Other' Is the Teacher: Implications of Teacher Diversity in Higher Education" (1999, *The Urban Review* 34. 3, pp. 359–383).

CHAPTER ONE

Introduction

LUCILA VARGAS

> It is an effect of history that in the academy, the voice of authority is distinctly male, white, and privileged. The implications are salient for teachers who do not reflect this social profile and particularly for those who, at the same time, are committed to the unveiling of the hegemony that configures the authoritative voices/discourses of traditional disciplines.
>
> —Magda Lewis (1999, 73)

THIS ANTHOLOGY COMPILES work narratives exploring the intricate dialectic of the self of woman faculty of color and the culture of the predominantly White college classroom. The anthology is about the unique pedagogical challenges faced by professors who look, and are, very different from the typical professor of the predominantly White U.S. campus. It is also about how we meet these challenges and find rewards in our teaching-learning. The anthology is guided by a basic question: What is it like for women of color to teach in predominantly White college classrooms? Thus the anthology also explores the larger problematic of how social distinctions shape classroom social life and teacher-student interactions.

This project began with a profound feeling of alienation. When I joined the ranks of assistant professors of predominantly White campuses, I was not prepared for the classroom challenges I would encounter. Despite over ten years of teaching-learning in predominantly White classrooms, I found myself reading everything I could on instructional techniques. I did learn something from these materials, but quite soon I turned to the literature on campus diversity, guided by a hunch that what I was dealing with was not a personal technical deficiency but a socio-political problem. In reading works on campus diversity, however, I noticed that they often address an intended reader who is White, and sometimes, White and male. There is a pervasive assumption in this literature that those who need to learn how to meet the challenges of the diversified college classroom are, primarily, White faculty. I had to dig very deep to find readings that spoke to teachers like me.

My initial hunch about the complex nature of the problem at hand was anchored in gatherings with other faculty of color, where I learned that we shared similar classroom experiences. It was also anchored in eye-opening findings about the status of women faculty of color in U.S. colleges and universities (see Chapter 2). Many women teachers of color are hired only as lecturers and part-timers; many never make it to the prized tenure-track positions. Only very few such assistant professors gain tenure. Indeed, at 54 percent, women faculty of color have a dismal tenure rate, the lowest among all faculty, and far lower than the 79 percent tenure rate of White male professors (Wilds and Wilson 1998, 41–43).

My search, then, shifted to critical pedagogical writings. This literature helped me see the classroom as a contested terrain and also helped me start making sense of the feelings I had. Ultimately, I concluded with Ellen Ellsworth (1989) that many of these writings assume a teacher far more powerful than I perceived myself to be. This assumption, I thought, is especially problematic when the teacher is a woman of color, because institutional discourses bestowing teachers with authority carry ambivalent statements about women of color. These discourses are so pervasive on the predominantly White campus that they have become "normal" as Erving Goffman would say (1963).

In my bibliographic journey I found dispersed, but nonetheless numerous, calls from scholars who for nearly twenty years have been alerting the academic community to the burden imposed by cultural mythology on women professors of color. As early as 1982, Jacqueline Jordan Irvine wrote:

> Many Black academic women complain that they are victimized for simply "not looking the part" and that they are limited by racist and sexist conceptions that depict the scholar and academic as White and male. Some students and faculty assume that every Black female on campus is a member of the custodial or clerical staff. Others assume that the Black woman faculty member was hired as a result of imposed affirmative action pressures—a "two for one," satisfying the demands of Blacks and women for more representation. Some of her peers believe that she will be rewarded in the institution simply because she is Black and female. (1982, 114)

References to the unique challenges created by the signs of gender, class, race, ethnicity, and nation inscribed in the bodies of women faculty of color kept surfacing in my readings on campus diversity. Although my search yielded a growing body of research on the topic, I found that most of the research on minority faculty dealt with institutional rather than classroom concerns. Then I turned to feminist scholarship. Feminist researchers have collected sound empirical evidence on the impact of gender in classroom practices (Wheary and Ennis 1995). They have also discussed the unique pedagogical challenges faced by feminist faculty, the rearrangement of classroom dynamics that occurs when a feminist instructs the class, and the ways in which feminist teachers re-vision and reorganize their classes (Lewis 1990). Nonetheless, while White feminist researchers have indeed looked at the pedagogical implications of the gender of faculty members, they have often neglected other social differences (Bronstein 1993). It is only recently that works paying specific attention to the multiple group memberships of women professors of color have begun to appear (Christian-Smith and Kellor 1999). For example, Frances A. Maher and Mary Kay Thomson-Tetreault (1994), in their ethnographic investigation of feminist classrooms, talk about how social distinctions shape classroom social life:

> The diversity of the classroom environments we have studied has shown us that position, perhaps more than any other single factor, influences the construction of knowledge, and that positional factors reflect relationships of power both within and outside the classroom itself. It has made an important difference in our study, for example, whether teachers and students were male or female, white or African American, heterosexual or lesbian. And those differences have varied according to the history, region, experiences, and "cultural practices" that brought participants to each classroom and positioned them there. (1994, 22)

I found these comments on positionality particularly germane to my inquiry, and they are at the core of the anthology. As defined by Maher and Thomsom-Tetreault, positionality is a "kind of 'metaknowledge,' locating yourself in relation to others within social structures, such as the classroom, that recreates and mediates those relationships" (1994, 202). This "metaknowledge" helped me to use my feeling of alienation for a qualitative research project based on semi-structured interviews with women faculty of color (see Chapter 3). My analysis of these interviews suggested that each professor's experience is unique. It varies according to personal characteristics and academic rank; it also varies according to contextual differences, such as discipline, type and size of classes taught, academic unit, and gender composition of the unit's faculty. Each of the participants in my research talked about her own experience in a quite different voice. Most thought that the interplay of their gender with their race/ethnicity/nation made a difference in their classroom, but two of the participants disagreed: "The type of classes I teach are conceptual—the students have little need to examine other aspects of my role," said one of these professors. Consequently, in the process of conducting this research it became clear that the best method for the problem I was trying to tackle was an approach that would allow examination of the teaching-learning experiences of women faculty of color without stripping these experiences of their specificity and situatedness.

Our Narratives

Feminist research highlighting issues of positionality is invaluable for investigating the problematic that we tackle in this anthology (see, for example, Talburt 2000). Our writing, however, better fits the tradition of reflective inquiry pursued by the critical feminist academics we cite throughout the anthology. Thus, we have drawn on postmodern approaches to ethnography to explore an intricate and opaque problematic (Ellis and Boshner 1996). These methods have been extensively used in educational research, including research on the experience of women in educational institutions (Chase 1995). These approaches have also been regarded in recent years as powerful tools for investigating social interaction and lived experiences (Angrosino 1989; Conquerwood 1991; Denzin 1989, 1997; Ellis 1997; Van Manen 1990). Furthermore, reflective approaches have also been regarded as particularly powerful for exploring how class, race, ethnicity, gender, sexuality, and nation are experienced by women in specific social contexts and locations (Anderson and Hill Collins 1995; Braine 1999).

Nonetheless, it is well known that some positivist researchers still view autobiographic methods with suspicion. In an interview conducted in 1986, Gayatri Chakravorty Spivak responded to these criticisms, bringing to light the epistemological incongruity of the argument against autobiography. She said:

> If one looks at the history of post-Enlightenment theory, the major problem has been the problem of autobiography: how subjective structures can, in fact, give objective truth. During these same centuries, the Native informant (was) treated as the objective evidence for the founding of so-called sciences like ethnography, ethnolinguistics, comparative religion, and so on. So that, once again, the theoretical problems only related to the person who knows. The person who *knows* has all of the problems of selfhood. The person who is *known* somehow seems to not have a problematic self (quoted in Suleri 1996, 343).

This anthology relies on the power of interpretive autobiography and other postmodern methods that use lived experience as a resource for apprehending social reality. The anthology compiles critical, self-reflexive texts that seek to shed light on the way a woman faculty of color experiences her interactions with students and the social life of her classroom. Despite the

fact that not all contributors would consider themselves feminists, all the essays assume feminist (standpoint) epistemologies. These epistemologies posit
that knowledge and knowing are predicated on one's positionality and identity, on the way one both constitutes oneself and is constituted by others.
Feminist epistemologies also view the interplay of one's gender, age, class,
sexuality, race, ethnicity, body, family, and nation as the footing for consciousness and cognition. Asserting that this interplay is the working surface
for all cognitive work, these epistemologies postulate that different social
groups experience the world from different standpoints, and, therefore, that
all claims to knowledge are partial and situated (Hill Collins 1991; Harding
1991; Moraga and Anzaldúa 1981).

The contributions to this anthology are autoethnographic texts. As
Carolyn Ellis explains, autoethnography is as "a turning of the ethnographic
gaze inward on the self (auto), while maintaining the outward gaze of ethnography, looking at the larger context wherein self experiences occur" (Ellis and
Boshner 1996, 227). Our texts are based on memory and documents; we
combined our own (and sometimes others') recollections of classroom events
with documents and archival material, such as memos, reports, letters, class
notes, school publications, newsclips, peer observations, and student evaluations of our teaching. Trying to be as faithful as possible to our classroom experiences, we reflected on these materials to identify patterns of meaning in
the events and processes that stand up in our memory. Lisa Chavez puts it
nicely in her essay: "I recreate classroom scenes to tell you a certain kind of
truth, to recreate how they felt to me, one very subjective human being. I
can't pretend the dialogue or detail is exact, but I can give you my story as a
woman of color teaching in predominantly White institutions, and what I
learned from that."

All the essays are interpretive and self-reflective narratives, but they are
very different from each other. Since we come from different cultures and
were trained in different fields, we recontextualize our experiential knowledge in light of different knowledges, different bodies of literature; we use
metaphors from different discourses to make sense of our personal teaching-
learning experience. Likewise, although all contributors juxtapose emotion
and analysis, we speak in different narrative voices; while some contributors
make use of dialogue and other creative forms of writing, other contributors
rely on more traditional ways of writing the social science text. However, although we have produced different texts, we went through similar research
and writing processes while writing these essays. Delores Black-Connor
Cleary begins her essay by stating: "I am hesitant to put myself forward or to
recount narratives of my experiences as an exemplar for others." Rashmi

Luthra says: "I have been writing for more than ten years, and yet this essay has been particularly difficult to write." Their comments resonate in many of the essays and in our e-mail conversations from the project's on-line discussion group. It was hard to write these essays for a number of reasons. None of us had done autoethnographic research before, and the level of self-disclosure that this project asked from us was unsettling at times. In particular, the project asked us to make public some of our student evaluations, an act of self-disclosure that many professors would dread. In Chapter 12, Zeinabu irene Davis explains why she ventured to make public at her institution the racist and sexist comments written in a recent evaluation of her course. She says: "This is not an easy choice—I hate rehashing these comments, but I feel that it is important that other faculty and the administration know that this is going on." Furthermore, the exercise of reflecting in a systematic way on our teaching-learning experience forced us into the unexpected. It forced us to delve into feelings that, perhaps, we did not want to acknowledge. It also forced us to probe our own assumptions about our pedagogies and teaching-learning practices. And it forced us to examine, as fairly as we could, the impact of systems of inequality on our classrooms, our work experience, and our teaching-learning selves.

The experiential knowledge on which we base our reflections comes from years of work experience in predominantly White institutions of higher learning. Most of the essays were written by faculty with more than five years of full-time teaching-learning experience. Being beyond the initiation phase of our careers as college professors is important. We have the experiential knowledge necessary to distinguish between those events and feelings that seem to be part and parcel of the work experience of the novice professor (Boice 1992) and those that seem to be specific to the work experience of women faculty of color. To eliminate other confounding variables, the anthology limits itself to contributions from scholars in two areas with a relatively high proportion of women: the humanities and the social sciences. Also, since the anthology is about the predominantly White college classroom, it does not include essays from faculty teaching in Tribal colleges, all-women colleges, or historically Black colleges. Despite these parameters, the anthology contains a rich variety of experiences because there are great differences among the contributors. The sixteen essays come from both U.S. native-born and immigrant faculty whose academic ranks cover the spectrum from lecturer to full professor.

Finally, there are two caveats regarding methodological matters. First, the main focus here is on the teacher's understanding of the way her students perceive her and her performance, rather than on students' views. The narratives contain many student voices, but these are not students' views *per se;* we, the authors, have selectively chosen quotes from documents to make a particular point or to illustrate a given argument. Students' views on the issues at hand are extremely important, and they should be the focus of further research, but they are beyond the problematic addressed in this anthology. Second, like other qualitative research, our research is not about generalizing. Some women professors of color might not identify with any of the teaching-learning experiences that we describe. We hope that they will make the time in their busy schedules to reflect upon their own experiences and that they will share those reflections with the wider academic community.

A Note on Terminology

In my earlier research on the topic, I used the term "Other Teacher" to talk about minority women faculty, and the expression became the initial reference for the anthology. The term "Other" has been widely used in feminist (de Beauvoir 1961) and postcolonial writings (Bhabha 1983; Said 1998), but the inspiration for my research came from Erving Goffman. According to Goffman, a "normal" individual deviates little from America's paragon, which he describes as "a young, married, White, urban, northern, heterosexual Protestant father of college education, fully employed, of good complexion, weight and height, and a recent record in sports" (Goffman 1963, 128). I argue that those women faculty who are not seen as White are likely to be perceived as Other Teachers in the predominantly White campus.

Largely for reasons of economy, we use the term "White" to refer to non-Latino White/Caucasian persons, their culture, and their institutions. To avoid referring to ourselves in the negative (i.e., as "non-White women faculty") most contributors use the expression "women faculty of color." Like other terms used to create identity constructs, it is a contested term and it has very porous boundaries. Here it is used as a descriptive category that includes foreign-born faculty from the "Third World" as well as non-White, native-born professors. For many White students—not to mention White faculty and administrators—the distinctions between these two groups are hazy at best. Since the social imaginary of U.S. mainstream culture uses race as a fundamental category for classifying individuals, for many White students there is little difference between, say, an African American professor and a Black immigrant faculty from Trinidad, or a Mexican American professor and an immigrant faculty from Mexico. The presupposition that many White students see native and immigrant women faculty as one group, "women faculty of color/Other Teachers," lies at the core of the anthology. A pivotal notion of this work, then, is that race, class, gender, and ethnicity are relational, political, and unstable categories.

The anthology's main point is that professors who are seen as Others in their campuses have classroom experiences that are quite different from the experiences of both their male counterparts and White faculty. Many of the students, faculty, and administrators of the predominantly White campus have little experiential knowledge of people different from them and therefore rely on another form of knowledge, the stereotype, to relate to women faculty of color. Then, based on stereotypes, they construe these professors as Other Teachers. These stereotypical constructions create unique teaching-learning challenges. One of the professors I interviewed for my earlier research used heart disease as a metaphor to explain the synergistic action of multiple social differences and their likely impact on an academic career:

> The more of those risk factors [for heart disease] you possess, the more your chances are of developing heart disease. It's the same thing that we're talking about here. You can sort of apply that approach to being Other. The more factors you have that make you Other, the more impact that it has on your life and on your accomplishments. So if you're a person of color, not from a strong economic background, English as a second language, female, with a handicap. I mean, the more, more layering you have, the more of those attributes you have, more of those characteristics or factors, it's like going up a hill with a weight. You're adding a weight. So those make it far more challenging to survive.

The idea that the metaphor of heart disease poignantly expresses is one of the brightest threads that bring the narratives of this anthology together. In the literature on campus diversity, it is often referred to as "double jeopardy," meaning that women of color have at least two traits that become burdens in the predominantly White campus. Social distinctions are not neutral differences. They set the boundaries for a particular, more or less privileged life experience, and, therefore, for a particular, more or less privileged work experience.

The Anthology's Outline and Major Themes

In contrast to the rest of the book, Chapter 2 is not a narrative but a more traditional social science piece. Its purpose is to provide a context for our autoethnographic narratives. It gives a sense of the picture of women faculty of color that emerges from survey studies done at the national level. It also reviews some lines of research that have dealt with the questions related to the anthology's problematic. Chapter 3 is the narrative of my own teaching-learning experience. This chapter also differs from the other contributors' essays in that I blended together the narrative on my own teaching-learning with my earlier research on the topic, which was based on interviews with other professors. I decided to put my narrative at the beginning of the anthology because my earlier research served as the springboard for the book. The organization of the remaining chapters is, as with most anthologies, rather idiosyncratic. I chose to organize them according to the major themes that weave these narratives together. Despite the autobiographic feeling of these contributions, the reader is likely to find echoes of one chapter in another. What follows is a brief introduction to the major themes that emerge from the narratives, the sounds and silences that we used to compose this anthology.

The Classroom as One of the Microtheaters of the Diversity Wars. There is a pervasive sense in this anthology that the predominantly White classroom becomes a highly contested terrain when the teacher is a woman of color. In Chapter 3, I draw on Michel Foucault and Erwing Goffman to argue that student resistance can play a crucial role in enforcing traditional standards and stifling efforts to diversify the faculty of higher education. I tell the story of a Mexican immigrant woman teacher who experienced great resistance from my undergraduate students during my first years as assistant professor. I also describe the tremendous impact that the process of doing this research has had on the social life of my classroom and the way I experience myself as a teacher.

Disrupting Traditional Notions of Identity. An underlying motif in the anthology's narratives is how our mere presence in predominantly White classrooms disrupts traditional notions of identity; how it forces both teacher and students to become intensely aware of the relational and unfixed nature of the teaching-learning Self. All contributors to the anthology agree that the mere entry of a woman of color professor into a predominantly White classroom challenges entrenched hierarchical systems of social distinctions. However, this disruption comes to the fore in the essay by Giselle Liza Anatol, an openly lesbian Black faculty who chose to concentrate on issues of sexuality rather than on issues of race/ethnicity and gender. In Chapter 4, Anatol, who is of Trinidadian descent, foregrounds the interplay of her sexual orientation with other aspects of her identity to sharply illuminate how disruptive the mere presence of women faculty of color can be for traditional notions of identity. She uses a short story by Shani Mooto, a Trinidadian writer, to tell how she deals with challenges related to self-presentation, self-disclosure, and passing in the classroom. "As a brown-skinned, lesbian daughter of upwardly mobile immigrants, in what ways do I pass?" she asks. She describes how she uses her coming out as a lesbian in her classroom as a pedagogical moment for teaching and learning that identity is far from being absolute, stable, and natural. Since Anatol's is the only essay discussing the classroom challenges faced by lesbian professors, it indirectly reveals the meager attention paid by the rest of the essays to the privileges enjoyed by all heterosexual faculty, including those who are women of color.

Teaching White Students about White Privilege. Another theme that surfaces in most of the chapters is the tremendous challenge it is, for many of us, to teach about race and White privilege to White students. Lisa Chavez's essay dramatically reveals how strenuously engaging and unavoidable this challenge can be. As Chavez says in Chapter 5, race is always an issue, either manifest or submerged, in a classroom of a professor whose body is read as Indian. She describes herself as "the Chicana who doesn't speak Spanish, the Indian who doesn't know her tribal background, the Norwegian who doesn't look White." She narrates how emotionally charged her classroom has been when the discussion has centered on issues of race, prejudice, and privilege. Chavez relies on the work of critical feminists such as Audre Lorde, Patricia Williams, and bell hooks to contend that a teacher's anger is a proper response to students' bigotry. She points out that the acceptable way of expressing emotion in higher education settings is class based; then she argues that for a working-class professor like her, socialization into academe has included internalizing a central middle-class habit: avoiding anger. Chavez, who is also a poet, maintains that the pressure to assimilate into academe's bourgeois culture restrains the desire and ability of faculty like her to engage students "in passionate and rigorous argument."

The Emotional Demands that Cultural Diversity Courses Make upon the Teacher. In Chapter 6, Kimberly Nichele Brown says: "We often talk about the good the trailblazer does for those that come after her and even those that she challenges, but we rarely discuss the psychic damage done to the trailblazer once the path is on fire." Her words reflect a point that it is also made by other contributors to the anthology: the hidden emotional work involved in teaching-learning cultural diversity in the predominantly White classroom. Brown vividly describes the confrontation and challenge that occurred in her classroom when she taught, for the first time, an African American literature course. Brown is a Black professor whose teaching practices have been informed by radical feminist pedagogy. She uses one of the course's readings, Audre Lorde's "Uses of Anger: Women Respond to Racism" (1984), to frame her narrative. Because racism and oppression are often the core concern of African American, postcolonial, and other non-White authors, Brown's essay helps to illustrate the difficult emotional demands that cultural diversity courses make upon the teacher.

Paradoxes Involved in Our Practice of Liberatory Pedagogy. A major concern in many of these essays is the paradoxes we face when striving to practice liberatory pedagogy in the predominantly White classroom. Rashmi Luthra's essay highlights the tension between emancipatory pedagogical theories' disembodied ideal of the teacher and her own reality as a teacher with a "brown, small" female body. Luthra, who says that she "grew up thinking of myself as Punjabi or Indian," uses the metaphor of the minefield to talk about the challenges she has faced in her efforts to negotiate power and relinquish authority in the classroom. In Chapter 7, she says, "Whether a particular course lends itself to discussions of cultural politics or not, I always face a tension between the disembodied ideal I would like to enact in the classroom, that of liberatory pedagogue, in the tradition of Paulo Freire, Jonathan Kozol, Henry Giroux and others, and the embodied reality of the classroom, with its subterranean hostility, suspicion, and rejection." She describes the challenges that her Indian descent poses to the teaching of subjects such as global politics and the role of the United States in sustaining global inequalities. She also explains how the distrust that some of her students have expressed regarding her knowledge is encouraged by her university's legacy of ethnocentrism. Luthra's essay points to a fundamental concern of this anthology: the need and importance of naming "the presence of racism, sexism and ethnocentrism within the academy."

The Weight of the Institutional Context on Our classrooms. The weight of the institutional context on both our teaching-learning practice and our interactions with students is another of the distinguishable threads that weave these chapters together. Since the focus of the anthology is on pedagogical rather than institutional issues, as the anthology's editor I kept asking contributors to limit their discussions of issues such as hiring, promotion, and relations with colleagues and administrators to a minimum. Nonetheless, many of the contributors subverted the parameters I had set for the book. Through the telling of their own stories, contributors shed light on the tremendous impact that the institutional context may have on the teaching-learning experience of women faculty of color. Xue Rong's essay is compelling in this respect. In Chapter 8, Rong describes her journey as the first woman of color teaching in a school that was not prepared to make the institutional changes required by a faculty that was no longer all-White. Rong, who grew up in China, draws on socio-cultural, contextual theories (Hsu 2000) to highlight issues related to her socialization into the cultures of her new academic environs. To understand her own teaching-learning experience, Xue argues, it is necessary to look at her socialization into academic and local subcultures. She describes how this socialization affected her classroom performance.

Cecilia Manrique's essay also highlights the weight of the institutional context on her relations with students. In Chapter 9, she points out academe's schizophrenic view of women faculty of color: on the one hand we are sought by colleges and universities because we are seen as a "two-fer" (a woman and a minority) in terms of diversity goals and policies. On the other hand, the same institutions that hire us because they need to transform their racist and sexist cultures fail to recognize that we are brought into a campus culture that, most likely, will resist our presence on campus. Manrique's contention concerning the blithe assumption that the academic playing field has been leveled resonates in the rest of the essays. Manrique, who was raised in the Philippines, describes the multiple mechanisms that became activated to oppose her presence on campus. They have included subtle and overt discriminatory behavior on the part of both faculty and students: "The hallowed halls of academia are not spared from prejudice and discrimination, as some may have already concluded," says Manrique. They have also included the stigma of being seen by students and colleagues as an "affirmative action hire." "How dare you have a 'ferner' teach me American Government!," said one of her students to her dean. But one of the most powerful of such mechanisms, argues Manrique, are "those all-important, magical student evaluation scores!" Her essay shows the lengths that she had to go through to balance her "below the department average" evaluation scores ("I would get a 4.3 when the department average was 4.34!"). Manrique's chapter brings into light a pervasive sense in the anthology: student evaluation scores, which have become crucial factors in merit, tenure, and promotion decisions, can effectively push women professors of color out of predominantly White campuses. Manrique's strategy for achieving full-professor status was to work harder than her colleagues (and husband, who is also a Filipino professor) to be sure that her scholarship and service records were stellar.

Class as Both Structural Enabler and Structural Constrainer. The essay by Fay Yokomizo Akindes foregrounds the crucial role that class plays in student-teacher interactions. She sees her own experience growing up as a working-class girl as a bridge that allows her to forge connections with her working-class students. As do many of the essays in this anthology, Yokomizo Akindes's essay combines ideas from the pioneering work of Brazilian educator Paulo Freire with concepts from postcolonial theorists. In Chapter 10, Yokomizo Akindes, "an American Japanese Buddhist from Hawaii," talks of her teaching-learning experience as a sustained effort to help her students unlearn the oppressive ideology of superiority/inferiority that colonialism teaches to the colonizer. In her role as facilitator, she relies on listening and experiential learning to help her students achieve higher levels of under-standing. Through field trips, journal-writing, and other tools for encouraging empathy and self-knowledge, she strives to disrupt dichotomies in her class-room. Since Yokomizo Akindes characterizes her teaching-learning experi-ence as "overwhelmingly positive," this chapter is especially useful for appreciating the centrality of the structural elements that may enable women faculty of color to succeed. It is noteworthy that Yokomizo Akindes's stu-dents are not the middle- or upper-class students typical of most predomi-nantly White campuses; most of them are working class. This chapter throws an oblique light onto the constraining/enabling power of class in the teach-ing-learning experience of all working-class academics.

The Meaning of Cultural Diversity in Our Classrooms. "Much of what I do pedagogically is derived from my own cultural experience," say Delores Black-Connor Cleary, an Okanogan-Colville professor. Her statement cap-tures a sentiment that permeates other essays. In Chapter 11, Black-Connor Cleary shows how her tribal values guide her classroom practices. She also points out that her cooperative approach to teaching-learning is often at odds with dominant pedagogies, which are based on individualism and competi-tion. She mentions that her approach is at times mistaken by both students and colleagues as poor teaching. Misunderstandings about the cultural be-havior of teachers like herself, she argues, is compounded by an additional burden often carried by faculty of color: teaching-learning about social ine-quality. Cleary explains how difficult it is for a teacher like herself, whose professorial authority is fraught with doubt, to teach about cultural diversity, because this subject is intertwined with the country's hidden history of op-pression of racial and ethnic minorities.

Striving to Arouse Students' Interest in Cultures Other Than Their Own. Another motif in the stories that we tell is our strong desire to arouse stu-dents' interest in societies and cultures other than their own. This desire con-stitutes a defining element of many of the courses taught by both foreign-born and U.S.-born contributors. In Chapter 12, Zeinabu Davis illustrates how this desire frames her film history course. Davis is an African American professor and a pioneer Black filmmaker. As she explains, in U.S. universi-ties, students usually learn a version of film history that disregards the cine-matic production of countries other than the United States. By contrast, in Davis's course students are exposed to a broader range of films. For example, students learn that "the use of color is very different among the national cinemas of the world." Davis says: "It is my obligation to take the opportunity to discuss the use of color from other cultures." The desire that professors like

Davis feel brings remarkable teaching-learning opportunities to the classroom, but it also adds a new degree of challenge for both teacher and students. As Davis and other contributors argue, student resistance to the diversification of the curriculum is sometimes expressed in racist and sexist comments on their evaluations of our courses.

Learning to Deal with Special Classroom Challenges. A point that all the narratives share is that we have learned to deal with the special classroom challenges we face in a rather erratic way. Because for many of us this learning has been a painful trial-and-error process, we feel that novice Other Teachers can benefit from our suggestions on how to deal with such challenges. Lou-Ann Crouther, an African American professor, dedicates much of her narrative to offering advice. In Chapter 13, she highlights the importance of systematically studying the subject. "I would suggest that Other Teachers read a number of the works about the challenges faced by women and minorities," she says. Like many other chapters, Crouther's includes brief discussions of specific works that she has found helpful. Her chapter also describes her own classroom practices, many of which seek to preempt inappropriate student behavior. She gives detailed accounts of how she helps her students become aware of what is expected of them in terms of classroom manners and deportment. "They are subjects I knew about when I went to college, but these are different times, and I do not expect my students to have the same assumptions about university protocol as I did," states Crouther.

Making the Academy Conscious of Itself. All the essays aspire to help make predominantly White institutions of higher learning more critically aware of themselves. In Chapter 14, Anne B. Onyekwuluje looks at White academe as a social system that structures the interactions between herself, a Black woman professor, and her students. Like many other contributors to the anthology, Onyekwuluje says that she teaches through the current politics of race, class, and gender. Then she poignantly asks: "Who should be held responsible for students' negative perceptions about race, class, and gender?" Maintaining that "almost all predominantly White institutions upheld the White male consciousness that so many students adopt as their own," she posits that all members of these institutions should be accountable for the adverse political climate in which most Black women professors teach. Inspired by bell hooks, Onyekwuluje makes a strong call for progressive social change. It is only under hooks's visionary "new sociology of community," Onyekwuluje argues, that "the presence and experiences of difference can be recognized and valued within academe." She envisions a teaching-learning space "based on equality and equity for all selves and souls." This vision would require that all students, faculty, and administrators work jointly for the shared goal of truly diversifying higher education. Onyekwuluje's call might seem utopian. However, the magnitude of the social change needed for creating a friendly campus climate for women faculty of color would indeed require the transformative power of a utopian vision.

Reconstituting Our Teaching-Learning Selves. A major theme running throughout the book is that although the White campus has often been a hostile environment for many of us, we have found safe spaces where we have been able to emotionally reconstitute our teaching-learning selves. These positive teaching-learning environments are mentoring students and teaching certain courses. Diana I. Rios, a "U.S.-born Latina," highlights this point in Chapter 15. She uses the concept of "cultural stranger," which has been widely used in interpersonal communication research on foreigners (Gudykunst 1998) to argue that many White students' perceptions of teachers like herself are based on ethnocentric beliefs. Then she touches on what seems to be part and parcel of many of the experiences that we describe: feelings of isolation and estrangement fueled by hostile student behavior. Since for her the classroom has often been a site of struggle, she says that she needed coping mechanisms. One of her most important coping mechanisms has been mentoring students and teaching a seminar in her specialty. She highlights the positive role that teaching a seminar in her trained specialty played in her first years as an assistant professor.

The Impact of Our Memories on Our Classrooms. In Chapter 16, Priti Kumar uses Gloria Anzaldúa's (1987) symbols and metaphors to convey the sense that our memories, our past lived experiences, inescapably come to the classroom with us. "We humans cannot shed our past like the snakes shed their old skins," says Kumar. Her memories include strong remembrances of India, the country of her birth; recollections of travels and migrations; and memories of graduate school at Utah. She describes graduate school as "the hardest cultural crossing" for her. This painful experience, she says, shaped her teaching-learning practices, which are grounded on her conscientious effort to "never undervalue and thus undermine my students' knowledge base." Like the story told by Anzaldúa's Mestiza, Kumar's life story is fraught with marginalization and duality. With great effort, Kumar has been able to turn her own duality and marginality into teaching-learning resources. Her multiple border crossings, Kumar argues, have made her a more caring and insightful teacher. Kumar and other contributors encourage novice women faculty of color to see the memories of their own multiple "border crossings" as bridges, that is, as structures that provide passage over the cultural gaps that separate us from our predominantly White students.

Joint Appointments, Dual Teaching-Learning Experiences, and "Native Infor-mants." Many faculty of color are hired under a joint appointment that combines some time in their trained specialty and some time in a department or program related to their race, ethnicity, or national origin. Several of the contributors who hold such appointments describe the effects that joint appointments have had on their teaching-learning experience. Ryuko Kubota, who was born in Japan, draws on Pierre Bourdieu's concept of capital to examine the dual nature of her teaching-learning experience. In Chapter 17, Kubota describes the contrasting experiences that she has had as an academic with a joint appointment. While her cultural and linguistic capital has been valued by the students of the Curriculum of Asian and Asian American Studies (where half of her appointment is), her students at the School of Education have not shown the same appreciation. Kubota's dual experience is shared by other contributors to the anthology. Liza Chavez, for example, borrows the term Native informant to talk about the authority that she was accorded by students when she taught a course focusing on U.S. minority cultures. Chavez puts it this way: "The moment I walked into that small room in the basement, I was the authority. Those students, even those who already knew me, took one look at my brown skin and Indian features and decided I was the genuine article, the true 'Native Informant' there to give them inside knowledge about Indians."

As Kubota underlines in her essay, because of the relational nature of power and cultural capital, a teacher's authority, power, and prestige are fluid and contingent on the specific context in which teaching-learning takes place. Insisting that women teachers of color need to use alternative instructional strategies, she advances a counter-hegemonic pedagogy. Her pedagogical proposal converts the traditional view of difference as a lack into a view of difference as a resource, an asset for promoting critical multiculturalism.

Understanding Our Students' Situations and Feelings. As many of the contributors do, Fredi Avalos-C'deBaca foregrounds the emotional or affective dimension of the classroom. In Chapter 18, she suggests a strategy to deal with this dimension. Combining critical feminist thought (Lorde 1984; Schewsbury 1987) with theories of emotional intelligence (Goleman 1995), she maintains that teachers should use emotionality as "a creative force for learning." Then she argues that the key to effectively using such force is to understand our students' positionalities, to empathize with them. Avalos-C'deBaca, a Chicana Mestiza professor deeply committed to social change, points out that when the teaching-learning concerns social injustice, "instructors must remain sensitive to the levels of personal, social, and moral anxiety that this knowledge may cause students, particularly those who come from conservative political or religious backgrounds." Echoing other essays, Avalos-C'deBaca talks about the emotional effort that women faculty of color often have to make to empathize with White, middle-class students. She shows the extent of her own empathy when she states: "I am continually humbled by the courage many students exhibit in their willingness to confront these issues by recognizing their own conscious and unconscious participation in structures of oppression." This chapter advances what Freire would have called a "hopefully critical" approach for dealing with student resistance (1994, 144).

Finally, Chapter 19 contains Kristina Casto's response to the narratives. Casto is one of my master's students, and she was the research assistant for this project. As a White woman student, she looks at classroom interactions and pedagogical choices from a different perspective than the rest of the contributors. However, she says, "Witnessing the intense struggle that many of the contributors to the anthology went through in articulating their classroom experiences has made me more sensitive to the intense emotionality and vulnerability that comes with the teaching experience, particularly to those who are perceived as Other." Since the dialogue that Casto and I had during the process of editing the anthology helped shaped the final product, her voice should be included in this product.

Difficulty in Acknowledging Our Own Privileges. One of the unmet challenges of these essays is the need to acknowledge and reflect on our own privileges. We are acutely aware of gender and the marks of race and ethnicity inscribed in our bodies, but we make cursory remarks about the privileges that come with an able body. While some contributors mention the disadvantages of having a "petite" body for establishing professorial authority, none of us talks about fat as an issue. Some contributors nearly ignore the special advantages that a middle-class upbringing and educated parents bestow upon them. For some contributors who learned English as children, accent is inconspicuous. For some who are heterosexual, sexuality is invisible.

Likewise, while many contributors point out the constraining side of the institutional context of our teaching, we often fail to recognize the elements of this context that have enabled us to succeed. All contributors tell success stories. Most of us have successfully negotiated the initiation phase of an academic career; many of us are tenured and a few are full professors. However, while we stress the constraining elements of the specific contexts and circumstances where our teaching-learning takes place, we tend to underplay the elements that have enabled us to succeed. This is definitely an area that calls for further reflection and writing.

What Have We Learned, What Can We Share?

A major idea running throughout the chapters is that one of the essential abilities that a woman professor of color needs to develop to succeed in the predominantly White classroom is to recognize and deal effectively with the unique classroom hurdles that she is likely to face. Although there is little research on faculty of color regarding these issues, the research on students of color suggests that we may be headed in the right direction. Among the traits that have been identified as predictors of success of college students of color is the ability to understand and deal with racism. "Research has consistently shown that students of color who understand racism and are prepared to deal with it perform better academically and are more likely to adjust to predominantly white campuses than those who are not prepared to do so"(Wilds and Wilson 1998, 6).

A second major idea in the anthology is that to succeed in the predominantly White classroom, women faculty of color also need to recognize, and use, the unique teaching-learning opportunities that their mere presence in the classroom creates. As Kubota rightly argues in her essay, we, Other Teachers, should see our own "marginality as an asset." Elsewhere (Vargas 1999) I have argued that the most important lesson students learn in the classrooms of women faculty of color may not be the course content; rather, it may be how to work and play in multicultural settings. Many middle-class, White undergraduates have never been in social situations led by people of color. When sorting out how to behave in the classroom of a woman teacher of color, these students have no experience to draw upon. To be able to use the unique teaching-learning opportunities that are available to us, we need to listen to Avalos-C'deBaca when she argues that we should "remain sensitive to the levels of personal, social, and moral anxiety" that social and economically privileged students are likely to experience in our classrooms.

Costs and Benefits of Our Presence
in the Predominantly White Classroom

When students have never seen women of color in leadership positions or as sources of mainstream knowledge, our mere presence in the classroom is deeply disrupting. What is needed to use those disruptions as teaching-learning moments may be more than what a teacher alone can do. Nonetheless, in predominantly White campuses, the delicate and challenging task of teaching-learning how to work and play in multicultural environments has rested, by and large, on the shoulders of faculty of color. Most novice women faculty of color are likely to be unaware that the issues we discuss in our narratives will be a substantial part of their work. The psychological consequences of such an unexpected experience can be potentially devastating for them, because they are likely to be already subjected to other stressors (Boice 1992, 254). Dianne Bartlow, Virginia T. Escalante, and Olga A. Vásquez have pointed out the multiple sources of anxiety for women of color in academia:

> Working within the system, women of color confront a variety of common sources of anxiety. Some of these stressors are inherent to the phase of the newly initiated: of finding oneself in an unfamiliar, unwelcoming, and often oppressive culture. Others are the direct result of confronting a system that on the one hand is in dire need of a dramatic reconstruction and on the other holds steadfastly to a threatened power structure based on hegemonic notions of truth, language, and knowledge. (1993, 268)

Preparing herself cognitively and, most important, *emotionally* to confront what most likely will be a stressful teaching experience should be a priority for the novice woman professor of color. She will need a great deal of institutional support to be able to use the unique opportunities available to her. However, the benefits that such institutional support would accrue are considerable. The American Council on Education's latest annual status report on minorities in higher education stresses the benefits of racial and ethnic diversity in institutions of higher learning. The report highlights three types of benefits. First, it highlights the benefits to individual students; these include greater openness to challenge and diversity, reduced levels of ethnocentrism, and gains in critical thinking skills. Then, the report points out the way in which ethnic and women's studies have transformed teaching, research, and service. According to the report, scholarship in these areas has transformed "the nature of what is studied, how it is studied, and how excellence is defined in particular disciplines" (Wilds 2000, 6). Finally, the report stresses the benefits of diversity to the economy and the private sector. These are related to the development of competencies that graduates must possess to work in the global work environment (competencies include domain knowledge and cognitive, social, and personal skills). According to the report, cross-cultural competence is "the most critical human resource need" in the globalized economy:

> It involves some domain knowledge (in relation to other cultures), as well as social skills and personal traits that enhance cross-cultural communication and cooperation. This skill enables workers to function effectively in an increasingly diverse marketplace. (Wilds 2000, 7)

One African American woman professor that I interviewed for my earlier research eloquently talked about White students' need to develop cross-cultural competence and the role the university should play in creating a space where the teaching-learning of this competence can occur:

> These White students, who are trained by these White males, and then they go out and they want to work in a major city, then more than likely their boss will be a person of color, you know, and that's what happens in my profession. But I think there's that level of having to live in a multicultural environment, many of our students, who graduated in May are now in such an environment....So I think that it's not so much about affirmative action as it is of the university playing a role model in terms of how you have a physical faculty that represents different ethnic groups, that help prepare students for a multicultural environment at work, at play.

It is our hope that the anthology will be a resource for all concerned with enabling the diversification of the professoriate of higher education. When writing these narratives, we often addressed all faculty and administrators, especially those with the decision-making power necessary to effect change in the situations that we describe. But most often we imagined our readers as novice women minority faculty and female graduate students of color learning the ropes of college teaching. Limited mentoring by senior faculty is one of the factors that have been consistently identified as contributing to the slow progress of minority faculty in higher education. We hope that, along with the writings of the critical feminist writers who we draw upon to compose our narratives, this anthology will be a resource for novice women faculty of color.

The larger conversation on the problematic that we address has mostly centered on the special challenges that result from being construed as Other Teacher. This anthology hopes to add an emphasis on the unique teaching-learning *opportunities* that, *given the proper institutional support,* may be available for women faculty of color in the predominantly White campus. It has been suggested that the double jeopardy faced by these professors is one of the factors contributing to the gloomy picture that emerges from the available data on the country's professoriate (see Chapter 2). What we would like to suggest is that by failing to seriously engage with the issues dealt with in this anthology, students, faculty, staff, and administrators are squandering precious opportunities for fostering multiculturalism in predominantly White campuses and in society at large. Multiculalism is not only a set of beliefs. It is also a set of practices.

Works Cited

Anderson, M., and P. Hill Collins. 1995. *Race, Class, and Gender: An Anthology*. Belmont, CA: Wadsworth Publishing.

Angrosino, M. V. 1989. *Documents of Interaction: Biography, Autobiography, and Life History in Social Sciences Perspective*. Gainsville: University of Florida Press.

Anzaldúa, G. 1987. *Borderlands/La Frontera: The New Mestiza*. San Francisco: Aunt Lute Books.

Bartlow, D., V. T. Escalante, and O. A. Vasquez. 1993. "Exploring New Frontiers. Women of Color in Academia." In *Women in Mass Communication*, edited by P. Creedon. Newbury Park, CA: Sage.

Bhabha, H. 1983. "The Other Question." *Screen* 24 (6): 18–36.

Boice, R. 1992. *The New Faculty Member*. San Francisco, CA: Jossey-Bass.

Braine, G., eds. 1999. *Non-native Educators in English-language Teaching*. Mahwah, NJ: Lawrence Earlbaum Associates, Inc.

Bronstein, P. 1993. "Challenges, Rewards, and Costs for Feminists and Ethnic Minority Scholars." *New Directions for Teaching* 53: 61–70.

Chase, S. E. 1995. *Ambiguous Empowerment: The Work Narratives of Women School Superintendents*. Amherst: University of Massachusetts Press.

Christian-Smith, L. K., and K. S. Kellor. 1999. *Everyday Knowledge and Uncommon Truths: Women of the Academy*. Boulder, CO: Westview Press.

Conquerwood, D. 1991. "Rethinking Ethnography: Towards a Critical Cultural Politics." *Communication Monographs* 58: 179–194.

de Beauvoir, S. 1961. *The Second Sex*. New York: Bantam.

Denzin, N. K. 1989. *Interpretive Biography*. Newbury Park, CA: Sage.

———. 1997. *Interpretive Ethnography*. Thousand Oaks, CA: Sage.

Ellis, C. 1997. "Evocative Autoethnography." In *Representation and the Text: Reframing the Narrative Voice*, edited by W. G. Tierney and Y. S. Lincoln. Albany: State University of New York Press.

Ellis, C., and A. P. Boshner, eds. 1996. "*Composing Ethnography*. Walnut Creek, CA: Sage.

Ellsworth, E. 1989. "Why Doesn't This Feel Empowering? Working Through the Repressive Myths of Critical Pedagogy." *Harvard Educational Review* 59 (3): 297–324.

Freire, P. 1994. *Education for Critical Consciousness*. New York: The Continuum Publishing Co.

Goffman, E. 1963. *Stigma*. Englewood Cliffs, NJ: Prentice-Hall.

Goleman, D. 1995. *Emotional Intelligence: Why It Can Matter More Than IQ*. New York: Bantam Books.

Gudykunst, W. 1998. *Bridging Differences: Effective Intergroup Communication*. 3rd Ed. Thousand Oaks, CA: Sage.

Harding, S. 1991. *Whose Science? Whose Knowledge: Thinking from Women's Lives*. Ithaca, NY: Cornell University Press.

Hill Collins, P. 1991. *Black Feminist Thought: Knowledge Consciousness and the Politics of Empowerment*. New York: Routledge.

Hsu, R. Y. 2000. ""Where's Oz Toto?": Idealism and the Politics of Gender and Race in Academe." In *Power, Race, and Gender in Academe*, edited by S. Lim and M. Herrera-Sobek. New York: Modern Language Association.

Jordan Irvine, J. 1982. "The Black Female Academic. Doubly Burdened or Doubly Blessed?" In *Stepping Off the Pedestal. Academic Women in the South*, edited by P. Stringer and I. Thomas. New York: Modern Language Association of America.

Lewis, M. 1990. "Interrupting Patriarchy: Politics, Resistance, and Transformation in the Feminist Classroom." *Harvard Educational Review* 60 (4): 467–488.

———. 1999. "The Backlash Factor: Women, Intellectual Labour and Student Evaluations of Courses and Teaching." In *Everyday Knowledge and Uncommon Truths*, edited by L. K. Christian-Smith and K. S. Kellor. Boulder, CO: Westview Press.

Lorde, A. 1984. "The Uses of Anger: Women Respond to Racism." In *Sister Outsider: Essays and Speeches*. New York: The Crossing Press.

Maher, F. A., and M. K. Thomson-Tetreault. 1994. *The Feminist Classroom*. New York: Basic Books.

Moraga, C., and G. Anzaldúa, eds. 1981. *This Bridge Called My Back. Writings by Radical Women of Color*. Watertown, MA: Persephone Press.

Said, E. 1998. "Edward Said: The Voice of a Palestinian in Exile." *Third Text* 3 (4): 39–50.

Schewsbury, C. M. 1987. "What Is Feminist Pedagogy?" *Women's Studies Quarterly* 15 (3 & 4): 6–14.

Suleri, S. 1996. "Woman Skin Deep: Feminism and the Postcolonial Condition." In *Contemporary Postcolonial Theory. A Reader*, edited by P. Mongia. London: Arnold.

Talburt, S. 2000. *Subject to Identity. Knowledge, Sexuality, and Academic Practices in Higher Education*. New York: State University of New York Press.

Van Manen, M. 1990. *Researching Lived Experience: Human Science for an Action Sensitive Pedagogy*. London, Ontario: State University of New York Press.

Vargas, L. 1999. "When the 'Other' is the Teacher: Implications of Teacher Diversity in Higher Education." *The Urban Review* 31 (4): 359–383.

Wheary, J., and R. H. Ennis. 1995. "Gender Bias in Critical Thinking: Continuing the Dialogue." *Educational Theory* 45 (2): 213–224.

Wilds, D. J. 2000. Seventeenth Annual Status Report on Minorities in Higher Education. Washington, DC: American Council on Education.

Wilds, D. J., and R. Wilson. 1998. Sixteenth Annual Status Report on Minorities in Higher Education. Washington, DC: American Council on Education.

CHAPTER TWO

Why Are We Still So Few and Why Has Our Progress Been So Slow?

LUCILA VARGAS

STATISTICS CONCERNING RACE and ethnicity in the U.S. professoriate are slippery. Most studies on faculty of color do not distinguish between native-born and foreign-born professors, largely because the data-collecting instruments used by colleges and universities many times fail to distinguish between the two groups. This practice helps institutions appear to comply with the demands of native-born minorities for more representation. Nonetheless, what is indisputable is that minorities, and especially minority women, are still severely underrepresented in the academy. Given these data limitations, the profile of minority women professors I sketch in this chapter is based on statistics that refer to native and immigrant women faculty combined. However, I have added a brief discussion on the specific circumstances of immigrant women faculty at the end of the chapter's first section.

Many of the few women of color who teach in U.S. institutions of higher learning are likely to be employed as adjunct or part-time instructors. Non-Latino White women and faculty of color make up more than their share of the new "migrant faculty."[1] These teachers are often hired under short-term contracts and move frequently from one campus to another. Without a doubt, this is one of the most disturbing employment patterns of recent years. For the year 2000, faculty working under contract are estimated to make up nearly half the higher education workforce (Moody 2000, 32). Although many of these "part-time" instructors carry full-time teaching loads, they do not enjoy the material and symbolic rewards that come with "full-time" faculty status.

The representation of women professors of color among full-time faculty has improved slightly in the last few years, but it remains well below their representation in the general population. The American Council on Education estimates that in 1995 (the most recent year for which comprehensive statistics are available), faculty of color held only 12.9 percent of the more than 538,023 "full-time undergraduate faculty" teaching positions in higher education. Men outnumbered women in all racial/ethnic groups (the gender gap is particularly large among Asian American/Pacific Islanders). Accordingly, the absolute numbers of women faculty of color were extremely low. There were 12,988 African American women, 7,287 Asian American/Pacific Islander women, 5,078 Latinas, and 894 Native American women (Wilds and Wilson 1998, 102). Furthermore, many of these women professors hold non–tenure-track positions, and only about one of every two of the few women of color who succeed in securing a tenure-track position is ever tenured.

Women professors of color gain tenure at a significantly lower rate than other groups. While the tenure rate for White males was 79 percent, it was 66 percent for men of color, 63 percent for White women, and only 54 percent for women of color (Wilds and Wilson 1998, 41–43). Women of color remain at the lowest rungs of the ladder: Only 2.1 percent of all full professors are women of color (Wilds and Wilson 1998, 42). The dismal tenure rate for women of color suggests that this group may be facing extraordinary internal stressors; these are "the subjective, internally motivating aspects of life that add or detract from job satisfaction" (Tack and Patitu 1993). It also suggests that there may be workplace factors, such as salaries, interpersonal relations, and working conditions, that are effectively deterring this group from advancing. Indeed, extra service work, marginal professorial status, limited mentoring by senior faculty, and lack of recognition for research with a minority focus have been implicated in the slow professional advancement of women minority faculty (Justiz, Wilson, and Björk 1994; Turner and Myers 2000). The research on the topic, however, has largely neglected factors related to classroom climate and teacher-student interaction, which are the focus of this anthology.

Women faculty of color lag behind their male counterparts in most measures of formal status. This is also the case for White women. Reviews of studies that include both minority women faculty and White women faculty conclude that women "tend to be segregated by discipline and by institutional type; to be disproportionately represented at lower ranks; to get promoted at slower rates than their male colleagues; to participate less in governance and administration; and to be compensated at a rate that averaged only 85 percent of that of their male colleagues"(Goodwin and Stevens 1996, 272). However, there are some important differences among racial/ethnic subgroups.

The only racial/ethnic group with a higher proportion of women employed as full professors than men is African Americans (19 percent vs. 17 percent) (Astin et al. 1997, 12–13). African American women are only slightly more likely (19 percent) than Asian American/Pacific Islander women and White women (18 percent for both) to be full professors. On the other extreme of this axis are Latinas and Native American women, who occupy the lowest academic ranks. The proportion of women of color who teach as instructors or lecturers is 37 percent for Latinas ands 41 percent for Native American women. Accordingly, these subgroups also have an extremely low representation at the full professor level; only 9 percent of all Latina women faculty and 12 percent of all Native American women faculty are full professors. By contrast, 43 percent of the White male professors and 36 percent of the Asian American/Pacific Islander male faculty are full professors, and only 11 percent of the former and 6 percent of the latter teach as instructors or as lecturers. Moreover, except for the lowest rank, where the proportion of men is relatively low, women's salaries are consistently lower than the salaries of their male counterparts. Whites and Asian American/Pacific Islanders have the greatest gender gap in salaries (Astin et al. 1997, 16–17).

Gender discrepancies are partially explained by age, education, and field of study. White men have the highest median age of all subgroups (49 years), followed by African American women, whose median age is the highest among all groups of women (48 years). Asian American/Pacific Islander women have the lowest median age of all groups (42 years), followed by Latino and Asian American/Pacific Islander men (44 years). The median age of Native American and White women is the same as for African American men (46 years). Like African American women, Latinas are older than their male counterparts (45 years) (Astin et al. 1997, 6).

Regarding education, male professors tend to be more educated than their female counterparts in all racial/ethnic groups. Native American women professors have the lowest rate of Ph.D/Ed.P. (37 percent), followed by African American women (42 percent) and Latinas (44 percent). By contrast, the rate of Asian American/Pacific Islander women holding a Ph.D or Ed.P. is considerably higher (61 percent) than any other subgroup of women. With respect to field of study, which is linked to salary differences, all women of color have higher rates of representation in the humanities than their male counterparts, but the rate of representation among Latinas is extremely high in the humanities (43 percent). Asian American/Pacific Islander women hold a relatively high rate of degrees in the physical sciences (Astin et al. 1997, 9), and African American women have a relatively high rate of degrees in the life sciences (18 percent) and the social sciences (15 percent) (Astin et al. 1997, 11). Native American women faculty hold degrees that are more evenly distributed among different fields than any other subgroup of women faculty. Thus, it seems that this is a case of sectoral segregation, since the humanities include fields such as English and foreign languages, which are known to offer low salaries and relatively limited resources.

Another factor that is often cited as explaining gender inequalities is that women have greater family responsibilities than men. Over three-quarters of all faculty are currently married, but the representation of single faculty is higher among women in all racial/ethnic groups. Also, women are more likely to have been divorced than men. Asian American/Pacific Islander men have the highest proportion of currently married faculty (89 percent), followed by Asian American/Pacific Islander women (70 percent). This is a big departure from the marriage rates of both Native American women (52 percent) and African American women (55 percent), who have the lowest rates of all subgroups. Further, Native American women have the highest rate of divorce of all subgroups (38 percent). For Latina faculty, the proportion who are currently married is nearly the same as for White women (65 percent vs. 66 percent) (Astin et al. 1997, 7). In short, as in many other occupations, balancing work and family responsibilities seems to be harder for women professors than for their male counterparts, but it seems to be especially difficult for Native American and African American women.

Class appears to be a factor in the discrepancies among racial/ethnic groups, but class fails to explain gender discrepancies. The national survey of the Higher Education Research Institute gives an indication of the socioeconomic class of women faculty in its data on parents' education level. Women faculty have more educated mothers than male faculty and, apart from Asian American/Pacific Islanders, women also have more educated fathers. The highest representation of faculty whose fathers had a college degree was Asian American/Pacific Islander men (54 percent), followed by Asian American/Pacific Islander women (46 percent), White women (40 percent), and White men (37 percent); the lowest rate here was for African American men (16 percent). Within subgroups of women, the fathers of African American women are the least likely to have a college degree (24 percent), followed by the fathers of Latinas and Native American women (Astin et al. 1997, 7–8). These statistics suggest that class may be an important factor in explaining the difference between Asian American/Pacific Islanders and other faculty of color. Most studies concur that the Asian American/Pacific Islander experience in academe has been closer to the White experience than to the minority experience (Brown 1988, 2).

As I mentioned above, these figures conflate the experience of native-born and immigrant faculty. Non-European immigrant faculty have been joining the U.S. professoriate in higher numbers since 1965, when the country's laws and patterns of immigration changed. The new wave of immigrants from the "Third World" included highly educated individuals who would fill the need for more faculty of color created by a combination of factors, such as the shortage of Ph.D.s, the expansion of many colleges and universities, and, especially, the demands of social movements for a more inclusive educational system. Although economic opportunity is one of the major reasons for all Third World migration, economic opportunity is not the main reason women professors come to the United States. In their survey of immigrant faculty, Cecilia Manrique and Gabriel Manrique found that, while most male respondents stated that their standard of living would be lower in their country of origin than in the United States, women faculty said that such standards would be higher in their country of origin (1999). For women immigrant faculty, then, the decision to migrate has more to do with the prospect that life in the United States offers the opportunity to escape from the oppressive gender roles of their home countries.

What Might Explain the Slow Progress
of Women Faculty of Color in Academe?

The slow progress of women of color in higher education seems to be over-determined by a number of factors related to gender inequality, class under-privilege, and racial/ethnic minority status. The synergistic action of these factors is likely to produce accumulative disadvantages that may explain the low numbers of women of color in the professoriate, their extremely low tenure rates, and their overrepresentation in the lower academic ranks. These disadvantages include those they accumulate before joining the ranks of the professoriate and the tests and challenges they encounter as junior faculty.

Most women of color join the professoriate with cumulative disadvantages that begin early in life and that defy traditional social science measures. Most women of color accumulate further disadvantages as students, especially as graduate students. Shirley M. Clark and Mary Corcoran state that both White and minority women are likely to face the following disadvantages as graduate students: inequality regarding financial aid, no parity in enrollment in the most prestigious graduate programs, lack of mentors and role models, and exclusion from collegial networks of advice and patronage (which are usually composed of White male faculty) (1996, 129). In addition, as minority students, women of color must cope with their racial/ethnic minority status, which is a rich source of internal stressors. These challenges seem to contribute to the current slowdown in doctoral production among minority women. They are also likely to be important factors in the choice taken by many of the few minority women who succeed in attaining a Ph.D/Ed.D. to not pursue an academic career.

Those who do choose to become professors most likely encounter familiar challenges, such as lack of mentors and a chilly climate,[2] plus the challenge of developing strategies to cope with their racial/ethnic minority status in the faculty culture they join (Aguirre and Martinez 1993; Sandler and Hall 1986; Sandler and Hall 1982). Some minority faculty have argued that racist attitudes among non-Latino White faculty and administrators impede the hiring and, especially, promotion of faculty of color.[3] Other academics argue that women of color "are not likely to be a part of either the 'old boy' or even the 'new woman' feminist networks"(Browne Graves 1991, 6). In her qualitative study on women faculty of color, Francis V. Rains concludes:

> Life in the academy is challenging, hectic and stressful for most faculty, regardless of gender or ethnicity. When socially constructed, contradictory expectations and demands generate benefits for some White faculty, while the consequences generate costs for some women faculty of color, it adds a layer of strain, intensity, and pressure for these women that absorbs valuable time and energy that could be committed to more scholarly pursuits. It would seem that at Everwhite University, equity of access did not always materialize into equity of treatment in the area of collegial relations. Sandler and Hall (1986) note the chilly climate that many White women in the academy endure. I posit that for many women of color the climate is not chilly, it's a cold sword upon which they must dance, often barefoot, ever faster and faster to survive. (Rains 1999, 167)

Rains's conclusion resonates with the findings of many other investigations about minority professors. As of this writing, the most comprehensive work on the topic is *Faculty of Color in Academe* (Turner and Myers 2000). It reviews, and largely confirms, the findings of numerous other studies regarding factors associated with the slow professional advancement of academics of color. Particularly important factors discussed by Caroline Turner and her collaborators are extra service work, marginal professorial status, a hostile work environment, limited mentoring by senior faculty, and lack of recognition for research with a minority focus. Significantly, even though the parameters of the study were not set to systematically explore pedagogical questions (or the interplay of race, ethnicity, class, and gender), the authors found some evidence that issues related to teacher-student interaction appear "to be of particular concern to female faculty of color" (Turner and Myers 2000, 92).

Coupled with the growing body of literature on women academics, the literature on minority faculty provides ample evidence of the various institutional challenges women professors of color are likely to face. On reviewing the literature, however, it becomes evident that, as Sherryl Browne Graves correctly points out, most research has paid little attention to the multiple group memberships of women faculty of color (1991, 4). Often, the research on women fails to distinguish between White women and women of color. Likewise, most research on minority academics does not examine gender, racial, and ethnic differences; nor does it distinguish between native and foreign-born professors. "Most data treat minority faculty members as one group; as a result, the situation of non-White women is often obscured," states Linda K. Johnsrud in her review of the literature on women and racial/ethnic minority faculty (1993, 5).

Except for studies concentrating on African American women academics (Benjamin 1997; Gregory 1995; James and Farmer 1993; Moses 1989), there are very few studies on the variegated experience of women faculty of color. Worth mentioning is *Perspectives on Minority Women in Higher Education* (Brodie 1992), which combines interpretive essays with more traditional historical and qualitative studies on Latinas and African American women.[4] Several chapters add to the pile of testimonials and anecdotal evidence, which is dispersed throughout the literature, of the classroom challenges faced by these academics. In her contribution to this book, Mary Ann Williams captures a feeling that permeates the literature on minority faculty:

> Students challenge professors to give them their money's worth (or a grade that makes sitting through the class or showing up for the final exam worthwhile). Challenges come in many forms. They are certainly a function of race, gender, and subject area. Students/people assume that a male math/science/business professor (white or black) will know his subject area and be involved in "serious" work. A white female will often experience some resistance, but a certain level of competence can be presumed.
>
> As an African American female (with a smile) and an arts background, I encounter a "you got a be kidding" look that takes over the students' faces when I enter a classroom. Most white males and females distrust the African American woman's knowledge base and certainly feel a need to challenge her authority. (Williams 1992)

There are numerous comments similar to Williams's in the literature on the minority faculty experience. Also, the literature on the organizational culture of higher education sheds some light on issues of student resistance to these professors. For example, in their study on faculty socialization in academe, William G. Tierney and Estela Mara Bensimon quote a Latina professor talking about the support that she and other Latina junior faculty received from senior Latina professors: "[They] would say to us: 'Look, this is what we went through, formally and informally.' I was shown how to put together a class, how to handle problems in the classroom. They told us: 'You're a Latina and you're going to have white male students who have never seen a person like yourself in authority. This is how we deal with these types of things" (1996, 111). However, comments on teaching challenges and classroom social life are often embedded in broader discussions on professional socialization, acculturation, and work environment. The literature on minority faculty shows a conspicuous imbalance between institutional and pedagogical issues. Nearly all the studies deal with institutional issues, such as lack of mentors, tenure, and promotion. In addition, most of the research on women professors of color focuses on African Americans. Latinas are sometimes included, but other groups have been largely ignored in this research.

Another body of research, the research on instructional communication, has the potential to illuminate the classroom experience of women academics of color, but it has also neglected issues related to power and social distinctions.[5] Researchers in this field have explored the effect of teacher characteristics (e.g., dynamism, disclosiveness, delivery skills, nonverbal expressiveness, teacher immediacy) on teacher effectiveness.[6] They have found, for example, that immediacy plays a strong role in effective teaching. Instructional communication researchers have also found that students' perceived homophily with their teachers increases the latter's chances of being listened to: "If the students perceive that our attitudes and values are more similar to than different from theirs, the greater probability we have of influencing their attitudes, values, and, ultimately, behavior" (Sorensen and Christophel 1992, 43). Leading researchers James C. McCroskey and Virginia P. Richmond argue that immediacy is culturally anchored: "Much of immediacy is a function of nonverbal behavior, and it is very well established that nonverbal behaviors have different norms and impacts in different cultures" (1992, 114). Despite these findings, however, as McCroskey and Richmond rightly point out, "Most empirically-based communication theory is heavily biased in the direction of what is normative for the White, middle-class, American culture. Almost all of the research in instructional communication has been conducted within this cultural context" (1992, 113–114). Furthermore, as Jon F. Nussbaum points out, "the circular nature of teacher-student interaction has not entered into the research. This is most evident in the education and communication research that ignores the effects that students have on teacher behavior" (1992, 178).[7] Academics of color such as Katherine Grace Hendrix have argued that the instructional communication research has largely failed to acknowledge that "just as every professor isn't male, every professor isn't White"(1997, 28).

In sum, the status of women faculty of color in the U.S. professoriate is clearly lacking. The reasons behind their extremely low numbers, dismal tenure rate, and overrepresentation on the lower rungs of the academic ladder are numerous and complex. The literature on minority faculty has pointed out important factors that prevent the advancement of this faculty. Most of this literature, however, has concentrated on institutional concerns, and therefore it has not sufficiently considered the pedagogical implications of diversifying the U.S. professoriate. The research on instructional communication has the potential to illuminate these issues but, by and large, it has failed to contextualize classroom interactions within their larger social, economic, cultural, and political milieu. We hope that this anthology will shed light on the submerged pedagogical effects of bringing women faculty of color into predominantly White college classrooms.

Notes

1. Throughout the book we use the term "White" to refer to non-Latino White/Caucasian persons, their culture, and their institutions.

2. The term "chilly climate" is widely used in the literature to refer to a hostile campus environment for women. It became popular with Bernice Sandler and Robert Hall's (1982) studies on campus climate commissioned by the Project on the Status and Education of Women of the Association of American Colleges.

3. More than a decade ago, Yolanda T. Moses (1989) and Maria de la Luz Reyes and John Halcón (1988), for example, discussed how racism among White faculty and administrators hinders hiring and promotion of Latinos. Moses combined the findings of other research concerning Black women in higher education with her own survey data to offer a comprehensive view of the double jeopardy faced by such faculty. She also proposed a number of strategies to tackle various problems.

4. The last section of this book deals with international experiences.

5. Some of the research on instructional communication has also paid attention to central issues discussed by the contributors to this anthology, such as power, authority, and student resistance in the classroom. However, most researchers in this field have used the terms "power" and "control" to refer to influence. Ann Staton, for example, defines power as "a teacher's potential to influence the attitudes, values, beliefs, and behavior of students." She defines control as the teacher's actual influence (1992, 168).

6. For reviews of the literature in this field published between 1983 and 1990, see Nussbaum (1992) and Power, Nitkavic, and Koerner (1996).

7. The research of Donald L. Rubin and his collaborators (Rubin 1992; Rubin and Smith 1990) sheds some light on issues related to the impact that students' perceptions of teachers might have on classroom social life. He has conducted a series of studies on the effects of non-language factors (such as accent and ethnicity) on undergraduates' perceptions of international teaching assistants.

Works Cited

Aguirre, A., Jr., and R. O. Martinez. 1993. *Chicanos in Higher Education: Issues and Dilemmas for the 21st Century*. Washington, DC: The George Washington University, School of Education and Human Development.

Astin, H. S., A. L. Antonio, C. M. Crees, and A. W. Astin. 1997. *Race and Ethnicity in the American Professoriate, 1995–1996*. Los Angeles: Higher Education Research Institute, UCLA.

Benjamin, L., ed. 1997. *"Black Women in the Academy. Promises and Perils*. Gainesville, FL: University Press of Florida.

Brodie, L. W. 1992. *Perspectives on Minority Women in Higher Education*. New York: Praeger.

Brown, S. V. 1988. *Increasing Minority Faculty: An Elusive Goal*. Princeton, NJ: Educational Testing Service.

Browne Graves, S. 1991. "A Case of Double Jeopardy? Black Women in Higher Education." *Initiatives* 53 (1): 3–8.

Clark, S. M., and M. Corcoran. 1996. "Perspectives on the Professional Socialization of Women Faculty. A Case of Accumulative Disadvantages." In *Faculty and Faculty Issues in*

Colleges and Universities, edited by D. E. Finnegan, D. Webster and Z. F. Gamson. Needham Heights, MA: Simon & Schuster.

Goodwin, L. D., and E. A. Stevens. 1996. "The Influence of Gender on University Faculty Members' Perceptions of 'Good' Teaching." In *Faculty and Faculty Issues in Colleges and Universities*, edited by D. Finnegan, E. D. Webster and Z. F. Gamson. Needham Heights, MA: Simon & Schuster.

Gregory, S. 1995. *Black Women in the Academy: The Secrets to Success and Achievement.* New York: University Press of America.

Hendrix, K. G. 1997. Student Perceptions of Verbal and Nonverbal Cues Leading to Images of Black and White Professor Credibility: Unpublished paper.

James, J., and R. Farmer, eds. 1993. *Spirit, Space and Survival: African American Women in (White) Academe.* New York: Routledge.

Johnsrud, L. K. 1993. "Women and Minority Faculty Experiences: Defining and Responding to Diverse Realities." *New Directions for Teaching and Learning* 53: 3–16.

Justiz, M. J., R. Wilson, and L. G. Björk, eds. 1994. *"Minorities in Higher Education.* Washington, DC: American Council on Education.

Manrique, C., and G. Manrique. 1999. *The Multicultural or Immigrant Faculty in American Society.* New York: The Mellen Press.

McCroskey, C. J., and V. P. Richmond. 1992. "Increasing Teacher Influence Through Immediacy." In *Power in the Classroom: Communication, Control and Concern*, edited by V. P. Richmond and J. C. McCroskey. Hillsdale, NJ: Lawrence Erlbaum.

Moody, J. 2000. Tenure and Diversity: Some Different Voices. *Academe*, May-June, 30–33.

Moses, Y. T. 1989. *Black Women in Academe.* Washington, DC: Project on the Status and Education of Women. Association of American Colleges.

Nussbaum, J. F. 1992. "Effective Teacher Behaviors." *Communication Education* 41 (April): 167–180.

Power, W., R. Nitcavic, and D. Koerner. 1996. "Teacher Characteristics: A College Level Perspective." *Communication Education* 39: 227–233.

Rains, F. V. 1999. "Dancing on the Sharp Edge of the Sword: Women Faculty of Color in White Academe." In *Everyday Knowledge and Uncommon Truths: Women of the Academy*, edited by L. K. Christian-Smith and K. S. Kellor. Boulder, CO: Westview Press.

Reyes, M. L., and J. J. Halcon. 1988. "Racism in Academia: The Old Wolf Revisited." *Harvard Educational Review* 58 (3): 299–314.

Rubin, D. L. 1992. "Nonlanguage Factors Affecting Undergraduates' Judgments of Non-Native English-speaking Teaching Assistants." *Research in Higher Education* 33 (4): 511–531.

Rubin, D. L., and K. Smith. 1990. "Effects of Accent, Ethnicity, and Lecture Topic on Undergraduates' Perceptions of Nonnative English-speaking Teaching Assistants." *International Journal of Intercultural Relations* 14: 337–353.

Sandler, B., and R. Hall. 1982. *The Classroom Climate: A Chilly One for Women?* Washington, DC: Project on the Status and Education of Women, Association of American Colleges.

———. 1986. *The Campus Climate Revisited: Chilly for Women Faculty, Administrators, and Graduate Students.* Washington DC: Project on the Status and Education of Women, Association of American Colleges.

Sorensen, G. A., and D. M. Christophel. 1992. "The Communication Perspective." In *Power in the Classroom: Communication, Control and Concern*, edited by V. P. Richmond and J. C. McCroskey. Hillsdale, NJ: Lawrence Erlbaum.

Staton, A. Q. 1992. "Teacher and Student Concern and Classroom Power and Control." In *Power in the Classroom: Communication, Control and Concern*, edited by V. Richmond and J. C. McCroskey. Hillsdale, NJ: Lawrence Erlbaum.

Tack, M. W., and C. L. Patitu. 1993. *Faculty Job Satisfaction: Women and Minorities in Peril.* Washington, DC: The George Washington University, School of Education and Human Development.

Tierney, W. G., and E. M. Bensimon. 1996. *Community and Socialization in Academe.* Albany, NY: State University of New York Press.

Turner, C. S. V., and S. L. Myers. 2000. *Faculty of Color in Academe: Bittersweet Success.* Boston: Allyn and Bacon.

Wilds, D. J., and R. Wilson. 1998. *Sixteenth Annual Status Report on Minorities in Higher Education.* Washington, DC: American Council on Education.

Williams, M. A. 1992. "The Ultimate Negotiation: Communication Challenges for African American Women in Higher Education." In *Perspectives on Minority Women in Higher Education*, edited by L. B. Welch. New York: Praeger.

CHAPTER THREE

My Classroom in Its Context: The Struggle for Multiculturalism

LUCILA VARGAS

Abstract

AS I REFLECT on my experience as a Mexican immigrant woman teaching media and communication studies, I examine the social life of my classroom in the context of the struggle for multiculturalism. Drawing on Erving Goffman and Michel Foucault, I explore questions related to student resistance and to the mechanisms by which systems of inequality in U.S. society strive to reproduce themselves on the predominantly White campus. I posit that students can play a crucial role in resisting social change and enforcing traditional standards. I see student resistance to my teaching as one of the tactics by which social opposition to the diversification of institutions of higher education is articulated at the local level. Throughout the essay, I describe my teaching practices and my students' responses to them. I stress the strategies that help me cope with student resistance. But I also highlight how this strategy enhances the teaching-learning process that takes place in my classroom and the joy that I find in my work.

"We always write over the written," says Michel de Certeau (1996, 51). I thought about de Certeau's assertion as I decided how to write about my teaching experience on a predominantly White campus, because this experience has been intertwined with a previous research project. Since the process and product of that project (Vargas 1999) are an integral part of the story about my teaching, this chapter cannot be anything other than a way of telling the same tale. In this chapter, I draw upon Erving Goffman and Michel Foucault to posit that the predominantly White classroom becomes a contested terrain when the teacher is a woman of color and that students can play a crucial role in resisting social change and enforcing traditional standards. I also address the two questions of my earlier project: (1) How, in this presumably contested terrain, do the larger society's systems of inequality struggle to reproduce themselves? and (2) What are the specific ways in which student resistance to teacher diversity complicates the teaching-learning process? In this chapter, however, I address these questions by relying on autobiographic and autoethnographic techniques. Hence, the questions here are situated within the context of my own work experience as a Mexican immigrant professor. I also describe my pedagogical approach and some of the classroom practices that have helped me to find joy in my teaching.

For the first project, I collected data through fifteen individual interviews and a group discussion with women faculty of color plus nineteen written questionnaires with open-ended questions. I also transcribed 267 comments from 568 student evaluation forms. To write this chapter, I revisited these data and also used other documents about my teaching, such as my syllabi, class notes, peer observations of my teaching, and my course and teaching evaluations of the 1999–2000 academic year. I should note that I analyzed most of my student evaluations while I was still untenured and thus my reading of these documents was probably colored by a keen awareness of the potential impact that they could have on my life.

Erving Goffman and Michel Foucault

My approach to the study of the interactions between women faculty of color and their students combines Erving Goffman's attention to concrete, everyday events with Michel Foucault's theorizing on power and social reproduction. Foucault posits that in post-industrial societies, power is diffused and dispersed, rather than concrete and localized. "It is never localized here or there," Foucault states, "never in anybody's hands, never appropriated as a commodity or piece of wealth" (1980, 28). Disputing the conceptualization of power as something concrete and exercised from above, Foucault contends that "power in its exercise goes much further, passes through much finer channels, and it is much more ambiguous, since each individual has at his disposal a certain power, and for that very reason can also act as the vehicle for transmitting a wider power" (1980, 72).

Foucault proposes an "ascending analysis of power" that begins at the local, everyday level. In order to understand politics, he argues, one must scrutinize the subtle mechanisms and minute procedures sustaining power at the microlevel. "One of the first things that has to be understood," Foucault states, "is that power is not localized in the State apparatus and that nothing in society would be changed if the mechanisms of power that function outside, below and alongside the State apparatuses, on a much more minute and everyday level are not changed" (1980, 60).

Numerous post-structuralist theorists and postmodern researchers have drawn on Foucault's thought to theorize questions of pedagogy and schooling. Yet concrete tools to investigate what Foucault called "the microphysics of power" remain elusive. I find that Erving Goffman's analyses (1959; 1963; 1974) are a useful hermeneutic for examining the microphysics of power in the classroom. His astute observations of the way people manage everyday encounters offers a valuable reservoir of insights for analyzing classroom social life. Anthony Giddens says that "Goffman's emphasis on trust and tact… generates an analytically powerful understanding of the reflexive monitoring of the flux of encounters involved in daily life" (1986, xxiv).

Using ritual and drama as metaphors to understand social life, Goffman examines the various behaviors that take place in specific settings or situations.[1] From detailed observations of micro-events that occur in specific locales such as restaurants or hospital wards, Goffman infers tacit ground rules guiding participants' actions. Because the classroom is a setting where well-established rituals are performed and where social interactions are highly routinized, Goffman's social theory is quite appropriate for analyzing the interplay between classroom dynamics and teacher diversity. Therefore, drawing on Goffman, I look at everyday classroom events as capable of revealing the subtle mechanisms by which the larger society's systems of inequality (e.g., racism, sexism, classism, ableism, etc.) reproduce themselves. Drawing on Foucault, I view teacher-student interaction as one of those sites where some of the offensives and counter-offensives of the administrative initiative to diversify the faculty of higher education occurs. With Goffman and Foucault, I assume that the unconscious plays a crucial role in everyday social life and therefore in my interactions with students. As Joe Sprague rightly asserts, classroom interpersonal encounters "cannot be considered as a result of conscious cognitive choices without regard for the interplay of factors like class, race, gender, sexual orientation, and able-bodiedness that shape each encounter" (1992, 17).

My Self

My story is rooted in my own immigrant experience as a brown, first-generation college graduate (with a "heavy" Spanish accent). I was born and raised in Mexico, close to the U.S.-Mexican border. Like my mother and many other members of my family before me, I too crossed the border. Unlike my mother, who went back home after a few years in *el otro lado* (the other side), I have stayed in the United States for twenty years. Both of our experiences are typical of the Mexican economic migratory experience, which is fraught with contradictory desires to be a part of *El Norte* (the North). I resisted giving up my native Mexicanness until, while doing my dissertation fieldwork in Chiapas, I overheard a Mexican boy saying *"Ahi va la pocha"* (There goes the *pocha*). *Pocho/a* is a derogatory term used in Mexico to refer to Mexican Americans. The comment brought home the idea that national and ethnic identity are not only fluid but also contingent on our relationships with others. Now I make sense of my life by placing it in the space of the Third World diaspora.

My story is atypical in that I did not come to do menial work like most Mexicans, but to teach. I enjoyed a quasi-diplomatic status while teaching at the Extension School of Mexico's National Autonomous University in San Antonio, Texas. Years later, I would take my first job as assistant professor at a midwestern university and would soon realize that I would not have the same authority as a mass communication teacher that I had enjoyed as a Spanish instructor. I have been teaching in a large journalism school at the flagship campus of the North Carolina system since 1994. I was granted tenure and promoted to the rank of associate professor in the Summer of 2000. I am the school's first woman of color ever to earn tenure and the second ever to hold a tenure-track position. My predecessor was an African American woman who left before earning tenure. Among the school's thirty-three full-time faculty are two African American men, one man from China, and one man from India. Women make up about one-third of the faculty. Most of my colleagues have some kind of professional experience in journalism or related applied arts. I do not, and this matters at the school. My background in philosophy and Latin American studies seems to be irrelevant to the professional aspirations of most of our undergraduate students.

In addition to teaching a graduate seminar in Communication for Social Change, I have been teaching International Communication, Women and Mass Communication, and Current Issues in Mass Communication. All my courses are "conceptual" (as opposed to the valued "skills courses"). This also matters because in professional programs such as journalism, students are encouraged to see their education in quite instrumental terms. Most students in the Women and Mass Communication class are eager to learn about the subject matter, but most students in my other two undergraduate courses have little motivation to learn about things that—I suspect—they see as largely irrelevant to their future careers. Nearly all my students are White and middle class; increasingly, they are also women. Most were raised in the Black Belt, a region with a historical legacy of racial prejudice and sharp economic differences between Whites and African Americans (Wimberley and

Morris 1997). Many come from small towns where people have reelected, time and again, one of the nation's most conservative senators, Jesse Helms. Most people in the area did not have any experiential knowledge of Latinos until recently because Latinos did not begin to settle in the region until the 1990s. There are Latinos now on our campus: mostly men doing construction work. Many locals have seen Latinos as a threat and there have been overt manifestations of racism and xenophobia, including a rally led by former Ku Klux Klan Grand Dragon David Duke at a nearby town, Siler City. Since I came to UNC-Chapel Hill, I have felt the power of this context to shape the social life of my classroom.

My first years as assistant professor were fraught with angst, in part because of the teaching challenges that I later describe, but also because of my difficulties in adjusting to life outside of Texas (where Mexican culture is part of everyday life) and my family's stressful emotional times. Some of these hardships were related to my dual-career marriage, which is one of the life-style stressors that contribute to job dissatisfaction among women faculty (Tack and Patitu 1993, 46–48). My personal troubles were part of my teaching context and perhaps my feeling of alienation at school was fueled by loneliness and a deep longing for home.

My Pedagogy

My philosophy of teaching has been informed by the tenets of emancipatory pedagogy (Freire 1970; 1973) and critical feminist thought (Ellsworth 1989; hooks 1994; Ng 1995). My teaching-learning practice, therefore, assumes a constructivist stance regarding knowledge and knowing (Harding 1991; Hennessy 1993), and it is rooted in a commitment to transformative learning and social justice. These principles guide my classroom practices, which are student centered and inquiry oriented.

My efforts to implement my pedagogy in a classroom with over fifty juniors and seniors (who I suspect may harbor subconscious xenophobic feelings) have tested my own tolerance. Should I encourage students to draw upon their own sexist and racist cultural experiences? Should I foster a classroom climate for student voices, even though it is possible that some of those voices are fueled by contempt for Mexicans? Should I strive to empower students who I perceive as overprivileged? Added to these dilemmas are my own submerged fears and insecurities. I think that the anxiety of the novice teacher before the first day of classes was in my case entangled with the insecurity of women and the uneasiness of Mexican immigrants in the United States.

Certainly I have not overcome my personal angst and my ambivalence toward critical pedagogies, but, as I explain later, I have carved out a space in which I can foster transformative learning. For example, one of my students wrote: "I liked how she constantly challenges/questions students; it makes us think!" Many times I use the feminist metaphor of teacher as mother and draw upon my love and longing for my son to relate to the young men in my classes. Nonetheless, I still struggle to come across as an authoritative teacher. One of the classroom observations done by my colleagues captured the Achilles' heel of my teaching:

> The key problem we identified in Lucila's class was one of style, not substance or method. By way of explanation, Chuck suggested a line from King Lear about his daughter, Cordelia: "Her voice was ever soft, gentle and low, an excellent thing in woman." Admittedly sexist, the line captures the essence of the problem we identified in Lucila's class.

Other peer observations of my classroom teaching and many of my student evaluations also mention my "soft voice" and hint at my failure to come across as an authoritative professor. Creating an impression of professorial authority in my undergraduate classes has been difficult for me. By contrast, teaching a graduate seminar in Communication for Social Change has been a joyous fulfillment. The class's success has to do in part with the fact that it plays on my intellectual and interpersonal communicative strengths. It is a suitable space to engage students in inquiry-oriented exercises. It is the appropriate specialty to explore creatively a fascinating problematic. And it is a course in which I can draw on my interdisciplinary background. Most important, this space has been "a community of learners" where I have often experienced Freire's dialogic pedagogy. A space in which I have been often the learner and the students have been the teachers. This has resulted from my good fortune of having small groups of bright and motivated students. As has been true of most of the students whom I have advised on theses and dissertations, the students of this seminar have empowered me to be an effective teacher. I have felt appreciated as a teacher, cared about as a learner, and frequently also loved as a person.

I yearn to be that kind of teacher all the time. Yet in my undergraduate classes, the challenge of being a Latina faculty has been compounded by the difficulty of applying a student-centered pedagogy in classes of over fifty students. In these courses I have had mixed results. On the one hand, I have learned to be a relatively successful teacher, enjoying these classes and feeling touched by students' sudden realizations of, say, the interconnection between thought and language or the role of mass media in gender identity formation. On the other hand, teaching these classes persists as a challenge. I still get the occasional student evaluation characterizing me as a "horrible instructor," despite my having learned a variety of strategies to mitigate student scorn.

Students regularly give me high marks on accessibility and enthusiasm. Some said that I am passionate about the subject matter. Their impressions arguably stem in part from my Latin American communicative style, characterized by facial expressions and body movements that some students may interpret as extreme emotions. Some students enjoy this and other "exotic" aspects of my persona and rely on notions of cultural difference to negotiate my "unique" teaching practices. For instance, one student stated: "Professor Vargas has a unique perspective since she is a Latina. I learned a great deal from her. Her assignments are pertinent and insightful." My Latinness is sometimes a resource, sometimes an obstacle.[2] One of my students candidly wrote: "She seemed to display a strong sense of bias because of her background." Another wrote: "I often felt that she let her own opinions and biases get in the way of class subjects."

It is possible that for students not open to cultural and political differences, my "Latin" looks and communicative style, coupled with my critical political views and student-centered pedagogy, signify lack of objectivity. A recurring theme in my student evaluations is that I am very "opinionated." Given that the positivist notion of objectivity is the cornerstone of U.S. mainstream journalism's ideology, a journalism teacher's lack of objectivity is no minor problem. Some students see my expert opinion (and sometimes even the facts and theories in my lectures) as unsubstantiated beliefs. One student wrote: "The instructor is extremely biased and rarely showed both sides to an issue. She often presented her opinions as fact and sometimes graded in the same manner." Thus, according to some students, my subjectivity (which is seen as an insufficiency) colors all my teaching practices, including my grading. A question of epistemology thereby becomes an indictment of professional ethics (I am an unfair teacher).

I am aware of the inherent risks of asking students to leave their cultural comfort zones to explore issues of social justice; I am sensitive about the risks of asking them to face the dissonance between their previously taken-for-granted views and their new understandings. I also appreciate how upsetting my critical views are for some students. "The main distraction and area of dissonance for me in the class," wrote one student, "was the instructor's opinions on what are referred to as 'politically correct' areas (third-world issues, minority and women's issues)." Yet I believe that my being a Mexican immigrant woman contributes greatly to delegitimizing my knowledge. Following Foucault's contention that power is sustained at the local level by subtle mechanisms and minute procedures, I submit that some students help reproduce the social order by unconsciously expecting me to behave according to the symbolic construction of Mexican immigrant women that circulates in U.S. society. Because a prominent feature of this construction is subordination, I believe that some students feel that I should not criticize any aspects of the U.S. society. In extreme cases, these students construe my efforts to promote critical thinking as bashing White culture. Their comments have an admonishing tone: "Prof. Vargas," wrote one student, "puts too much emphasis on cultural differences for this course not to be a cultural diversity class. Also, she should respect Americans if she's going to live here." Another expressed his/her criticisms this way:

> When I signed for this course, I had no idea what kind of angle that the class would be taught from. While learning about global communication from a different perspective is helpful, the constant bashing of the United States and its culture was enough to make one ill. I can only hope that in the future the professor will realize how fortunate we are to live in such a great country & to afford such a fine institution.

I read these comments as overt efforts to reproduce established social hierarchies and ideologies. Relying on Foucault's thought, I see student evaluations both as instruments of institutional and societal surveillance and as technologies that create social distinctions. Consequently, a major challenge for me has been to create a classroom environment in which my otherness becomes a resource instead of a barrier for transformative learning. One exercise I developed is to ask students on the first day of classes to tell me about their experiences with professors of color and with non-native faculty, and, more specifically, with Mexican immigrant faculty. This exercise enables me to introduce issues of critical (standpoint) epistemology and teacher diversity. It further sets the stage for later comments about intercultural communication and students' interactions with me.

For many students, the most problematic aspect of my otherness is my "heavy" Spanish accent. In the same way that some educators still label Latino and Black children who do not speak Standard American English as "slow" or stupid, some students label me as incompetent (Farley 1988, 306). I myself used to see my accent as a personal deficiency. Now I do another exercise in which I use the encoding-decoding model of communication to challenge students to take responsibility for their part in our communication. Unlike the transmission model, which assumes that a concrete "message" is sent from an active "sender" to a passive "receiver," the encoding-decoding model stresses the role of the "reader" in the decoding of a "text." I explain that utterances (including mine) can be seen as "texts" that listeners have to "read" and that people have different levels of listening skills and cognitive processing. Then I go back to the discussion about the uniqueness of their learning experience with me, combined with a discussion on accents (including the prominent southern accent of many students). Finally, I invite them to take on the challenge of further developing listening skills that will help them to communicate with the world's millions of English speakers with accents different from their own. Many students have told me that they like these exercises, and it seems that they have helped some students to open up to foreign-born teachers. For example, one student wrote: "She is excellent—it was interesting to have someone teach of a different language and a different country." But many other students resent my asking them to take more responsibility for our verbal interactions than they would like to: "She talks too soft & w/a terrible accent that no one can understand. When confronted with these problems she says the class has a problem!" wrote one student. Comments such as this one reveal that my efforts to subvert prevailing notions of linguistic hierarchies are not always successful. I see these comments, in Foucauldian terms, as counter-offensives. These students are articulating at the local level the tenets of the national political movement against immigrants and bilingual education.

The Social Life of My Classroom

My student-centered teaching practices, combined with my fears and insecurities, have not always been the most effective teaching strategy for the circumstances of my teaching. I have identified two major problematic aspects: lack of control and ambiguity of instruction. Ambiguity comes with the package of emancipatory pedagogies; it is difficult for students not used to such teaching practices to accept a non-directive role on the part of the instructor and to grasp the significance of multiple ways of knowing—not to mention the difficulty in problematizing absolute truths and universal values. Effectively coping with these various sources of ambiguity is not easy for many students, and they become confused and frustrated. I will return to this point later. Here I focus on issues of control.

Control is a major concern for most novice teachers, but I think that it was particularly challenging for me. I attempted to relinquish my institutional power while struggling with the contradiction between the power of being a professor and the signs of subordination inscribed in my body. Following Goffman's analysis of social life as drama, I learned to interpret the events

that take place in my classroom as theatrical performances.[3] These performances are shaped by the interplay between the classroom's interpersonal dynamics and the larger social, cultural, political, and economic forces that
surround and permeate my classroom. Goffman distinguishes between "expressions given" and "expressions given off" during a performance. While the
former are intentional and are often carefully rehearsed, the latter are largely
unintentional and are often unconscious. Goffman's insights helped me see
that my ability to control the class, therefore, relies not only on my deliberate
actions and words, but also on the behavioral expressions that I unintention-
ally "give off." The behavioral expressions that may have undermined my efforts to establish myself as an authority figure are components of what
Goffman called the "personal front" of a performer. They include "clothing;
sex, age, and racial characteristics; size and looks; posture; speech patterns;
facial expressions; bodily gestures; and the like" (1959, 24). I have striven to
be more aware of my personal front, especially during the first classes (I definitely shift my language style toward a formal register and wear a suit during
the first two weeks). Moreover, I stress my teaching experience and other
scholarly accomplishments when introducing myself to the class. But doing
this is not easy, because as a Mexican, lower-middle-class girl, I was not only
taught, but disciplined, to be humble. Underneath, sometimes I feel like an
impostor.

My impostor complex is undoubtedly due to gender oppression, but I
think is by and large a class issue. Many working-class women academics,
contend Michelle M. Tokarezyk and Elizabeth A. Fay, "have an impostor
complex; they fear that they've scammed others into giving them doctorates
and academic positions and constantly have to prove themselves and others
that they are worthy" (1993, 17).[4] I am a social climber, and this fact is hard
to conceal on a campus where my brown body signals the lowest-status occupations on campus. Goffman's *Stigma* (1963) is a treatise on how difficult it is
for stigmatized individuals not to behave according to society's expectations
of them. Like other stigmatized individuals, I have even occasionally questioned my legitimacy. Doubts about one's self-worth, which are often manifestations of internalized oppression, were expressed by four of the junior
professors I interviewed in my earlier research project. One of them explained:

> I think the things that make it [being a professor] harder are sometimes internal to
> me, but they're also external. I've noticed this more in women and in people that are
> different than the mainstream. We are just constantly second guessing whether we're
> good or not. *It just drives me nuts* how I do that and I see my colleagues do that....But

that constant perception by other people, that the fact that you happen to be a minority and female and you are where you are means that's why you got where you are. And that just undermines everything you do. And it starts to seep into yourself and it's really hard to, sort of, stand up straight and say no that's not the reason why. I got here because of these qualities I have. So that constant second guessing of yourself and self-doubt and, sort of, ego dysfunction, that I think being different, not being White and male, sort of, drives a lot of people, and it's a constant struggle internally to not believe that. That's probably the hardest thing. Sort of this pervasive self-doubt.

Even though I grew up a member of Mexico's mainstream culture, my own experience has also been a constant struggle against internalized oppression. It has been very hard for me to admit that my own teaching practice has been undermined by my own shyness and self-doubt. I have often used the excuse of having to teach in English (a language I learned as an adult) to hide, especially from myself, my harsh feelings about my teaching. My self-doubt is entrenched in the widespread sexism of the Mexican society in which I grew up, in the U.S. culture's undercurrents of contempt for Mexicans, and in the enlightened racism of the UNC campus; but, again, it is mostly a class issue. Internalized class oppression is a formidable obstacle because of its insidious nature. One of the most upsetting incidents at UNC occurred when I went to get my first ID card. I was given an ID identifying me as staff instead of faculty. The incident was so upsetting because it told me, loud and clear, that social mobility for dark-skinned people is never quite complete.

Since I come from stigmatized groups and my appearance and expressive behavior definitely fail to fit the persona of the "normal" professor, I have encountered repeated difficulties getting accepted and treated as a legitimate member of academe. While doing this research, however, I found great comfort in learning that my personal troubles resonate with similar experiences of many women professors of color. One of the professors I interviewed stated that students perceive her as Other because of "the manner in which they address me, and the lack of respect accorded to me in the class." Another one wrote that she was seen as Other because "I'm an African American in a position of authority that some have not expected." A Latina wrote a poignant comment on this: "They see a petite brown young faculty member. They must adjust their perspectives. Many students do not make the adjustment needed and do not take their professor seriously. They cannot believe that the person before them has a Ph.D., or is an expert in the area of study." Comments such as these demonstrated to me that my own classroom challenges had to do more with social and political concerns than with my own personal deficiencies as instructor.[5]

For example, consider the seemingly easy task of defining each class session as a "class" rather than, say, just a "gathering." Despite my institutional authority, my power to define the situation depends on the collaboration of all members of the university community. This collaboration, in turn, rests in part on people's perception of me as a real (not a token) professor. One of Goffman's central concepts refers to people's struggle to define (or "frame," in Goffman's terms) social situations in which they become involved. Part of this struggle has to do with the limitations imposed on an individual's agency by multiple factors, including other individuals' agency, and her by own social location and unintentional expressive behavior. For me, the struggle to define the parameters of my interactions with students has taken convoluted twists.

I cannot conceal my color, my accent, and many other aspects of my otherness on the predominantly White campus, and this conspicuous otherness has an impact on the way my professional competence is perceived in the classroom. Goffman theorizes that the members of most professions need to dramatize their work in order to convey a sense of professional competence to others. A key element for a successful dramatization is the ability to perform one's work in such a way that the routine matches the idealized image held by society about a given performance. Because nobody exactly matches the ideal, a good performer "tends to conceal or underplay those activities, facts, and motives which are incompatible with an idealized version of himself and his products," says Goffman (1959, 48). For me, then, "putting on a good show" in the classroom has not been an easy task. Teachers like me need an unusual mastery of our professional role to offset the contradictory signals that our personas give off. One of the professors I interviewed put her finger right on it: "The only way you get away with it is being more than average. That is, being the walk-on-the-water different minority, where it's obvious that you are so good and so different. Then you become the celebrity. But if you're just average Joe, forget it."

I feel that some students frame me as incompetent in our first encounter. For example, my teaching assistant told me that a White woman student asked her, just after the very first class, if I were qualified to teach the course! Students' first impressions not only weigh heavily on student ratings (Brooks 1985); as self-fulfilling prophesies they can also shape the way the course develops. Teachers might find themselves in what Goffman calls a "frame trap." He says that "the world can be arranged (whether by intent or default) so that incorrect views, however induced, are confirmed by each bit of new evidence or each effort to correct matters, so that, indeed, the individual finds that he is trapped and nothing can get through. The notion of the frame trap is conventionalized in the interrogation joke 'Have you stopped beating your wife?'" (Goffman 1974, 480).

For teachers whose native language is not English, like myself, frame traps are especially likely. It is well documented that many undergraduate students avoid taking classes taught by non-native speakers of English (Rubin and Smith 1990). Not surprisingly, the most frequent negative comment about my performance in the classroom refers to my "thick accent." There is little research on these issues, but studies on international teaching assistants have revealed that undergraduates' preexisting social stereotypes have a strong effect on how they rate these instructors' teaching performance.[6]

Some of my students fail to appreciate performances that are not given in Standard American English. When I invited a Brazilian Xavante videomaker to my International Communication class, one student complained in the evaluation form: "Many of the (guest) speakers had trouble speaking English." On another occasion, when I invited the head of the British Broadcasting Standards Council to this class, students' comments on her talk centered on *their* trouble with *her* British accent. Although this kind of student resistance is profoundly discouraging, fortunately I have been able to see that exposure to otherness can have a transformative learning effect. Here are other student comments on the Xavante videomaker's talk: "Thank you for arranging this lecturer. It was an extremely valuable experience." "Having this speaker really enhanced my understanding of indigenous cultures and their points of view. It really enforces the common beliefs among humanity."[7]

Securing cooperation from my students has been a further test of my abilities. As with all dramatic performances, a successful class requires the audience's cooperation to create and sustain an atmosphere of make-believe. Some hostile or resentful students have refused to exercise what Goffman called "audience tact":

> When performers make a slip of some kind, clearly exhibiting a discrepancy between the fostered impression and a disclosed reality, the audience may tactfully "not see" the slip or readily accept the excuse that is offered for it. And at moments of crisis for the performers, the whole audience may come into tacit collusion with them in order to help them out (1959, 231–232).

I believe that some students' ideas of what a "normal professor" and a "Mexican woman" are have kept them from exercising audience tact during some of my performances. The stereotypes of people of color that circulate in American society persist among many college students (Gordon 1986). Such prejudices have not only prevented some students from tactfully overlooking my mistakes but may have predisposed them to find fault where there was none. Securing students' cooperation has also been a challenge for me because professors rely on the established boundaries between faculty and students to keep discipline in the classroom. Those established boundaries tend to fade in my classroom. For example, it took me a while to learn how to tactfully point out to some of my male students that they should not touch my shoulder when they approached me with a question. One time I tried to appropriate one of the disciplinary techniques used by a White woman colleague to enforce discipline by exposing unacceptable behavior in the classroom. The class session after I had subtly (or so I thought) exposed the behavior of a woman student, I found her waiting for me in front of the class with a defiant manner. Obviously, I cannot always rely on my White colleagues to be role models. Discipline actions on my part are like a balancing act: I have to be authoritative enough to command, yet even a little authority in my part offends some of my students. Although many students—even some who evaluate my teaching poorly—express that I am "very nice," a few others say that I am "rude and inconsiderate."

Students' Responses to My Pedagogy

One of the first things I noticed about my teaching evaluations was its bipolarity. Students often disagree on their assessments of the course and my performance. After much reflection on this apparent contradiction, I realized that these documents (which are invaluable records of institutional and societal change) embody feelings and judgments about the diversification of the faculty. To make sense of a Mexican immigrant woman professor, my students must draw on their own life experiences and sense of identity. For some of them, my professorial authority might be reassuring, but for others it might be profoundly threatening. Later, I concluded that such bipolarity also revealed the degree of learning that occurred during the semester. As Magda Lewis points out, "We need to understand that a class, multiply divided in debate, included as this debate is carried into course and teaching evaluations, is a learning class" (Lewis 1999, 77).

Students' responses to me and my teaching practices can be grouped in three general categories: acceptance, confusion, and hostility. In my classroom, a student's status as a minority is a fairly good predictor of a positive response. U.S. minority students and foreign students often express appreciation for having me as their teacher and/or adviser. Likewise, White students with some type of outsider status themselves often feel an affinity with me. Some working-class students, gay and lesbian students, and especially students with critical views seem to enjoy my classes. Along with students' real or felt marginal status are crucial contextual factors that enable students to enjoy my classes. A foremost factor is the course's content. Despite its large size, my Women and Mass Communication class always has many more happy students than my other undergraduate classes. The course's content easily lends itself to problematizing taken-for-granted notions about social distinctions and hierarchies, including traditional classroom hierarchies. Because nearly all students in this class are women, the class is a safe space for us to talk about troubling gender issues. Students quickly learn to use what they learn in class to make sense of their daily life. Further, since I am heterosexual and look "feminine," and have been a wife and a mother, I discuss issues of sexuality from the privileged stance of a woman who has fulfilled society's mandate for women. Moreover, I simply like teaching about gender and media more than I like teaching about global media trends; despite the fact that my formal training is in the latter, my passion is in the former.

The second and most common student response has been confusion. I have seen many students become puzzled and frustrated when they take classes with me. These feelings are probably brought about by numerous factors, especially my critical views. I think, however, that two factors are crucial: my pedagogy and their low expectations of a class with a Mexican woman. My class evaluations contain comments revealing how my pedagogical practices disconcert many students: "People got *too* uptight in class—weird/non-productive discussions/fights." Often, disconcerted students state that the class lacks structure and that it is disorganized. Some disapprove of my attempts to reposition myself as a co-learner and ask me to play a more traditional role: "*Too* much class discussion—teacher didn't always teach," wrote one student. And another wrote: "Her teaching method is incredibly timid and apologetic." Some disconcerted students fail to see the value of some of my teaching practices, such as peer evaluations: "Why did we do so much peer evaluation?" asked one of them at the end of the term, despite my efforts to help them see their tremendous value. My non-directive teaching is at times met by resistant students who insist on getting step-by-step instructions from me: "Requirements for things were not clear," complained one student. And some students have no use for my creative assignments: "The book reviews puzzled me. I didn't understand the point of the exercise."[8]

The other critical factor unsettling many of my students has to do with their low expectations of a class with a Latina teacher. One of the most frequent complaints in my student evaluations is that my classes are too demanding. "Way too much work, attendance policy is unfair, grading is ridiculous. Quizzes are ridiculous," wrote one student. As another Latina faculty remarked, I think that some students expect our classes "to be a pushover and become angry when they are wrong."

I try in various ways to help students reflect on their own unconscious attitudes and behaviors regarding social distinctions, especially class, race, ethnicity, gender, and national origin. For example, I ask them to pay attention to the representation of Latinos in television. I would like to believe that for some initially distraught students a class with me turned out to be an enlightening encounter with their own prejudices. Some of my evaluations mention that my classes are an "eye-opening experience." My favorite comment in this respect is this: "Mrs. Vargas is an excellent instructor. Probably one of the best that I have had at this university. She has opened my male dominated eyes & views." Another student candidly admitted: "At first I was skeptical, but I really liked Prof. Vargas and think she's a great teacher." Comments such as the last one suggest that some students resist the new situation in transformative ways. But for those students whose integrity is threatened by the situation, the encounter with me provokes a negative response, an inclination to "not learn" from me.[9] The most extreme resistance to my teaching has been open harassment from students with reactionary cultural politics. They have expressed anger and resentfulness. I think they find it quite difficult to accept that the university has bestowed me, a woman of color, with powers of surveillance and discipline over men and over Whites. The worst harassment I have endured is a handful of hate messages written in the anonymous forms that I use for gathering student feedback throughout the semester. (It is difficult to convey the inexplicable shame I felt when I got them.) Some of my formal student evaluations, which students know will be seen by other faculty, contain less inflammatory but nonetheless resentful comments. "This course," wrote one of my students, "was a waste of time, her lecture content was unclear and pointless. She didn't clarify anything she taught. I think she should not be teaching at any university. She cannot be understood, her speech is unclear and inaudible. I think that she doesn't know what she is talking about whatsoever." Students with reactionary politics have expressed, in various ways, their resentment of my power to upset their work, their time, and their grades. Often, these students are White men. Fourteen of the professors I interviewed also stated that they have experienced rejection from White male students. One of them said: "I've had at least three occasions when White male students have felt that I had nothing to offer them in terms of their education....But I don't know whether that's a reflection of this campus or just a reflection of the way society is." I used to think that White male students were more likely than their female counterparts to express their hostility in overt behavior, but I have discovered that gender may not be the strongest predictor of hostile responses.

My feelings about White males were grounded in an extraordinary experience with two White male students. During my second year at UNC, I had two extremely conservative White male students who questioned everything that could be questioned. Much of the material I was using was prepared by two White women veteran faculty. Among much useful material, there was a faulty grading system for group projects that my colleagues have used for years without major problems. In my class, the two White male students discovered the subtle error, rallied the class against me, and complained to the administration. I had to change the entire class's grades. After this incident, I decided to be as specific as possible about grading procedures in my syllabi and to never discuss graded tests or other assignments in class. Now I invite students to come by my office (a safer place than the classroom) and to offer an informed and compelling argument for their grievances. Although I am very firm regarding the course's rules and grading procedures, I am quick to recognize when I have made the slightest mistake. Most important, I focus the conversation on the content and purpose of the assignment, which gives me the opportunity to engage students in learning.

Conclusion

By examining the social life of my classroom in the context of the current struggle for multiculturalism, I interpret hostile student resistance to my teaching as one of the tactics by which social opposition to diversifying institutions of higher education is articulated. "Each offensive from the one side," says Foucault, "serves as leverage for a counter-offensive from the other" (1980, 163). As I described above, some students think that I have nothing to offer to them, and there have been some dramatic incidents in my classroom, but dramatic incidents are probably just the tip of the iceberg. Although students' resistance toward women faculty of color is sometimes expressed in overt behavior (and we can tell revealing stories about such behavior), most challenges to our knowledge and authority are acted out in subtle ways. To grasp the subtle mechanisms of social reproduction that are likely to delay the professional progress of women faculty of color, it is necessary to give careful thought to the politics of today's college classroom. As the literature on faculty diversity reveals, both men and women faculty of color have been pointing out the various ways in which cultural mythology slows their professional advancement. Listening to our narratives is a first step for developing institutional strategies to deal with the challenges discussed in this essay.

Lucila Vargas teaches in the areas of communication and social change, international communication, and gender, class, race, and ethnicity and the media. She has a Ph.D. from the University of Texas at Austin, and she is now a tenured associate professor at the University of North Carolina at Chapel Hill. Her book, *Social Uses and Radio Practices: The Use of Participatory Radio by Ethnic Minorities in Mexico*, is an ethnographic account of grassroots communication. She has also published research on U.S. Latinos and the media.

Author's Note

I wish to thank my colleagues Ryuko Kubota, Enrique Murrillo, Xue Rong, Chuck Stone, and the faculty who participated in my initial research project for their insights and encouragement. I am also grateful to the numerous students who commented on various versions of this paper. Some of the most useful observations came from graduate students who read and discussed the paper with me in the space provided by Tom Bowers in his pedagogy seminar.

Notes

1. Another metaphor Goffman uses to understand social life is the "game."
2. There is some hard data supporting my thinking. Rose Weitz and Leonard Gordon, who surveyed the image of Black women among 256 White non-Latino undergraduates, found that they "primarily view Black women as threats: loud, aggressive, argumentative, stubborn, and so on"(1993, 27). Weitz and Gordon also determined that Anglo students "assign different emotional evaluations to the same trait depending on whether they are characterizing women in general or Black women"(1993, 29). Identical patterns were found regarding students' attitudes toward Mexican American and Jewish American women.
3. Goffman examines lecturing as a performance in *Forms of Talk* (1981), but he focuses on speech rather than power issues.
4. The effects of the impostor complex is a frequent topic in feminist scholarship on women in higher education. Larissa A. Grunig, for instance, argues that the "imposter syndrome" causes women professors "to downplay or dismiss their accomplishments" (1993, 280).
5. Recognizing that I had much to learn regarding teaching techniques, I did attend several workshops offered by UNC's Center for Teaching and Learning. While they did not help me to cope with the political problems that I describe here, they helped me to deal with other classroom challenges. Additionally, they also proved to be useful for the tenure review. One of the outside reviewers commented that these workshops demonstrated my efforts to improve my teaching.
6. Rubin and Smith (1990) found that the strongest predictors of teacher ratings were undergraduates' *perceptions* of the instructor's accent. Even more, Rubin's research on East Asian instructors (1992) suggests that preconceptions shape students' perceptions; the sampled undergraduates stereotypically attributed a foreign accent to East Asian-looking teachers who spoke Standard American English.
7. These positive comments come from the forms that I regularly use to gather student feedback on guest speakers.
8. This assignment is not a traditional book review. It asks students to pretend that they work for a publishing company. Their task is to write a 600-word memorandum recommending changes for the second edition of one of the course's textbooks. This is an early assignment in the semester and it seeks to encourage students to look at the entire textbook with a critical distance, aided by two book reviews written by experts in the field.
9. Kohl argues that students respond to schooling situations that threaten their integrity by resolving not to learn (Kohl 1991).

Works Cited

Brooks, D. M. 1985. "The First Day of School." *Educational Leadership* 43: 76–78.

de Certeau, M. 1996. *La Invención de lo Cotidiano. 1 Artes de Hacer.* Translated by A. Pescador. México: Universidad Iberoamericana.

Ellsworth, E. 1989. "Why Doesn't This Feel Empowering? Working Through the Repressive Myths of Critical Pedagogy." *Harvard Educational Review* 59 (3): 297–324.

Farley, J. E. 1988. *Majority-Minority Relations.* 2nd. ed. Englewood Cliffs, NJ: Prentice Hall.

Foucault, M. 1980. *Power/Knowledge.* New York: Pantheon.

Freire, P. 1970. *Pedagogy of the Oppressed.* New York: Continuum.

———. 1973. *Education for Critical Consciousness*. New York: Seasbury Press.

Giddens, A. 1986. *The Constitution of Society*. Berkeley: U. of California Press.

Goffman, E. 1959. *The Presentation of Self in Everyday Life*. New York: Doubleday.

———. 1963. *Stigma*. Englewood Cliffs, NJ: Prentice-Hall.

———. 1974. *Frame Analysis: An Essay on the Organization of Experience*. New York: Harper and Row.

———. 1981. *Forms of Talk*. Philadelphia: University of Pennsylvania Press.

Gordon, L. 1986. "College Students' Stereotypes of Blacks and Jews on Two Campuses: Four Studies Spanning 50 Years." *Sociology and Social Research* 70 (3): 200–201.

Grunig, L. A. 1993. "The 'Glass Ceiling' Effect on Mass Communication Students." In *Women in Mass Communication*, edited by P. J. Creedon. Newbury Park, CA: Sage.

Harding, S. 1991. *Whose Science? Whose Knowledge: Thinking from Women's Lives*. Ithaca, NY: Cornell University Press.

Hennessy, R. 1993. "Women's Lives/Feminist Knowledge: Feminist Standpoint as Ideology Critique." *Hypatia* 8 (1): 14–34.

hooks, b. 1994. *Teaching to Transgress: Education as the Practice of Freedom*. New York: Routledge.

Kohl, H. 1991. *I Won't Learn from You*. Minneapolis: Milkweed.

Lewis, M. 1999. "The Backlash Factor: Women, Intellectual Labour and Student Evaluations of Courses and Teaching." In *Everyday Knowledge and Uncommon Truths*, edited by L. K. Christian-Smith and K. S. Kellor. Boulder, CO: Westview Press.

Ng, R. 1995. "Teaching Against the Grain: Contradictions and Possibilities." In *Anti-racism, Feminism, and Critical Approaches to Education*, edited by R. Ng, P. Staton and J. Scane. Westport, CT: Bergin & Garvey.

Rubin, D. L. 1992. "Nonlanguage Factors Affecting Undergraduates' Judgments of Non-Native English-speaking Teaching Assistants." *Research in Higher Education* 33 (4): 511–531.

Rubin, D. L., and K. Smith. 1990. "Effects of Accent, Ethnicity, and Lecture Topic on Undergraduates' Perceptions of Nonnative English-speaking Teaching Assistants." *International Journal of Intercultural Relations* 14: 337–353.

Sprague, J. 1992. "Expanding the Research Agenda for Instructional Communication: Raising Some Unasked Questions." *Communication Education* 41: 1–25.

Tack, M. W., and C. L. Patitu. 1993. *Faculty Job Satisfaction: Women and Minorities in Peril*. Washington, DC: The George Washington University, School of Education and Human Development.

Tokarezyk, M. M., and E. A. Fay, eds. 1993. *Working-Class Women in the Academy. Laborers in the Knowledge Factory*. Amherst, MA: University of Massachussetts Press.

Vargas, L. 1999. "When the 'Other' is the Teacher: Implications of Teacher Diversity in Higher Education." *The Urban Review* 31 (4): 359–383.

Weitz, R., and L. Gordon. 1993. "Images of Black Women among Anglo College Students." *Sex Roles* 28 (1/2): 19–34.

Wimberley, R. C., and L. V. Morris. 1997. *The Southern Black Belt*. Lexington, KY: TVA Rural Studies, University of Kentucky.

CHAPTER FOUR

"Passing/Out" in the Classroom: Eradicating Binaries of Identity

GISELLE LIZA ANATOL

Abstract

IN MY EXPERIENCES as an instructor at public and private universities in the Northeast as well as in the Midwest, in classes of ten nervous freshmen or ninety students of varying ability and levels of jadedness, I have discovered that so much of teaching is performance. Regardless of how good my acting is, however, I am placed into certain roles by my audience. I therefore continue to think and rethink my self-presentation and the process of passing. As a brown-skinned lesbian daughter of immigrants, in what ways do I pass? In this chapter, I examine my active and passive performances at the front of the classroom, employing an extended discussion of Shani Mootoo's short story "Out on Main Street" as an interpretive lens through which one can consider notions of ever-shifting, unfixed identity.

> Perhaps it is the case, then, that my identity is not what I am but what I am passing for.
>
> Samira Kawash (1996, 73)

My first act of sexual self-disclosure at the midwestern state university where I have been teaching since August 1998 came as much as a shock to me as it did to my students; the words seemed to tumble out of my mouth of their own accord. Because I was encountering rather atypical hesitance from this vocal group of freshman and sophomores during our discussion of Shani Mootoo's (1993) short story "Out on Main Street," I asked them to take a time-out from considering the work at hand and create lists of the first images that popped into their minds when they heard the word "lesbian." I hoped that as they shared their ideas, they might get over their initial shyness of actually saying the taboo "L" word. I also anticipated gaining a stronger sense of the students' stereotypical assumptions, beliefs, and level of exposure to the Queer so that I could better direct their analysis of the text.[1]

In contrast to the honors freshmen I had taught the semester before, the students in this Spring 1999 Introduction to Fiction course represented a more accurate cross-section of the undergraduate population. Some were very bright and motivated; several hoped to be English majors. Quite a few, however, were merely fulfilling their sophomore English requirement. I had a higher percentage of students of color enrolled in this class than in any other to date—eight (ascertainable to me) out of thirty five—and three students who identified themselves as struggling to attend classes while working full-time. Earlier in the term, I had found that eliciting the students' personal experiences and using some childhood stories of my own had been instrumental to the class's overall comprehension of the ideas and situations presented in the sometimes-alien narratives of the course.[2] Although many academics wince at the idea of sharing personal information with their students, I find that this practice of disclosure—appropriately done—can stimulate a great deal of thought. It has the potential to wrench students out of certain ruts of presumption as well as their passive comfort with acting as the inert vessels of transmitted information.[3] Recent constructivist views of education emphasize that people learn most by constructing and reconstructing their own already-formulated ideas of the world; therefore, if an occasional personal example helps to illuminate a point more compellingly than one from the assigned text, I encourage students to use it. I am confident that this practice of making connections to various spheres of life aids them not only in retaining the material but in seeing and seeking its applicability to other courses and the world outside of the university setting.

The first five or so students to speak about their conceptions of lesbians were all women.[4] One exclaimed that the idea of a woman approaching her and trying to kiss her sickened her. Another stated, "I think of two women together...*You* know. I don't know what they do...I don't *want* to know what they do...You know." She twisted uncomfortably in her chair, and seemed unable to go farther in either speech or thought. Like the student before her, she believed that homosexual identity centered on the sexual act—a deliberately amorphous, horrifyingly unvisualized/unvisualizable act. In striking contrast to this invisible performance of sex, however, was the preconception of the highly visible, clearly marked Queer body: a third student suggested that lesbians wore very short hair, "guy's" clothes, and combat boots.

I thought about my shorn head. I also thought about my tailored blazer and long skirt. I began, "What I find fascinating about this discussion is that you are all speaking with the assumption that there are no gay people in our classroom. In a class of forty, statistically speaking, there should be at least one or two gay people among us." The students looked nervously around to try to determine whom it might be. Where was the mysterious Queer who had sneaked by their sexuality sensors and "passed"? This indistinguishable presence revealed that using the physical body as a site of identic interpretation was a troubled, if not impossible, process.

Passing, in terms of ethnicity or sexual orientation, can help to avoid the enclosures of xenophobia and homophobic stereotyping in much the same way that Martha Cutter argues that racial passing can be "a subversive strategy for avoiding the enclosures of a racist, classist, and sexist society (in order to) become truly liberating" (Cutter 1996, 75). The liberation in which I am interested, however, is not only my own but also the liberation of the minds of the students. As I discussed issues of sexuality with this group of young scholars, I recognized that I had a radically productive opportunity for this type of liberation, but only if I revealed the "pass."

Literary critics Kathryn Conrad and Julie Crawford have argued that the act of simply wondering about the sexual identity of others can be ideologically transformative for students; it "can lead to intellectual curiosity about the stability of normative categories of all kinds" (Conrad and Crawford 1998, 153). My own students' agitated attempts to pinpoint the queer, however, only seemed to reinforce the conventional boundaries of a grounded, ordinary Self lying in stark opposition to a strange (i.e., "Queer") Other. In order to truly achieve the conceptual challenge that I desired, the explicit declaration of my sexual identity was necessary.

I therefore continued on: "You know, your professor is gay." (As I heard two front-row students gasp and watched all eyes bulge wide, I experienced a moment of alarm and wondered if this indeed was the appropriate coming-out moment.[5]) I quipped: "I fooled you with my lipstick, didn't I?" Some students laughed, and I felt a small sense of relief.

Part of my anxiety at this first pedagogical coming-out experience at the University of Kansas was that I feared that the students might believe I had "tricked" them by asking for their opinions before divulging my identity. In some ways, I think that the shock of being caught with their pants down, so to speak, was effective for helping the students to recognize the true force of their false assumptions. One must be accountable for one's opinions, know what they are based upon, and be ready to back them up (typically, in class, with evidence from the text we are discussing). This is one of the major premises of all the courses I teach. At the same time, however, I panicked that I had ruined the atmosphere of trust that had carefully been built up over the first half of the semester. The next time I prepared to come out to a class—this time a group of forty Literature for Children students in the spring of 2000—I again asked the members of the class to share opinions, but this time worded the question as follows: "What are the stereotypes of lesbians that exist in U.S. society?" This alteration allowed the students to "hide" from me as an authority figure, but not necessarily from themselves, behind the metaphorical veil of "other people's" presumptions and beliefs.

In the necessary stage of bringing the conversation back to the assigned short story in the aforementioned Introduction to Fiction class, I connected the reading and misreading of my appearance to the ways the characters' bodies are read and misread in Mootoo's work. I realize that while English professors must urge and push students to scrutinize the assigned readings in a course, the students far more readily scrutinize us as we stand in the front of the room or sit at the head of the circle.[6] And as Conrad and Crawford note, "A first step towards understanding the implications of disclosure is understanding the extent to which the teacher is read as one of the texts of the classroom" (1998, 156).

To think about this dynamic in another way: In my experiences at both public and private universities, in the Northeast as well as in the Midwest, in classes of ten nervous freshmen or ninety students of varying levels of ability and jadedness, I have discovered that so much of teaching is performance. I prepare myself to walk into a classroom in much the same way that I primed myself to walk onstage in the children's theater shows of my undergraduate career. Regardless of how good my acting is, however, I will be placed in certain roles by my audience. For the rest of the term that I first taught the Introduction to Fiction course, I found myself thinking and rethinking my self-presentation and the process of passing. As a brown-skinned, lesbian daughter of upwardly mobile immigrants, in what ways do I pass? In this essay, I examine my active and passive performances at the front of various groups of predominantly White midwestern students, eventually employing an extended discussion of Mootoo's story as an interpretative lens for considering notions of ever-shifting, unfixed identity. I will address how my means of maneuvering in an academic space and various moments of revelation and disclosure can be pedagogically transformative.

*   *   *

In January 1836, the Richmond *Whig* published the following advertisement:

> 100 DOLLARS REWARD. Will be given for the apprehension of my negro Edmund
> Kenney. He has straight hair, and complexion so nearly white that it is believed a

stranger would suppose there was no African blood in him...escaped under the pretence of being a white man. (quoted in Ginsberg 1996, 1)

Kenney, like countless others who could also "pass" for White, fled slavery's horrors and entered a world of freedom and social privilege. More than sixty years later, two decades after emancipation, African Americans were proclaimed "separate but equal" by the Supreme Court. Homer Plessy, a man with one Black great-grandparent, and thus "Negro" by law, had generated tremendous anxiety when his white complexion allowed him to buy a first-class train ticket and gain entrance to a Whites-only railroad car. In the 1896 *Plessy v. Ferguson* decision, the justices determined that the Fourteenth Amendment meant political, but not social, equality, reaffirming the principles of segregation and thus leading to the adoption of Jim Crow laws throughout the South. As a result, there were increasing numbers of "passers"—African Americans who denied their Black racial ancestry and legal definition in order to achieve a measure of social and economic success.

The practice of passing called the American system of racial categories and hierarchies into question, especially the notion that the categories of "Black" and "White" were in binary opposition, mutually exclusive, and unequivocally essential.[7] By extension, identity as a whole—not solely in terms of race but also in terms of the numerous aspects of its formulation—was effectively exposed as imposed and/or self-created, potentially adopted or rejected, highly mutable and multiple, and largely about visual "specularity." In other words, identity was theoretically removed from the realm of the absolute, the intrinsic, and the natural when it was shown that the clearly visible traits interpreted as "fact" could just as easily be misinterpreted: "Passing forces reconsideration of the cultural logic that the physical body is the site of identic intelligibility" (Ginsberg 1996, 4).

Nella Larsen's novel *Passing*, originally published in 1929, tells the story of Irene Redfield, who passes occasionally to gain access to particular stores, restaurants, seating arrangements, and the like, and Clare Kendry, who has left both community and past behind in order to marry a wealthy White businessman. At one point, Hugh Wentworth, a friend of the Redfields, proclaims, "I couldn't pick some of 'em [African Americans passing for White] if my life depended on it." Irene responds, "Nobody can. Not by looking" (Larsen 1986, 206). Similarly, Clare's husband believes that he can visually distinguish Black from White: "No niggers in my family. Never have been and never will be" (171). The irony, of course, lies in the fact that his wife of twelve years is one of the disparaged group of Others. Both conversations resonate in a scene from Jamaican author Michelle Cliff's *No Telephone to*

Heaven. The White manager of a Georgia hotel asks the light-complexioned Boy Savage if, "by any chance," he is Black, because "niggers...ain't welcome. It ain't legal" (Cliff 1989, 55). The manager casts his "trained eye" over the visage of the Jamaican immigrant, but is bewildered by thin lips, British-tinged accent, and skin that is "colored...but a manner that was quite white" (Cliff 1989, 56). In both Larsen's and Cliff's narratives, the visual markers of a supposed racial identity are unmasked as flimsy and unsound. In our U.S. society, where "justice is blind" but "seeing is believing" and evidence is typically visual proof, the inability to rely on the view before one's eyes wreaks havoc.[8]

These literary scenes provide a key element for the analysis of my position in the classroom. Students bring certain assumptions to the space the moment they see me because they can read a racial identity and a gender identity onto my appearance. Unlike Anneliese Truame (1994), who explains that she must verbalize her identities to make her experience visible because she wears her Anglo/Amerindian/Mexican ethnicity, physical limitations, and sexual orientation as unmarked categories, as a medium-brown-complexioned African American woman, there are certain ways I cannot pass. Conjectures about what it means to have a visibly Black English professor, what it means to have a female English professor, and, finally, what it specifically means to have a Black woman in front of the classroom cannot be avoided once I step up to the lectern on the first day of the term.

I am pleased to note that a supportive university environment makes my task much easier in several ways. Unlike many of my peers who teach at other institutions around the country, I am not the sole face of Blackness in my department; I am not even the only Black woman professor among the English faculty. Although I have had lamentably few African American students enrolled in my classes (or any students of color, for that matter), I am extremely fortunate to be part of a department that is committed to diversifying its instructors. Within a year of my 1998 appointment as an assistant professor, two other Black senior colleagues were hired. Together with other English professors who focus on African American literature, we have passed several new courses into the curriculum and thereby strengthened the university's offerings in African Diasporic Studies. Hopefully these changes will generate more interest among students of color and attract a more varied student body.

I would argue that by our mere presence, we three African American English professors have the potential to challenge many dominant views of the academy. As two women and one man; two senior scholars and one junior; as a grandparent, a parent, and a childless woman; as an African American from the deep South, an African American from the Midwest, and a Caribbean American from the Northeast, we represent a wide variety of experiences and approaches to literature, to scholarship, and to students. We also are important visual evidence of difference within the Black community.

At the same time, however, each semester—both during my three years at the University of Kansas and during the three years of my doctoral candidacy that I taught at the University of Pennsylvania—I have to keep my fingers crossed in the hope that when students see me, they will not be caught in the web of stereotypes of women of African descent that have survived through the centuries. As literary critic Hortense Spillers writes:

> Let's face it. I am a marked woman, but not everybody knows my name. "Peaches" and "Brown Sugar," "Sapphire" and "Earth Mother," "Aunty," "Granny," God's "Holy Fool," a "Miss Ebony First," or "Black Woman at the Podium": I describe a locus of confounded identities, a meeting ground of investments and privations in the national treasury of rhetorical wealth. (Spillers 1987, 65)

The names in quotation marks, like our very bodies themselves, are so bound up and enshrouded by myths that it is nearly impossible for the Black female subjects who hold them to come to light. Because of these myths, I do not actively pass; rather, I am passed. Image and Self diverge as the physical body in front of the classroom is observed by untrained eyes. And if I allow the representation of my Self to be conceptually manipulated by others, remaining in the space they expect me to occupy in a particular way, I risk being "frozen by the look that sees me in stasis" (Truame 1994, 209).

Of course, this conceptual manipulation is not always in our control. For example, although I have had colleagues who teach in jeans and T-shirts, I always dress professionally for class. One reason is to visually demonstrate my respect for the students and the seriousness of our endeavors; another has to do with the "onstage" performance that I mentioned earlier. I found the "costume" necessary to assert my position of authority in the classroom because when I first began teaching at the University of Pennsylvania, I was only six years older than my students. What I found striking in the University of Kansas Spring 1999 Introduction to Fiction class was how my intent seemed to be lost on my students; many of them commented on my clothing on their midterm course evaluation forms. At least five of them complimented my outfits before assessing the reading materials, assignments, paper grading, or discussions. They seemed obsessed by image, surface, and form above and beyond content. I was instantly reminded of Patricia J. Williams's description of a particularly bad set of evaluations in which her law students remarked on her "neat" clothes and braids arranged over her "great bald dome of a skull." The African American legal scholar laments: "I marvel, in a moment of genuine bitterness, that anonymous student evaluations speculating on dimensions of my anatomy are nevertheless counted into the statistical measurement of my teaching proficiency" (Williams 1991, 95).

I dedicate myself to helping students learn to read texts, however, and so, although the path is difficult and often frustrating, I plunge into the task of teaching them to delve below the surfaces that they think they see. I cannot say that I am new to this experience of trying to make people see me. Although I was born in a predominantly African Trinidadian community in Brooklyn, New York, I have been raised in Euro-American, middle-class neighborhoods for most of my life. I was usually one of two or three Black students in my elementary and high school classes. And before moving to Philadelphia for my graduate studies at the University of Pennsylvania, I attended Yale for my bachelor's degree—a fact I consistently hid from non-Yale acquaintances lest they read me as "snob." As one is sure to recognize, this position of racial isolation simultaneously bespeaks a life of definitive privilege—not only in terms of the financial advantages that allowed my family to reside in these neighborhoods and me to attend these schools, but also the social privileges that exposure to these environments provided. In many ways, this middle-class experience grants me a point of connection with numerous University of Kansas students (and, I suspect, colleagues as well) who might otherwise find me completely alien.

At the University of Kansas, I have designed my freshman honors seminar, a course on masterpieces of world literature that I teach each fall, around the theme of Caribbean Literature: Mimicry or Culture? Texts from the European canon are paired with Caribbean revisions and rewritings of them. When I mention my Trinidadian parentage to the students, I usually notice a few raised eyebrows. Whereas meeting a first-generation African American was commonplace for students on the distinctly east-coast, urban campus of the University of Pennsylvania, West Indians are rather hard to come by in the Midwest. Identifying myself by ethnicity and heritage thus has a tremendous effect on the students whose exposure to African Americans might be minimal or nonexistent aside from the images perpetuated by the media. My presence calls into question stereotypical equations of complexion with experience (Black = urban, Black = ancestors from the American South, etc.).

To continue this lesson on stereotypes, during the second class meeting I require the first-year students to write short essays on what they think of when they hear the word "Caribbean." The images elicited from this exercise are not difficult to predict: palm trees swaying in balmy breezes; empty beaches bordering clear, turquoise waters and cloudless blue skies; cruise ships and luxury hotels; (White) sunbathers; tropical drinks served in coconuts; steel drums and reggae music; friendly dark-skinned people with dredlocks and carefree attitudes wearing colorful clothing; a slow-motion and relaxing way of life. After sharing the lists, I ask the students to consider where these images come from and why these scenes might be the most popular. Recognizing the tourist economy, U.S. political races, and other factors starts to open some of their eyes to reasons for the generation of these stereotypes. In addition, I do not doubt that my legibility as a Caribbean American woman who has a shorn head instead of dredlocks, who wears black more often than any other color, and who speaks quite quickly and demands much of them in class also aids in the disruption of the conventional exotic images.

It is interesting to note, however, that while my heritage and the students' general lack of familiarity with the history, culture, and literature of the region tends to situate me as a dangerously absolute authority on the Caribbean texts, I have encountered the most resistance during our discussions of the assigned Shakespeare play, *The Tempest*. In other classes I teach regularly—a Major Authors course on Toni Morrison's fiction, for example, or the African American–focused Border Lands, Border Crossings—my expertise goes unquestioned; I am legitimated by the color of my skin and the presumed "authentic" connection to African American literature and culture. I also experience remarkably little resistance in the Literature for Children course, possibly because students, anticipating an exceptionally light reading load and elementary discussions, are surprised by the rigorous literary, historical, and cultural analysis I expect them to perform.

In the case of Shakespeare, however—much more so than with Wordsworth, Homer, or Brontë, the other canonical authors whose works I use in the freshman seminar—students often consider their former high school instructors' interpretations as inviolable. Others seem so deeply wed to the notion of bard as "master" that they balk at any criticism of his words. They have been captivated by what Williams identifies as "the authority of what this culture considers 'classical'" (Williams 1991, 84), holding the play on high as if there is only one, easily perceived, objective reading. They refuse to challenge, or even interrogate, its meanings. I sometimes wonder, however, whether their halting approach to a postcolonial analysis would be quite so intractable if one of my White male senior colleagues were teaching the text.

This first-year seminar is the one in which I become most aware of the nature of my power in the classroom. Like Williams, I have a "place in an institution that is larger than myself, whose power I wield even as I am powerless, whose shield of respectability shelters me even as I am disrespected" (Williams 1991, 96).[9] However, because of the roles I "symbolically and imagistically bring to bear in and out of the classroom" as a Black female professor, my position is "particularly aggravated in [a] confusing, oxymoronic hierarchic symbology" (Williams 1991, 97).

*   *   *

As I stated above, because I am brown-skinned, there is little possibility that students will mistake me for White. I do not say *"no possibility"* here since I have been told that I "sound White"—a comment that always stuns me in its lack of consciousness of what it means to conjoin accent with race rather than with geography—and I have had blind students in the classroom. Both details further hint at privileges I possess—those privileges that enable me, in some ways, to circulate in academic spheres more freely than those whom the students "read" as coming from "lesser" socio-economic class back-grounds (a trait often interpreted through accent) and those privileges that permit me to move about less hindered than my differently abled colleagues. However, while my students will not visually perceive me as White, they al-most always mistake me for straight. In this way, I am one of those academics to whom doris davenport (1994) refers when she identifies Black lesbians pos-sessing "visible invisibility." The title story of Shani Mootoo's (1993) collec-tion *Out on Main Street* provides an interesting way for taking into account these issues of identity and disclosure for lesbians of color.

Mootoo's short stories come from a variety of perspectives: One of the protagonists is a young married woman who has immigrated to North Amer-ica to join her husband; one is a White woman in an abusive heterosexual relationship; one is a young child with a philandering father. The shifting viewpoints of the narratives play on the notion of passing, forcing the reader to consider questions of whose voice—if any, including the author's, or the Self's, by extension—is "real." As the text travels back and forth between narrative poles, the reader must also perceptually slide and negotiate the ideological terrain in order to determine who the speaker might be and how she is to be interpreted.[10]

"Out on Main Street" focuses on the experiences of two Trinidadian-born women of Indian descent who have immigrated to Canada. Main Street represents a cultural center for them, a place where they visit for traditional music, clothes, jewelry, and delicacies: "We does go Main Street to see pretty pretty sari and bangle, and to eat we belly full a burfi and gulub jamoon" (Mootoo 1993, 45). With this introduction, the author sets up an apparently fixed landscape of identity: one in which my students typically assume that the "we" is a single, indistinguishable group, alternately labeled "Indian," where race and culture mean one and the same thing.

However, the very next paragraph indicates that this supposedly stable category of identity is tenuous at best. The protagonists express hesitation about roaming freely on Main Street because they do not feel as if they truly belong to the local Indian community. The narrator proclaims: "We ain't good grade A Indians. We skin brown, is true, but we doh even think 'bout India unless…it come on de news" (Mootoo 1993, 45). The reference to skin color alludes to the practice of passing: In the same way that African Americans with extremely light skin can be read as White but identify as Black, the narrator's complexion causes her to be read as Indian even though she sees herself as Other and then is read as Other because she does not act "Indian enough." As ethnically Indian but nationally and culturally Trinidadian, she finds herself alienated from the "*real* flesh and blood Indian from India" (Mootoo 1993, 47).

The question of reality and "authentic" identity is an interesting one to consider in the classroom, especially for the "passing" lesbian and the "out" woman of color. When I reveal my sexual orientation during the discussion, I push my students to reevaluate their presumptions about all aspects of my "real" identity. When it comes down to it, what does a "real" lesbian look like? Speak like? Act like? What does an "authentic" Black woman sound like? How does she react to her students? The students' shock over my sexual self-disclosure, often translated by them as the inability to tell who I "really" am, is not only about *mis*-reading, and taking "wrong" for its oppositional "right"; it points to the very problem of binary and singular, narrowly defined readings.

I attempt to draw out this idea by making comparisons to similar instances in Mootoo's story. Most students easily recognize what the narrator has not—that the Indian people around her are also displaced, and the culture that she extols as "real" is as much a relocated culture as that found in Trinidad.[11] Besides deconstructing notions of authenticity, the story shows the diverse nature of an Indian community. It is not broken down into "real" Indian-from-India versus "fake" Indian-from-elsewhere; neither does it exist solely in opposition to a monolithic White community and culture. "Out on Main Street" thus begins to erase certain conceptions students may have concerning racial and ethnic oppositions.

I subtly urge the class to consider sexual orientation in the same way. The narrator, a butch with a walk "like a strong-man monkey," specifically claims that she does not wish to be a man but rather feels "like a gender dey forget to classify" when she goes out with Janet, who wears "high-heel shoe and make-up and…long hair loose and flying about like she is a walking-talking shampoo ad" (Mootoo 1993, 48). The passage, especially along with my sexual disclosure, has the power to subvert students' notions of a gender binary in which all human beings must be either "man" or "woman"—lesbians falling under the male category in terms of appearance, presumed behavior, and desire (i.e., "only men have sex with women") and gay men falling under the female category. The narrator's gender insecurity also accentuates the fact that like her racial identity, her gender identity—and by extension, that of the students—is significantly relational and crucially dependent on social recognition, or how "readable" she appears compared to Janet and other women who visually fit traditional roles.[12]

During my first time teaching the story at the University of Kansas, I discovered that the unwillingness of many students to stir from their conceptions of normativity did not allow them to engage independently with these theoretical principles at all. Early in the tale, the narrator identifies Janet as her girlfriend, expresses jealousy over the male attention that Janet receives, and describes her own crew cut, jeans, and sneakers. Most readers who are well socialized in the heterosexist U.S. mainstream would probably assume the narrator to be male. More shocking to me, however, was the fact that even after reading the section of the story in which the narrator is continually referred to as "Miss," a significant number of my students still believed the character to be male (or were quite unsure about her gender; they argued about it as they entered the classroom). The students read the initial visual clues and refused to stray away from their presumptions as they continually "passed" the character into their consciousnesses as male.

I therefore now encourage students in all of my classes to think about their positions of normativity by asking them to list all of the traits suitable for answering the question "Who am I?" After compiling a comprehensive slate of categories under which these various traits can fall,[13] we examine how identity is supremely relational and intertwined and by no means absolute. What does it mean to be White? Black? Woman? Queer? Tall? Middle class? At the end of Mootoo's story, the narrator's sexuality is thoroughly inflected with considerations of her racial, ethnic, and national subject positions. She prevents the assumption that her orientation is simply a separate and exclusive part of her, independent of the other facets of her identity—a point that I emphasize during the class discussion and to which I hope to draw attention here, in our considerations of the experiences of the Other Teacher. Each moment of tension at the narrator's heightened visibility in "Out on Main Street" is also a moment in which she firmly calls attention to herself as existent, real, and demarcating a particular yet ever-shifting space. The revelations of the expansive fields of her complex identity do not allow the narrator to be neatly defined, translated, represented, and then tucked into a small box (or closet). These moments echo the repeated "moments of surfacing" described by Truame as "useful in a continuing series of acts of struggle, not as end points in themselves or static representations" (Truame 1994, 209).

In this past semester's Border Lands, Border Crossings course, the notion of a dynamic, relational identity finally became clear when, of the sixteen upper-level students participating in the "Who am I?" exercise, only the three students of color included words describing race, ethnicity, or complexion on their lists. When I asked the class what this meant, after a great deal of mental struggle, a White student finally suggested that if he had been one of three White students in a class of all Black students, he probably would have identified himself in terms of race. I concurred: In a class of all male students, my position as female would likely be highlighted; in a class of all Black students, my ethnic identity and Caribbean parentage might play a more central role in the ways I define myself and am defined by others. The White students in the class were thus revealed not as "raceless," as one confessed she would like to see herself, but rather in the position of privilege that comes from being a member of the dominant culture. The supposed normalcy, "naturalness," authenticity, and primacy of Whiteness and, by extension, heterosexuality, or things such as masculine and feminine gender roles for men and women, respectively and exclusively, are thus exposed as socially determined and constructed.

And although I push students toward the recognition of this fact, I am simultaneously aware of how I profit by it in the classroom. I am relatively certain that one of the primary reasons I have not experienced any homophobic backlash after several rounds of disclosure has to do with my "femme" appearance. I am relatively tall (5'8") but have petite bone structure. As I stated earlier, my head is shaved, but I wear make-up and "feminine" clothing at work. When my Spring 2000 Literature for Children students listed short hair and men's clothes as signs of the stereotypical lesbian, I asked them if they believed I was a lesbian. "After all," I said, "I have very short hair and I am wearing a suit today." Several students insisted, "But it's a *feminine* hair cut" (which I find comical, considering that I get the "$8 Special" buzz cut at the local barber's, where I have to assert my space on line because I am the only female patron and the male customers typically assume that I am there waiting for a husband, boyfriend, son, or brother). Another student emphatically announced, "And that's a *linen* suit!" In other words, because I appear feminine, look quite young, and laugh a lot in class, students regard me as very accessible—which is often stressed as one of my best traits in evalua-

tions. I am not a threatening presence—militant lesbian *or* militant Black—
and I believe they accept me more readily because of this.

These principles are essential to raise, especially because some students
would like to ignore them in favor of a liberal humanist "we are all different
on the surface but the same under the skin" attitude. As Conrad and Crawford assert, we must beware a certain untheoretically grounded discourse on
the fluidity of identity. We must remain conscious of the ways in which
"identity categories are historically contingent and culturally specific points
to the constructedness of identity without denigrating the political and social
necessity and efficacy of those constructs and identifications" (Conrad and
Crawford 1998, 160).

Several weeks ago, I informed my mother that I had come out to several
classes here at the University of Kansas, and she worried about whether that
act of divulging personal information was "appropriate" for a professor. For
her—and, I suspect, numerous others—sexuality is a private affair, unsuitable
for most conversations, far less one that would occur in a college classroom.[14]
We discussed the issue for a while, and that evening I forwarded her the following e-mail from one of the students in that semester's children's literature
class. The message was sent to me after I came out during the discussion of
Lesléa Newman's (1989) controversial *Heather Has Two Mommies*:

> I really respect how candid you were in class about your own sexuality. It was im-
> portant I think because a lot of students I know have preconceived notions about
> gay people and they are often negative. I really hope that it helped some students in
> class think differently about homosexuality. I have a roommate who is extremely
> anti-gay and she actually has problems with my gay friends (X) and (Y) visiting me.
> That's a completely different story, but I do think that when you know someone per-
> sonally that's gay it is hard to maintain that prejudiced stance against them. I ap-
> plaud your honesty! (personal communication, April 2000)

At the end of the term, this student sent me another note: "I really enjoyed your class, you have been one of my favorite teachers at University of
Kansas. Thank you for making class so meaningful!" Both of these communications clearly lay out the issues of what is meant by "the personal is political," urging us to extend that statement to include the intellectual and the
pedagogical. By coming out to an entire classroom of students in the context
of teaching a piece of lesbian literature—or any literature with pertinent issues, for that matter—as well as speaking about my experiences with racism,
or xenophobia, or sexism, I maintain that all forms of identity are "topics of
intellectual relevance" (Conrad and Crawford 1998, 155) and social relevance.[15]

Williams has argued that inherent in the idea of neutral, impersonal academic styles is the false assumption of no risk. She continues: "The personal has fallen into disrepute as sloppy because we have lost the courage and the vocabulary to describe it in the face of the enormous social pressure to 'keep it to ourselves'—but this is where our most idealistic and our deadliest politics are lodged, and are revealed" (Williams 1991, 93). As a college professor, I am not only a role model for students of African descent, or queer students, or female students, but for straight White male students as well. I am also an importantly institutionally legitimized professional—a figure of authority, and thus, in some ways, normalcy—for all of the students in the classroom to see, listen to, speak with, and learn from. Hopefully, in the process, students will question all of their presumptions about identity.

An assistant professor of English at the University of Kansas, Giselle Liza Anatol specializes in Caribbean and African American literatures. She regularly teaches a freshman honors seminar entitled Caribbean Literature: Mimicry or Culture? She also teaches Introduction to Fiction, a Major Authors course on Toni Morrison's work, Literature for Children, and Border Lands, Border Crossings, a Topics in American Literature course with a focus in African American literature. Her current research project is tentatively titled *Mother Countries, Motherlands, and Mother Love: Representations of Motherhood in Contemporary Caribbean Women's Literature.*

Notes

1. Although there is some controversy surrounding the word "queer," I use it inclusively to represent a coalition of lesbians, gay men, bisexuals, and transgendered people.

2. I designed this course around the theme of "encountering the city." The goals were to improve students' skills in literary criticism and expository writing through an examination of short stories and novels that present different types of interactions in urban environments. Our discussions often explored the factors that affect these interactions and one's perspectives on city landscapes, such as race, ethnicity, age, socio-economic class, and gender.

3. In *The Alchemy of Race and Rights*, law professor Patricia J. Williams argues that her colleagues' preference for the impersonal "objective" above the personal "subjective" and their insistence on creating a binary between the "merely experiential" and things "relevant" to the law eventually requires students to devalue their own and other people's humanity for the sake of legal theory and their grades (Williams 1991, 87). She describes the "windy, risky plain of exposure that the 'personal' represents" (91), but insists upon occupying it in order to ensure her readers' and students' connection with her. She declares so-called personal discourse to be not the "denial of one's authority" that has so long been asserted but rather false power without the necessary "communion" with other beings.

4. After the women contributed their initial reactions, a male student insightfully remarked that he had never thought about how homophobia (my word, not his) was in some ways dictated by gender. He found the women's anxiety surprising and thought-provoking, given that most men he knew found lesbians fascinating but were exceedingly threatened about the idea of being in the presence of gay men.

5. In this way, I was almost as likely to suffer from "passing out" as my students! I borrow the idea and creative title pun from Conrad and Crawford.

6. No matter how hard I have tried to disrupt this power imbalance in certain situations, I have found that wherever I sit around a seminar table or in a circle of desks becomes the "head." The most common critique on my end of term evaluations is that I do not tell the students what the "right" answers are or that after raising a point of debate I do not reveal my own opinion. Unused to believing in their own command of the material, these students wait for a mystical moment of revelation—something they expect of the authority figure in the classroom, but which I refuse to give as I train them to think and analyze for themselves. In this act of refusing to be "the sage on the stage," I simultaneously attempt to resist being a type of "native informant," subject to the partial recognition discussed in terms of sexual identity by Anneliese Truame. She describes "the fixing nature of the gaze evident in the way that some of my heterosexual peers turn to look at me whenever they raise queer issues in class. That turning of the head is not an act of true recognition. On the contrary, it tends to mark the partial nature of someone's recognition of me. I am asked to validate this partial acknowledgment by filling in the established and circumscribed place for my participation as a lesbian by talking on cue" (Truame 1994, 209).

7. In her essay on George Harris's "Spanish masquerade," Julia Stern describes how *Uncle Tom's Cabin* author Harriet Beecher Stowe rejected the Black-White binary and disrupted rigid bounds of racial categorization by creating a character who plays the role of the Spanish gentleman, thus occupying a space of "neither," outside of the dualism. Thus,

Stern concludes, "race tells no essential truth about identity, for race is a sign and thus, interchangeable: until color is attached to structures of power, it does not and cannot figure, as George Harris's Spanish guise attests" (Stern, 1996, 122). In other words, the varied "readings" of George's complexion prove that a singular interpretation of any sign is a falsity, and "the definitive legibility of race is a delusion" (Stern, 1996, 123).

8. I teach both Larsen's and Cliff's novels in an upper level Topics in American Literature course entitled Border Lands and Border Crossings, which typically enrolls about fifteen students: upper-level undergraduate English majors and a few graduate students pursuing master's and doctoral degrees. Over the semester, the students and I examine literary journeys across the borders of U.S. society. On the most basic level, our project is to investigate the experiences of subjects who cross geopolitical boundaries and travel to and/or through the "land of opportunity." We also consider metaphorical border crossings, including ways in which categories of race, ethnicity, class, and gender are escaped, troubled, and revealed as less immutable than at first appears.

9. The notion of having a sheltered place suggests the power hierarchy beyond the student-teacher dynamic. As a tenure-track assistant professor, I need to be shielded from numerous pitfalls, ones that can come from above as well as those that come from below, if I am to survive in the institution.

10. Furthermore, the constantly shifting voices represent a type of ideological movement and thus are emblematic of the physical movement that has long defined the Caribbean geographical sphere. In the past, this movement included the seasonal travels of Amerindians, the forced migration of African peoples during slavery, the transport of Indian and Chinese indentured servants after emancipation to work on sugar plantations, and the exploits of European explorers and conquerors. In more contemporary times, this movement involves tourists traveling into the region and Caribbean migrants traveling outward to look for economic and educational opportunities. In this way, the collection's voice, style, and content signify a Caribbean outlook.

11. The shopkeepers who view Janet and the narrator with contempt for speaking English instead of Hindi, Punjabi, or Urdu, for instance, are actually from the Fiji Islands in the southwest Pacific and could be classified as just as "inauthentic" or "unreal" as the Trinidadian immigrants.

12. Significantly, the waiters in the Main Street restaurant ignore the narrator—making her invisible, voiceless, and with feelings of supreme powerlessness—while they ogle and flirt with Janet. It is those in social and political power—males in a patriarchal society, people of European descent in a White-dominated society, heterosexuals in a heterosexist society—who have the ability to symbolically erase those who stand lower on the social hierarchy.

13. Name, ancestry, position in family, religion, political affiliation, race, ethnicity, nationality, place of birth, place of residence, age, gender, sexual orientation, social class, economic class, occupation, skills, hobbies, interests, goals, personality, mood, and so forth.

14. Mary Mittler and Amy Blumenthal address similar concerns in their essay in *Tilting the Tower*. They consider how a professor's non-gendered references to a partner, family vacation, or first date are usually "innocent enough remarks," mentioned to students appropriately both in and out of class, and "not in and of themselves distracting to the teaching/learning process" (Mittler and Blumenthal 1994, 3). They wrestle with the

question of whether the professor's sexual orientation changes the context and if coming out in the classroom is truly a part of effective teaching.

15. And, as Kate Adams and Kim Emery attest, "people in the business of increasing knowledge shouldn't participate in hiding the fact that there are lesbians in the world" (Adams and Emery 1994, 26).

Works Cited

Adams, K., and K. Emery. 1994. "Classroom Coming Out Stories: Practical Strategies for Productive Self-disclosure." In *Tilting the Tower: Lesbians Teaching Queer Subjects*, edited by L. Garber. New York: Routledge.

Cliff, M. 1989. *No Telephone to Heaven*. New York: Vintage International.

Conrad, K., and J. Crawford. 1998. "Passing/Out: The Politics of Disclosure in Queer-positive Pedagogy." *Modern Language Studies* 28 (3): 153–162.

Cutter, M. J. 1996. "Sliding Significations: Passing as a Narrative and Textual Strategy in Nella Larsen's Fiction." In *Passing and the Fictions of Identity*, edited by E. K. Ginsberg. Durham, NC: Duke University Press.

davenport, d. 1994. "'Still Here': Ten Years Later. . ." In Tilting the Tower: Lesbians Teaching Queer Subjects, edited by L. Garber. New York: Routledge.

Ginsberg, E. K. 1996. "Introduction." In *Passing and the Fictions of Identity*, edited by E. K. Ginsberg. Durham, NC: Duke University Press.

Kawash, S. 1996. "The Autobiography of an Ex-Coloured Man: (Passing for) Black Passing for White." In *Passing and the Fictions of Identity*, edited by E. K. Ginsberg. Durham, NC: Duke University Press.

Larsen, N. [1928] 1986. "Passing." In *Quicksand and Passing*, edited by D. E. McDowell. Durham, NC: Duke University Press.

Mittler, M. L., and A. Blumenthal. 1994. "On Being a Change Agent: Teacher as Text, Homophobia as Context." In *Tilting the Tower: Lesbians Teaching Queer Subjects*, edited by L. Garber. New York: Routledge.

Mootoo, S. 1993. *Out on Main Street and Other Stories*. Vancouver, Canada: Press Gang.

Newman, L. 1989. *Heather Has Two Mommies*. Boston: Alyson Wonderland.

Spillers, H. 1987. "Mama's Baby, Papa's Maybe: An American Grammar Book." *Diacritics* 17 (2): 64–81.

Stern, J. 1996. "Spanish Masquerade and the Drama of Racial Identity in *Uncle Tom's Cabin*. In *Passing and the Fictions of Identity*, edited by E. K. Ginsberg. Durham, NC: Duke University Press.

Stowe, H. B. 1981. *Uncle Tom's Cabin, or, Life among the Lowly*. New York: Penguin Books.

Truame, A. 1994. "Tau(gh)t Connections: Experiences of a 'Mixed-blood, Disabled, Lesbian Student'." In *Tilting the Tower: Lesbians Teaching Queer Subjects*, edited by L. Garber. New York: Routledge.

Williams, P. J. 1991. *The Alchemy of Race and Rights: Diary of a Law Professor*. Cambridge, MA: Harvard University Press.

CHAPTER FIVE

Reading the Body Indian: A Chicana Mestiza's Experience Teaching Literature

LISA D. CHAVEZ

Abstract

DRAWING PRIMARILY FROM personal experience, I discuss issues of identity in the classroom and what happens when an Other Teacher focuses on issues of race in a predominantly White classroom. Beginning with my physical appearance, which is often read as Native American, I compare two classes in which my body caused students to read my race as motivating a political agenda, in which it raised issues of authenticity and cultural representation, and in which student perceptions about my race undermined my classroom authority. I also discuss the role of emotion in the classroom and the need for and the effects of challenging racist speech. Referring to my own experience and to the work of others writing about teaching and identity, I argue that Other teachers must teach our students about White identity and privilege before we can continue with a larger discussion of race.

> We are sometimes seen, it seems to me, as traveling icons of culture.... We are flesh and blood information retrieval systems, native informants who demonstrate and act out difference, often with an imperfectly concealed political agenda....We are walking exemplars of ethnicity and of race. What we are not, however, is objective, impartial purveyors of truth. (Karamcheti 1995, 138)

> Students come to the classroom equipped with their own cultural codes, which they impose on the text. I would like to...suggest that students bring their 'terms of reference' about the professor to the classroom also, and their 'reading' of the professor's body provides another textual consideration concomitant to the literary text. (Johnson 1995, 131)

In a 1993 article in the *Nation*, Wendy Kaminer mocks the academic habit of positioning oneself: "When I identified myself as a 'skeptical, secular humanist, Jewish, feminist, intellectual lawyer'...I was joking....This categorical self-portrait satirized the postmodern academic tradition of deconstructing yourself.... It still surprises me that people take such silly statements so seriously" (quoted in Bauer 1995, 67).

I don't believe that such statements are silly. To understand my experiences as a teacher, you need to know who I am. I am a Chicana Mestiza, the child of a Chicano father and a White (Norwegian American) mother. I was raised by my mother, who hovers between poverty and the working class (as she did during my childhood). I am one of the first in my family to be a college graduate. These things are already enough to make me an Other in an environment which is predominantly White and male and middle class. I am also an Other in academia because I am a writer in departments that are traditionally staffed by literary critics, and because I have an M.F.A. in creative writing rather than a Ph.D.[1] I am also privileged in many ways: I am able-bodied, heterosexual, U.S. born. I have a career that allows me to live well, that does not ruin my health, and that interests me. I started teaching as a graduate student in Alaska in 1987, and since then I have taught English in large and small state and private institutions and in Japan and Poland.[2] I am a poet and a writer of creative nonfiction.

The latter is important, because it will tell you something about the way I approached this essay. I tried many ways to write it, but many sounded hollow, as if my voice was coming through faintly, from far away. Finally I gave up and decided to write this in the way I would a piece of creative nonfiction. Understand, then, that I recreate classroom scenes to tell you a certain kind of truth, to recreate how they felt to me, one very subjective human being. I can't pretend the dialogue or detail is exact, but I can give you my story as a woman of color teaching in predominantly White institutions and what I learned from that.

*   *   *

In January 1992, I returned to Alaska after teaching in Japan. I desperately needed a job, so when I was offered a world literature class—a new requirement that the English department had not yet been able to hire a tenure-track person for—I was delighted. Because I had a B.A. from the department and had spent a year in the M.F.A. program before transferring, I knew the university well. The University of Alaska Fairbanks is the main campus of the statewide system, with about 8,000 students. According to

1995 statistics provided by the university's Office of Planning Analysis and Institutional Research (1995), 15 percent of the student body were Indian or Alaskan Native, 70 percent were White and roughly 7 percent were other minorities (categorized as Asian, Black, or Hispanic). The remaining 8 percent defined themselves as other or declined to state their ethnicity. These statistics seem relatively steady for the years listed, and I can only surmise that they were similar in 1992, when I was teaching—certainly my perception was that the university was predominantly White, and that Alaskan Native students constituted the largest minority group.

I don't know what the students thought when they saw me walk into the world literature class that first day, but I can imagine what they thought they saw. I am a Chicana Mestiza with light brown skin. There is not much evidence of my White mother in my skin color or features, and I look Indian—especially to those who have not had much contact with people of Mexican ancestry. I am Indian but I am also Latina and White, and because of my lack of knowledge of my tribal affiliation, I am not comfortable being seen as exclusively Native American—nor would it be an accurate representation of who I am. At the time, I also looked younger than my age of 31. What I think some of those students saw when I walked in the classroom that morning was a very young Alaska Native woman.[3] In a state where Native people represent the largest minority group, and where relations between Native and White are strained, my appearance was—for some students—already a problem.

The syllabus, I learned later, was a second problem. I structured the course around the theme of "Stories of Survival," focusing on works that dealt with various forms of resistance to oppression, many overtly political. I also included some American literature by groups that I felt were marginalized in the United States. I particularly wanted to include some work by Native American writers because I believed that students would see a connection between the writings of indigenous peoples worldwide.

That first day, I explained my rationale for the various books on the syllabus, and I told them a little bit about myself and my preparation. Finally, I told them about my ethnic background. Because many people had not heard the term "Mestiza," I talked a bit about how many people of Mexican descent were, like me, Indian too, though not exclusively. I told them I was not an Alaska Native. That done, we moved on to the readings.

I ran into trouble right away—because I juxtaposed creation stories from the Bible with other creation stories around the world, because I talked about White supremacy in South Africa when we read Nadine Gordimer, and because I aligned myself clearly with people of color. Then we read Leslie Marmon Silko's *Ceremony*, and that book was the match that lit the flame.

The novel is the story of Tayo, a mixed-blood Laguna World War II veteran who must find a way to restore balance to his life, and thus to his world. It is a difficult novel for those not familiar with Native American literature, for Silko's style is not linear but draws more on her own Laguna storytelling traditions. It is also a difficult novel in that it creates a vivid picture of racism, alcoholism, and despair. I expected the class to struggle with it—they did. But I did not expect the class to explode. That morning, as usual, our class was arranged in a large circle. Student A looked particularly tense and angry, though I started only by asking for initial impressions of the book.

"We shouldn't have to read this," she said, and her voice was so angry I could hear the tremor in it. The rest of the class was silent. "Why not?" I asked. "It's trash, that's why. Trash. I shouldn't have to read about these people." I could feel myself go very still and very angry. I tried to be calm. "What people?" She seemed to veer away, take another tack. "This drunkenness. It's disgusting."

I took a deep breath, tried to guide her and the rest of the class to a discussion of alcoholism as a symptom of despair. I tried to inject a bit of historical context into the discussion, to explain why despair might be the outcome of a national policy of genocide. I wasn't trying to silence her. Or perhaps I was. I knew what she was getting at, that she shouldn't have to read about about Native people, about people of color. I was trying to control my temper, but I also hoped I was helping others in the class understand the novel better, understand the characters' behavior, and to see their alcoholism as the novel portrayed it—a sign of the sickness in the world that needed to be balanced and healed by ceremony.

But my interruption only inflamed the woman's anger. "We shouldn't have to read any of this crap. This is a world literature class. We should be reading great literature, not trash." She looked around the room. "Come on," she said. "I'm not the only one who thinks this." A few other people met her eyes, then looked away, and I realized she was not alone.

"Nadine Gordimer is trash? A Nobel Prize winner? This novel," I said, holding my copy of *Ceremony* aloft, "this novel, one of the most well-known Native American novels, is trash?"

By now she was angry enough not to be cautious. "I don't need to read this. I see this every day in my job. They're all like this. Drunks. They make me sick."

"What's your job?" I asked.

"Emergency room nurse. They come in all the time. Drunk. " She looked around the room, but this time no one met her gaze. "I know all about this. I worked in Arizona before I came here. There too. Drunken Indians. Everybody knows what they're like. Worse than animals." She looked steadily at me, clearly including me in her condemnation of "them."

I was angry, which doesn't justify what I said next but does perhaps explain it. "You must be very good at your job," I said, and I could hear the bitterness in my words, the sarcasm. Some other students did too; I could see it on their faces, surprise, or anger at me for what they read—rightly—as an attack on this student.

I don't remember how the class ended. I remember challenging her more—asking her how she could justify her stereotypes. She said she'd never met any different, and though I argued, she shrugged, as if her experience was the world. The class ended, and though I know that not all the students agreed with her, no one spoke up against her. No one but me.

And that is a dangerous position to be in, one I have struggled with as a teacher. In this class, I felt that I had to challenge Student A; I couldn't let her racism stand. I still believe that. But this class has taught me that I must be careful how I challenge. For my students that day did not see this as an argument about racism, but as the teacher attacking a student, dismissing her viewpoint. I still believe that her racist views should be dismissed. But I also understand the power dynamics in the classroom better now. I felt this woman had power that day, speaking as she did from the privilege of her White skin. I aligned myself with people of color and therefore felt that her racist words and dismissal of Native lives put me in a position of weakness to her. I was sure that she meant to insult me personally when she made racist comments about Indians; she already knew that I had Indian ancestry. But I was still the teacher, the person who assigned grades, and for her and the class, that meant I was privileged, they powerless.

That blowup in class would have been bad enough had it been the end. It was not. A few days later, my department chair told me that Student A had made a complaint against me, both to the department and to the dean of liberal arts. The complaint was, initially, that the work I was teaching was not world literature (Student A suggested Shakespeare would be more appropriate in such a class). After a long discussion with the department chair, the underlying assumptions came to the surface: I was incompetent; I had a political agenda I was trying to force onto the students; I verbally attacked students in class; and finally, she didn't feel that she should be required to read Native trash just because she was unfortunate enough to have a Native teacher. Like other people before and since, she continued to read my appearance as exclusively Native—particularly Alaska Native—in spite of my explanation of my ethnicity.

I was lucky. My department chair defended me and also told Student A that she thought the problem was with Student A's assumptions, not me. That prompted the student's visit to the dean, which really frightened me, because while I didn't believe I had done anything wrong, I was not sure the dean would have any interest in protecting me, an adjunct instructor, from a determined student attack. Wouldn't it just be easier not to hire me again? But as I said, I was lucky—the dean was satisfied with the department chair's explanation of things. It went no further. Still, my entire teaching life was shaken to the core, and the class never quite recovered.[4]

*   *   *

When I think back to that time now, with the benefit of almost ten years more of teaching experience and the coursework for a Ph.D. in multicultural literature, I see myself as hopelessly naïve. Clueless, even. I had not quite anticipated how to deal with the controversy some of the texts would raise. I also did not know how to fit the works I had chosen into a context for the students, and I thought that close readings of the texts would be enough, because that was how I had been trained. I modeled my courses at that time after a favorite professor of British Romantic literature whose classes consisted of reading a lot and being whipped into discussion by his pointed questions and argumentative comments. Though he might summarize critical articles for us in class, we never read them ourselves. We all believed everything he said. He was wildly popular. He was also a middle-aged, tenured White man, though even I never thought of him that way—like my students, at that point I still saw his body as the norm, never thinking about how my own body would contrast with his.

I had no theoretical framework to guide me—I had done no reading on pedagogy, and little on race. I was truly an innocent. Unlike the White man I modeled my teaching on, I did not have the kind of authority in the classroom that he did. His appearance worked to signify his privilege, as mine worked against me. I looked like a Native woman, and some of these students, like Student A, had internalized racial stereotypes. They saw Alaska Natives as drunks, problems, people to joke about or avoid, not people who would ever have any any relation to their lives. For Student A, the fact that I had power over her in terms of grades and that I challenged her deep-seated prejudices in class was intolerable. I had no right to do so. The fact that I was not in fact Alaska Native was glossed over. I looked Native, therefore I was.

Student A would not have liked me more if she could have remembered that I was Chicana. Any person of color would have been a problem. But the fact that she identified me as Native exacerbated the problem, because it allowed her to dismiss me more easily. It also gave her a reason for attacking my choice of literature. I must have picked *Ceremony* only because it was by a Native writer—I was biased, in fact racist, for I let this book with what she saw as its attack on White people stand. With this shift, I could be attacker, she the victim.

My response to racism is anger. (Lorde 1984, 131)

Certainly, anger seems to me antithetical to the dialogue of teaching; yet anger is a real and present fact of the personal. (Karamcheti 1995, 144)

I see how I have been conditioned to avoid anger. While it is still my first instinctive response—one that I do not believe is wrong—I have learned from telling this story that most White people believe that while my anger is justified, it should also be controlled, hidden, disguised. Doesn't my anger inhibit my ability to teach, doesn't it stop communication? Lorde again: "When women of color speak out of…anger…we are often told that we are 'creating a mood of hopelessness,' 'preventing White women from getting past guilt,' or 'standing in the way of communication and action'" (Lorde 1984, 131). We learn to muzzle our anger. Recently, when discussing my feelings about racist comments in class, a White male colleague told me, "Of course you get angry, but anger doesn't help anything." So what does? Why is a student's racist comment a valid personal expression that I should not suppress (even if it is despicable) while my angry response is a stifling of classroom speech? What is the proper response to racist speech?

In *The Alchemy of Race and Rights*, Patricia Williams discusses her own struggle with such issues in the classroom and how challenging class-biased assumptions was called "trumping moves" to "silence" students (1991, 21). She was also told that her teaching style was "polemic" and thus "inappropriate" (32). Often the undercurrent of response to my discussion of this class seemed to be that perhaps I was wrong, that perhaps I should rethink my strategies when dealing with such issues so that I wouldn't "silence" students.

And that makes me angry. Most often, when I challenged student ideas, I meant not to silence them but to engage them in passionate and rigorous argument. Partially I learned this as a teaching style from other professors, but it is also a class-based mode of expression—in the predominantly White poor/ working-class culture my mother raised me in, people argued all the time, often quite heatedly, and while we might yell or even cry during these discussions, we saw those emotions as a sign that we were engaged in the discussion. Yet in a classroom in which many students are middle class, this heated sort of argument is thought of as rude and uncomfortable. bell hooks notes that "loudness, anger, emotional outburst, and even something as innocent as unrestrained laughter were deemed unacceptable, vulgar disruptions of classroom social order. These traits were also associated with being a member of the lower classes." As she goes on to say, people from different class backgrounds learn to "assimilate bourgeois values in order to be deemed acceptable" (hooks 1994, 178) and certainly I have found that this pressure is not just on students, but on teachers as well.

There is some irony in my class analysis. I know I tend to valorize what I see as the middle-class politeness-be-damned outspokenness of the poor and working class, but perhaps it was the discussion style of a working-class background that led Student A to be so outspoken in her prejudice, since I learned from her writing what her class background was. Now that I teach in a private institution that is almost exclusively middle- and upper-middle class (and mostly White), I rarely have those sort of direct confrontations; however, the "anonymous" comments on my teaching evaluations have been much more vitriolic, and since they are written and are part of my tenure file, they are perhaps more dangerous. The working-class students I taught in Alaska were no more or less racist than others I have dealt with, but they were more outspoken in their opinions.

I value outspokenness, but I also believe that students need to understand that words are powerful and have consequences, that ill-formed thoughts about identity can hurt, and that anger or pain is an acceptable, indeed almost inevitable, response. Yet how many times have I heard from (mostly White) colleagues that I need to not take racist comments so "personally"? While for the most part, my colleagues at various institutions have been sympathetic when I vent my frustrations to them, I have often been told even by the most supportive people that I need to just ignore it and not be too sensitive. This cry of oversensitivity is, of course, part of the backlash against discussing issues of identity, part of the whole P.C.-bashing[5] that has become part of our national culture. Even sympathetic and enlightened people sometimes fall into the overly sensitive trap. Yes, I probably am "sensitive" if that means I am quick to feel things, and feel them deeply. While it causes me pain, I value my so-called sensitivity, and sometimes a show of vulnerability improves classroom dialogue.

For example, in a composition class in Alaska, I got into a heated discussion about affirmative action with a student who insisted people of color got jobs undeservedly. I asked if other students (all White) agreed, but no one responded. To my chagrin, I began to cry. I dismissed the class. Later, a letter was slipped under my door from members of the class, apologizing and explaining that no, they did not agree with what had been said. In the following class, we discussed how these issues matter, and how misconceptions can affect people. It was not the only upset in that class. Another time, I missed an insensitive remark about Vietnam veterans, and when a student (himself a vet) pointed this out to me, instead of realizing his hurt, I dismissed it. I was wrong, and when I realized it, I apologized to him privately and publicly in the class, and we went on. It was a painful class, and I don't think I could stand for all of them to be like that. But at the end, I got some wonderful evaluations from students, many of whom said their entire thinking had been changed from seeing the vulnerability I and others displayed.

While it is often difficult, I believe we need to challenge bigotry in all its forms, regardless of the current climate in this country. In *The Rooster's Egg: On the Persistence of Prejudice*, Patricia Williams notes that if people of color "respond to or open discussion about belligerent or offensive remarks...we are called 'P.C' and accused of forcing our opinions down the throats of others" (1995, 40). Certainly my student evaluations have borne that out, regardless of how gentle I try to be in my challenges to racist assumptions and comments. Williams continues:

> It's great to turn the other cheek in the face of fighting words....But it's not a great way to maintain authority in the classroom or self-respect in the workplace—particularly in a society that abhors "wimps" and considers "kicking ass" a patriotic duty. In such a context, "just ignoring" verbal challenges is a good way to deliver oneself into the category of the utterly powerless. If, moreover, all our colleagues pursue the same path...then we have collectively created that peculiar institutional silence known as the moral vacuum. (1995, 40)

I agree with Williams. There are times I must speak out, even if it may mean "silencing" a student. I am not talking here about students who blunder into racist assumptions from inexperience while discussing race. What I am talking about here is the kind of clearly hostile bigotry I experienced with Student A.

In *Writing in Multicultural Settings,* Virgina A. Chappell also talks about challenging bigotry, but as a White teacher teaching predominantly White students. She discusses her students' comments "that some observers would have labeled racist" about Japanese American internment at Manzanar and quotes her teaching journal: "I don't want to squelch discussion. I don't want them to think they have to say what I want them to. If I truly believe in free speech and a free marketplace of ideas, then I have to let them explore their ideas without their feeling foolish or condemned." She says, "Rather than try to challenge or correct the generalizations and rationalizations I asked questions" (Chappell 1997, 175–176).[6] Perhaps Chappell is talking here of the kinds of students who really mean well, but her statement worries me because it expresses the non-judgmental attitude that allows bigoted comments to stand as if they were valid expressions of intellectual thought. How can students learn about race if their assumptions are not challenged? I do believe discussion is important, and I try to guide students into interrogating their assumptions and their own subject positions. Especially, I try to rely on other students in the class to help. But I also believe that I cannot let racist assumptions stand, even if it means the class will be uncomfortable or even painful.

Recognizing my own fear and pain has been useful. I now talk about my reactions and the possible reactions of students as we discuss race, and I try not to avoid the emotional but to explain it as a natural part of the learning process. An overt discussion of what we may *feel* as we read and discuss has been helpful.

I have also learned that any discussion of race must also include a discussion of Whiteness. In my earlier teaching I ignored White identity at my peril. Race must be discussed, because it is always an issue—at least in my classroom, with me as a teacher, especially one who often teaches about race through literature. And it must be discussed in a systematic way, beginning with a discussion of the White identity that White students have been socialized to ignore. White students must become aware of their own racial identity and race-based privilege. Now I begin any class that contains literature that focuses on race with an overt discussion of these issues. Peggy McIntosh's now well-known essay "White Privilege: Unpacking the Invisible Knapsack" (1989) is very useful for this. I also ask students to list (on paper) ways in which they fall into privileged groups and ways in which they fall into traditionally oppressed groups. I have asked students to consider a time when they felt judged on the basis of something they could not control and to think about the feelings that brought up. I ask them to return to that feeling when they are having difficulties with a particular expression of pain or anger at oppression. Beverly Tatum's work on White privilege and the formation of racial identity has also been critical in my thinking and teaching. Many of her ideas are included in her book *"Why are all the black kids sitting together in the cafeteria?" and Other Conversations about Race* (1997), and I use this book in class.

As a postcolonial person teaching postcolonial literature, my authority, too, is somewhat dependent upon my bloodlines, my physical and visible filiation with my subject matter. My authority is somewhat dependent on my status as native informant. (Karamcheti 1995, 142)

Sometimes a misreading of my body and identity has been an asset. My Native American literature class at Empire State College illustrates this. In 1997, I was studying for a doctorate in American literature, specializing in twentieth-century multicultural literature at the University of Rochester, and I taught at Empire State College, an alternative adult-education college that is part of the New York State system.

By then, I was a much more experienced teacher and had a better idea of what the difficulties of teaching any literature that discussed race would be. I knew the students would likely know nothing about Native American life and culture other than the false images our national culture is awash with. I had also recently been in a Native American literature class that had managed to touch very little on race or oppression or genocide, and I was determined to make sure that my class did not avoid necessary but difficult topics. I spent weeks combing through books and articles about Native history and culture, trying to narrow down my background information to what could easily fit into the time frame of my course—only seven weeks. Finally I was ready, and I went to meet the students. There were only six of them, all adults. Two of the students I already knew. All of the students were White, five women and one man, all of them over 30.

The moment I walked into that small room in the basement, I was the authority. Those students, even those who already knew me, took one look at my brown skin and Indian features and decided I was the genuine article, the true "Native informant" there to give them inside knowledge about Indians. In my opening lecture, I explained who I was and how I happened to be teaching this class. I introduced the term Mestiza, talked of the racial mix of Latin America, talked of my own racial mix, of my Mestizo father. I told them about my Norwegian American mother. To explain the diversity of Indigenous culture, I compared Native tribes to European nationalities: Tlingit are as different from Mohawk as French are from Swedes. In other words, I tried to express the complex nature of Native heritage in the Americas.

They all nodded eagerly and continued to identify me as a spokesperson for all things Indian.[7] During the class, I heard questions such as "Lisa, what do they do in this case in your culture?"

"Which culture?" I was always quick to reply. But it was clear that many of the students wanted to pin me down, wanted to put me into an uncontested category of Native, wanted to ignore that troubling Spanish last name or their knowledge of my White mother.

This European American way of seeing and understanding the world was something we struggled with in class, and perhaps my complex background was just the first step for the students in helping them learn to give up on dualities. They had to accept that I could be many things at once, that I was not just "Native" or just "Latina" (rarely do people see me as just "White"). Struggling with this helped them accept the worldviews of the writers we read—they had to give up on the idea of exclusion and focus on inclusion, on how disparate parts make a whole, to read and really understand books such as *Ceremony*. I was worried about that book, and some students struggled to understand Silko's circular and mythic structure. But they did not have the horrible reaction to it I had encountered in my earlier class, and we ended up having exciting conversations.

So what was different? First, it was a Native American literature class and was not a requirement. Students who were really interested in the subject took it, so particularly racist students were self-selected out. Then there was the fact that my body, perceived to be Native, was a plus in this class. It made me the Native informant, and though I tried to dispel that image—even introducing that term and explaining the problems with putting someone (especially me!) in the position of speaking for a culture—it also meant that the class went more smoothly than some others. I carefully prepared them for the kind of things we would be reading—we talked a lot about Native history in the United States, about U.S. policy and changing views of race, and about oppression. We talked about subject positions and White privilege. Some of it was luck—I was blessed with six students who were interested, articulate, and open-minded. Two in particular had taken courses in race and gender already and so were able to discuss these issues thoughtfully, which meant that I was not the only one in the classroom taking on difficult topics.

My evaluations for the class were among the best I have received, and yet I was never able to dispel the view of me as "pure Indian." I got a response from a student who loved the class and said there should be more courses on Native Americans, making sure that the teachers were "of that culture" like me. I smiled when I read it and wondered which culture she meant. In spite of the ways others read my body, there is no one culture that is mine, none that I could claim uncontested. I don't fit into the boxes: I'm the Chicana who doesn't speak Spanish, the Indian who doesn't know her tribal background, the Norwegian who doesn't look White. Sometimes, in exasperation, I see myself that way, a series of doesn't-fits. I understand why my background confuses people. Some days I think the pain of teaching about race costs me too much, and I wish I could stop. But on most days, I think "Just deal with it." America is too complex to fit in one category, and me, I'm as

American as they come. As my students struggle to learn to really see me, to learn from me, they are also learning to see the America that has always been before them: complex, diverse and beautiful.

Lisa D. Chavez is a Chicana Mestiza writer and teacher, born in Los Angeles but raised in Fairbanks, Alaska. She has an M.F.A. in creative writing from Arizona State University, and an M.A. in American literature from the University of Rochester. Her first book of poetry, *Destruction Bay*, was published in 1999, and her second book, *In an Angry Season*, was published in 2001. She has had poems published in many literary magazines, and her poems have been included in anthologies of Latina and American poetry. Her creative non-fiction has been widely published, and she is currently at work on a memoir of growing up in Alaska that focuses on issues of race, class and gender. She teaches at Albion College, a small, private liberal arts college in southern Michigan.

Author's Note

I would like to thank some courageous teachers who have shaped my thinking on issues of identity in the classroom: Dr. Deborah Grayson, Dr. Joyce Middleton, and my father-in-law, Dr. William Spohn.

Notes

1. Because I mention my doctoral studies in the essay, I felt I should explain that I did all the coursework and exams for the Ph.D. and was ABD (all but dissertation) when I decided not to finish the degree because I felt my energies were better devoted to poetry and other forms of creative writing.

2. I have taught at the University of Alaska Fairbanks, Arizona State University, the University of Rochester, Empire State College, Albion College, and the miscellany—an army base and air force base in Alaska, an English conversational school in Osaka, Japan, and for the Peace Corps in Poland.

3. Alaska's Native groups include Indian (Athabascan, Tlingit, Haida, and others); Inupiat and Yupik (who generally refer to themselves collectively as Eskimo if they are not specifically saying Yupik or Inupiat—the term "Inuit" was not much in use in Alaska by Native people); and Aleut. "Native" is used as a generic term to refer to all these groups--I use it to refer to anyone indigenous to the Americas.

4. This incident was the most overt problem in the class, though there were other battles over issues of race and, later, sexual orientation. Though my student evaluations from that class were so abysmal (and vitriolic) that I threw them away after reading them, I do remember that there were also a few students who I felt I had connected with. Still, my overwhelming memory of that class was negative, and it shows the ways in which a few resisting students can poison a class.

5. I don't have the space here to even begin to vent my frustrations with the phrase "politically correct" or the thoughtless way it is used in dialogue about race, class, gender, and sexual orientation in this country. For a good discussion of this term and the way it is used, see Griffin (1995).

6. Chappell, as a White professor, has a degree of privilege that teachers of color do not, though she does not acknowledge this in her essay. In another view of a White female professor discussing race in the classroom, Gail Griffin states that "the teacher's job is to break that silence, whether it comes from denial or ignorance or both. A White teacher in a predominantly White classroom has much less to lose than her colleagues of color in asking the questions, making the interventions that disrupt racist readings of black texts" (1995, 145).

7. It is not just White students who identify me as exclusively Indian, even after I explain my ethnicity. The summer after my disastrous world literature class, I taught composition for Rural Alaska Honors Institute, a program to aid rural Alaskan students in adjusting to college and life outside of rural Alaska. My class was entirely Alaska Native. In this class, though I again explained in detail about my identity, the students immediately adopted me, referring to me as a "Lower 48 Indian." They read my body as Indian, and far from being a problem, that meant they could trust me because I understood their experiences to a degree. Though I am not Alaska Native and did not share their varied cultural heritages, I did have an understanding of the kinds of challenges they would face, especially since my entire life in Alaska has been a time in which I have been misidentified as Alaska Native, both by White and Native people.

Works Cited

Bauer, D. M. 1995. "Personal Criticism and the Academic Personality." In *Who Can Speak?: Authority and Critical Identity*, edited by J. Roof and R. Wiegman. Chicago: University of Illinois Press.

Chappell, V. A. 1997. "'But Isn't This the Land of the Free?': Resistance and Discovery in Student Responses to 'Farewell to Manzanar'." In *Writing in Multicultural Settings*, edited by C. Severino, J. Guerra and J. Butler. New York: MLA.

Griffin, G. 1995. *Season of the Witch: Border Lines, Marginal Notes*. Pasadena, CA: Trilogy Books.

hooks, b. 1994. *Teaching to Transgress: Education as the Practice of Freedom*. New York: Routledge.

Johnson, C. 1995. "Disinfecting Dialogues." In *Pedagogy: The Question of Impersonation*, edited by J. Gallop. Bloomington, IN: Indiana University Press.

Karamcheti, I. 1995. "Caliban in the Classroom." In *Pedagogy: The Question of Impersonation*, edited by J. Gallop. Bloomington, IN: Indiana University Press.

Lorde, A. 1984. "Uses of Anger: Women Respond to Racism." In *Sister Outsider*. New York: The Crossing Press.

McIntosh, P. 1989. "White Privilege: Unpacking the Invisible Knapsack." *Peace and Freedom* (July/August): 10–11.

Office of Planning Analysis & Institutional Research. 1995. Factbook. Fall 1995–1999 Headcount by Ethnicity. Fairbanks: University of Alaska, Fairbanks.

Tatum, B. D. 1997. *"Why are all the black kids sitting together in the cafeteria?" and Other Conversations about Race*. New York: Basic Books.

Williams, P. J. 1991. *The Alchemy of Race and Rights: Diary of a Law Professor*. Cambridge, MA: Harvard University Press.

———. 1995. *The Rooster's Egg: On the Persistence of Prejudice*. Cambridge, MA: Harvard University Press.

CHAPTER SIX

Useful Anger: Confrontation and Challenge in the Teaching of Gender, Race, and Violence

KIMBERLY NICHELE BROWN

Abstract

THIS PAPER CHRONICLES my experience at Georgetown University, where I taught a literature course called Gender, Race, and Violence. The course focused on the revolutionary or retaliatory violence perpetuated by Black subjects on either real or imagined White oppressors. We examined the uses of anger and violence as rhetorical and structural devices and authenticating tools in the works of African American writers. In the classroom arena, where as professors we are taught to create "safe spaces" for our students, issues of gender, race, and violence disturb the safety of the classroom for all students, regardless of their racial background, because these topics tend to challenge our most basic beliefs. However, it is precisely in these moments of discomfort that I've found honest and frank discussions taking place. I feel that if we are ever to talk frankly about race and gender in this country, and even come close to ending racism, we must deal with the right of the oppressed to feel and express anger. Using classroom notes (written by several students), assignments, and lesson plans, I talk about the usefulness of anger by converting the discomfort found in moments where we discuss sensitive issues to opportunities for radical pedagogy.

> At the level of individuals, violence is a cleansing force. It frees the native from his inferiority complex and from his despair and inaction.
>
> Frantz Fanon, *The Wretched of the Earth*

> The act of violence kills more than the oppressor; it destroys also that image of passivity which was taken to stand between the individual and his authenticity.
>
> C. W. E. Bigsby, *The Second Black Renaissance*

In this essay, I narrate my experience as an adjunct professor at Georgetown University, where I taught a self-designed introductory African American literature course called Gender, Race, and Violence. Although I later taught multiple sections of this course, I've confined my discussion to an analysis of the first time I taught Gender, Race, and Violence. This first class focused on the revolutionary or retaliatory violence perpetuated by Black subjects on either real or imagined White oppressors. In this course, we examined the uses of anger and violence as rhetorical and structural devices and as authenticating tools in the works of African American writers. Because slavery informs most discussions about race, gender, and class in this country and marks the gap between African ideals and American socioeconomic practices, this course was framed by original slave narratives and contemporary renderings of slavery in the novel.

By the end of the class, students were to have obtained a basic understanding of how the combined effects of racism, sexism, and class status can affect African American subjects and inform most African American literature. Because of space constraints, this chapter centers on classroom discussions of White privilege and Audre Lorde's essay "Uses of Anger: Women Respond to Racism." I will end by briefly outlining some of the pedagogical strategies employed to teach a few of the other texts we read. Using classroom notes written by various "class historians" assigned each class period, classroom scenarios, assignments, and lesson plans, I describe the ways in which the discomfort found in anger can stimulate learning. I also examine how I attempted to turn uncomfortable classroom situations into opportunities for radical pedagogy.

Because of my classroom experiences, the questions I have sought to answer are as follows: How do I teach students to respect and understand the anger displayed by many African American authors and not reinforce negative stereotypes concerning Blackness? How do I highlight sensitive issues such as gender, race, and violence without making my students feel uncomfortable? And finally, is it possible to teach such topics without causing discomfort? I believe that in order for educators and scholars to address sensitive issues such as race and gender on open and honest terms, oppressed peoples must be allowed to voice their anger and those of the dominant group must be receptive to understanding such anger.

*   *   *

In *The Structuring of Emotion in Black American Fiction,* Raymond Hedin writes about the centrality of anger in the tradition of African American literature. He says:

> Anger has held a central, difficult position in this tradition. At the same time that Black writers have tried to change the racial attitudes of white readers, they have also become increasingly angry at those attitudes and at whites for their treatment of Blacks. But anger, a risky emotion in any argument, has been especially problematic for Black writers, given their awareness that inherent brutishness and lack of control have been alleged to the Black man from days of slavery on. (Hedin 1982, 37)

Although it is a justifiable response to oppression, Hedin's quotation shows that anger has traditionally been a difficult emotion for African American writers to negotiate. Writers of slave narratives, because they were representing the plight of all enslaved Africans and African Americans, had to be very careful about how they portrayed themselves and other Black characters to their White readership. Although it was important for a Black person to show a myriad of emotions in order to even be considered human, anger was the most difficult emotion for the slave narrator to mediate. To show too little anger would defeat the abolitionist program—a lack of anger would give credence to the widespread, yet erroneous, notion that Blacks were happy within the institution of slavery. To show too much would reinforce negative stereotypes of Blacks as bestial and savage.

Dialogues about anger and violence haven't progressed much since the era of the slave narrative. As a society, the majority of us tend to view African Americans as eternal victims of White oppression while simultaneously viewing "Black rage" as a psychotic and irrational response to racism. As a 31-year-old African American woman professor who has taught African American literature in predominantly White classrooms for over seven years, I have often found myself in a precarious position, similar to that of the slave narrators. I have found that my White students have been uncomfortable and sometimes hostile when confronted by the anger of African American writers studied in my courses.

As the epigraphs by Fanon and Bigsby point out, many African American writers see anger and violence as self-authenticating devices. Such writers openly express their animosity toward racism and racist Whites because, historically, Blacks have had to suppress anger in order to survive. However, many White students feel defensive, resentful, and even implicated when faced with such anger. To complicate matters further, I have also found that my presence as a 5'10" buxom African American woman who regularly dresses in black and often wears her hair in braids (or some other natural hairstyle) epitomizes the image of an "angry Black woman" for some of my students. For example, students often tell me that I intimidate them, although, ironically, not enough to keep them from telling me so. They sometimes perceive that I empathize with the writers' acrimony and either become antagonistic or become vested in proving to me that they are not racists. I sometimes, then, find myself defending my own position of authority as well as defending the authors and their texts.

Toni Morrison writes that "race is a very difficult thing to talk about, because the conversation frequently ends up being patronizing, guilt ridden, hostile or resentful. But for those interested in the study of literature and the writing of literature, it is something you have to confront and think about." In the classroom arena, issues of race, as well as issues of gender and sexual orientation, disturb the safety of the classroom for all students, regardless of their racial background. These topics tend to shake the foundations of our self-identity because they force us to confront our deepest prejudices. For example, many of my White students are unwilling to confront Black anger because it often places them in the position of "oppressor," and if they are uncomfortable with that label, they either feel guilt or anger. Conversely, many of my Black students tire of the pity they receive at being the "victim" of White oppression.

As a professor, I often feel that I suffer from what I call the "trailblazer syndrome" in these discussions. I envision the trailblazer as a person who is the first Black person to accomplish something that had been previously denied as an opportunity for African Americans. Although in the larger scheme of things I'm not the first African American to teach issues of race and gender, I sometimes consider myself to be a trailblazer because I am often either the first Black person or woman many of my students (White or otherwise) have ever had as a teacher. I am also often the first professor they've encountered who is so vehemently outspoken about issues of oppression. The discomfort I feel in the classroom stems from having to negotiate the differences between my students' impressions of me as an African American woman and who I really am as a person. It is precisely in these moments of discomfort, both my own and my students', that I've found that the most frank and honest discussions take place.

* * *

As both a master's and Ph.D. candidate in English at the University of Pittsburgh and the University of Maryland-College Park (UMCP), I taught both composition and several courses on African American literature. By the time I began as an adjunct professor at Georgetown University, I had taught nine courses on African American literature. Because of my extensive teaching background during my graduate career, my proposal for Gender, Race, and Violence was enthusiastically received by Georgetown's department head, who was anxious to see more diversity in the lower-level, writing-intensive literature courses offered by the university. During this time period, I was also working on my Ph.D. at the University of Maryland-College Park. I took the job at Georgetown primarily because my graduate school funding had run out at UMCP, but I relished the idea of teaching at a university that was markedly different from UMCP. While UMCP is a fairly large university, boasting of a highly diverse student population, Georgetown is an elite, Jesuit university, whose student population is predominantly White.

On the days when I was required to teach, I had to take two buses and the metro to get from my apartment in Hyattsville to Georgetown's campus. Hyattsville is a suburb of Prince George's County, a county that arguably has the largest Black population on the East Coast. My apartment was approximately five driving minutes from the Maryland/D.C. border. On my way to work, I rarely saw a White face until I reached the downtown area, and even then the number of commuting Black professionals was astounding. I have often marveled at the irony that our nation's capital is affectionately known in Black circles nationwide as "Chocolate City." However, like most major cities, Washington, D.C., has many segregated neighborhoods. It is quite possible for a student at Georgetown to ignore the enormous influx of Blacks throughout the city, given that the university is housed at the edge of an up-scale residential neighborhood that is not readily accessible by metro, which keeps the transient population to a minimum. Most of my students at Georgetown came from middle- to upper-middle-class families, and many were even more privileged than that. I have had students who studied over-seas in Asia and Africa as well as students who routinely vacationed in Europe. As a second-generation college student coming from a solidly mid-dle-class background (we vacationed in the Poconos or Virginia Beach), I was a little intimidated. I had been told that Georgetown students were often snobbish and elitist. To my delight, I found that students who had traveled widely were often more open to learning about other cultures and were aware that other populations had differing worldviews and practices.

My first class was predominantly White, consisting of only two African American students (one male and one female) and one woman who was of Japanese and White descent. I also had one openly lesbian student. One of the first things I asked my students to do was to define the main terms of our course (gender, race, and violence). Although the terms "gender" and "race" were vigorously debated, the most interesting conversation occurred when students attempted to define violence. Elizabeth (all students' names are pseudonyms), the class historian for that day, wrote:

Dom suggested that violence is an act of physical harm committed by somebody toward somebody else, while Erin added emotional and mental harm as possible outcomes. Mark believed that a "violent" act would have to be spurned by an emotion
(such as hate) and would have to be an intentional act; under this definition, boxing
would be an example of an act of aggression that remains non-violent. A suggestion
that violence is the result of a loss of self-control sparked the difficult question of
whether or not acts of war due to their calculated natures should be considered war.

It seemed as if students wanted to say that violence was really about intent,
especially given the fact that they were willing to label boxing as a "non-
violent" sport. To my students, if you intended to hurt someone, only then
had you committed a violent act. I brought up the phrase "to die a violent
death." Such terminology is used to describe someone who was murdered in a
particularly brutal fashion or someone who died a death that was unusually
painful, such as in a no-fault car accident. I suggested that if the end result is
that the victim is ultimately hurt, to label violence as something that is only
done with intent potentially denies the victim the right to be angry over her
or his experience. Because of my statement, we started talking about poverty
as violence and racism as violence. Thinking of violence in this manner encouraged students to think about the psychic damage or violence that can be
inflicted on those who live in poverty and those who must deal with racism,
sexism, or homophobia on a daily basis.

Because I am committed to practicing radical pedagogy, it was important
to me that my students were able to make connections between physical and
psychic violence caused by oppression. I have always believed that literature
can be used as a vehicle to talk about social issues and injustices. Through
the analysis of literature, I want my students to learn to think critically about
the world so that they might make it better. As a victim of racism and sexism,
I began teaching because I wanted to make a difference. Because I've been
taught traditions of African American protest and resistance, I sometimes feel
a moral obligation to continue that fight in the classroom. Very often thinking critically about another person's oppression requires that we interrogate
our own privilege. By discussing poverty and racism as acts of violence, I was
able to move my students into a discussion not only of White privilege but
also of privileges gained by being a member of a minority group.

In *Talking Back, Thinking Feminist, Talking Black* bell hooks writes:

When liberal whites fail to understand how they can and/or do embody white-
supremacist values and beliefs even though they may not embrace racism as prejudice or domination (especially domination that involves coercive control), they cannot recognize the ways their actions support and affirm the very structure of racist
domination and oppression that they profess to wish to see eradicated. (hooks 1989,
113)

I thought that it was important to develop an assignment that would unearth the "White-supremacist values and beliefs" my students had grown up with. However, I also believed that those from marginalized groups also have certain privileges stemming from our social positioning. Therefore, I asked my class to complete the following assignment for the next class session: "List 3–5 privileges you have because of your race. Then list 3–5 privileges you have because of your gender. Finally, address these questions: Have you ever felt oppressed or victimized? Is so, when? How did it make you feel? If not, what life experiences have you had that would account for never feeling this way?" I got the idea to develop this assignment after reading Peggy McIntosh's essay, "White Privilege and Male Privilege." McIntosh says:

> I have come to see white privilege as an invisible package of unearned assets that I can count on cashing in each day, but about which I was "meaning" to remain oblivious. White privilege is like an invisible weightless knapsack of special provisions, assurances, tools, maps, guides, codebooks, passports, visas, clothes, compass, emergency gear, and blank checks. (McIntosh 1995, 76–77)

McIntosh lists forty-six privileges of Whiteness. Before I shared McIntosh's list with my students, I wanted them to think on their own about the privileges they have because of their race and gender. Surprisingly, my White students generally found it easy to talk about the privileges they had because of race, while my two Black students found it difficult to think of anything about Blackness that they would consider racial privilege. Both my male and female students, regardless of race, found it easy to discuss the privileges of either gender. Melissa's class history highlights some of the things male students saw as their privilege:

> Kurt spoke of how a man can walk through the streets at any time and still not feel as afraid of being mugged or raped as a woman might…. if he is raped or mugged, the question, "Well, what was he doing there at that hour anyway?" never comes up. A man gets to keep his name when he marries. Wayne brought up the point that men don't have to go through PMS, abortion, or birth. As a White male, Sean says he can avoid racial and or gender discrimination. Trey talked about how the media was harder on women. For example, Oprah is often joked about for being overweight, but Jay Leno can be as fat as he wants and no one makes a comment.

I was pleased to see that the male students in my class took the assignment very seriously. I was worried that they would leave thinking "I'm glad I'm not a woman" rather than feeling emboldened to help eradicate sexism. Melissa recorded what students saw as the advantages of being female as follows:

> Brooke commenced on the topic of gender with the idea of Affirmative Action and
> how it allows women an extra edge. Angie stated that women are more privileged
> than men because they can give birth and because there is a stronger bond between
> a mother and a child. Also, it was mentioned that a woman at Georgetown can get
> free tutoring and can get into clubs and parties free. Most car insurance is cheaper
> for women than for men. Only a female can be "Daddy's little girl." Christine
> brought up that in certain instances a woman can cry and still not be considered
> weak.

Aside from the inherent flaw of considering being "Daddy's little girl" a
privilege, I was pleased with the women's responses. The most interesting discussion concerned whether or not we should see affirmative action as a *privilege* or a *right* for women. One student commented that to see it as a privilege
meant that White men aren't granted the same privilege. She thought that it
was better to see affirmative action as a corrective for the disproportionate
opportunities granted to White women and Blacks.

The discussion concerning White privilege was less surprising. Students
spoke of the ability to "blend in better"—thus casting Whiteness as the norm.
Most of the discussion concerning White privilege centered on material possessions and access to education. There was a painful silence, however, when
I asked what sort of advantages there were to being Black. My two Black students had been unable to come up with anything to list on their papers. One
of my White students, Melissa, timidly raised her hand in response to my
question. She mentioned feeling envious at the unity she sees among Black
people. At this statement, the Black male student agreed, but lamented that
most of the time Black unity is in opposition to Whites rather than joining
with Blacks because of a common culture. I could see that a few of my students felt hesitant to disagree with him because, as one of the few recogniz-
able minorities in the class, he had set himself up as spokesperson. Once I
interjected about my own positive experiences being Black, both Black students mentioned the security they felt when in predominantly Black situations. The Black male student who first spoke recanted his earlier statements
that most attempts at Black unity were a result of opposition to Whiteness by
recalling some moments in his life when he voluntarily sought out the company of other Blacks. I feel that it is important to stress privileges that so-
called oppressed groups possess so that members of these groups don't embrace victimization as a fixed component of their lives.

The final set of questions, "Have you ever felt oppressed or victimized? Is
so, when? How did it make you feel? If not, what life experiences have you
had that would account for never feeling this way?," proved to be the most
challenging for my White students to respond to. Some (women and men)

spoke of being mugged in D.C. as a moment of powerlessness. Some of my female students spoke of being sexually harassed and not reporting it for fear of reproach by their schoolmates. During classroom discussion, my Black students were strangely quiet. I felt uncomfortable about pressing them to disclose their painful experiences of being victimized. Because I grew up in predominantly White neighborhoods and attended predominantly White schools for my entire academic career, I know what it feels like to have your experiences stand for all Black experiences. I know what it feels like to have the most painful experiences laid bare for the scrutiny of White classmates, who are not always careful of your feelings when they probe for more information. Ultimately, I thought it was important for my White students to talk about moments when they felt powerless or victimized. To explore their own victimized moments would perhaps enable them to be more empathetic to others who experience oppression on a daily basis. My hope was that rather than seeing victimization as a "Black thing," students would see oppression as an assault on one's basic humanity.

I was very pleased with the discussions that came out of this assignment because I wanted my students to actively interrogate the freedoms that they had learned to take for granted. I felt that my students were beginning to understand the ways in which they were privileged and how that privilege can cause anger among marginal groups. I had hoped that such an interrogation would enable students to better understand why marginalized groups fought so hard to obtain these freedoms.

Although I would like to present all of my experiences with students in a positive and productive light, I have sometimes encountered students who are extremely resistant to my teaching style and to the types of course materials we read. I'd like to relay my experiences with one White female student who gave me particular difficulty when I taught that first section of Gender, Race, and Violence. For the purposes of this chapter, I choose to call this young woman "Anne"—as a derivative of "Miss Anne." "Miss Anne" is a generic label of Whiteness, like "Mr. Charlie or "The Man," that categorizes a particular brand of privileged White womanhood. The "Miss Annes" of slave narratives saw Black womanhood as subordinate and antithetical to that of their own. Like other concepts of White supremacy, Miss Anne's philosophy is based on the innate superiority of Whiteness and the denial of Black humanity.

I'd like to go back to the first class meeting to put my later experiences with Anne in a better context. As usual, on the first day of class, I requested that each student introduce her or himself and share an interesting fact about her or his life with the class. When I reached Anne, she revealed that she espoused a conservative ideology. The groans among her classmates were audible. Despite the wealth that abounded on campus, many of my students were self-defined liberals. I, however, attempted to give Anne the benefit of the doubt. She had, after all, elected to take a course that was clearly marked as one that dealt with the sensitive issues of race, gender and violence. Her presence in my class said to me that Anne might be more open-minded than her classmates thought.

Teaching and living in the Maryland/D.C. area has made me sensitive to regional differences in the protocols of communication. As a person born and raised in the Philadelphia area, I have been told by those outside of northern east-coast cities that I am blunt. Regional differences, coupled with the fact that I have been seen as intimidating because of my race and stature, have often caused me to use humor to make my students feel more comfortable talking about sensitive issues. This is my way of creating a "safe space" within the classroom. Paula Rothenberg explains the necessity of creating safe spaces:

> Creating a safe space is something most good teachers do instinctively in all their classes. In our course, potentially threatening in both form and content, it was critical. Students had to feel secure that their comments would be treated with respect whether or not the faculty member or the class agreed with them. The class had to feel confident that we would remain in control, directing classroom anger away from personal attacks on individuals or groups and focusing it on ideas or institutions. (Rotenberg 1990, 36)

Humor allows students to laugh at the stupidity of racist, sexist, or classist thinking. Humor also often alleviates the tension that arises when talking about such topics and thereby diverts classroom anger toward the institutionalization of such oppressions. However, my experiences with Anne taught me that things weren't as safe in the classroom as I had imagined.

Because of my teaching style, things ran smoothly between Anne and me for a brief period. Although I believe in teaching chronologically, in order to place texts within their historical contexts, I used Audre Lorde's essay "The Uses of Anger: Women Respond to Racism" to better situate the themes informing the course. Before reading this essay, I informed my students that Lorde was a Black lesbian, a feminist, and that she had died of cancer in 1992. I talked briefly about the feminist movement of the twenties and its exclusion of Black women. I mentioned that while White women won the right to vote in 1920, Black people in general didn't get the right to vote until 1964, when the Twenty-Fourth Amendment was instituted and poll taxes were ruled illegal. We discussed how Lorde's essay depicts the ways in which perceptions of race ultimately act as a barrier when Black and White women try to come together under a band of universal sisterhood. In a paper first published in 1981, Lorde wrote:

> After fifteen years of a women's movement which professes to address the life concerns and possible futures of all women, I still hear, on campus after campus, "How can we address the issues of racism? No women of Color attended." Or, the other side of that statement, "We have no one in our department equipped to teach their work." In other words, racism is a Black women's problem, a problem of Color, and only we can discuss it. (Lorde 1984, 125)

We then moved to a discussion of traditional ways of viewing anger. Carolyn, the class historian for that day, wrote that "several students offered various interpretations of the Lorde piece—the most significant being the idea that anger is traditionally admissible only when expressed by men." For Lorde, voicing her anger is a way to authenticate herself. I pointed out to the class that Lorde makes clear that she doesn't want her essay to be taken as a theoretical discussion. Rather, she wants it to be seen as her way of expressing her anger for the benefit of her own growth, and she offers up her insights to enable others to grow as well. I read then the following quote to the class to facilitate a discussion about White guilt:

> My anger is a response to racist attitudes and to the actions and presumptions that arise out of those attitudes. If your dealings with other women reflect those attitudes, then my anger and your attendant fears are spotlights that can be used for growth in the same way I have used learning to express anger from my growth. But for corrective surgery, not guilt. Guilt and defensiveness are bricks in a wall against which we all flounder; they serve none of our futures. (Lorde 1984, 124)

Lorde goes on to give examples of some of the things that make Whites feel defensive or angry. I asked my students what they thought of this quotation. Anne, who apparently felt implicated, launched into a long tirade, essentially claiming that Lorde was a racist. Although many students admitted to feeling chastised and even guilty after reading Lorde's text, several students attempted to interject and defend Lorde's positioning. But they were vehemently shot down by Anne's biting comments to the contrary.

Once class was over, Anne asked if she could speak with me. A White male classmate, Kurt, who seemed to be waiting for Anne, stayed to listen. Anne told me, once again, that she thought Audre Lorde was a racist and that she was offended that, as "cool" as I seemed, I would force her to read such nonsense. As in class, when I asked her to point out specific passages that revealed Lorde to be a racist, she was unable to do so. Not believing that I, or Lorde, had the power to work Anne into such a frenzy, I asked what was the underlying cause of her hostility. At this point, her friend spoke up. Kurt told me that Anne was reading the essay the night before and became enraged by Lorde's words. She then proceeded to share certain passages with a group of male and female friends in an adjoining dorm room. To her dismay, Anne was verbally attacked by these students, all of whom were White. She got into a series of shouting matches with the group and was told that she was a racist by several of its members. Now, I'm thinking, "If it walks like a duck and quacks like a duck"... I believe that most Whites in this country have an aversion to overt displays of racism, while they often explain away more covert manifestations of the same thing. Ultimately, I believed that if a group of White people could brand Anne a racist, then she probably embodied racism in its extremity.

Anne chimed back in at that point and insisted that she wasn't a racist, she just didn't like to talk about race. This, of course, puzzled me, and I reminded her that the course was called, Gender, Race, and Violence. I asked, as politely as I could, what she thought we'd be talking about in class. Anne stated that she didn't know, but she had read Toni Morrison's *Beloved* in another class and they hadn't *once* discussed race. I thought briefly about looking up her former teacher to ask how it was possible to teach *Beloved*, a novel about former slaves coming to grips with what it means to be Black in the wake of emancipation, without talking about race.

Anne must have read something in my face because she shouted, "Stop looking at me like that!" In calm dismay, I asked her how she thought I was looking at her. Her response: "Like I'm a dumb little White girl who doesn't know anything." I thought that Anne was projecting her own insecurities about confronting materials with which she was unfamiliar. I also assumed that she felt somewhat overwhelmed and offended that I, as an African American, had authority over her as an instructor. I tried to explain these things to her in as diplomatic a fashion as possible. However, in the next instant I saw that I wasn't very successful.

All of the books and articles I've ever read instructing me in the ways of relinquishing my authority so that students feel empowered came back to mock me as Anne stood in front of me, shaking in rage, her finger pointed in my face. Not only did Anne disregard my authority and the respect my position would have garnered had I been older, White, and male, she *assumed* the authority to *put me in my place.* She openly chastised me, stating, "You need to learn how to talk to people." The rest of her words were eclipsed by a rising rage I actively attempted to stifle. With what could be considered the most restraint I've ever shown in my life, I managed to calmly, yet coldly, tell her that she had no right to tell me what I needed to do. I accused her of functioning under the spell of some sort of White arrogance that surpassed my wildest imagination. I reminded her that during classroom discussions she had been allowed to voice her opinions as she saw fit and that I should be afforded the same respect and courtesy. And the rest of my words trailed off into hissing admonishments of "how dare you..." and "don't you ever..." until she was as visibly shaken as I felt inside.

Eventually, we were able to have a more civil and less emotionally charged conversation, in which Anne revealed that she didn't like to have her views challenged. At that point she ironically felt more comfortable to share some of her views with me. Anne believed that most people were poor because they didn't work hard enough. She believed that racism was virtually nonexistent while simultaneously believing in reverse discrimination. Anne also believed that Blacks made up the bulk of welfare recipients and were therefore a drain to her tax dollars—a penny of which she had yet to earn, given that she was supported by her family's wealth.

Kurt took up much of the slack, painstakingly explaining the holes in her arguments. While her friend tried to convince her that the class would probably be good for her, I secretly hoped that she would in fact drop the course even as I too encouraged her to stay. In my mind's eye, I saw the countless classroom afternoons drift by consumed by constant attempts to challenge Anne's thinking to the detriment of my other students, who were more eager to embrace ideas that might challenge their own. I believed that the future discussions I would have with Anne would just be debates (two differing worldviews butting heads within the space of the classroom) that would eventually annoy and exasperate both myself and my other students. I felt that such discussions would make us stray from analyzing the texts themselves, which was the case when we discussed Lorde's essay, and would make the class be about her insecurities as a White person or even about my need to claim authority as a Black person. Anne, as well as my opposition to her position, would become the central focus of a class geared toward the centering of Blackness. The thought made a knot in my stomach.

I have come to believe that racism, like alcoholism, is a sickness that can only be treated when the suffering person is ready. Anne was definitely not ready—and although such a class would have potentially benefited her, it would have severely damaged me. We often talk about the good the trailblazer does for those that come after her and even those that she challenges, but we rarely discuss the psychic damage done to the trailblazer once the path is on fire. Acting in the position of trailblazer for "Miss Anne," I'm hopeful that future African American professors will find her to be more amiable. Although Anne offered her sincere apology for her hostile and erratic behavior, I didn't feel as if I had won anything. To my guilty relief, she did in fact drop the class, presumably to take one that talked about Black texts without discussing race or racism.

The next class period, Anne, of course, was not there, but she haunted our further discussions of Lorde's text. Anne's comments labeled her a racist. Against her extreme words, another student making an occasional slip, such as calling an African American person "colored," didn't seem too bad. Now that she was gone, students no longer had Anne to shield them from being implicated as racists in their own right. In the class period following Anne's outburst, I asked students to be honest about how they really felt about Lorde's essay. Although no students reached the level of intensity that Anne had, many did admit to feeling that although Lorde wasn't a racist, she didn't like White people. When pressed to give specific examples of Lorde's racism, again, no one was able to do so. However, many felt that the overall tone of the text suggested a dislike of Whites.

Since I really enjoy reading Audre Lorde, my initial impulse was to counter my students, to show them how wrong they were. Instead, I did the opposite and asked them to explore reasons why Lorde might not like White people. Asking this question proved to be more successful because students were willing to concede that, given the scenarios she highlights in her text, that she has a right not to like White people, or at least the White people she described within her text. This concession enabled me to talk about the antebellum period, when slaves weren't allowed to express their anger, and thereby acted as a segue to discussing the primary texts of the course.

Our first text was Frederick Douglass's 1845 narrative. I asked the students to discuss the ways in which Douglass mediates his anger both as a character and as a writer. My intention was to make a distinction between Douglass the writer and Douglass the character in order to get students to see the autobiographical self as a constructed one. According to John, the class historian, one student discussed how Douglass (the writer) discusses his inability to put his emotions into words that would accurately describe his feelings of horror after witnessing a terrible whipping of another slave. This student asserted that Douglass was trying to show his readers that some of the atrocities of slavery were too horrible to describe. Another student commented that Douglass refrains from using emotionally charged language and instead uses metaphors to convey his anger. One student pointed out that as a character, Douglass shows a tactful negotiation of anger in the scene with Covey. Here he was referring to the most famous scene of the narrative in which Douglass fights with the overseer Covey and wins. We discussed the ways in which Douglass's negotiation of anger was very masculine, relying on the prevailing assumptions of manhood as being defined by physical prowess and the notion of self-defense.

Harriet Jacobs's *Incidents in the Life of a Slave Girl* (1857; reprinted as Jacobs 1987) presents a more female approach to negotiation of anger. In this text, Jacobs expresses her anger about the rape and sexual molestation of slave women. Jacobs must present this sensitive issue to a predominantly White female audience in order to highlight the widespread rape that occured within the master/slave relationship. When we discussed *Incidents in the Life of a Slave Girl,* many students wanted to talk about Jacobs's relationship with her master, Dr. Flint, and her White "lover," Mr. Sands. Some students wanted to read her consensual relationship with Mr. Sands as being better than her relationship with Dr. Flint because it was Jacobs's choice to have sex with him. In response, I made them read Barbara Omolade's essay, "Hearts of Darkness," and pointed them to the passage where she states, "All sexual intercourse between a White man and a Black woman irrespective of her conscious consent became rape, because the social arrangement assumed the Black woman to be without any human right to control her own body." This quotation was met with silence. Wynne, a White male student, expressed discomfort at Omolade's expressed belief that all relationships between Black women and White men during this time period could be labeled rape. Angie, a woman of both Japanese and White descent, countered that if Black women weren't considered to be equal to Whites and the White man, whether he was her master or not, could just "take it" without consequence, then the Black woman essentially had no choice. Janie was able to connect Omolade's essay with Jacobs's situation by pointing out that when Jacobs conferred the title of "Mister" to Mr. Sands, she was subtly demonstrating her subordinate relationship to his positioning as a White man.

Although one can argue that there were Black women during the antebellum period who did elect to sleep with White men of their own volition and that there were love relationships between the two races in question, I tried to get students to see that Omolade was attempting to show the ways in which Black women were oppressed because of the interrelated oppressions of being *both* female and Black.

Another text that facilitated wide discussion was Richard Wright's *Native Son.* In *Native Son,* Bigger Thomas, a poor Black urban youth, accidentally murders Mary Dalton, the daughter of the affluent White family for whom he works. Bigger then deliberately chops off Mary's head and stuffs her body into the furnace to avoid capture. Wright, like Morrison, attempted to upset the safety of the text by creating an unsympathetic character as the protagonist. After the disappointment he felt about the sentimental reaction of his White readers to *Uncle Tom's Children,* Wright stated, "I swore to myself that if I ever wrote another book, no one would weep over it; that it would be so hard and deep that they would have to face it without the consolation of tears." My students, like the first readers of Wright's novel, felt a certain affinity toward Mary Dalton. They believed her to be a woman that ultimately meant to do well by Bigger. Ironically, many accepted the idea that Bigger's socioeconomic situation caused him to commit murder and therefore made him less culpable for his actions. They were, however, less forgiving of Bigger's hatred toward Mary and her boyfriend Jan.

We analyzed the scene prior to Mary's murder to try to determine the source of Bigger's hatred. Students pointed out passages in which Mary and Jan made Bigger feel uncomfortable by insisting that they ride up front with him when he was chauffeuring them and by forcing Bigger to take them to a restaurant he frequented in his own neighborhood. Many students didn't understand why this made Bigger uncomfortable, let alone hateful of Mary and Jan. One student even suggested that Bigger should feel grateful that they wanted to be his friend and to treat him as an equal. The arrogance behind this statement is that access to Whiteness is a privilege. The underlying assumption this student makes is that Blacks should welcome the chance to be friends with Whites and that such a gesture automatically assumes equality and not just another chance to Other the Black subject in question.

I pointed out that Bigger becomes *embarrassed* to be seen with Mary and Jan in his neighborhood—that his primary concern at that moment was not how he appeared to the two of them, but how he appeared to the other Blacks. My comment made many of my students uneasy because they were used to thinking of Whiteness as a trait that all marginalized groups aspire to. Also, they were not used to being thought of as Other. bell hooks writes about her classroom experiences when White students realize that Whiteness is also scrutinized by Blacks. hooks writes:

> Their amazement that Black people watch white people with a critical "ethnographic" gaze, is itself an expression of racism.... Many of them are shocked that Black people think critically about Whiteness because racist thinking perpetuates the fantasy that the Other who is subjugated, who is subhuman, lacks the ability to comprehend, to understand, to see the working of the powerful. Even though the majority of these students politically consider themselves liberals, who are antiracist, they too unwittingly invest in the sense of Whiteness as a mystery. (hooks 1997, 168)

By explaining Bigger's anger and hatred of Mary and Jan as a reaction to being othered, students were better able to find places in the text that illustrated why Bigger might have felt essentially othered by Mary and Jan's comments. For example, one female student pointed to the quotation where Mary states her desire to see the inside of a Negro home: "I just want to *see*. I want to *know* these people. Never in my life have I been inside of a Negro home. Yet they *must* live like we live. They're *human*." The student likened Mary's comments to that of an anthropologist. I liked this woman's comment very much, because to position Mary as anthropologist also positions Bigger as her test subject. Mary isn't as interested in befriending Bigger as she is in studying him.

We ended the course with Anna Deavere Smith's *Twilight—Los Angeles 1992*, a text in which Smith constructs monologues from taped interviews of people after the LA riots. Smith's method of using multiple voices asks the reader to play a very interactive role. The multiple voices used in the text provide the reader with "psychological through-lines" that highlight the underlying philosophies of each character.

As their final exam project, I asked students to create their own five-minute monologues by interviewing a person about an incident in her or his life that made the person think differently about race, gender, class, or violence. I got the idea for this assignment from my friend and colleague, Virginia Bell. I chose this assignment to end the course because in teaching Gender, Race, and Violence I was concerned with getting my students to step outside of their own worldviews and insecurities in order to listen openly to other points of view. Role-playing, to a certain extent, allowed them to do this. The monologues I received were based on interviews from people of various backgrounds. Students were able to interrogate their character's beliefs while simultaneously defining their own.

* * *

Currently, I am an assistant professor of English at Texas A&M University and face new challenges when teaching issues of race, gender, class, and sexual orientation on a campus that is overwhelmingly and devoutly Christian and heavily steeped in traditions that go back to the Old South. While I have found my current students to be more hospitable than the students at Georgetown University, many of them haven't had much exposure to issues of diversity. The student population is one of the largest in the nation (over 43,000 students), but African Americans account for less than 2 percent, and Latinos constitute less than 11 percent. I would like to see our student population more readily reflect the diverse populations within Texas, let alone the rest of the nation. Should I ever teach my course on gender, race, and violence again, I would offer my Texas A&M students a more multicultural approach to the same themes to give voice to more underrepresented groups. I would include people such as the Chicana writer Gloria Anzaldúa to further decenter Whiteness within the classroom. Most of my students view Whiteness as the norm and anything else that falls outside of that parameter as being Other. In teaching a course on gender, race, and violence, my goal was to challenge, or problematize, discourses concerning the victimized Black Other by historicizing both political and individual responses to racist oppression. I also attempted to widen the category of Other to include Whites. I believe that if we are ever to talk frankly about racism, sexism, and classism in this country, we must deal with the anger of marginalized persons who have the right to feel and express that anger in the face of oppression.

My approach to pedagogy, much like my desire to write this essay, is to get people to be receptive to the multiplicity of voices that make up our nation. Being receptive entails listening to the things we might not want to hear. It involves listening to the anger of oppressed groups even when the message might be painful. Being receptive also means being willing to be uncomfortable and to use this discomfort as a tool to change both the world in general and how we talk about multiculturalism in the academy in particular. Multiculturalism should mean more than just the token inclusion of "different" bodies; it should mean the embracing of differing worldviews.

Kimberly Nichele Brown did her graduate work at the University of Pittsburgh and the University of Maryland-College Park. She is now is an Assistant Professor of English at Texas A&M University. At Texas A&M, Brown has taught courses on African American, Caribbean, and contemporary world literatures, as well as a film course entitled Slavery in the Cinematic Imagination. Her work has been published in *Other Sisterhoods: Literary History and U.S. Women of Color.*

Works Cited

Bigsby, C. 1980. *The Second Black Renaissance: Essays in Black Literature.* Westport, CT: Greenwood.

Douglas, F. 1993. *Narrative of the Life of Frederick Douglass, an American Slave.* Edited by D. W. Blight. Boston: Bedford Books.

Fanon, F. 1963. *The Wretched of the Earth.* New York: Grove Press.

Hedin, R. 1982. "The Structuring of Emotion in Black American Fiction." *Novel-A Forum on Fiction* 16 (1): 35–54.

hooks, b. 1989. *Talking Back, Thinking Feminist, Thinking Black.* Boston: South End Press.

———. 1997. "Whiteness in the Black Imagination." In *Displacing Whiteness: Essays in Social and Cultural Criticism,* edited by R. Frankenberg. Durham, NC: Duke University Press.

Jacobs, H. 1987. *Incidents in the Life of a Slave Girl.* Cambridge, MA: Harvard University Press.

Lorde, A. 1984. "The Uses of Anger: Women Respond to Racism." In *Sister Outsider.* New York: The Crossing Press.

McIntosh, P. 1995. "White Privilege and Male Privilege: A Personal Account of Coming to See Correspondences through Work in Women's Studies." In *Race, Class, and Gender: An Anthology,* edited by M. L. Anderson and P. H. Collins. Belmont, CA: Wadsworth.

Morrison, T. 1987. *Beloved.* New York: Plume.

Omolade, B. 1994. *The Rising Song of African American Women.* New York: Routledge.

Rothenberg, P. 1990. "Teaching Racism and Sexism in a Changing America." In *Politics of Education: Essays from Radical Teacher,* edited by R. O'Malley, D. Rosen and L. Vogt. Albany: State University of New York Press.

Smith, A. D. 1994. "Twilight—Los Angeles 1992." New York: Anchor Books.

Wright, R. 1998. *Native Son.* New York: Perennial Classics.

CHAPTER SEVEN

Negotiating the Minefield: Practicing Transformative Pedagogy as a Teacher of Color in a Classroom Climate of Suspicion

RASHMI LUTHRA

Abstract

IN THIS ESSAY I describe the ways in which racism, ethnocentrism, and sexism have worked through the larger academic environment and, more specifically, the classroom environment to shape my daily lived experience as a woman teacher of color. Further, I delineate the tensions between the disembodied ideal of the liberatory educator that I seek to emulate and the embodied realities of the classroom that constrain the pedagogical options available, especially for the woman teacher of color. My account is based on reflection on my nine years of teaching, a close reading of student evaluations, and teaching artifacts such as syllabi, discussion notes, and selected lecture notes. In addition, I have relied on published autobiographical accounts of other women teachers of color.

I have been writing for more than ten years, and yet this essay has been particularly difficult to write. It has forced me to look squarely at the ways in which the academy reproduces racism, genderism, ethnocentrism and a variety of other isms that serve to circumscribe our lives as academics. The paralysis preceding the act of writing has reminded me starkly that teaching, writing, speaking, everything we do in the academy, is infused by the global politics of race, gender, ethnicity, and nationality. I asked myself, Will I be perceived as simply whining, as masking incompetence with discussions of pedagogy? The intensity with which I approached these questions evidenced traces of an environment in which the very credibility of particular kinds of individuals, their very competence, is already in question from the moment they walk in the door. As Espinoza says, "We cannot afford to make mistakes because everything we do is scrutinized with such attention to detail and minutiae that it would paralyze most creative people" (as quoted in Srivastava 1997, 113–114). When one is written into the margins, then one enters the situation differently from the beginning, whether it is a meeting, a conference panel, or a classroom. One can certainly work to make oneself credible, authoritative, and so forth, but one is always working with, against, or around the already-present doubt and suspicion. In this essay, I will be focusing mainly on the implications of this climate for the classroom.

We are discouraged by the fabric of the academy and the institutions with which the academy intersects from naming the ways we are constructed as teachers by the racist, sexist, and ethnocentric society in which the classroom is steeped. We are disciplined in a multitude of ways to deny the existence of, internalize, and even legitimize the oppressive structures that surround us. We are supposed to pretend that the classroom is a neutral, safe space and that we enter it as disembodied, neutral educators (hooks 1994).[1] As a result, we spend a great deal of energy dealing with the tensions between the attempt to be a disembodied teacher creating a safe space for students and the reality of being an embodied teacher in a space that is already infused with contradictions and conflicts, a space that can be more appropriately seen as a battleground than a safe space (Himley et al. 1997; Vargas 1999).[2] Margaret Himley reminds us that students "do not leave their class or race or sexual loyalties at the door anymore than we do" (1997, 129). Lucila Vargas points out that students can serve to reproduce established social relations in the classroom setting. These and other authors problematize the classroom space in ways that provide an opening for my own analysis here.

From the moment I walk into a classroom at the University of Michigan-Dearborn, I am a brown, slight woman, an Asian American woman professor, an anomaly. Before they know I am of Indian descent, that I was once director of the Communications Program, that I am a feminist, that I have just hit my 40s, they have read me as a contradictory sign, an Asian American woman professor. Whether I like it or not, whether I choose to emphasize it or not, my range of pedagogical choices and responses has been constrained. The circle has been drawn around me (Hoodfar 1997; Reyes 1997).[3] Every aspect of my performance is then foregrounded by this initial perception. I can and do work hard to minimize the damaging effects of this initial perception, even to use it as a source of energy. I sometimes try to relegate it to the background and at other times bring it to center stage as a way of lending emphasis to questions about border-crossing, interculturalism, and so forth. But the point I want to make is that the gulf is always there to reckon with, and it takes additional effort, an additional investment on my part, to deal with it. When I say this, I am not suggesting that these are the only dimensions along which I am perceived, or that I perceive myself in these ways. I am merely saying that in this particular pedagogical context, the ascription of gender, race, ethnicity, and national origin does matter every day in the classroom. To displace the seeming essentialism of the essay, let me say that I recognize that my identity as well as that of my students, is constantly shifting, fragmented, and contradictory. In fact, it has taken me a very long time to perceive at all that a color, an ethnicity, may be attached to me in the classroom and that this could associate me with marginality in some way. Before coming to the United States at the age of 21, I had spent my teenage years struggling to come to terms with my privileged class and caste position in India and my privileged class position in the Philippines. I had worked hard to see the unseen struggles of the less privileged (Martin and Mohanty 1986; Mohanty 1994). I have dealt with the pain and guilt that comes from recognizing the consequences of one's own privileged position. Because of my personal history, it has been all the more difficult, therefore, to recognize the possibility that I myself may be written into the margins in the present context. This is compounded by the fact that I have grown up thinking of myself as Punjabi or Indian, and only in my 20s did the language associated with a different kind of identity, that of "Asian American" and "woman of color," become accessible to me. These different aspects of my identity continue to sit together uneasily, never quite reconciled with each other.

I teach in a multidisciplinary humanities department in which, out of forty-five faculty members, there are three women of color (two of Indian descent, including me, and one African American woman) and one Hispanic man. The students, who are mainly undergraduate, are not generally accustomed to being taught by men or women of color, and this may lend particular poignancy to the dilemmas I face. The student body itself is predominantly White (about 70 percent of the student body is White) on the campus as a whole, which is significant considering the diversity of the overall population in the Detroit metropolitan area and the presence of a large Arab population in Dearborn. The ghettoization and polarization of racial and ethnic groups in Dearborn and Detroit has made race and ethnicity an ever-present absence. Questions regarding race, ethnicity, gender, and globalization sit uneasily just under the surface. This presents both danger and opportunity for the woman teacher of color. There are many potential "political moments" waiting to be exploited for further discussion, for exploration of the connections between self, other, and society (Himley et al. 1997). But the risks involved in tackling such political moments, and the pedagogical strategies available to the teacher when riding the wave of such moments, are partly conditioned by the race, ethnicity, and gender of the teacher.

Whether a particular course lends itself to discussions of cultural politics or not, I always face a tension between the disembodied ideal I would like to enact in the classroom—that of liberatory pedagogue, in the tradition of Paulo Freire, Jonathan Kozol, Henry Giroux, and others—and the embodied reality of the classroom, with its subterranean hostility, suspicion, and rejection. As Homa Hoodfar, Maria de La Luz Reyes, and others point out, the liberatory pedagogy literature does not provide the language to understand the tensions experienced by the woman teacher of color. Ironically, while geared toward transformation of society, liberatory pedagogues often take for granted that the norm is the White teacher, the male teacher, and even the White male teacher. When at some level I am rejected for my body (brown, small, of middle age, not "one of us"), it takes an extra effort to summon up the sheer courage, the love, and the total engagement required to practice liberatory education. When my attempts to make the classroom a place where assumptions and premises can constantly be challenged bump repeatedly against students' suspicion regarding my legitimacy, the resultant friction wears me down (Reyes 1997).[4]

I am well aware of the potential rewards of relinquishing authority in the classroom, the exciting possibilities that are opened when a two-way dialogue occurs in the class, and when teachers and students can both take risks to discover, learn, and unlearn together. As a liberatory educator, I strive to create the spaces where such mutual learning-teaching can take place. But the delicate process of negotiating power in the classroom, the dialectical process of relinquishing and using authority, is substantially complicated by the presence of a teacher of color in a classroom of predominantly White students. Authority can be relinquished more easily when its presence can be assumed in the first place.

If teacher authority is on shakier ground at the outset, as I believe it is for women teachers of color, experimentation with the power dynamic in the classroom becomes much riskier (Hoodfar 1997; Ladson-Billings 1996; Vargas 1999). Homa Hoodfar describes how her students respond more positively to "critical thinking" when she purposely distances herself from them and consciously asserts her authority as a teacher. She is keenly conscious at such times that she is retreating from the practice of critical pedagogy but is forced to use this strategy to elicit student engagement with issues of racism, sexism, ableism, heterosexism, and so forth. As a woman teacher of color, her pedagogical options are narrowed. I know I have sometimes retreated to a banking model of education as a response to the fear that a riskier approach might yield negative student evaluations or student complaints (Freire 1995).[5] As a woman teacher of color, as someone who enters the academy with one's credentials tainted by suspicion, I have never felt that I could afford to put myself at the mercy of administrators who are in a position to take a student's word against mine (Ng 1997).[6] Deep down, I have not felt assured that no matter how hard I work to be the best teacher I can be that my word would prevail.

I have paid for the need to maintain this high level of credibility in many ways; it has generally led me to avoid confrontation and to teach more conservatively than I would like to (Hoodfar 1997; Srivastava 1997). There are other risks entailed in practicing liberatory pedagogy as a woman of color. As Johnson puts it quite eloquently, "the racial/gendered subject simply avoids the potential for violence to her history, background and culture." We may be tempted as women of color to seek refuge in the classroom, and in doing so, our "revolutionary inclinations" may sometimes be reduced to a "mere gesture" (as quoted in Srivastava 1997).

The negotiations surrounding authority are conditioned in part by the context of a particular course. In Communication Research Methods, I had my authority questioned in a systematic way for several semesters in a row. Student evaluations pointed to my inability to clearly explain the content, my inability to communicate clearly. This was curious in light of the fact that during the same time period, evaluations in my other courses, particularly Critical Media Studies, frequently referred to my eloquence in class. At the time, I was giving a fairly difficult in-class midterm to the students in the Research Methods class. When I dropped the in-class midterm from the course, changing the emphasis to papers and projects, the complaints about lack of ability to communicate went away. I still lecture in that class occasionally, and my style during lectures is similar to what it had been before. Students no longer complain of lack of clarity. This has led me to believe that it was the degree of authority I was presumptuous enough to exert as a woman teacher of color that was partly responsible for the negative evaluations. At the time the evaluations were written, I was untenured and particularly vulnerable in the face of such feedback. Now that I am tenured I can distance myself from the self-doubt, the tendency to read everything in individual terms, that the tenure process itself encourages. I am able to put the evaluations in a larger perspective that takes into account the presence of the larger culture in the classroom.

By far the most difficult course for me to teach, and the one closest to my heart, has been International Communication. Discussions of the global economic order, global inequities, and the historic attempt to restructure the world communication order are inevitable in such a course, and it is during these discussions that I feel distanced from the students the most. I attempt to tap into their sense of themselves as global citizens, as intercultural beings, as cosmopolites. But because I am in some senses a stranger, my efforts are received with suspicion. When I encourage the students to look at ways in which the United States is complicit in sustaining global inequities, my credentials as a United Statesian are questioned (Valdivia 2000).[7] At these moments, I am othered acutely, made to feel like an outsider. Although many students remark in evaluations that the course has opened their eyes to global/international issues in important ways, a few reject me in toto, using phrases such as "I do not care for this style of teaching" or "I hated this class with a passion." I remember feeling wounded when I read the last comment about four years ago. Its intensity was astounding at the time. I remember going into a period of deep self-doubt. I was in the midst of being evaluated for tenure, exhausted by the pressures of directing the Communications Program, teaching a heavy load of courses (initially three-three while directing the program, later two-two while directing the program), dealing with the emotional pulls and pushes I have alluded to throughout this essay, and raising two children. It was also a period during which my credentials as director were being questioned by my colleagues in the Communications Program. I became an easy target for one student comment because I was feeling an overall sense of rejection at the time. I remember thinking hard about the source of the intensity of that comment. But at that moment of sheer physical and emotional exhaustion, the answers always led in the direction of my own possible incompetence; what was obscured was the presence of the larger cultural and social forces in the classroom that shaped the whole dynamic, contributing in large part to the hatred expressed by one student.

I have made substantial changes to the International Communication course over time. I have added elements of intercultural communication (the interpersonal aspects) to the course, partly to soften the political edges. I now carefully foreground my discussions of global politics so students' sense of patriotism is disturbed only minimally. I use the word "we" often when referring to U.S. citizens, to Americans, although I often slip into the "we" mode when discussing India as well. Even with the changes, I sometimes get accused of media-bashing when we look at ways in which powerful Western news agencies have defined the terms historically, and I am accused of U.S.-bashing whenever U.S. cultural, economic, or military power becomes the subject of conversation. While I am still alive to "political moments" in the classroom, and excited by the dissension that arises, I am equally dreading of it. The knot in my stomach is a constant companion when I teach, although it is looser since I received tenure.

Other courses I teach have been less problematic in terms of the classroom dynamic. I have received much more appreciation and love from the students in Critical Media Studies, Introduction to Women's Studies, Survey of Mass Communication, Press Law and Ethics, and Feature Writing (which I have taught once). The evaluations for these courses have been tremendously positive, and I have been much freer to experiment pedagogically and to relinquish authority in the classroom in useful and exciting ways. I will probably be analyzing for a long time the reason for the differences, but at this point my understanding is that these are not perceived to be courses for which a woman of color could not have the requisite expertise (as may be the case with Communication Research Methods, a core course every Communication major must take), and they do not pose a challenge to the students to become less ethnocentric (as does International Communication). In Introduction to Women's Studies, I do encourage students to critique the predominantly White mainstream rubrics within which the discipline has developed, but it is done in the context of team-teaching, and so I am not seen as the only one challenging students' assumptions. Also, students entering Women's Studies courses have a relatively greater predisposition to engage with multiple perspectives than do other students.[8]

I have taught Introduction to Women's Studies three times, and each time I have received very positive comments, such as "Dr. Luthra is an *unbelievably* well qualified, well versed, well educated professor which I feel is an *incredible* asset to U of M-Dearborn. I strongly intend to seek out her courses in my college career." I have felt freer to experiment in this course, because I've had a friendly woman colleague as co-teacher every time (the first two times the co-teacher was a White woman professor senior to me, and the third time it was a White woman professor junior to me). Yet even in this course, there are subtle ways in which my status as a woman professor of color conditions the responses of the students. The last time I taught the course, a year ago, provides the best example of the complicated and unexpected ways a teacher's gender and color inflect the pedagogical process. As I've mentioned, I taught this class with an untenured White woman professor. I was already tenured at the time. My co-teacher suggested as we planned the course that she could initiate discussion in certain areas because she would be seen as more familiar by the students, as more like them. As the class unfolded, she very naturally became the anchor teacher and I the second teacher. Although we were both present for every class session and both actively participated in all discussions and my co-teacher made strenuous efforts to highlight my higher formal status, my experience, and so forth, the students looked more often to her for instructions, vested more authority in her than in me. This was despite the best intentions on everyone's part. My presence was certainly appreciated in the classroom, and the students and we as teachers learned a lot and experienced a great deal of satisfaction overall. My secondary status was manifested in the slightest of ways, but it was something I found hard to shake off. The irony is that my co-teacher, the students, and I were all complicit in this process. As conscious as we were of the ways in which our differences could enter into the classroom dynamic, we simply slipped into the cultural grooves along with the students because this allowed us to "get on with the class." It takes a constant and conscious effort to teach against the grain in such situations, to make visible and overturn the cultural assumptions that stubbornly inform even something as seemingly innocent as team-teaching a Women's Studies course.

The Critical Media Studies course is the one that has provided me with the greatest freedom, pedagogically speaking. It has been a self-feeding cycle of freedom to experiment, positive evaluations, and more freedom to experiment. I have not met the kind of suspicion and hostility I find in teaching some of the other courses. We have had many volatile discussions in this course over the years on different aspects of popular culture, on feminism, on racism. On occasion male students have truncated discussions of feminist theories by refusing to engage with what they perceived to be "feminazi" approaches; at other times students have asked me three-fourths of the way through the course why we are taking popular culture so seriously, and dissecting it in such great detail, when it is basically just entertainment.

I have had my share of frustrations to deal with in the course, but there is a difference. The frustrations appear to be the right ones to tackle, the ones any teacher would tackle. I am not reminded in class of a "B" for brown or "W" for woman hung around my neck. When we have heated discussions, there is a greater sense of honesty and a greater sense of engagement with the issues at hand. Overall, the students are not as prone to use "silences as weapons" in this class as students are in some of the others (Ladson-Billings 1996). Whereas in the International Communication course I often feel I *am* the issue even though no one is willing to admit it, this is not the case in the Critical Media Studies course. I am not entirely sure why, but I suspect it's a combination of reasons. As I've said earlier, the students do not a priori question my credentials to teach this course as they might in Communication Research Methods. We rarely address global politics in the course except obliquely, which does not provide the impetus to peg me as "other," as "stranger," as is the case in International Communication. We do address race and gender in the class often, but we tend to examine them as a community looking within, avoiding the "us" versus "them" dynamic that develops in International Communication, where I easily fall into the "them" category. I am not racialized as acutely in Critical Media Studies as I am in International Communication.

I strongly suspect that this has to with the fact that South Asians, and Asians in general, are not identified as the "problem," the "underclass" within the United States. Because of its generally high level of affluence relative to other populations of color in the United States, the South Asian population, along with some other categories of Asian Americans, has been projected to be a "model minority." This mythic representation has served to obscure the actual economic diversity within South Asian communities in the United States, and has also exacerbated the political division between South Asians and other populations of color. In the context of the classroom, the model-minority myth probably serves to insulate the South Asian woman teacher to some extent; so, for example, during discussions of race, we are not automatically read as "other."

The history of Asian Americans has created particular kinds of citizenship dilemmas, and these provide the backdrop for the classroom dynamic. The internment of Japanese citizens during World War II is just one stark reminder of the mercurial status of Asian citizenship in the United States. The recent treatment of Wen Ho Lee, the Asian scientist accused of spying, is another such reminder. The International Communication course is structured in such a way as to call up the suspicion regarding Asian American loyalty and patriotism that lies just under the surface. The Critical Media Studies course does not tap into this suspicion, neither does it tap into a different kind of suspicion attached to the racialized underclass, a suspicion that the underclass will threaten the privilege of the White majority. As a South Asian American woman professor, I am not easily identified with the underclass.

The institutional culture at the University of Michigan-Dearborn contributes in some ways to the ethnocentrism the students exhibit. The university has inherited a strong traditional Western core curriculum, and efforts to deal with multiculturalism in the past fifteen years or so have been framed by this legacy. As an example, although the university has existed since 1959, only now is an attempt being made to start a Center for Arab American Studies, despite the existence in Dearborn of one of the largest concentrations of Arabic-speaking people outside of the Arab world. There are other, subtler, ways in which racism works within the academy, such as tokenism. Persons of color can be made to stand in for an entire group. For example, if one woman of color stains her credibility within the department or college, other women of color are perhaps unconsciously positioned against this "fact." Whether the relation is one of analogy (you're just as unreliable or undependable as her) or contrast (you're nothing like her, even though you have the same background), other women of color can be made to feel they are on probation in some sense. This may extend to the whole grouping regardless of gender, such as when all teachers or students of Indian descent are lumped together.

I am not suggesting that the University of Michigan-Dearborn is unique in this regard. In some ways it may provide greater openings for meaningful multiculturalism than other universities, and in other ways it may provide fewer such possibilities. Rather, the point about institutional culture is meant to emphasize the existence of widespread institutional racism, genderism, and ethnocentrism as the environment within which we attempt to carry on liberatory pedagogy, anti-racist and anti-imperialist pedagogy. As Aruna Srivastava asks, "How does anti-racist teaching work in a racist institution?" Cornel West, Chandra Mohanty, bell hooks, Aruna Srivastava, and many others suggest that we challenge the racism inside and outside the classroom, that we behave as "intellectual freedom fighters" (Cornel West, as quoted in Srivastava 1997), as "healers" (hooks 1995).

However, this essay has pointed to the inevitable tensions involved in trying to enact any of these positions as a teacher of color, the disproportionate risks one assumes, the energy one spends in negotiating suspicion and hostility. Yet another dimension is the way in which our own responses are conditioned by the cultural and classroom environment. My love for students and for teaching is in constant struggle with the equally real forces of fear of rejection and anger that I experience as a teacher. These are not the kinds of forces I am encouraged to name in my annual reports or in any other forum in the academy, but they constitute a constant undercurrent in my teaching. As Karamcheti says insightfully and courageously, "Certainly, anger seems to me antithetical to the dialogues of teaching, yet anger is a real and present fact of the personal" (Karamcheti, as quoted in Srivastava 1997). When the institution and the classroom encourage one to deny one's identity, anger may be a rational response. I have asked, just as Homa Hoodfar asks, "whether there would be greater engagement with the themes of imperialism, alternative feminisms, and other critical issues if I did not embody them" (1997, 224), and the possibility that this may be true has angered me indeed. But as with student evaluations and the process of evaluation by colleagues, the anger and frustration must be understood within the larger institutional and societal context to avoid a narrowly individualistic interpretation.

Once again, I would like to undercut the dichotomous implications of my argument, that pedagogical shortcomings have to be interpreted either as societally determined or as individual failings. I fully acknowledge that I am imperfect as a teacher and that some of the difficulties arise from my inability to break the entrenched habits of banking education; that even when I embrace new ideas, I may be attached to old ways of "practicing teaching" in some instances (hooks 1995, 140–141). And yet I am cautioning against the greater tendency within the academy to attribute such failings *only* to the individual rather than seeing them as a result of *both* societal and individual factors.

I have devised various strategies to deal with the obstacles I face in my teaching. I have described some of these already, in this essay and elsewhere. In an article in *Journalism and Mass Communication Educator,* for example, I have described useful ways to incorporate gender perspectives into the teaching of International Communication (Luthra 1996). In a recent semester, for instance, I brought in an example of a confrontation between Afghani women refugees in Pakistan and UN mission members sent to gather information from them. In a widely distributed e-mail, the Afghani women were expressing their outrage at the cultural and political insensitivity exhibited by the UN representatives. I used this as a way to discuss power dynamics between international agencies, powerful industrialized countries, and Third World peoples, particularly Third World women.

More than anything else, what has helped me is to structure the courses in a way that enables students to take responsibility for their own learning. I state explicitly during the first day that we will be working together to make the course a success, that the class dynamic depends as much on them as on me. Almost every course involves independent research, allowing the students to grapple with the issues on their own. In International Communication, I have added team projects that take place throughout the semester. I assign the project about two weeks before the team is due to present it to the class, and I select topics based on questions/problems/issues in which the students have shown the most interest. I also assign individual projects that allow students to work through various aspects of the course on their own. At least one of the projects involves student immersion in a cultural situation other than their own, asking them to write reflexively about the experience, tying it into the concepts taken up in class. Another project usually involves comparative news analysis, leading to insights regarding the factors shaping the news framing process in different countries. I also ask students to pose questions after giving thought to the discussions in class. I ask them to identify the issues and questions that most concern them. We then attempt to tackle the questions together. I allow students to voice the perspectives and viewpoints at which they have arrived.

Sometimes these are the perspectives that I myself would have enunciated, but it displaces the hostility and suspicion when classmates arrive independently at these conclusions. I build on certain enunciations to good effect, using them to pose further questions and lines of argument. I also try to introduce the complexities that underlie every concept, such as cultural imperialism. While presenting the cultural imperialism thesis and its historical underpinnings, for example, I start to simultaneously introduce critiques of the thesis. Students feel freer, as a result, to take more complex positions themselves, moving away from simplistic binaries. This also creates an atmosphere that encourages self-critique.

I have felt freer to relinquish authority in these ways as I have been able to take my own competence, my own considerable skills as a teacher, for granted. I have learned to use the gestures of authority even as I relinquish authority in other ways. All of this has taken an enormous toll in terms of time and energy. And yet I recognize that I have had at my disposal certain resources, particular privileges, that others may not be able to take for granted. My command of English has helped. The fact that my accent is very close to the normative U.S. accent has shielded me from being dismissed out of hand by students. In addition, the fact that I am heterosexual and able-bodied has provided a set of shared assumptions with many of the students, assumptions that can lie unawakened most of the time until I consciously choose to disturb them. In these realms I signify the unmarked category, just as in the areas of gender, race, ethnicity, and nationality I signify the marked category.

Many of us have survived the minefields, some by leaving the academy and others by finding ways to be whole within the academy or by negotiating livable compromises (Reyes 1997). Although my commitment has been tested numerous times, many long-term and daily satisfactions, rewards, and reassurances have sustained me. The overwhelmingly positive response in some courses has been a reminder of my potential as a teacher and my strong love for teaching. The satisfaction of being an integral part of the process of creating the communications major has been immense. The fact that I had a supportive chair (of humanities) when I was director of the Communications Program and simultaneously going through the tenure process helped in no small measure. My network of feminist colleagues and friends outside of Dearborn has been an invaluable lifeline during difficult times. Even in the International Communication course there have been various sources of sustenance. Students have gotten fired up to pursue the topics further in independent studies, in graduate work, and in other arenas. For one student, for example, the dream of being a peace ambassador was born. Many of my Arab students have found ways of making their identities and histories visible in the class in a way that they cannot do in most other courses. Some of them have been vocal for the first time in my class, saying they find it difficult to join discussions in other courses. Many students have been astonished at the paucity of certain kinds of information in the U.S. media and at the ways in which newsframes incorporate particular ways of seeing, how economic, political, military, and other power relations influence these newsframes. They have been excited to discover strategies to widen one's base of knowledge on world news, to discover that the same event can be covered in widely different ways in different countries. Often the students have challenged me in very productive ways, and we have all grown from the experience. They have posed the burning questions, they have engaged with the issues head on. Why is it that various governments are so concerned about cultural imperialism when the people enjoy and freely adopt popular culture emanating from the United States? What are some useful strategies that can be adopted to preserve aspects of local cultures that are beneficial? I thrive on challenges presented to me in the classroom when those challenges occur within a frame of engagement with the substance and process of the class. The class burns with energy at such moments. It is these moments that sustain me. Students and colleagues who enjoy my presence in the academy, who acknowledge my basic strengths and talents while honestly dealing with my weaknesses, have enabled me to stay on and to derive meaning from my work. It is not because of the institutional and cultural environment but despite it that we have occasionally been able to create honest relationships and establish mutual trust and respect. When we have managed to go against the grain in these ways we are testing the hegemonic formation, poking and prodding at it when ruptures and openings permit. This is yet another way in which teaching is inherently political. We are immersed in a racist, sexist, and ethnocentric environment; whatever we choose to do or not to do with regard to these factors has implications for either the further solidification of the formation or the (however slight) loosening of that environment.

The very writing of this essay provides another such opening. If, as liberatory pedagogues, we urge our students to understand the ways in which they are constructed by oppressive structures and how they might together remake the conditions within which they find themselves, we ourselves must begin by examining the ways we are shaped by the oppressive structures within the academy and how we might work to remake the conditions within the academy. In naming the presence of racism, sexism, and ethnocentrism within the academy, and the ways they impinge upon the classroom, a fruitful beginning may be made.

Rashmi Luthra teaches communications in the humanities department at the University of Michigan-Dearborn. She is currently a tenured Associate Professor. She teaches International Communication, Critical Media Studies, Communication Research Methods, Survey of Mass Communication, and Introduction to Women's Studies. Her research areas include women and development communication, women's movements and media, and women's interpretations of culture/media. She has published widely in journals and in anthologies.

Author's Note

I would like to thank Lucila Vargas for initiating this project and for including me in it. I also thank Camron Amin for his feedback on portions of the essay. Thanks also go to the Office of Institutional Research and to Chris Roehl for statistical information required for the essay.

Notes

1. bell hooks calls attention to the legacy of repression, the mind/body split that we have inherited from "our professorial elders," who have generally been White and male. She says we cannot teach wholeheartedly if we attempt to enter the classroom as "disembodied spirit" (1994, 113).

2. The premise of *Political Moments in the Classroom* is that the classroom is not a safe space. It can more usefully be seen as a city, incorporating the heterogeneity and the irreducible and unassimilable differences characteristic of the city (Himley et al. 1997). Lucila Vargas (1999) astutely uses Foucault to theorize the classroom as a site where the "offensives and counteroffensives" of the battle to diversify the faculty occur.

3. Homa Hoodfar (1997), Maria de La Luz Reyes (1997), and many of the authors cited here, help to problematize the concept and practice of liberatory pedagogy in useful ways. They write in contradistinction to much of the liberatory pedagogy literature, which neglects to ask about the complex interactions between the gender, race, ethnicity, and so forth of the teacher and students and how this informs liberatory teaching. Elizabeth Ellsworth, in a groundbreaking article (1989), points out another important blind spot in the practice of critical pedagogy. She says that by adopting particular notions of "empowerment," "student voice," "dialogue," and "critical reflection," critical pedagogues might unwittingly be exacerbating the very conditions we are trying to work against, including racism, sexism, and classism.

4. In Maria de La Luz Reyes's interviews with Chicana faculty members, she discovered that most of them felt their relationships with White students were strained and that their authority was constantly challenged. They were more likely to receive hostile and cruel comments on their evaluations, and these evaluations left a "bitter, long-lasting sting" (1997, 29).

5. Roughly speaking, the banking model of education connotes students as passive consumers and the teacher as the repository of information, the wielder of authority, who transfers information/knowledge as packages to the students. Liberatory or democratic education is the exact opposite of this. It starts with the premise that students are active subjects and that the students and teacher participate together in the process of knowing the deeper significance of an object, or the object-world, in an open-ended and mutually empowering process of discovery.

6. Roxana Ng (1997) describes how a student who was upset about her class on minority groups and race relations complained to the administration about her teaching at a meeting at which Ng was present. By maintaining a neutral stance, and by asking Ng to seriously consider the student's request that she state her perspective explicitly in the course outline, the administrator ended up further delegitimizing her. It is precisely the fear of this kind of reception that has steered me toward a more conservative approach in my teaching than I would like.

7. I owe the use of this term to Angharad Valdivia, who explains that "I use *United Statesian* instead of *American* because common and by now nearly global usage of the latter word embodies the process of imperialism" (2000, 175).

8. Homa Hoodfar (1997) explains that she has met student resistance in Women's Studies courses in which she problematized the notion of "universal sisterhood" and introduced Third World women's perspectives. I have experienced this as well over the years, but I

believe that in the team-teaching context this has been minimized. Hoodfar describes how the tension in one such course evaporated after she invited a White female colleague to give a guest lecture on women in Uganda halfway through the term. I believe I benefit from this kind of legitimation by association in the context of the team-taught courses.

Works Cited

Ellsworth, E. 1989. "Why Doesn't This Feel Empowering? Working Through the Repressive Myths of Critical Pedagogy." *Harvard Educational Review* 59 (3): 297–324.

Freire, P. 1995. *Pedagogy of the Oppressed.* New York: Continuum.

Himley, M., K. LeFave, A. Larson, and S. Yadlon. 1997. *Political Moments in the Classroom.* Portsmouth, NH: Boynton/Cook.

Hoodfar, H. 1997. "Feminist Anthropology and Critical Pedagogy: The Anthropology of Classrooms' Excluded Voices." In *Radical Interventions: Identity, Politics and Difference/s in Educational Praxis,* edited by S. de Castell and M. Bryson. Albany: State University of New York Press.

hooks, b. 1994. "Eros, Eroticism, and the Pedagogical Process." In *Between Borders: Pedagogy and the Politics of Cultural Studies,* edited by H. Giroux and P. McLaren. New York: Routledge.

———. 1995. *Killing Rage.* New York: Henry Holt.

Ladson-Billings, G. 1996. "Silences as Weapons: Challenges of a Black Professor Teaching White Students." *Theory into Practice* 35 (2): 79–85.

Luthra, R. 1996. "International Communications Instruction with a Focus on Women." *Journalism and Mass Communication Educator* 50 (4): 42–51.

Martin, B., and C. T. Mohanty. 1986. "Feminist Politics: What's Home Got to Do with It?" In *Feminist Studies: Critical Studies,* edited by T. de Lauretis. Bloomington: Indiana University Press.

Mohanty, C. T. 1994. "On Race and Voice: Challenges of Liberal Education in the 1990s." In *Between Borders: Pedagogy and the Politics of Cultural Studies,* edited by H. Giroux and P. McLaren. New York: Routledge.

Ng, R. 1997. "A Woman Out of Control: Deconstructing Sexism and Racism in the University." In *Radical Intervention: Identity, Politics and Difference/s in Educational Praxis,* edited by S. de Castel and M. Bryson. Albany: State University of New York Press.

Reyes, M. L. 1997. "Chicanas in Academe: An Endangered Species." In *Radical Interventions: Identity, Politics, and Difference/s in Educational Praxis,* edited by S. de Castell and M. Bryson. Albany: State University of New York Press.

Srivastava, A. 1997. "Anti-Racism Inside and Outside the Classroom." In *Dangerous Territories: Struggles for Differences and Equality in Education,* edited by L. G. Roman and L. Eyre. New York: Routledge.

Valdivia, A. N. 2000. *A Latina in the Land of Hollywood and Other Essays on Media Culture.* Tucson: The University of Arizona Press.

Vargas, L. 1999. "When the 'Other' is the Teacher: Implications of Teacher Diversity in Higher Education." *The Urban Review* 31 (4): 359–383.

CHAPTER EIGHT

Teaching with Differences and for Differences: Reflections of a Chinese American Teacher Educator

XUE LANG RONG

Abstract

IN RECONSTRUCTING MY experience as an education professor from unique socio-cultural, linguistic, political, economic, ideological, and philosophical backgrounds, this reflective piece integrates three major approaches: a self-study approach, a cultural-contextual interactive approach, and a reflective constructivist approach. I explore what constitutes the socio-cultural context of university teaching. Then I look at how this context has affected my teaching positions and performance, and how I have learned to recognize the effects from hidden aspects of this context. I also examine the ways in which I have gained strength and developed strategies to cope with this environment and, at the same time, begun to push for necessary institutional changes.

> How can we reveal the unity in diversity, the sameness in differences, and how can we engage long-term intractable differences and conflicts in ways productive to humans and not necessarily with the goal of winning and defeating? How can we live together with different moral positions without hatred, violence, or imposition and without permissiveness and amorality?
>
> Johnnella B. Butler (Butler 2000, 24)

I invite you to walk in my shoes. When I teach, I usually represent the only diversity in the classroom. The multiple diversities I present to my students fall into demographic categories not typical of the average university professor: an East Asian–looking woman, from a developing country—a socialist country—and an immigrant speaking English with a foreign accent. Moreover, my attributes may not seem to the average person to mesh with my specialty within the teaching field; I do not teach Chinese language, history, or literature, nor do I teach computer science, biology, or physics. I teach social studies methods classes that prepare pre-service teachers for state public secondary schools. To top it off, I live in a region of the country with historically low (or no) immigration, and among people who have rarely seen any Asians, foreign or native. As an Asian American academic with a background in teacher training, I was a true "outsider" when I started my job here.

In the early 1990s, like many minority and women professors, I entered a classroom with predominantly White students and worked alongside an almost totally White faculty. The growing presence of minorities and women has caused significant demographic shifts in the teaching force nationwide. As suggested by Johnnella Butler (2000), the hope is that such recruitment will create diversity not only in statistics but also in the form of transcultural, transethnic, and transnational changes in institutional structures. Those changes, Butler hopes, would allow for the sharing of perspectives and experiences from a variety of racial, ethnic, class, and gender groups, a melding that would become part of an illuminating scholarship and participatory pedagogy.

After a decade of minority hiring, a timely and important question has been raised by Shirley Lim and Maria Herrera-Sobek: "What are the challenges, problems, proposed solutions and transformations that face the university when faculty members from traditionally underrepresented groups enter academia?" (2000, 1). With this question in mind, I have chosen to focus here on analyzing my teaching experience. Reflecting on my struggle, adjustment, and affirmation, my essay—which is both descriptive and interpretive—attempts to explore the following questions: How does the sociocultural context affect faculty teaching positions and performance? How can junior faculty develop strategies to cope with the realities of academic life and, at the same time, push for necessary institutional changes? To respond to these interrelated questions, the analysis of my experience adds one more piece to the totality of the larger reality of minority women faculty in the nation's universities. It also sheds light on a series of questions with a much wider scope: What problems and difficulties concerning teaching have minority women encountered in predominantly White institutions? How have we overcome these difficulties? Finally, how has our entry as minority women transformed the classroom, the institution, and ourselves?

I am traditionally a quantitative researcher; writing about myself has not been easy for me. I struggled with the concept of objectivity in writing this essay, but I came to realize that I am not required to tell this story from all sides. I am telling my story from my angle and with my own bias. I understand that a story written wholeheartedly and sincerely from the perspective of one person may be seen as distorted by other people. However, the voices of minorities and women are rarely heard at many institutions. My experiences, perceptions, and interpretations may be key to a more complete and balanced understanding of the complexities and contradictions of life and of career advancement for underrepresented groups in American higher educational institutions. Though I have not been objective, I have tried to be fair. Furthermore, my story is neither a "standard version" of an Asian American or a woman faculty's experience, nor can it be generalized beyond my own situation. I've known many Asian American women faculty who have had quite different experiences, either because they were not immigrants (and didn't speak English with an accent), were not living in southeastern regions of the United States, were teaching different subjects, or simply had different personalities or worldviews. But I still have faith that my story will be useful for sharing information and for empowering, healing, reconciling, and for envisioning a new future.

I use my personal experience and autobiographic voice (Creswell 1998; Davies 1999) and frame my story by cultural-contextual, interactive theories. These theories emphasize that analysis of the experiences of women and minorities teaching in higher education must be grounded within the larger national, regional, and local socio-economic, political, and cultural context in which universities are located (Hsu 2000). Because many hidden contextual factors (in the academic unit, in the school, in the university) affect what happens inside the classroom, the ways in which a new faculty is socialized into these subcultures may significantly affect his or her performance. The socio-cultural dynamics of the region and local area where a faculty member works and where most of his or her students hail from must also be acknowledged.

According to cultural-contextual interactive theories, the classroom is an important site of institutionalized socialization. This socialization process is vital for new faculty. Here, new faculty get to know the curriculum, the program, and its outcomes. Most important, they get to know the students and the dynamics of school culture. Teaching has many domains—content knowledge, organizational skills, pre-teaching preparation, instructional approaches, and an awareness of and an adjustment to the socio-cultural context of the institution. My personal experience has been that when academic units deal with teaching issues, the technical domains are often emphasized over an understanding of the socio-cultural context and individual conformity is prioritized over institutional adjustments. This is partly because the socio-cultural context is a largely hidden factor, one not widely recognized or willingly acknowledged by many administrators and senior faculty who went through their junior faculty years many years ago, when faculty and students were more homogeneous. It is also partly because new faculty often must improve their teaching (by whatever means) at a faster pace than the pace at which institutional change is taking place. Junior faculty members face a rigidly formed time line of four to six years after their first entry to shape their evaluable teaching performance for the purposes of contract and tenure reviews. By contrast, the institution usually has no explicit time frame for the transformation of its practices.

The story of why I was hired as an assistant professor at the University of North Carolina at Chapel Hill does not differ significantly from the reasons so many other women of color have been hired. Annette Kolodny (2000) has suggested that many institutions have hired women and/or minorities because of external pressure to comply with affirmative action goals or to fulfill the diversity expectations of professional organizations. The National Council for Accreditation of Teacher Education and the State Department of Public Instruction visited my School of Education in 1992. Visitors raised serious questions about the demographic composition of its faculty. At that time, the student population was about 70 percent female, while only 10 of 46 faculty members who were tenured or on the tenure track were female (less than a quarter) and only two senior faculty members were African American men. There was no junior minority faculty and there had not been a woman of color on a tenure line since the school was set up in 1913. The lack of diversity stirred anxiety among some faculty and continued to raise many concerns for the next accreditation visit that was scheduled to take place in 1997. In 1993, in addition to an African American male professor, five women faculty, a record, were hired. This hiring brought the proportion of women faculty to 30 percent. To the best of my knowledge, when I was hired, I was the first minority woman faculty, the first Asian American person, and the first immigrant in the more than 80-year history of the School of Education. In 1995, three more minority women (two African American and one Asian American) and a Caucasian woman were brought on. Like so many Research I institutions around the country, the hierarchy in the School of Education consisted of mostly White men at the full professor level and mostly minorities and women at the lower stratum.

There were faculty in the School of Education who had actively and persistently advocated diversifying the faculty body. However, others had not yet internalized the need for a more diverse faculty body at a school that prided itself on being a teacher-training institution. The situation at that time seemed to confirm what Kolodny (2000) has argued: Hiring to achieve diversity was viewed as "adding women and minorities" without senior faculty's programmatic attention to the recontextualization of institutional socialization. The expectations of the administration were communicated to the new faculty members; however, the newcomers' expectations, requests, and queries were not sought by the administration.

In this way, institutional preparation for the adjustments and changes necessary for harmonious relations between these two diverse faculty cohorts were not a part of the agenda of the School of Education. The result, as Kolodny (2000) has suggested, was that many new faculty members either didn't know what role they were supposed to play or were concerned they might not be able to play these assumed roles in the traditional social context because of their very different backgrounds. The voice of dissatisfaction provoked broad and continuing ideological and philosophical discussions among the senior faculty that led to several reviews of faculty tenure and promotion policy. These reviews later resulted in some important procedural changes, including the broadening of the definitions of teaching and research in the faculty policy manual and the creation of two models for assessing faculty teaching. These changes more or less eased the tension and laid the groundwork for junior faculty mentoring, which I discuss below.

Several incidents during my first year led me to question why I was hired and may partially have shaped my colleagues' and some of my students' initial perceptions of me. Was I hired for affirmative action alone, for my own merit alone, or for some combination of the two? Of course, I never received a straightforward answer, but there were campus-wide talks at that time about how favoritism had brought in less-qualified candidates. An instructor who claimed he was in the candidate pool for my job but who hadn't gotten an interview treated me very rudely. I once received an angry comment from a student evaluation that charged that I was a typical example of the kind of professors hired for affirmation action. In her view, I was only qualified to teach kindergarten. This attitude not only came from misunderstanding, ignorance, and possible racial bias, but it also reflected the tendency toward scapegoating minority and woman faculty for the increasingly fierce competition in the U.S. higher education job market. The tight job market actually resulted from a decade-long higher education budget cut, downsizing, and corporatism (Bramen 2000).

If some, even a small percentage of, faculty and students believed my hire was tokenism and not based on merit (Tierney and Bensimon 1996), such perceptions and attitudes would translate into rejection in the classroom. In talking with several colleagues, I later realized that I did not even contribute much to the state's affirmative action plan: affirmative action in my state only included African Americans and American Indians. The recruitment of Hispanic Americans and Asian Americans in this state did not fulfill affirmative action requirements; instead, it only improved cultural diversity. This ambiguity raised several difficult questions: Are Asian Americans a minority? What kind of minority are we in the context of American or regional racial politics? These are important questions. My experience has told me that how people respond to these questions affects how they interpret policy and how they treat Asian American faculty. Kul Rai and John Critzer (2000) point out that racial politics in higher education are determined and shaped by Black experiences, on the one hand, and White experiences, on the other. Asians are perceived to be either like Whites or not like Whites or like Blacks or not like Blacks. This perceptual confusion was formed in a racially binary society.

Because of immigration, the patterns of U.S. racial composition in the last three decades have been heading in a truly polyethnic direction. The question of how Asian Americans should be treated in relation to affirmative action has tested the limited Black-White framework (Nakanishi and Hokoyama 2000); it has, therefore, stirred a national debate on discrimination, diversity, and meritocracy in higher education, and it has challenged the current status quo in racial politics in the United States (Takagi 1992). The continuing debate is clarifying many misconceptions about Asian Pacific American faculty. One misconception, noted by Don Nakanishi (1993), is that Asian American faculty who encounter problems in their employment or promotion are more inclined than other minority faculty to walk away and not contest any unfair treatment. This image of Asian American educators as passive and permissive has invited intimidation and aggression from students, colleagues, and administration, resulting in a difficult classroom situation for many Asian American faculty.

My Teaching and Perceptions of Asians and Asian Americans

Asian American scholar Ruth Hsu (2000) once wrote: "The place of minorities in academe is fraught with undesirable compromises and battles, in which we are routinely devalued, erased, and attacked, in which almost every aspect of our daily experiences with students, scholars, and administrators is embroiled in a hierarchical power structure constructed along axes of race, gender, sexuality, class, and age" (2000, 185). This may not be an overstatement. Students' perceptions of an instructor's competence play an important role in determining how they behave in the classroom. Their perceptions are affected not only by who the instructor is but also by who the students are. Their perceptions are further influenced by how they believe their instructor's colleagues perceive him or her as a teacher and as a colleague. Finally, mainstream media images of Asians, Asian Americans, Third World countries, and socialist countries have considerable impact on how students see Chinese peoples in general and their Chinese American instructors in particular. Each instructor presents a demographic profile (race/ethnicity, gender, nationality, accent, age, sexuality, geographic origins, etc.) and a professional profile (academic rank, teaching experience, doctoral-granting institution, academic reputation, etc). These profiles signal the instructor's various academic and personal strengths and suggest his or her status (as, for instance, a member of a minority group, a woman, and an immigrant) in the power structure of a specific academic unit and in a larger society.

Overall, Americans' perceptions of Asians are ambivalent: On the one hand, the "model minority" myth that was created by the media in the 1960s claimed that Asian men made good workers, Asian women made desirable wives, and Asian children made diligent students. On the other hand, there are the gangster images of Chinese and Vietnamese youths, the widely publicized deaths of Chinese from illegal immigration activities, and the images of nerds best-suited for crunching numbers, frying microchips, or stalking quarks in American Academe (Takaki 1989; Walker-Moffat 1995). Unfortunately, this typification of Asian Americans not only affects the general public but also makes many Asians in America believe these things of themselves and of their children (Chua 2000).

In addition to the misconceptions, the main problem facing Asian faculty in my region of the country may be ignorance: This state historically has had very low immigration rates, and the majority of the native residents have no frame of reference for dealing with Asians or Asian Americans. Although the Asian population has grown rapidly in the last two decades, the Asian American population has remained small. Data from the 1990 U.S. Census indicated that Asians or Asian Americans counted for about 1 percent of the state population in 1990.

My Asian background puts me at odds with some colleagues who have had no real knowledge of or contact with Asian women, especially Asian American female scholars, and who apply stereotypes to the Asian faculty they deal with. I once heard a woman academic refer to an Asian American doctoral student as "the Pacific chick" at a conference. One student told me she had never talked to any Asian people before she met me. On the one hand, it may be a problem if students have never seen a person like me in authority. On the other hand, it may give me the opportunity to communicate to students my own perceptions of who I am and what I am.

Who am I and how do I perceive myself? The journey from a Chinese to an Asian American requires constant adjustments involving the deconstruction and reconstruction of a person's ethnic identity through the process of

acculturation. As described by Du Boisian (Butler 2000), this process of ra-
cialization involves an internalization of the stereotype projected by the
dominant group and therefore creates a self-other dichotomous existence. As
an immigrant, how I perceive myself is largely affected by how I was raised.
Since I grew up in China and was not raised as a member of a domestic minority in the United States, the development of my self-identity has not been
significantly affected by internal colonization. Before I came to the United
States, there were many things I was not aware of: the racial tension, the discrimination against Asian Americans, and the glass ceiling for minority professionals. I was very naïve about what it meant to become an Asian
American, that is, what it meant to become a member of a U.S. domestic minority. I knew nothing about public perceptions of Chinese in the United
States. All I knew was the perception I had of myself from my experience in
China, and my self-identity didn't fit well the U.S. image of a "typical Asian
woman" (and whose does?).

Because I grew up in socialist China, was raised in an educated and all-
girl family, and was schooled in girls-only middle and high schools, I always
had passions for literature and the social sciences, but I also did quite well in
math classes. My experience mirrored the Chinese government propaganda
at that time, which proclaimed that "women were holding up half the sky;
equal pay for equal work; and girls can do everything boys can do." I never
shied away from sports: I was very athletic, representing my school and competing in many sports. I was not a so-called family-oriented Chinese woman: I
was always single-mindedly pursuing a career. This past experience has provided me with a solid self-confidence and a strong desire to challenge the
deeply rooted stereotypes of "academic nerdity" or "oriental feminine pas-
siveness and permissiveness," and to resist the imposition of an identity as
"invisible person and outsider."

After many years' teaching in U.S. universities, I've gradually realized
that my difference from the stereotyped Asian image in U.S. popular culture
may cause my students and colleagues much confusion and trap me in a dilemma: A passive Asian female instructor may be considered as lacking competence and leadership, while an Asian female instructor with solid
confidence can be viewed as confronting, bitchy, and unreasonable. To make
things worse, when I first started teaching I didn't realize the perceptual gap
between my students and myself and therefore was unable to act on it. Since I
didn't lack confidence, my major efforts in initial adjustment were not about
redefining and refining myself but about developing tactics to fill the perceptual gap.

It is difficult to determine whether I would have had stronger or weaker self-esteem or whether I would have had more or less confidence if I had been born to a family with less education and a working-class background or if I had been disabled in some way. Considering the experiences of my fellow Chinese academics whose long journey involved the transition from an impoverished childhood in a small Chinese village to a very successful professorship in an Ivy League university, my speculation is that coping strategies must be tailored to fit each individual's circumstances in order to produce the best adaptation. The adaptation process will be segmented and even sometimes contradictory for people with different backgrounds.

Becoming a Better Teacher

I have searched the literature for help in understanding my situation. Because there have been very few Asian Americans in schools of education, and especially in the field of teacher education, there is little ethnographic research about Asian professors. I have realized that I am in a situation for which there are no specific blueprints to guide me. I have to be creative, self-sufficient, and flexible, constantly directing and redirecting myself. When I read research on the "ivory tower," I am curious about what people mean. I have never felt my teaching had anything to do with the "ivory tower" image. My teaching has a strong clinical perspective, and my program is a public school–based program (mentoring, co-teaching, yearlong practica and internships, and school-based research). I've seldom had opportunities to debate my students on theories at an abstract level in my classroom; instead, I've relied on demonstration, modeling, and evaluation. My teaching responsibilities also have involved a huge amount of student advising work (from undergraduates to doctoral students in many different programs) and an exhaustive yearlong admission process, plus a great "hidden workload" (Tierney and Bensimon 1996).[1]

As I reexamine my experience, I am convinced that successful teaching depends on the selection and application of appropriate procedures, derived in part from an awareness of the characteristics of the student population, a recognition of a school's physical and human environment, an understanding of its academic programs, and a familiarity with the learning resources available at the university and in the community. Because of my immigrant background, I have to make an extra effort to reach out to students, colleagues, and local educators.

The Authority Issue in the Classroom

As I mentioned above, when I began my current job I was the only minority woman faculty in my building and one of a few minority women faculty on the university campus. People on campus mistook me for a foreign student, a staff member, or a visitor. On many occasions, such as taking a photo for my university ID, checking out a book, or getting a campus parking map, I was ignored or was treated with rudeness, flirtation, or intimidation. It took me a while to figure out what was going on, that at a traditionally White university, staff and students might not be used to having authority wielded by a woman of color. Several of my undergraduate students told me that they'd never had any contact with any Asian person in their entire life, much less one in a position of authority. One of my students complained to my face that I should not be permitted to hold so much power over her career.

My classroom situation has improved since then, partly because I am a more skillful and more confident teacher after nine years of university teaching, and partly because the cultural context in my program, the school, and the university has changed. (My gray hairs and my facial wrinkles may also help.) The previous program was an undergraduate program where I was the only minority and the only junior faculty. Although my undergraduate students were good students in many ways, some of them didn't have experience beyond the state border. As deficient as my students were in national and international exposure, and sometimes in maturity, from time to time I felt fifteen weeks was not long enough to help them construct the cultural knowledge in teaching and develop a true sense of pluralism that I considered necessary for all teachers. The program I am working for now is a graduate teacher education program and has many women faculty, including many junior faculty and two other minority women. I feel I can comfortably share my stories and experience with many of my colleagues during program meetings and in informal conversations, and the fact that I am now working with graduate students exclusively has made a significant difference. Most graduate students have clear professional goals and are serious about constructing knowledge. My current students have received an undergraduate degree in the social sciences or humanities from large universities where they likely took courses with diverse faculty. Because they were nurtured in a more pluralistic learning environment and have seen male and female faculty of all colors and of many nationalities, they are relatively sophisticated in terms of cultural awareness and sensitivity. My teaching evaluations had improved long before I entered the current graduate program, but I don't know if I would have had the feelings of freedom and joy to work with my students in the classroom if we hadn't made this program change.

My lecture-style teaching method may also have contributed to poor teaching evaluations early on. I was raised and trained in Chinese schools that leaned toward authoritarian and lecturing styles in terms of classroom interaction. The teaching culture and philosophy in my program has encouraged me toward a student-centered, hands-on approach. This approach provides for many shared learning experiences, not just for students but also for the instructor who has accepted the challenge of rethinking the student-teacher relationship and has traded in sole authority for the role of the informed facilitator who learns with his or her students (Lim and Herrera-Sobek 2000). This approach allows me to become the kind of instructor I always hoped to become: a professor who creates a learning environment in which students feel comfortable enough to voice their thoughts, ideas, and intellectual concerns (Hwang 2000).

As elaborated by Sandra Gunning (2000), instructors using the student-centered approach often experience a shift in power away from themselves when they invite students to participate actively in the learning process. Inviting students to participate in class planning, organizing class activities, and other related decision making begins the process of student empowerment. Small-group activities also give many non-traditional students or underrepresented groups voices that might be lost within a large group. My own experience has demonstrated that when students recognize that I intend to empower them and invite them to share power, the line between instructor and students in the class becomes blurred. Students tend to take a closer look at the materials selected for class, and they tend to listen more thoughtfully because their own insights have been valued. They also tend to see the instructor's input as a contribution to the shared learning process rather than an authoritarian "lecture." The instructor's classroom behavior—agreeing and disagreeing with reason and respect—tends to model the students' behaviors (McKeachie 1994).

Now I struggle with a question I cannot answer: Do I feel I am more respected by students after I have given away much of my authority to students? The authority issue seems to fade from my central concerns when I think and rethink my teaching. Of course, style alone can't explain my perceptual change; many other contextual factors (such as longer years of experience with university students, higher levels of freedom and confidence in the classroom, changes in the academic unit, and a larger academic community) may also help empower me and make me feel I am appropriately respected by most of my students.

Dealing with the Foreign Factor

Many Asian American Studies scholars have detected what they believe to be a special racism against Asian immigrants that can be traced to the arrival of the very first cohort of Chinese immigrants to North America. The social and political exclusionism of U.S. policies, they say, have made Asians the exotic Orientals and permanent aliens (Ong 2000).

As an Asian faculty with a foreign background, I may have different (if not more) difficulties in the classroom compared to my colleagues without this background. A foreign appearance accompanied by an accent may immediately discount an instructor's credibility unless one teaches subjects such as Greek or Chinese history. As one immigrant friend explained, "Many Americans believe if a person doesn't speak Standard English that person must be stupid." My accent caused me some initial difficulties in the classroom (and may still be a hidden factor). In my experience, the main reason an accent makes immigrant faculty unpopular is that it inconveniences the listeners (although most students may not admit that). Students have to make an extra effort to understand what the instructor is saying. I knew a native speaker of English who was hired from a British university in the early 1990s and was accused of speaking poor English. On the other hand, the reaction to a person's accent may connect to the listener's sense of power, status, and social contract and to the listener's own cultural identity. During my many years of observations in the classroom, my accent aroused some students' emotions (both positive and negative) because of their recollections of how they themselves were treated badly because of their own accent— whether foreign or regional—and they may project their own positions on me. For instance, more than one student told me that listening to me reminded them of watching others treat their immigrant parents rudely because of their Asian accents.

Students' reactions to foreign accents may also be influenced by the ethos of the institution, and their behaviors in my classroom may be modeled by the behavior of their peers in other classrooms (and sometimes by the behavior of their instructors). Several international students have complained to me about how they were treated in the classroom. One told me that she had been completely ignored in one class for the entire semester and that nobody, including the instructor (who always invited students to participate in discussion), noticed her desire to talk in the classroom. Another foreign student told me that a few students tried to discount the credibility of her arguments by pretending not to understand what she was saying or by simply cutting her off when she was still talking. Even the instructor had once jumped in and requested that she make her comments quick and simple. These incidents were embarrassing and discouraging. Yet they were not isolated incidents. I have heard over and over again similar complaints from Asian American and Hispanic American students in my building and across the campus.

I have rarely shared my personal story with my students. But to empower them (and myself as well), I have shared one story several times in the classroom and in my office: Many years ago, when I was a doctoral student, I attended a professional conference at which I saw no other Asians. I was to make my first solo presentation. Although I was thoroughly prepared, I perceived that my presentation was not going well. I still remember the moment I started to talk. I could see the expressions of surprise, discomfort, and hostility that appeared on some of the faces in the audience. At that moment I realized a harsh reality: I will always encounter this kind of situation, unless I decide never to speak publicly. And here I am. In the last thirteen years, I have taught over forty courses and made over fifty presentations and speeches on the local, state, national, and international level. If I can do it, then you can do it. And you can do it with a sense of humor and forgiveness.

My foreignness has raised other issues, too. Several times during class discussions, when my comments and critiques have directly criticized America or Americans (as many social scientists and as many of my students have), I immediately feel the tension resulting from students' perception of me as a non-American. Some of my students (and some of my colleagues) have also assumed that immigrants from communist countries must be pro-Communist. Similar situations have also occurred in graduate seminars: The opinions that students and instructors contribute are culturally loaded. Some linguistic-minority students had the feeling that their comments were viewed as odd, insignificant, or irrelevant. The advice I gave to these students was: "This happens to almost every person who speaks English with an accent, including myself. If you believe you have a point to make and that point contributes to the discussion, then exercise your right to voice yourself. Be consistent and persistent, even though it sounds like a very lonely or even desperate voice." I also admitted to them that after so many years in U.S. universities, I myself still have to fight these feelings from time to time. To understand what I was doing and why, I prefer not to think of myself as a role model who has to carry such a heavy psychological burden. I simply want to empower my students and be empowered by those who have shown me their incredible courage by using tactics to challenge the unfair classroom practice and challenging their own evaluation of their worthiness.

While I rarely share my personal experiences in the classroom, I refuse to let other people define me with ethnic identity, stereotypes, and misconceptions. I conscientiously communicate to my students my own perceptions of my accent, my ethnic identity, my competency, my teaching philosophy, and my work ethic during the first class of each semester. I don't shy away from the collective ethnic conscience that is part of me, and I also personalize myself by acknowledging my unique background, experience, and character. I continually clarify any confusion whenever I feel it emerge. I believe open communication provides benefits for all parties participating.

Evaluating Yourself

I feel fortunate that I always have a very clear sense that I need to hear about my own teaching directly from my students. In spite of the limitations of the socio-cultural context, there is room for them to help me improve. If communicating my own perceptions is one way to reach out to my students, seeking evaluation from them is another way to reach the same goal. I don't feel official evaluations are very helpful for me. I prefer monitoring my own teaching through midterm interviews with each student and by talking with students immediately after class. I also have developed my own survey instruments with specific quantitative questions and open-ended qualitative questions on all aspects of my course. Because I explain the importance of answering these questions, most students answer them sincerely and seriously. The results have been valuable; many useful details have helped me revise and modify my courses each year. My colleagues, who have served as my official or unofficial mentors, brought these evaluation ideas to me.

The Multiple-Mentor Experience

Mentoring was one of several factors that pulled me through my pre-tenure "dark period" without much bitter recollection. The socialization process in a university usually provides its members with ample informal networks of academic, administrative, and political information; collegiality and positive social contact; intellectual exchanges; and other valuable opportunities (Bramen 2000). These networks are critical for newcomers; however, getting newcomers into the loop can be a struggle. Starting a new job requires the rapid gathering of large amounts of accurate academic, demographic, and interpersonal information about the institution and the academic unit. In many institutions, mentoring is a collegial way to get junior faculty oriented effectively (Luna and Chullen 1995; Welch 1992).

The multiple-mentor experience I had was very similar to the one described by William Tierney and Estela Mara Bensimon (1996). One mentor may be good for one or two things but not others, and most new faculty have a long list of needs in teaching, research, academic-unit politics, and so forth. Additionally, in my schools, people were very busy and guarded their private time very carefully, so I had to find different mentors for my various concerns. In this essay, I will focus on how mentoring helped me improve my teaching, since that is the focus here.

The student evaluations of the methods course I taught for the first time at this university were not positive. In my second contract review, I received praise for my research and service, but harsh criticism for my undergraduate teaching from some of my colleagues. I wrote a response that questioned ignoring socio-cultural factors in evaluating my teaching and expressed my concerns about the lack of policy adjustments from the administration and senior faculty in response to newly hired diverse faculty. I had heard other junior faculty also note the ineffective communication between new faculty members and administration, and I requested that a systematic mentoring system be put in place.

After that incident, I realized I needed to see how instruction took place in my colleagues' classrooms to develop a familiarity with my school's learning environment and teaching culture. I worked with several non-minority senior male and female faculty who came to my classes many times to observe my teaching. We had pre-observation conferences and post-observation conferences. We shared our impressions and comments regarding their observations and discussed the strategies I used and the rationales behind them. Based on our discussions, we came up with some adjustments and modifications I might want to make in my planning and teaching.

This was helpful. However, I feel I benefited more from sitting in my colleagues' classrooms to observe how they taught classes. I learned about them as educators—strategically, tactically, and philosophically. Their teaching styles were often different. Because I observed so many of them, I also learned about the teaching culture in my building. I believe I saw something subtle and philosophical that told me more about the instructors themselves than about their instruction. The underlying philosophy of their behaviors seemed to imply the belief that the best classroom is one in which both students and teacher are learning. Understanding this philosophy helped me understand why too much emphasis on the instructor's authority may prevent instructors from learning, including learning about themselves. This also suggests that whether disagreement leads to hard feelings or to innovation depends on the leadership provided by the instructor for the classroom interaction (McKeachie 1994). The shift from my old lecturing style to a more student-centered classroom interaction has empowered me as an instructor, though I don't think I recognized its profound meaning at that time. Other useful strategies I learned from my colleagues during my observations included using multiple methods of student evaluation; making the final product of the course a useful portfolio for the student; peer learning and coaching; and the constructive use of autobiography and narrative inquiry.

I agree with Tierney and Bensimon's (1996) contention that mentoring can occur at various levels and on virtually any occasion and that junior faculty can seek mentors across race, ethnicity, and gender. I would have liked to have been closely mentored by an Asian woman faculty or another minority woman, but as the first non-White woman hired for a tenure-track job in this school of education, I didn't have that opportunity. I acknowledged the so-called White hypocrisy of academic "liberals" (Butler 2000; Tierney and Bensimon 1996); at the same time I also saw many colleagues who showed me their general kindness, their deep concern for fairness, and their strong desire for change. For example, one of my unofficial mentors, an African American senior faculty member, helped me understand the racial-class stratification in American society and what it means to children's education. He also helped me recognize the hidden factors related to the socio-cultural context and made me understand the causes of my initial difficulties in the classroom, the classroom reality for minority faculty across campuses, and what I should and should not do to better my teaching. Almost all senior faculty women in my building gave me advice, and several White male senior faculty showed concern for my progress and regularly checked back with me. Two White women faculty mentors from my doctoral-granting institution also kept in close contact. They still continue to provide advice, suggestions, empathetic listening, and encouragement. I found I felt very comfortable talking about problems in my classroom with people who knew me well and whose advice and integrity I could trust. These two women faculty shared with me their classroom stories, current and past. Conversation with them gave me a reality check and helped me realize I was not the only one who had to spend forty hours a week dealing with teaching concerns. They also helped me distinguish between common problems for many instructors and specific ones for myself because of my cultural, racial, and national backgrounds. Hillary Clinton claimed that it takes a village to raise a child; my past experience told me that it takes an academic community to welcome and mentor a junior faculty, especially a faculty member who comes from a historically underrepresented group.

My experience has also taught me that seeking mentoring is a two-way effort: A junior faculty reaching out to colleagues may find that some of his or her colleagues share that desire to connect. Commonalities that might form the basis of a mentoring relationship abound—gender, teaching interests, research methodologies, office locations, doctoratal-granting institutions and so forth. The cultivation of collegiality and the giving and receiving of guidance requires a serious investment of time on both sides of the mentoring relationship (Chua 2000). However, the outcomes may have more lasting importance to junior faculty, to their mentors, and to the institution than most people think. Such relationships can help establish a professional civility that includes mutual understanding and respect. Mentors might begin to contemplate what junior faculty experiences reveal about the culture of an academic unit (Gunning 2000), and junior faculty may realize what they need to do to foster a better academic and human environment in the future.

Although mentoring is a method of institutional socialization, that socialization is not equivalent to social life. Mentoring for me is more professional than personal. I can still remember the feelings of marginalization, isolation, powerlessness, and loneliness that accompanied the many long hours on weekdays and weekends I spent working in my windowless office. I cannot be sure how much of these ill feelings came from my racial, gender, immigration, and cultural backgrounds and how much of them came from my personality, my junior faculty status, my research topics and methodologies, and my hobbies and other interests.

I do not have the delusion that something that worked for me must work for many other people, because each person brings different strengths and weaknesses to his or her respective institution at different times and under different conditions. Moreover, I am one of those for whom the promotion and tenure system seemed to work. Honestly speaking, tenure has changed my view of the tenure and promotion process: Feelings of cynicism and powerlessness partially shadowed my pre-tenure memory, and I believe I gained a more balanced view of academic life and U.S. society at large upon achieving tenure. I am living in a world with both a glass ceiling and increasing opportunities; sometimes I have to take bold action to break the blockage but I also remind myself to be fair and patient. On the one hand I feel that my life has meaning and is fulfilling. On the other hand, I am aware that for an Asian American woman, teaching in a predominantly White university is not a career full of joy.

I have an Asian friend who is a scientist and who entered higher education at almost the same time I did. She taught for three years in a research university before deciding to quit her job and join an industrial company. She said the lack of sensitivity (at all levels of university administration) in dealing with the subtleties of racial discrimination against Asian faculty was perhaps the most important dynamic that drove her away from teaching in higher education. In addition to occasionally blatant racial discrimination and xenophobia, she believed Asian Americans have had to deal with White hypocrisy and, from time to time, the racism of a few minority faculty members who have bash other minority faculty, especially immigrant faculty. In her case, the administration either was not able to see the problems or chose not to deal with them. For this reason, I strongly agree with Tierney and Bensimon (1996) that there is an urgent need for those for whom the current system is not working (or at least not working as well as it might) to address change. When we depend on colleagues' kindness and humanity alone, minority women faculty succeed only by chance. From my own experiences and those my friends and colleagues have shared with me, I believe that talented and dedicated minority and women faculty, without the necessary systemic and institutional supports, may miss out on any real opportunity to grow into mature and competent professionals. These invaluable human resources for higher educational institutions are thereby squandered.

At the heart of the development of my academic self is a constant realization of the internal struggles between developing an awareness of societal perceptions and stereotypes and resisting the internalization of the stereotypes. There is also a constant effort to find strengths and strategies to bridge the gaps between realities, principles, tactical compromise, and opportunistic overcompromise. I don't know to what extent this piece is revealing of myself and to what extent it is revealing of my colleagues and my institution. Nevertheless, I hope what I've shared here helps us toward the ultimate goal as described by Ruth Chua (2000), that is, transforming the ivory tower and changing all of us.

Xue Lan Rong is a tenured Associate Professor in the School of Education at the University of North Carolina at Chapel Hill. Born in Hong Kong and raised in Beijing, she received her B.A. in Chinese literature from the Beijing Capital Normal University, and later her M.A. in global education and her Ph.D. in social science education from the University of Georgia. She has substantial experience in teaching, administration, and research in China, including several years teaching in rural villages with scant resources. She has also taught at various levels of schools in the United States. Xue Lan Rong has written numerous journal articles, book chapters, and the book *Educating Immigrant Students: What We Should Know to Meet the Challenge* (1998).

Note

1. Student teaching supervision is a very time-consuming job that usually requires long commutes and work with mentor teachers in many schools and various school districts I have worked with teachers in twenty schools in six school districts since 1991, and it can be very emotionally charged. It takes me an average of about fifteen hours per week for a three-credit-hour supervision course, and many of these fifteen hours are in the late afternoon and at night. My duties involve not only academic advisement but also advising on a licensure process that is complicated by requirements and that has been changed constantly in the past several years. Furthermore, in addition to the regular faculty service to the School of Education, the university, and the professional associations and journals, school of education faculties are required to provide an incredible amount of service for local schools, for the school district, for the state, and for surrounding communities. In my unique case, I have given formal and informal advice to most (if not all) international students from Asian countries in my building. All these hidden workloads gave much joy and meaning to my job but also took away time from maintaining my physical and mental health, my relationships with family and friends, my professional networking, and my research.

Works Cited

Bramen, C. T. 2000. "Minority Hiring in the Age of Downsizing." In *Power, Race, and Gender in Academe*, edited by S. Lim and M. Herrera-Sobek. New York: Modern Language Association.

Butler, J. E. 2000. "Reflections on Borderlands and the Color Line." In *Power, Race, and Gender in Academe*, edited by S. Lim and M. Herrera-Sobek. New York: Modern Language Association.

Chua, C. L. 2000. "A Stranger in the Department." In *Power, Race, and Gender in Academe*, edited by S. Lim and M. Herrera-Sobek. New York: Modern Language Association.

Creswell, J. W. 1998. *Qualitative Inquiry and Research Design*. Thousand Oaks, CA: Sage.

Davies, C. A. 1999. *Reflexive Ethnography*. London: Association of Social Anthropologists.

Gunning, S. 2000. "Now That They Have Us, What's the Point?: The Challenge of Hiring to Create Diversity." In *Power, Race, and Gender in Academe*, edited by S. Lim and M. Herrera-Sobek. New York: Modern Language Association.

Hsu, R. Y. 2000. "'Where's Oz Toto?': Idealism and the Politics of Gender and Race in Academe." In *Power, Race, and Gender in Academe*, edited by S. Lim and M. Herrera-Sobek. New York: Modern Language Association.

Hwang, S. M. 2000. "At the Limits of My Feminism: Race, Gender, Class and the Execution of a Feminist Pedagogy." In *Power, Race, and Gender in Academe*, edited by S. Lim and M. Herrera-Sobek. New York: Modern Language Association.

Kolodny, R. 2000. "Raising Standards While Lowering Anxieties: Rethinking the Promotion and Tenure Process." In *Power, Race, and Gender in Academe*, edited by S. Lim and M. Herrera-Sobek. New York: Modern Language Association.

Lim, S. G., and M. Herrera-Sobek. 2000. "Introduction." In *Power, Race, and Gender in Academe*, edited by S. G. Lim, and M. Herrera-Sobek. New York: Modern Language Association.

Luna, G., and D. L. Chullen. 1995. *Empowering the Faculty*. Washington DC: George Washington University Press.

McKeachie, W. J. 1994. *Teaching Tips*. Lexington, MA: D.C. Heath and Company.

Nakanishi, D. T. 1993. "Asian Pacific Americans in Higher Education: Faculty and Administrative Representation and Tenure." *New Directions for Teaching and Learning* 53: 51–55.

Nakanishi, D. T., and J. D. Hokoyama. 2000. "Preface." In *Transforming Race Relations*, edited by P. M. Ong. Los Angeles, CA: The LEAP Asian Pacific American Public Policy Institute and the UCLA Asian American Studies Center.

Ong, P. M. 2000. "The Asian Pacific American Challenge to Race Relations." In *Transforming Race Relations*, edited by P. M. Ong. Los Angeles, CA: The Leap Asian Pacific American Public Policy Institute and the UCLA Asian American Studies Center.

Rai, K. B., and J. W. Critzer. 2000. *Affirmative Action and the University*. Lincoln, NE: University of Nebraska Press.

Takagi, D. Y. 1992. *The Retreat from Race*. New Brunswick, NJ: Rutgers University Press.

Takaki, R. 1989. *Strangers from a Different Shore: A History of Asian Americans*. Boston: Little, Brown.

Tierney, W. G., and E. M. Bensimon. 1996. *Community and Socialization in Academe*. Albany, NY: State University of New York Press.

Walker-Moffat, W. 1995. *The Other Side of the Asian American Success Story*. San Francisco: Jossey-Bass.

Welch, L. B. 1992. "Introduction." In *Perspectives on Minority Women in Higher Education*, edited by L. B. Welch. New York: Praeger.

❧ CHAPTER NINE

A Foreign Woman Faculty's Multiple Whammies

CECILIA G. MANRIQUE

Abstract

IF ACADEMIA IS to continue as an effective vehicle for social mobility for un-
derprivileged people, and if academia is to help American society maximize
the benefits it gets from the various groups that makes it up, then practices
and policies of inclusion, tolerance, and opportunity are needed. Third World
immigrant women in academia embody many of the concerns, problems, and
potentials that arise from the mix of gender, race, and foreign origin. In this
chapter, I discuss some of the experiences and issues faced by that new kind
of Other Teacher—the Third World foreign woman professor. I draw upon
my own work experiences as well as upon years of research on the immigrant
faculty experience (Manrique and Manrique 1999).

It was January 29, 2000, in a major midwestern city. My daughter was swimming at a
state swim meet and, as part of the tradition, we stayed in a hotel so that we did not
have to wake up at 5:00 AM to make the two-hour trip to the Cities in order to
make it to 8:00 AM warm-ups. That morning I went down to get breakfast. While
waiting for the elevator, I happened to stand beside a hotel cleaning lady's cart sans
cleaning lady. Out of the room closest to the elevator came a White woman who
looked at me and said: "Could I please have a towel?" Assumptions like these make
me boil. I cannot wear a tag all the time that says "Cecilia Manrique, Ph.D.!" These
are times when I want to make it known that I have educated thousands of Americans about their own political system! But in my nicest voice and with my nicest
smile I said, "Sorry, I don't work here!"

The fact that women face obstacles in American society has gained attention as a result of the women's movement. That women faculty face obstacles in higher education associated with their gender is a topic that has

merited considerable attention (Hensel 1991; Richardson 1974; Rosen, Werner, and Yates 1974; Simeone 1987; Swoboda, Roberts, and Hirsch 1993; Welch 1990). That women of color face greater obstacles in higher education associated with both their gender and their race or ethnicity is a topic that has also merited attention (Tang and Smith 1996; Turner and Myers 2000; Wyche and Graves 1992). That foreign women of color face even more obstacles associated with their gender, race, and foreignness is one that should merit more of our attention (Gabaccia 1992; Manrique and Manrique 1999). As a group, immigrant women in higher education, particularly the non-Europeans who are part of the recent (post-1965) wave of immigration to the United States, face many of the same obstacles as native-born women of color. However, they may encounter different obstacles because they are "strangers from a different shore" (Takaki 1989).

Because campuses in America today reflect the increasingly multiethnic composition of society, it is important that immigrant women be part of programs aimed at greater inclusiveness in universities. Aside from the talent and skill that immigrant faculty, both men and women, can contribute, their highly visible roles on campus allow them to be role models for today's diverse student population. This may be particularly important for female students of color who still have a limited number of role models on campus to look up to. And this may be particularly important for predominantly White academic institutions where students have had limited opportunities to interact with a diverse faculty, staff, and student population, as do many students in "lily-white" midwestern institutions.

In this chapter, I take a look at the experiences of yet *another* type of *teacher* in a predominantly White college or university setting—the *Third World woman faculty* member who may have many more whammies, burdens to bear, or strikes against her in her life as an academic. I am not writing this chapter in a vacuum. Nor do I base it purely on a single individual's experience. I would like to think that it is part of a collective—my collective experience as well as that of the many women with the same background I have encountered who have shared their experiences with me. My background and theirs color much of this perspective.

Current trends in affirmative action aside, it has been quite ironic for foreign women in academia that the characteristics that may lead universities and colleges to hire us can be the same factors that are used against us once we are hired. Thus, the three characteristics that make us unique in academe—gender, ethnicity, and foreign origin—are both pluses and negatives. Immigrants are often highly educated and motivated individuals. Therefore, regardless of gender, race, or national origin, women immigrant professors have the potential to make significant contributions to their adopted country. In addition to the expertise that all faculty are expected to have, non-European immigrant women enrich universities in other ways. Our perspectives provide balance to the dominant perspectives in traditionally male-dominated institutions. Our ethnicity provides diverse cultural perspectives that are important as students learn to function in an increasingly multicultural, multi-ethnic and multinational workplace. Furthermore, the very presence of immigrant women on campus can provide role models for students from majority and minority backgrounds. Our different national origins reinforce learning of cultures beyond the country's borders, thus providing a broader perspective for students who start out with very parochial backgrounds. For these important reasons, as well perhaps as for mandated reasons such as affirmative action hiring, women immigrants may be sought out by colleges and universities.

But there are also forces that work against non-European immigrant faculty. The very factors that may make us desirable to colleges and universities may also be used against us. In addition to gender, race and ethnicity, immigrant women also have to contend with our "alienness." But our alienness does not mean that we are from a different culture or that we look different. We are also viewed as competitors and, worse, as intruders. Thus, when they are seen positively, gender, ethnicity, and national origin can be multiple crowns for women immigrant faculty. But when these differences are seen negatively, the same characteristics become multiple whammies that non-European immigrant women faculty are hit with as we strive to succeed in American higher education institutions. And we face these issues when it comes to the hiring process, the experience in the classroom, the merit and retention process, and the tenure and promotion process. These are some of the experiences that I would like to take a look at in this chapter.

Who Am I?

First of all, I am originally from the Philippines, a former Spanish and then American colony. This means that I was educated in schools patterned after the American educational system. I saw Jane run and told Spot to Go! Go! Go! I even sang songs about snow before I finally experienced it when I was 17 and came to the United States as the official Philippine representative to the World Youth Forum. I learned English at school and at home and am truly bilingual in that I think and dream in both English and Pilipino, my native language. My getting a private school education was a conscious decision on the part of my parents to put their earnings and savings into educating their children so that we could do better. I am not from a rich family. In fact, we were the "poor relatives" of some of my cousins, who used to mock us because we were not as well off as they were. I, therefore, do not come from a position of privilege, and that may explain part of my drive to excel. But once I got that private education, I became part of an elite group in my country that could command a job and a salary that could pave the way to a position of eventual privilege.

Second, I obtained graduate degrees in institutions of higher education in the Midwest, and within those institutions I did not experience feelings of racial prejudice or discrimination. I either blended in successfully because the institutions were truly diverse, or I was so involved in my own world that my life then did not allow for the opportunity for such issues to arise. My graduate school friends were mostly, if not all, White, and color was no barrier to them as we struggled through the readings, projects, papers, comprehensives, and late nights together in the library or at the local 24-hour Denny's.

Third, I have been teaching in higher education in the United States continuously for thirteen years, although prior to that I had taught part-time for five years. Thus, I have more than fifteen years of teaching experience. I have taught in large institutions and small colleges. I have taught in public as well as private institutions; some conservative and some liberal. Some are in the Midwest, others on the East Coast. My current institution is in the Midwest. It is considered a mid-sized comprehensive four-year university with more than 8,000 undergraduate students; for most of them, this institution was their first choice within the state.

I have taught in the fields of political science, computer science, and economics. I have taught small and large classes as well as introductory and upper-division courses. The classes that I have taught include survey courses in American government, comparative politics, and international relations. They also include specialized courses for juniors and seniors in Asian, African, Latin American, and Middle Eastern government and politics; women and politics; international political risk analysis; ethnic politics in American society; and research methods.

Many of the students in my current institution come from the state of Wisconsin and the neighboring states of Minnesota, Iowa, and Illinois. They can be described as predominantly middle class. Many of my students in my early years of teaching were first-generation college attendees, and many struggled in classes that expected a lot from them. I have taught in departments where I was the only woman or the only Other woman. In my current job, I am the only minority in the department. It is essential to point out that the experiences outlined here do not necessarily belong to only my experience with one academic institution. Since I have done extensive research on immigrant faculty, this essay does not necessarily reflect just my experience; my writing has been influenced by the experience of many Other Teachers who have crossed my path.

Why Am I Here? Reasons for Coming and Staying

One of the reasons why students come into my classroom is because of the stories I have to tell within the context of the topics that I cover in American government: affirmative action and immigration policy. For many of them, the thought of leaving family, friends, and familiarity and taking all one's worldly possessions in two suitcases to the opposite part of the globe is just unthinkable. They are amazed when I talk about the privileges that I had to give up to stay in the United States of America: a prestigious position with a top salary and the services of a chauffeur, cook, *lavandera* (laundry woman), and *yaya* (live-in baby sitter for children). Given my story of privilege of having gone to an all-girl American missionary-run private school and getting an elitist education with doses of liberation theology, the big question is *why* and *how* did I make that decision to immigrate? It was not an easy one, but I followed my heart. My then boyfriend, who is now my husband, decided to fulfill his deceased mother's dream that he get an American education. When he left, I followed and the rest is history.

Because of our backgrounds and our experiences in the Philippines, where I had no feelings of being discriminated against, settling in this country served as a wake-up call, especially for me. As my FOB (fresh off the boat) or FOA (fresh off the airplane) status wore off, I settled into the academic rat race. I needed to secure a position close enough to where my husband was teaching; I also needed a position that would lead to permanence (tenure) and movement in the ranks. I began to realize that it was not going to be a smooth ride because I carried certain baggage with me that would not make my life easy.

How Are You? Disguised Civility in Academia

Many of my experiences with the hiring and retention process have had an impact on my perceptions of the workplace as well as of what I am all about. That is the reason why it is important to focus attention upon the various experiences that have had an impact on my teaching, the life of my classroom, my classroom behavior, and my interactions with students.

Surprisingly enough, working in academia—in what can be considered the bastion of open-mindedness, liberalism and tolerance—is not what one is led to believe it is. After more than twenty-five years of comfort with myself, I began to have nagging doubts about who I was, where I was from, and why I was here. Was it just me? Was I just imagining things? Or were there really signs that I would need to struggle with my place in academia? There have been times when I have come close to bringing my situation before affirmative action. However, the problem with reporting acts of racial prejudice and discrimination is that among academics, they are seldom blatant; more often they are subtle and covert. Perhaps this is because of the "disguised civility" that regulates behavior in academe at least insofar as issues of race and national origin are concerned. What you will notice are innuendos about your national origin or slight racial slurs, but one is never directly insulted. And as is often the case, when a colleague makes a disparaging remark about a race or nationality in the presence of another who is a minority or a foreigner, the person making the remark is too quick to exclude present company from the generalization or feign ignorance about the statement's impact on others. It is somehow assumed that one can completely separate one's self from one's race or national origin. If I take offense at such a statement, I quickly point it out to serve as a teaching moment even for colleagues who are so sure of themselves and their benevolence that they cannot conceive of themselves as hurting others by their statements.

Even in cases of workplace discrimination in which the college or university reverses a decision to side with the aggrieved faculty (after an appeal or a lawsuit has been initiated, of course), the reversal is usually made on the basis of an error in the process. Admitting to knowingly committing acts of discrimination or prejudice is seldom done (Leap 1995). And that was what I tried to avoid—a lawsuit, even though that has been the way to have one's voice heard. Did I feel that I was silenced or marginalized? Not necessarily so. I find solace in the fact that suing is not the way of the Filipina. I extract my "revenge" in other ways, such as proving my worth to the institution and the system.

On My Hiring

The extent to which discrimination occurs in hiring practices is often difficult to measure. Anecdotal evidence points toward how it can take place. I often wondered what goes on in these proceedings, and the best way to know is to be a part of such processes. I have been part of various search and screen committees where members tread very carefully because of affirmative action guidelines. Institutions are worried about being sued and therefore go out of their way to make sure that the process is acceptable. But I have been in situations where I have wondered why I did not get hired over some other woman who did not have her doctorate in hand while I did. Was it because despite my having the doctorate she had a much better record than me, even when she had not completed her degree? Was it because she was White and I was not? Was it because the institution could pay her a lower salary than me?

And there have been situations when colleagues in a search committee have explicitly indicated that they are not going to take a look at a person's file because he or she has a foreign-sounding name. When I questioned them about why they were automatically rejecting the applications of people with foreign-sounding names, the response was "This person may not know how to speak English!" My next question was, "Then how did you come to hire me?" And the response was, "We liked your credentials on paper. We were not sure if you could speak English, so we gave you a call." I passed that test. But think of all the people who had been rejected purely on the basis of their names. That is why I have tried to act as a conscience for the group when I work on search committees; I have been very aware of this first pass and the basis committee members sometimes use for rejecting a candidate. It is legitimate to reject a candidate because he or she does not have the proper qualifications, but it is outright discrimination when candidates are rejected because they do not have the right last name or because committee members speculate that he or she may not know how to speak English.

On the Job and That Ever-Revolving Door

Getting one's foot in the door and being hired for a job is only the first step. However, I have always had to contend with the fact that I was the first woman hired in an all-male political science, computer science, or economics department. Therefore, people constantly viewed me as their "affirmative action hire," their "token woman" or their "token minority," and their "two-fer," meaning that they got two for the price of one (a woman and a minority). Some joke that I am a good hire because statistically they can count me in two categories, which makes the institution look good on paper. I have even been counted as Hispanic because of my last name to improve statistical records. I have to live with the stigma of frequent reassurances from my colleagues that I was not an affirmative action hire, even though I was told at the time of my hire that I had excellent qualifications and I was perfect for the job because of my multiple backgrounds in political science, computer science, and economics. But the more my colleagues "reassure" me that I was not an affirmative action hire, the more I feel that I am one. In point of fact, some departments hired me in order to infuse technology in their curricula, requiring me to set up computer labs and develop courses in quantitative analysis using computer software packages that no one else in the department was familiar with. That I am fully aware of, but outsiders may not be. So I live with that constant burden, which at times I can explain, at times becomes apparent when they become familiar with my accomplishments, and at times I just have to bear.

Subtle or covert signs of discrimination show up. One colleague showed me a passage about why a woman should not be allowed to teach and it included reasons such as a woman lacks intelligence, her teaching might inspire lust, and when allowed to teach she would turn the world upside-down. Another colleague was upset that I was chosen by students to serve as faculty advisor to an honor society and blurted out that "This is the problem with affirmative action, you women are taking over what should belong to us!" I politely pointed out that the students' choice had nothing to do with affirmative action. They just recognized that my visibility on campus (I had established a reputation for being a hard worker) would be valuable to an organization that was just starting out.

The hallowed halls of academia are not spared from prejudice and discrimination. Colleagues and administrators are more subtle in their approach to discrimination. This is not to say that immigrant faculty do not experience blatant acts of racial prejudice. However, the perpetrators of most of these are students rather than colleagues on the faculty or the administration. An Asian faculty member was repeatedly called "gook" to his face; another faculty member who had just been appointed chair received a swastika in the mail; a faculty member found a sign on his door saying "Foreigner go home!"; and an African faculty member was directly questioned about how inferior foreigners can give low grades to American students. Early in my teaching career, when I still did not have gray hair, I looked just as young as most of my students and, being vertically challenged, I was smaller than many of them. I compensated for such shortcomings with a loud voice and fast speech. At one academic institution, my department chair recounted to me that after my first day in the classroom one of my students went straight to the dean and said, "How dare you have a 'ferner' teach me American Government!" It was dismissed as a comment by a "redneck," the student left the class and I remained in my classroom. But it was only the first sign of trouble in academia for me in my second full-time teaching job. One student told me that I had an accent she could not learn from. She stayed the whole semester and did not get very good grades, but she must have had the satisfaction of pulling down my student evaluations for that course. When it comes to accents, I am always reminded of what a former chancellor tells students time and again when they complain about hiring foreigners with accents, "You will just have to listen a little harder, just like you would for a person from New York or Texas." I remind students to think about who has the accent by determining whether there is a standard for the proper speaking of English and what it is. If there is no standard, then could I also complain that my students have an accent that I cannot teach to? It becomes a powerful teaching moment on the topic of ethnocentrism, especially since many of my students do not realize that by insisting that their English is the only language spoken here, that by thinking that their culture is better than others, and by thinking that they are better than others and have a right to prejudge them, they are guilty of prejudice and discrimination.

I also impose a lot of rigor in my courses. I am still one of those professors who expect my students to read the text before coming to class so that we can engage in real discussion, to write a full-length paper for the course (complete with footnotes and bibliography), and to do well in exams that include objective questions to test factual knowledge and essays to develop analytical skills. And I do expect my students to write in proper English even though I am not their English teacher. There are students who resent this "foreigner" judging their essays. They just want me to grade on "content" and not on their English. And I point out to them that "content" may not come across if you cannot express yourself properly. But since many got by with little factual knowledge and bad writing in their formative years, it becomes quite difficult to impose these expectations. I have become one of those instructors who are written up in residence hall bathrooms walls as "If you want to learn take Manrique. If you want an easy A do not take Manrique!" They contrast me with those who are easy teachers who provide copious handouts, notes, and study guides; give easy take-home exams; and hold their hands every step of the way in the guise of accommodating different learning styles in order to justify their giving a high percentage of A grades to students in every class. I have not been willing to sacrifice standards, which has irked some colleagues who have "mentored" me to spend less time on scholarship and service and more time on "improving" my teaching. It has been a real dilemma for me, because I have always felt that I may have to sacrifice my principles in order to obtain those high student evaluations coveted by my peers. My contention has been that regardless of what I do, my student evaluation numbers will hover around where they are (around 4 out of 5) for three reasons: the nature of the field that I teach (material changes constantly; new preparation is required every time the course is taught; it is usually a required course that people do not like to take and do not take seriously; and the subject matter is difficult); my reputation for being a hard grader; and who I am in the classroom (a woman, non-White, and foreign).

In order to overcome some of these difficulties, I have found myself adapting certain strategies in the classroom and varying my teaching methodology. One strategy is to dress professionally when I teach so that I place myself in an acceptable role for the students who tend to question my qualifications and my credibility. On the first day, I introduce myself and lay my cards on the table (I have a doctorate from the University of Notre Dame and mention my other degrees. I talk about my experiences in different institutions and let them know that I have expertise in three fields). On the first day and every teaching day I come to class prepared. Students get a syllabus on the first day so that they know what to expect, and I tell them that they are free to decide whether they can take the demands of the course or not. It is really not that much hard work if they get into the habit of doing it. And I guarantee that they will learn. I also assure them that within the first two weeks of classes I will learn names and be able to put names and faces together. Students consistently say in their evaluations of me that I am one of very few professors who actually gets to know their students by name in and out of the classroom. I am approachable if they choose to come and see me. I am willing to partake in their learning and other aspects of their lives such as writing letters of recommendation, acting as a reference, and so forth.

In terms of methodology, I do not just "chalk and talk." I do not spoon-feed my students with lecture notes or tell them what is going to come out in the exam, expecting them to spew back to me what I have given to them. It has been very hard not to succumb to pressure to participate in these practices. To this day I constantly get asked "Do we have to know this? Is this coming out in the test?" I am still one of those professors who expects their students to know everything when they come in to take an exam. Because of my computer science background, I have been able to adapt information technology in all my general education and upper-division political science classes so that students get more than a political science education. Some have been grateful after graduation for what they have learned regarding electronic mail, surfing the Internet, and creating Power Point presentations and Web pages, because they have been able to make use of them in the workplace. Some of these students have even served as pioneers in the field.

In terms of student support, I can claim that I attract a certain following of students—those who want to be challenged; those who do not mind the work; those who are willing to be educated beyond what they already think they know. The hardest thing to do in the classroom is to educate those who think they already know everything. What I really want them to learn to do is to think for themselves, to be analytical and to make the connections between what they read and what they experience around them. White students as well as students of color come to my classroom because they feel that they are getting their money's worth and a good education because of the rigor I impose in the classroom. We work together to discover new things. I incorporate the tools of information technology into my curriculum; my students must use the Internet and learn how to use computers. I treat White and non-White students alike so that no one can claim that I provide preferential treatment to one group or the other.

And yes, those all-important, magical student evaluation scores! There are some institutions that attach a lot of value to them so that merit, retention, promotion, and tenure depend on those numbers. Some even manipulate evaluations for people they like and use them as a tool of punishment for people they don't like. Although one needs to establish a good record, one should keep a balance with scholarship and service in order to survive the academic rat race.

Early in the game, I realized that in a department of so-called teaching superstars, I was not going to be able to compete and get ratings of 5 out of 5 or even come close to that. In fact I usually came "below the department average. "I would get a 4.3 when the department average was 4.34! I usually had to fight for the wording of my merit, retention, promotion, and tenure packets whenever such language was used, because it tends to be misleading. I usually had a very strong scholarship and service record to balance the "below-average" student evaluation scores. I had also established an excellent record with colleagues outside the department and in other parts of the institution who were aware of the rigors of my teaching, my productivity in terms of research and scholarship, and my active involvement in service to the institution, my profession, and the larger community. Thus, being "below the department average" in terms of student evaluations did not mar my process of retention, tenure, and promotion from assistant professor to full professor, which I was able to do in six years. In some cases, I came out near the top of the list of people to be promoted. However, it also meant that I had to establish a sound record in all areas so that no one could deny me that right to be promoted. Despite the general support that I felt from the institution about my accomplishments, I did start an affirmative action file and documented incidents of manipulation just in case someone tried to "snake" me.

It also helped that I had a support structure outside the small circle of the department. Having worked previously for the Academic Computing Services department in the institution certainly helped cultivate friendships outside the department. I could count on these friends and colleagues for moral support whenever the going got rough. I could seek advice from them regarding steps to take should there be stumbling blocks along the way. The friendships I have cultivated among colleagues have been a source of strength as well. Both White and non-White members of the faculty and administration have encouraged me to move forward and acknowledge the contributions that I make to the institution through their kind written and verbal comments. Members of the faculty and administration have provided me with mentors and role models, including the support of our first woman chancellor, who has been instrumental in bringing an honor society on campus that recognizes student academic achievement. My being chosen to be the faculty advisor by students certainly helped enhance my status and visibility within the institution as one who has high-achieving students on her side.

It certainly helped not to feel the isolation within the institution that I believe was felt by a few other foreign women who had left the institution in search of "friendlier" environments. Some of them may have encountered difficulties in courses that were "American," such as American history, American government, and American literature. The notion that a foreign-born faculty could teach a course that pertained to the United States was alien to some students. A variant of this problem is exemplified by faculty who are slotted by their departments to teach only those areas consistent with their origin (e.g., Asian history or Latin American politics), even if they are fully qualified to teach other areas. These are the instances where the multiple crown of gender, ethnicity, and national origin becomes a multiple whammy for non-European immigrant women. And such may be the case for women who go from one job to another in search of the ideal job, thus participating in the revolving door in academia for women in various fields. Being one of a few dark flowers in a lily-white institution can be very lonely indeed. In fact, as a result of this revolving door, in my few short years in the institution I have become one of the "senior" non-White woman faculty members.

And of course the invaluable support of my husband and my family became one of the most important crutches of my shaky life in academia. If I had not had someone and something to go home to after the conflicts and frustrations of the workplace, my situation would have been difficult to handle. Being able to share the joys and travails of teaching with people who understand and share the same standards is a relief.

That Incredibly Elastic Yardstick

There were a few other issues on campus that I found myself mixed up with by virtue of being who I am. The first had to do with the definition of diversity that we would like to bring about on campus. There were those who insisted that bringing in native-born (rather than foreign-born non-White) faculty should constitute the extent of diversity that is encouraged by the campus. I entered the debate by writing memos to parties concerned, including the chancellor, that objected to the manipulation of the nature of diversity because of the interests of a few. It is hard enough to encourage Other faculty to settle in La Crosse, whether they are native-born or foreign-born. Did we want to limit our options further? Some members of the campus also resented the number of foreign students that we recruited; they argued that the number of African American students we recruited was not sufficient to justify the recruitment of students who were not born in the United States. I stood on the side of encouraging both, since they all make contributions to diversity that would be equally valuable to the campus.

Another issue had to do with raising the bar for new faculty. After I had gone up for promotion to Associate Professor, there were those who wanted to increase the number of years in one level before one could seek another promotion. The rationale was that there were too many people who were being promoted with only a few years of service in rank. This was an expression of queen bee syndrome, in which proponents wanted the "new ones" to go through the same hardship and number of years they had to in order to reach their status. Once again, I wrote several memos objecting to such a proposal on the grounds that it discouraged the really good professors to come up for promotion whenever they felt they had established a good record after a few years in rank. I can understand the fear of some that should a person get promoted and tenured the individual might no longer make productive contributions and end up in what some have termed semi-retirement. But enterprising faculty members should not be penalized for what others have gone through. Needless to say, changes have not been made to the promotion criteria in terms of years served in rank.

Thus, some of my experiences on campus tended to be colored by the factors of gender, ethnicity, and national origin. One such rude awakening can be the recognition that one is considered to be a "three-fer." Hints, or even direct statements, that in hiring a non-European immigrant woman the department got a three-for-one deal are not uncommon. Many a time a colleague in search of a member for a committee has called me to say "You are perfect because you are a woman and you are not White!" And I will often retort "Is that all? Or is it my qualifications you are interested in also?" And there have been times when I have turned down an appointment because I felt that my gender and race were the only factors that they took into consideration, not my qualifications for the position.

I have often voiced my frustration about what seemed to be differing standards by which faculty are rated. There were times when I felt that not only were the standards for me different but they were also being changed in the middle of the game, in effect making it harder for me to meet departmental and institutional criteria either for promotion or tenure. This incredible elastic yardstick may take the form of the varying emphasis placed on the teaching, research, and service components—a problem that is more acute in institutions that are not heavily research oriented. Or it may take the form of redefining what are the "admissible" journals for publications; what are "admissible" research activities that constitute scholarship; and what are "admissible" activities that constitute valuable service.

The changing yardstick is probably experienced by many women and/or minority faculty, but for immigrant faculty this can be further compounded by assertions that as a foreigner one needs to understand the system better. Or if one complains, suggestions are made that the foreigner just does not fit in. In addition, questions that relate to one's "foreignness," such as student concerns about speech accent, whether such concerns are real or not, give those who wish to denigrate immigrant faculty another means of stretching the yardstick.

In the process of jumping through the academic hoops to obtain tenure and get promoted, one may be asked to sacrifice principles when it comes to maintaining high standards in one's classroom. One may be "advised" that to maintain viability in the department one must have a feel for the "students' needs" because they are the customers. And when one sees that yardstick being stretched for people who get great student evaluations (because they give mostly As to students and have C as their lowest grade; teach to the test and indicate to students exactly what they have to study for by providing study guides, past tests, and all kinds of aids for students to memorize from; and give take-home essays where there are hints of what the answer should be), one wonders why sticking to principles is so difficult to do.

Perhaps because of the incredible elastic yardstick that I had to somehow measure up to, I have felt that I have had to try much harder to prove myself professionally. This may simply be an act of self-preservation. I made it a point to amass a professional record that would make it clear to the university that they could not win a lawsuit (if I was denied tenure or promotion). Thus, in my nine years at the current institution, I have put together a total of sixteen binders for merit, retention, promotion, and tenure decisions (which seemed to be coming at me every six months). I have done this so that no one could say that I was not worthy because I did not have a good record of teaching, scholarship, and service. As highly motivated and highly qualified as I am, there have been times when I have thought that the system has made it harder for me to succeed. One simply has to compare my situation with that of my husband, who did not have to go through many of the situations I have had to. The system sometimes marginalizes immigrant women and makes it hard for them to find affirmation of their professional worth. Suggestions that one is a "three-fer" and that one does not yet measure up to the standards (even though such standards are impermanent) can gnaw at the individual. That I was driven to work harder because of this may be a positive side effect, but on the other hand, this cannot be totally comforting to the individual who must endure problems associated with gender, ethnicity, or national origin.

Where Are We Going?

Today's non-European immigrant faculty, both men and women, have an important role to play in the continuing struggle of society to cope with the current wave of immigrants. In many institutions, non-European faculty may represent the first significant personal contact that many students have with non-Europeans. That these non-Europeans are in positions of authority over the students may also be a new experience for them. Although these encounters may not be completely smooth, as my experiences and our study (Manrique and Manrique 1994) showed, it can be stated that the longer the Other Teacher interacts with students, the better the relations between them will become. In the majority of instances, immigrant faculty win over all but the most skeptical or hostile of students.

Immigrant women, because they must also overcome inherent biases against their gender, have a tougher nut to crack. But where they succeed, they break down even more barriers for immigrants. By the nature of their highly visible jobs, these faculty members counteract negative stereotypes that students may have of women from other cultures. And whether willingly or unwillingly, these faculty serve as role models for the diverse students on U.S. campuses. I have found myself filling various roles including that of role model, mediator, and advisor for students of non-European origin. And whether I actively sought such roles, or whether such roles were thrust upon me by circumstances, I have tended to accept them as excellent opportunities to educate myself and others around me.

Universities and colleges play a significant role in the continuing evolution of a diverse American system. In addition to providing a means of access and assimilation into society for immigrants, colleges can also help to condition the kinds of interactions that occur among people of different origins. When campuses tolerate, or create, an atmosphere that is hostile to immigrant faculty, students learn that it is acceptable to denigrate the new immigrants. When changing and different standards are applied to immigrants, this only reinforces stereotypes that the new immigrants are indeed different from the native-born population. And when women immigrants are hit with the multiple whammy on campus, efforts to level the playing field for all women are damaged.

Unfortunately, continuing research reveals that universities and colleges have much work to do with regard to non-European immigrants. In our study (Manrique and Manrique 1994), faculty reported encountering instances of discrimination and prejudice across the various segments of campus; this suggests that campus atmosphere is a greater problem than we realize. For immigrant women, it is interesting to note that those who treat them unfairly or are their antagonists are just as likely to be native-born women as they are to be men. Many immigrant women also tend to be isolated from effective support networks. In fact, this is one price of immigrating that immigrant women constantly refer to. They give up the support of the strong network of their extended family and community in their country of origin when they come to the United States. There is little to replace that support network (other than their immediate family, perhaps), when they take on faculty positions.

As both American society and American campuses become more diverse, colleges and universities will have to face up to the problems and the potential that immigrants bring. This will require both proactive measures that create a campus atmosphere conducive to the acceptance of diverse peoples in place of the "chilly climate" (Chilly Collective 1995) that often prevails and reactive measures to confront intolerance where it manifests itself. Some of these measures could involve the following: early identification programs for potentially diverse faculty; programs to ensure retention of minority faculty, especially in a majority White community; efforts to provide a positive and encouraging institutional atmosphere; efforts to make available financial support packages, especially for research and publication; efforts to create opportunities for networking; efforts to recruit a critical mass of like people who can support each other culturally; open and frank discussions concerning racism and sexism; and concerted and systematic efforts to incorporate gender and race in the curriculum. These are just some of the measures that can be used to make life more palatable for foreign women faculty who find themselves in majority White academic institutions. The history of immigrants and immigration in the United States suggests that changes will not be smooth but that in the end, the American cuisine is large enough to accommodate a more inclusive variety of immigrant salads. The prospects for the future of immigrant women in academic employment settings center on change from within. This change requires effective strategies to recruit, retain, train, retrain, and develop immigrant non-European women academics, recognizing us for the great national resource we represent.

It was June 3, 2000. My husband and I had been invited to the wedding of a former student who had gone on to a prestigious law school, graduated, and is now working for a law firm on the East Coast. Since the wedding was in town, we decided to attend. The bride's mother sought us out at the reception, came up to me with her sincerest smile and said, "I have been longing to meet you. My daughter has spoken so highly of you. Thank you very much for all that you have done to turn her into the wonderful lawyer that she is now." The woman did not see me for the color of my skin but for the role that I had played in her daughter's life! It was a welcome contrast to comments made in the past. Somehow this makes being in the teaching profession all worth it!

Cecilia G. Manrique is a Full Professor who teaches in the political science/public administration and women's studies departments at the University of Wisconsin-La Crosse. She has a doctorate in political science from the University of Notre Dame. Her areas are comparative politics and international relations, especially having to do with the developing world. She has published in the field of incorporating technology in the political science classroom and is the author of *The Houghton Mifflin Guide to the Internet for Political Science* (1999), which is now in its second edition. Her most recent publication (co-authored with Gabriel Manrique) is *The Multicultural or Immigrant Faculty in American Society* (1999). She was named University of Wisconsin System Woman of Color in 1996 and YWCA Coulee Region Outstanding Woman in 1997.

Works Cited

Chilly Collective, eds. 1995. *Breaking Anonymity: The Chilly Climate for Women Faculty*. Ontario, Canada: Wilfrid Laurier University Press.

Gabaccia, D., eds. 1992. *Seeking Common Ground: Multidisciplinary Studies of Immigrant Women in the United States*. Westport, CT: Greenwood Press.

Hensel, N. 1991. *Realizing Gender Equality in Higher Education*. Washington, DC: ERIC Clearinghouse on Higher Education.

Leap, T. L. 1995. *Tenure, Discrimination and the Courts*. 2nd ed. Ithaca, NY: Cornell University Press.

Manrique, C., and G. Manrique. 1994. Immigrant Faculty in U.S. Colleges and Universities: American Higher Education and the New Wave of Immigration. Paper read at Midwest Business Economics Association, 1994, at Chicago, IL.

———. 1999. *The Multicultural or Immigrant Faculty in American Society*. New York: The Mellen Press.

Richardson, B. 1974. *Sexism in Higher Education*. New York: The Seabury Press.

Rosen, D., S. Werner, and B. Yates, eds. 1974. *"We'll Do It Ourselves: Combatting Sexism in Education*. Lincoln, NE: University of Nebraska Printing Office.

Simeone, A. 1987. *Academic Women: Working Towards Equality*. South Hadley, MA: Bergen & Garvey.

Swoboda, M. J., A. J. Roberts, and J. Hirsch, eds. 1993. *"Women on Campus in the Eighties: Old Struggles, New Victories*. Madison, WI: University of Wisconsin System.

Takaki, R. 1989. *Strangers from a Different Shore: A History of Asian Americans*. Boston: Little, Brown.

Tang, J., and E. Smith, eds. 1996. *Women and Minorities in American Professions*. New York: State University of New York Press.

Turner, C. S. V., and S. L. Myers. 2000. *Faculty of Color in Academe: Bittersweet Success*. Boston: Allyn and Bacon.

Welch, L. B., ed. 1990. *Women in Higher Education: Changes and Challenges*. New York: Praeger.

Wyche, K. F., and S. B. Graves. 1992. "Minority Women in Academia." *Psychological Women's Quarterly* 16: 424–437.

CHAPTER TEN

The Pacific Asianized Other: Teaching Unlearning among Midwestern Students

FAY YOKOMIZO AKINDES

Abstract

THIS CHAPTER IS an autoethnographic account of my experiences as a Pacific Asianized woman teaching communication and culture at a small public liberal arts college in southeast Wisconsin. My background as an American Japanese Buddhist from Hawaii marks me as different from my students, many of whom are White Christian women. Common threads among us, however, are class and gender. I am a first-generation college graduate from a working-class family, as are 65 percent of my students. Central to my teaching work is helping students to disrupt dichotomies and dichotomous thinking; in short, to unlearn lifelong lessons.

Learning is easy; it's unlearning that is difficult. Consequently, teaching to unlearn is more problematic than teaching to learn. How do college professors, for example, help students to unlearn what the dominant culture has conditioned them to believe: that class differences are nonexistent in the United States, that their Whiteness signifies superiority over the Other or, conversely, that their Otherness relegates them to the margins? This essay addresses pedagogical issues of power and control, specifically in the context of a decolonized Pacific Asianized (American Japanese) subject teaching at a midwestern university. How does unlearning colonization influence the teaching and learning process? How do I infuse my experiences of (de)colonization among students who have been indoctrinated to believe that they are superior to others, superior to me? How do I help them to recognize and take responsibility for their White privilege? How is my presence as the Pacific Asianized Other disruptive to the hegemonic system of education?

My teaching style dispels what Brazilian critical pedagogy theorist Paulo Freire (Freire 1993, 54) calls "banking education," in which the professor deposits information into students' empty vaults. As Freire writes, "The solution is not to 'integrate' [the oppressed] into the structure of oppression, but to transform that structure so that they can become 'beings for themselves'" (55). In other words, students must actively participate in their own education, and they do this by developing their critical consciousness, as opposed to conforming to preexisting oppressive structures of learning. My assumption is that White people (many of my students) are not exempt from oppression. In this sense, my teaching work is potentially a radical act of resistance.

Situating Myself

My academic home is the University of Wisconsin-Parkside in Kenosha, located between Milwaukee and Chicago. There are some 5,000 students at this public university, which was built in 1968 next to a wooded park. The architecture is stunning: five red-brick buildings connected with glassed corridors; once you enter the building there is no need to leave. This could be viewed as a convenience, especially in winter, but it also confines students indoors when the weather is inviting. Eighty-three percent of Parkside's students are from the southeast Wisconsin region; a smaller number of students are from northern parts of Wisconsin, the suburbs of Chicago, or other states and countries. It is a commuter and "suitcase" campus; students (and faculty) do not "hang out" on campus except to attend classes. According to a survey conducted at Parkside, 65 percent of the students are first-generation college students with neither parent holding an associate or bachelor's degree. During the late 1990s, the largest increase in students, in terms of age range, was among students between the ages of 35 and 54.[1] These "non-traditional" students live round lives, juggling families, full-time jobs, and community service. I teach in the communication department, which has the third largest number of majors (some 145) in the College of Arts & Sciences and a disproportionately small staff of six full-time faculty, including five females and one male. The department chair is a woman. As an American Japanese woman from Hawaii, I am the only non-White faculty in the department. Parkside's students and faculty of color together constitute 16 percent of the student and faculty population. African American students make up the largest group of non-White students, and Asian professors, many of them Chinese and Indian nationals, represent the largest "minority" faculty group. There are, however, a large number of Blacks and Hispanics on the university staff in areas of service. This residual pattern of White dominance over those of color suggests how difficult it is to move from positions of servitude to positions of power. In addition to the institutional structure, how students relate to me may be influenced by the courses that I teach: Communication Theory, Intercultural Communication, Cyberspace Communication, Asian Americans and Media, Broadcasting and Society, and Gender, Race, and Class in Media. The theory course is a basic core requirement; the other courses are upper-level electives for juniors and seniors.

What first attracted me to Parkside's communication department was its explicit social constructivist philosophy; it is grounded in the assumption that reality is socially constructed and, therefore, open to de- and re-construction. The implications of this philosophy in the classroom are liberating both for students and professors; it means that teaching and learning hold transformative possibilities. This idea can also be threatening for those who are anchored in a paradigm that justifies a system of oppression; since they benefit from the existing system, they have no impetus to change it.

By the time students enter my classroom, they have been indoctrinated by a lifetime of messages, stereotypes, and prejudices. This includes an educational hegemonic system that reproduces and maintains the dominant power structure by inscribing passivity among students in relation to authority. In other words, students are conditioned to unquestioningly accept "facts" relayed by a professor at the lectern. Yet education is not a neutral practice but one laden with deeply embedded values; because it is ideological it works at an unconscious level. Moreover, professors, whether they admit it or not, teach according to particular worldviews that shape their understanding of knowledge and existence. When students at UW-Parkside enter my classroom, how do they see/meet me? How do I see/meet them? Many of them have little interpersonal experience with Pacific Asian women, yet they *have* encountered the likes of me on television, in movies, magazines, and other forms of popular media. What are these popular images and how do they subjectivize me? According to Deborah Gee's documentary *Slaying the Dragon*, there are three popular media stereotypes of Asian women: the sinister dragon lady, the sexually submissive geisha girl, and the "Connie Chung," referring to the token minority news anchor (*Slaying the Dragon* 1988). How have these stereotypes influenced how my students perceive and relate to me in and out of the classroom? Although students do not enter the classroom empty of knowledge, many do lack any experiential knowledge of Pacific Asian women. On the first day of every class, I unpack my baggage, contextualizing my life so that students see the person who is the Other.

Personalizing the Other

I was born in January 1959; the first 17 years of my life were spent on Molokai, a slipper-shaped island in Hawaii. Molokai is 10 miles wide by 38 miles long, with (still) no traffic lights, one school for intermediate and high school students, a leper colony on a remote peninsula, and fishponds dating back to the thirteenth century (Spalding 1984). The island is home to 6,000 people, including a large Native Hawaiian population and an immigrant Filipino population that has lingered after the closure of Dole and Del Monte's pineapple plantations in the 1970s. I participated in 4-H for six years and spent weekends learning homemaking skills, such as sewing and baking. My high school basketball team name was The Farmers. We bought fresh corn from pickup trucks parked on the side of the road (corn seed research is popular on my island). I was also a first-generation college student in my immediate family. Daddy was of the working class. When he was not reading, installing, and maintaining meters for the electric company, he fished, played the guitar, watched televised wrestling, and chain-smoked cigarettes. My parents both grew up in homes where Japanese was the primary language. My first language was Pidgin English, which linguistically is Creole, the lingua franca of Hawaii; it is a "chop suey" language of English, Hawaiian, and Asian words and gestures that was developed during early days of trade between Hawaiians and *haole* and was complicated during the plantation era.[2] Roughly from the mid-1800s to the mid-1900s, the plantation era necessitated a common language for predominantly Asian indentured field laborers to communicate with Portuguese and Hawaiian *luna* (foremen) and *haole* owners.

Today when I drive to work each morning, I pass Lake Michigan (which I pretend is the Pacific Ocean), cornfields, cabbage patches tended by Mexican workers, a log cabin, a red tractor with a "For Sale" sign on it, intersections with stop signs on each corner, and fields with red barns and silos in the distance. Initially it was an exotic landscape to my eyes. After three years of living in Kenosha, however, it is decidedly not entirely foreign to someone from Molokai. I have learned to see the common threads that stitch my new habitus to the one I grew up in. Bourdieu describes the habitus as a durable system of "structured, structuring dispositions" that translate into everyday practices, "things to do or not to do, things to say or not to say" (1993, 480). Beneath the superficial differences between Kenosha and Molokai are similarities inherent in a habitus in which many people have a recent immigrant genealogy; where livelihoods are dependent on the land, blue-collar, or service occupations; where multigenerational families are tightly knit and do not always embrace outsiders. When I lived on Molokai I felt like an outsider, not only because our family was Japanese in a predominantly Hawaiian community but also because my parents were born on another island. Similarities between Molokai and Kenosha, however, do not coalesce. Molokai is a *colonized* island and Kenosha is not. This is an important point, because it positions me as a colonized subject; during the past eight years or so I have been unlearning colonization (decolonizing myself), and this inevitably influences my teaching work. In other words, I help my students to unlearn years of conditioning and to become critical thinkers, to embody education as a liberatory practice (Freire 1993). Today I find myself on the U.S. continent teaching *haole* students from a (de)colonized Pacific Asian standpoint, one that strives to be inclusive, accepting of difference, and critical of a Eurocentric bias. The irony has not escaped me.

Hidden Histories

When I first moved to Kenosha, I often combed the classified ads for bargains to furnish our house. One ad caught my eye immediately. It was an ad searching for "Jap memorabilia from WWII." It historicized my ethnicity in a specific time period and reminded me that for some people I still wore the face of the enemy. The ad was also a reminder of hidden histories related to the U.S. concentration camps for American Japanese during World War II. Ten thousand Japanese on the West Coast were ordered out of their homes and imprisoned in ten different barbed-wire camps in desolate sites as far east as Arkansas. Most of those imprisoned were children, and two-thirds were U.S. born. Ironically, the young men in these families were drafted or asked to volunteer to fight in the war on behalf of the country that had stripped their families of American civil rights. I first learned of the camps while an undergraduate at the University of Hawaii-Manoa when I was the age of many of my students. This was a startling revelation for me, not only because my family is Japanese American but also because Grandpa's sister, Aunty Mildred, was interned in Poston, Arizona. This was a hidden history that my family never discussed, suggesting why Asians are stereotyped as the model minority: We keep our mouths shut about shameful acts of injustice. The model minority stereotype—hardworking, quiet, compliant—actually emerged after World War II and is still invoked by my Pacific Asianized body.

Although I soon discovered that many of my students have a limited understanding of American history (*none* of the thirty-four students in my Asian Americans and Media class had any knowledge of the camps), I was still conscious that among some of their family members I represent the "yellow peril" of their past. One of my students confessed that her father and grandfather both served as World War II navy commanders in the Pacific and forbade anyone in the family to purchase products from Asia. Another incident that hit close to home was learning that Ron Ebens, the man who bludgeoned Vincent Chin to death with a baseball bat, was originally from a small town in Wisconsin. The documentary *Who Killed Vincent Chin?* (1988) is modeled after Akira Kurosawa's masterful *Rashomon*, skillfully problematizing the violent incident from different points of view. In the documentary, Ebens insists that he is not a racist. Despite eyewitnesses, Ebens and his accomplice son served no prison time for committing this brutal 1982 murder in Detroit. They were sentenced to three years' probation and a $3,000 fine for smashing the skull of a "China-man" who they mistook as a "Jap." In the documentary Ebens says, "The system worked the way it should've worked right down the line" (*Who Killed Vincent Chin?* 1988). Eben's son had recently been laid off from a Detroit auto plant because of increased competition from Japanese companies. When my students watch this documentary they must confront ugly truths of injustice coiled around issues of race and difference. We problematize the title, asking Who killed Vincent Chin? and Would he be alive today if he was not Asian?

Disrupting Dichotomies

The central aim in all of my classes is to disrupt dichotomies—to unsettle the dominant logic of either/or with alternative possibilities of both/and. Consequently, it is difficult for me not to consider issues of identity and difference as understood through the interlocking lens of gender, race, and class. By disrupting dichotomies, my teaching objective is to be inclusive: How can I create and sustain an environment where all students, ideas, and standpoints are included in the dialogue? How do I help my students understand the necessity of disrupting dichotomies and dichotomous thinking? How do I help my students claim their responsibility to dismantle invisible systems that privilege some and oppress others? How can I engage all students to be active learners as opposed to passive receptacles that absorb a normalized point of view? Active learners fully immerse themselves and participate in and out of the classroom. They take a personal responsibility for and interest in delving into the material, questioning it; making sense of it; in short, experiencing the thesis-antithesis-synthesis of learning.

While teaching Asian Americans and Media, a White female student who I will call Crystal emerged as an active learner. She adopted a passionate interest in the Japanese American internment camp experience during World War II and decided to research the archives of the local daily newspaper, the *Kenosha News*, and its coverage of the camps during the period of December 1941 to December 1944. She then interviewed five individuals who read the *Kenosha News* during that time period to assess their understanding of the issue. What she learned was not entirely surprising: The news coverage was limited, biased, and relegated to the back pages of the newspaper. Her research participants' awareness and understanding of the camps reflected the narrow and one-sided news coverage. Rather than stop there, Crystal arranged a screening of the video documentary *Children of the Camps* (1999), that we had viewed and discussed in class, for three of her research participants. In the post-screening discussion that she facilitated, one of the participants, who was 25 at the time of World War II and believed the Japanese were a threat to the United States, said, "I can't believe how in the dark I feel. I take back what I said earlier. I can't believe our government did this." The project was a transformative learning experience not only for Crystal but for her research participants as well. She identified the interviewing process as "the most enlightening part of the project. It put real faces with the people that lived on the outside of the internment camps of the United States and didn't know what was going on." Included in Crystal's research paper was an article from the *Kenosha News* that she rewrote based on her new knowledge of the internment camps. This multifaceted research project enabled Crystal to experience the thesis-antithesis-synthesis trajectory of active learning. Moreover, the social and historical constructedness of reality was de- and reconstructed.

Model Minority

While my Pacific Asianized body may represent the "yellow peril" to some eyes, to others it may convey positive stereotypes of hard work, diligence, and intelligence. As one of my students mentioned, the quiet study dorm at the University of Wisconsin-Milwaukee (which he attended prior to enrolling at Parkside) was known as the "Asian tower" because many of its residents were Asian. This stereotype is reinforced in popular media with bespectacled Asian characters cast in business and professional roles, albeit usually as non-speaking atmospheric characters. The stereotype is positive when contextualized in the role of professor and may influence how students perceive my role of authority in the classroom. Why have Asians been labeled in such a positive way and what are the consequences in the context of college teaching and learning?

Ebens's assumption that Vincent Chin was Japanese reflects a general tendency to categorize all Asians into a monolithic group. Yet, as my students learn, the histories and circumstances that brought individual Asian groups to the United States makes their experiences distinctly different. The first Asians to arrive in the United States were the Filipinos and, since they were colonial subjects of Spain, they were classified as White. The Chinese, who were responsible largely for the construction of the first transcontinental railroad, were considered half human (as were Black slaves) and were legally restricted from voting, owning land, or bringing their wives to the United States. The experiences, then, of these sojourners are radically different from the experiences of Hmong refugees, many of whom settled in Wisconsin during and after the Vietnam War. As my students learn, refugees cannot visit home while living in the United States because of limited life choices. Because of this tendency to lump all Asians into a monolithic group (as is the tendency with any group), my students may mistakenly perceive me as representative of all Asians, particularly since many of them have little or no previous personal contact with Asians. If all Asians are, therefore, smart, obedient, and the "model minority," then my role as professor is logical and naturalized.

A Question of Style

What distinguishes how I teach from how a White male or female professor might approach teaching? Beyond specific activities, I believe it is the style in which I frame activities and engage students in learning that sets me apart. Comments that resurface again and again in student evaluations say, "I absolutely love your teaching style." "You have a very unique style of teaching." "Your teaching style is unique. I love it!" It is difficult to describe or explain what this style is, since it is an embodied style that does not translate well to words on a page. My teaching style emanates from my lived experiences on rural Molokai, in cosmopolitan Honolulu, the border city of San Diego, at graduate school in the Appalachian foothills, and, now, living and working in southeastern Wisconsin. It is a style that emerges from my lived experiences as the former wife of a White man from California, the current wife of a Yoruba man from the elite educated class in Benin, and "Mama" to two African Asian American children. My lived experiences shape my consciousness as a teacher, enabling me to translate theoretical concepts into everyday practice.

In his provocative book *The Colonizer and the Colonized*, Albert Memmi (1965, xvi) describes his colonial positionality by saying, "I was a sort of halfbreed of colonization, understanding everyone because I belonged completely to no one." To be colonized, then, is to be a hybrid subject, to be neither this nor that, but both/and. This multiple consciousness, although unsettling in its ambiguity, is also a source of strength as Said implies: "The more places you have been, the more displacements you've gone through....As every situation is a new one, you start out each day anew; the more experiences seem to be multiple and complex and composite and interesting for that reason" (1998, 48). To start each day anew, drawing on multiple experiences, is how I constitute my hybridized self, one that I have grown to appreciate as rhizomatic, a perpetual in-betweenness of becoming, with no beginning or end, with seemingly disparate connections (Deleuze and Guattari 1980). My lived experiences, then, inform my understanding of teaching and learning and explains why much of my teaching is grounded in experiential learning.

Understanding is not a transparent or monolithic phenomenon; it is a multifaceted one. Wiggins and McTighe identify six facets of understanding in the context of learning: explanation, interpretation, application, perspective, empathy, and self-knowledge (1998). Although all six facets are present in my teaching, empathy and self-knowledge are particularly evident in my cultural communication classes.

Field trips are an effective way to teach empathy, to provide a lived dimension to course material by placing students in someone else's shoes. When teaching intercultural communication, for example, I organize an hour-long bus trip to Mitsuwa Plaza in Arlington Heights. The plaza is designed specifically for Japanese expatriates; therefore, most of the workers, products, and customers are from Japan. There is a supermarket with an expansive fresh produce and seafood department, a food court, a bookstore, a liquor store with a variety of sake (rice wine) and Japanese beer, a travel agency, a video rental shop, a bakery, a pottery store, a fashion boutique, and gift shops. Students spend a few hours shopping, observing, and experiencing an environment where they are the Other. It is usually in the bookstore, where they are confronted by books (which open right to left), magazines, CDs, and signage in foreign characters, that they feel most displaced. Some students quickly exit; others experience the discomfort and browse until they find the English section marginalized in the corner. When we meet again as a class, we spend time discussing the field trip, sharing observations of people and products, and reflecting on feelings of displacement and Otherness. For some students the field trip remains the single most important event during the semester because it fully immerses them in an environment that marks them as different.

In *Asian Americans and Media*, we spent a Sunday afternoon attending the Chicago Asian American Film Showcase at The School of the Institute of Art. Students not only viewed independently produced Asian American films; they also had the opportunity to hear the filmmakers speak in a public forum as well as informally in the lobby. This was another event where many of my predominantly White students, a few who have never been to Chicago, found themselves the minority in a theatre filled with Asian Americans. The embodied experience was important in reifying the cultural production of films that re-present Asian Americans as multidimensional human beings. One of my White male students could not join the rest of the class on the field trip and attended a Saturday night screening alone. Although he was one of the few Whites in a theatre full of Asians, he did not experience the discomfort felt at predominantly Black events and he wondered why. Historical differences influence intercultural communication and contexts, reminding me that, perhaps, my experiences as the Other Teacher at Parkside might be markedly different if I was a Black woman.

These two examples suggest how my Asian American identity is foregrounded in my teaching. I am aware that students may be hesitant to speak negatively about their observations or experiences knowing that I am implicated in the Asian American culture. This has not been a problem. I openly confess my ignorance about certain aspects of Asian culture (I, myself, do not speak Japanese) and position the Mitsuwa field trip as a learning experience for me as well. Furthermore, my teaching exemplars are not limited to Asian American culture. I also draw on Yoruba, Arab, Cuban, Hawaiian, Irish, French, and other cultures.

Teaching and learning are rhizomatic with seemingly disparate connections among concepts that illuminate, make visible, make traceable, the trajectory of understanding. I have learned to "listen" to students, individually and collectively, and to steer the course according to these cues. For example, during my four-week summer course on intercultural communication this year, I arrived one morning to find most of the students dressed in shorts and sleeveless tops. After a week of overcast days, this particular day was gloriously sunny. One of the three male students in the class jokingly suggested that we hold our class at Pets Park (short for Petrified Springs Park) next to the university. The students were delightedly surprised when I agreed that it was a great idea. We walked to Pets Park and formed a triangle with three picnic tables. On this particular day we were discussing *A Small Place* by Jamaica Kincaid (2000). Each table constituted a small group discussion, after which I sat on the grass and facilitated a large-group discussion. It was one of the best classes all summer. The students demonstrated ownership of the class and I complied.

If I had to characterize my teaching style with one dominant characteristic it would be silence. Silence is unsettling and "loud" to some students. Yet it is a language that provokes self-reflection and knowledge. As Katagiri writes, "Silence means you have to be you as you really are—what is just is of itself" (1988, 6). Students have commented to me how powerful silence can be, how my silences in the classroom have taught them strength, how silence speaks answers that only you yourself can hear.

Journal-writing is a pedagogical tool that I have found extremely effective in transformative learning, specifically in Gender, Race, and Class in Media. Journal-writing is similar to poems and dreams: "In them you put what you don't know you know"(Rich 1979, 40). For this reason, I encourage my students to write in a stream-of-consciousness style while also integrating three areas: the personal (experiences, memories, observations), the popular (media), and the theoretical (assigned readings).³ Students' journals are safe places to write, question, remember, and reflect. I collect journals every three weeks and carefully read each one, commenting in the margins, posing questions, engaging in a private dialogue with each student. The journal is not only a learning tool for the student; it also provides me with an assessment of how students are engaging with the course material. What concepts are they struggling with? What needs clarification in class? What questions emerge that need addressing? Students often write with candor what they cannot voice in class. I extract provocative passages from journals and read them anonymously to the class to extend or spark discussions.

My assumption that journals are a safe site for critical exploration was refuted last year when a female student in her 30s, whom I will call Jasmine, refused to release her journal to me, claiming that it was too personal. She explained that as an African American woman, she was raised to be wary of "giving away" personal stories and that she did not trust anyone, including me, to read her work. Jasmine went on to say that since "the professor" did not reciprocate with a personal journal, the relationship was an imbalanced one. She reminded me that despite my attempts to flatten the power hierarchy, my position as professor ultimately overshadows the student. What this suggests to me is the need to take similar risks as my students, to expose confessional narratives that also situate me as vulnerable (hooks 1994). This is something I already do in class discussions and, to some extent, in my comments to students within the margins of their journals. For example, I have shared my fear of acting out internalized racist behavior in the context of my family, of buying imported gruyere cheese with WIC coupons as resistance to a dehumanizing social structure, of escaping an abusive relationship as an undergraduate. In keeping with my flexible attitude toward grading criteria, I suggested that Jasmine edit her work and submit only the entries that she felt comfortable sharing. She was an excellent student who participated generously in class discussions and, as the only Black student, often carried the burden of responsibility to enlighten some of her White classmates. Her refusal to release her writing to me signified, ironically, her political agency as a Black woman coming to terms with her identity. She troubled the academic system in which students produce and submit work in return for a grade, negotiating the private (personal stories) with the public (teacher's assessment). Journal-writing is, I still believe, an effective pedagogical tool for understanding facets of empathy and self-knowledge (Wiggins and McTighe 1998) and, consequently, it can be a liberatory practice, as Jasmine demonstrated.

Journal-writing demands considerable time and engagement on my part. I collect journals every three weeks and spend approximately fifteen to twenty minutes reading and commenting on each one, sometimes faced with inscrutable handwriting. Yes, it would be easier to read word-processed work, but I have found handwritten journal entries to be more spontaneous and thoughtful. An average class is twenty-five students; assessing journals usually takes some six hours of work. This, in addition to teaching two other classes with twenty-five to forty students each.

Teaching from an interpretive paradigm that privileges empathy and experiential learning is time intensive. Students are graded through reflection papers, essays, and take-home examinations (essays), which all require individual reading and assessment. Because of this, I am in the office five days a week. My husband, Simon, who is also an assistant professor on Parkside's tenure track, and I are tag-team parents. We alternate days to chauffeur Adelana and Tunji to and from school. Twice a week, I work into the evening, usually to nine, sometimes later, to work on research projects that, in my case, are writerly acts. It is also not unusual for Simon and me to retreat on weekends. We are most productive at our Parkside offices, surrounded by books and expansive views of sky, as opposed to home, where housework and children distract us. The price paid, then, for being a teacher that values qualitative and interpretive styles of learning is solitary confinement in order to create engaging activities and handouts and assess student work.

There are other side effects: my Hawaii family now receives New Year's instead of Christmas presents from me (no time to shop in early December), the buttons on my summer shorts have popped because of the extra weight I've gained, and our house is in constant disarray. Although my tenured colleagues comment that I'm neglecting my family, I think just the opposite. The "scaffolding" of teaching and research that I'm so heavily engaged in today ensures my family's security. My work toward tenure is critical; my working-class background is devoid of a trust fund as a safety net. Of course, it does not mean that I fully accept this tag-team parenting arrangement and the excessive work involved with being a professor. As I write this, I question the humaneness of a patriarchal institution that once assumed that a woman's place was in the home. We could argue that this assumption still drives policy today.

Structural Support

Chosen acts of teaching—how I design my courses and the material I choose to focus on—are interdependent with the institutional context of my teaching. The University of Wisconsin system, including Parkside, has established an aggressive diversity plan that includes recruitment *and* retention of professors and students of color and the inclusion of diversity issues in the classroom. All Parkside students are required to complete a three-credit diversity course; three of my courses fulfill this requirement. Being in a department with a predominantly female faculty also translates into a nurturing environment, although gender is just one modality in an interlocking system that includes race and class. It is not uncommon, for example, for women (and people of color) to internalize and uphold dominant patriarchal values, sometimes with regard to other women (and people of color). Furthermore, being the only non-White faculty has resulted in occasional "imposed invisibility" and "designated visibility" (Rains 1999, 153). The curriculum that our department fosters translates well into supporting my presence as a professor of color. Cultural understanding and an aim to promote diversity, in terms of worldviews, are consistent throughout our department's curriculum. One of our electives, Communication and Ethnicity, focuses on a different ethnic group each semester: African Americans, Asian Americans, Hispanic Americans, and Native Americans. Enrollment is usually around thirty students. One of my graduate school friends who teaches communication at a similar state institution in the Midwest commented that were his university to offer such a course, only a handful of students would enroll. His comment positioned Parkside as atypical and progressive.

Those at the university who have demonstrated interest in my teaching and research activities have been older White men, in particular the former and current secretary of the faculty and an English professor who chairs the faculty committee for research and creative activity. They have helped me to navigate institutional obstacles to the pursuit of my scholarly aims and, consequently, have disrupted presuppositions of the "big, bad" White patriarchy. They may regard my Pacific Asianized female Otherness as deficient and in need of White male guidance, and their positions of power reify the institution as a patriarchal structure, but it is difficult for me *not* to see them simply as decent human beings.

Infinite Layers of Identity

There is a constant self-reflexivity in teaching which requires an acceptance of who I am as a person and how this influences my teaching style. How do my "infinite layers"(Trinh 1989, 94) of identity—soft-spoken Pacific Asian feminist *sansei* Buddhist from a working-class home now married to a Beninoise with two African Asian American children—influence my teaching worker role in and out of the classroom? As someone who is constantly negotiating her multiple identities and who has crossed multiple borders, I have grown comfortable with the idea that my life is becoming. It is not fixed but is something that is continually in transformation. Perhaps this explains why I am tolerant of students who are sometimes resistant to the point of rudeness (not acknowledging my presence, "dissing" class assignments, clinging to passivity) because I have confidence that, in time, their critical consciousness will develop. For example, the first course that Donald enrolled in with me was Cyberspace Communication. He spent the first two classes joking in a 13-year-old smart-alecky sort of way. I quickly sassed him back. Subsequently he enrolled in two classes with me, Intercultural Communication and Gender, Race, and Class in Media, both of which address identity and difference. Although he exhibited some signs of resistance, he soon learned to listen to his peers (and me) and engage in thoughtful discussion. Recently he stopped by my office to reflect on his classroom experiences (he graduated this spring). He confessed that he initially questioned my credibility to teach and tested me with derisive remarks. The turning point for him was seeing the comprehensive reading packet I had produced and how I was able to speak knowledgeably about the material. What he did not say, and what he may not want to admit, is that my being a Pacific Asian woman prejudiced his expectations of me. As bell hooks writes: "Our very presence is a disruption" (1990, 148).

Student Evaluations

The only comment I have ever received that explicitly took issue with my "race" was handwritten on a student evaluation form for Gender, Race, and Class in Media. In response to the question, "What was the worst thing about this course? What could be improved?" the student wrote:

> It attacked students and made most feel uncomfortable. I don't think a minority should teach this subject. They bring too many feelings to the topic and tend to side with the minorities ganging upon the Whites for things they cannot help and are not a party to!

It hurt me to read this comment because it suggests that as a minority professor I am unable to treat fairly students who are different from me. The implicit message here is that it is acceptable for a White professor to side with

White students because s/he is maintaining the normalized power structure with Whites in the center and "minorities" in the margins. This comment further troubles me because it relinquishes any responsibility from White students to confront social inequalities as a result of historical events. In other words, White students may not have chosen to be born into families where they may inherit land or other generations-old wealth, but they are benefiting from a system that historically denied non-Whites the same privileges. As one of my colleagues likes to say, if you are not fighting racism, then you are racist.

This student's comment contrasts sharply with this narrative, written by a White female student (a non-communication major) who also enrolled in Gender, Race, and Class in Media. She nominated me for an award sponsored by Parkside's Womyn's Center (Voss 1999):

> Fay tackles some of the most pressing and controversial topics within the world of communications in an unbiased way, forcing her students to observe the world around them with a critical view, that prior to entering her classroom, many of them have probably not encountered before. Social injustice, poverty, racism, gender and power struggles, sex and sexism, and any other social constraint and or system are shown in varying aspects by Fay; and it is then left up to the student to process on their own, in a critical perspective. Fay is both challenging and fair, and somehow manages to keep a keen balance between the two.

Students who have been most vocal about supporting my teaching represent a spectrum of backgrounds, including "non-traditional" females and males, students of color who feel an unspoken alliance with me, and students with liberal political worldviews. Marginalized students find their way to my office: the Hmong student whose sister has run away from home and whose parents are growing apart, the shy White male who was arrested for possession of marijuana, the former minister who struggles with a multiple personalities disorder, the White working-class male student who works at a pool hall and has not made any friends during his several years at Parkside. There is the White male student who wants to conduct research on grunge music, the quiet White female student who wants to research queer theory and the representation of homosexuals in the media, and the Polish American woman in search of her roots after studying Asian Americans. There's the White woman who is petrified by the thought of public speaking and, despite her exceptional writing skills, embodies the imposter syndrome. I jot down one of my favorite quotes by Eleanor Roosevelt: "Nobody can make you feel inferior without your consent." I hand her the paper and confess that I carried these words in my wallet through my undergraduate years when I, too, battled a fear of speaking in class. At some point in time, it seems, we are all marginalized.

Yet however marginalized I may be, there is always someone who is situated even deeper in the shadows. Would my encounters with Parkside students be as positive as they have been if I was an African American woman, an "out" lesbian, or a woman who spoke with a noticeable foreign accent? One of my African American colleagues has shared stories of classroom interactions with White students that suggest that my experiences of Otherness are relatively mild. She confronts overt and inferential racism nearly every day from students as well as from administrators, colleagues, and strangers. Being in public spaces with African Americans has given me a taste of the existential experiences as a Black person. Many people confuse the body (the signifier) with the signified, "reading" color as fixed racist stereotypes and doing it innocently without critical reflexivity. Consequently, Black women professors must prove themselves intelligent enough to be in positions of authority over White students (Alexander 1994; Hamlet 1999; Pope and Joseph 1997). Stereotypes of Asians as the "model minority," conversely, privilege my body with assumed intelligence that naturalizes my position as professor. Moreover, as an able-bodied, heterosexual, married woman with children, the system, to some extent, works for me to the exclusion of Others.

Summary

Feminist *sansei* Mari Matsuda reminds me that my teaching work is a radical act of resistance (1996). It is an act of resistance because someone from my cultural and class background historically was not expected to teach at a "mainland" college and publish academic papers; we were expected to reproduce the workforce for Hawaii's sugarcane, pineapple, or tourist plantations. In other words, I was expected to stay in my place as a Japanese woman whose ancestors were indentured field laborers. Instead I have migrated across class and geographic boundaries to "disrupt dichotomies" and teach students in predominantly White classrooms to unlearn life lessons. Yet it is not just the structure of the act (my chosen occupation) but the products of my agency that make my teaching work radical. I aim to change the way my students view the world and their place in it.

Response to my teaching has been overwhelmingly positive. According to the chair of my department, my teaching evaluations were high—"the strongest start of a new member of the department in memory" (Leeds-Hurwitz 1998). My evaluations, both quantitative and qualitative, have been consistently strong since joining the University of Wisconsin-Parkside in 1997. Moreover, enrollment in my elective classes, even ones taught on Saturday afternoons, evenings, and during the summer, have attracted full rosters of twenty to thirty students. Several factors contribute to my generally positive experiences as the Other in the classroom. There are limited historical encounters between people in the southeastern Wisconsin region and Japanese Americans; students, therefore, have no prior direct contact or experience with which to prejudge me. My personal identity as someone born and raised in Hawaii complicates my Japanese American identity and, to some extent, exoticizes my Otherness as someone from "paradise" and all that this discursive structure implies (pleasure, passivity, earthiness). The nature of my classes, several of which revolve around cultural identity and difference, privileges my Otherness and legitimizes my role of facilitator. One of my students, for example, said my being a "minority" gave credibility and legitimacy to my teaching of identity and difference. He recognized that my lived experiences provided insights that escaped White professors. At the same time, my students have responded favorably to the "non-controversial" classes I teach, such as Cyberspace Communication and Communication Theory, where my Pacific Asian identity is not directly implicated in the course material. Furthermore, my Americaness, as manifested in my language fluency (I don't speak with a foreign accent), body language, and popular culture literacy, collectively positions me as an approachable and accessible figure. My working-class family background and experiences growing up in a rural environment serve as a bridge to my White students and, at times, transcends race and ethnicity. It aligns my working-class students with me; we are the Other in an institution of higher education that has historically privileged wealthy White males. The structural organization of my department, the nature of the classes I teach, the nature of the students I teach, and the coherence between my students and me all contribute to my generally positive experiences as a Pacific Asianized Other teaching Midwestern students to unlearn.

Fay Yokomizo Akindes is Assistant Professor of Communication and Co-Director of the Women's Studies Program at the University of Wisconsin-Parkside, where she teaches cultural and media studies. Her research problematizes culture and identity in Hawai'i and the United States, and appears in *Diegesis, Discourse, Qualitative Inquiry*, and a few book anthologies. She was born and raised on Molokai.

Author's note

Merci beaucoup to Simon Adetona Akindes, my most merciless critic.

Notes

1. The survey was conducted by Diana Sharp, Ph.D., executive director of Academic Support Programs and Institutional Research at UW-Parkside. Demographic information on Parkside students and faculty was compiled by Dennis Irwin, UW-Parkside's Internal Auditor.

2. *Haole* is a Hawaiian word for "White person." It literally translates into "without breath" and was used to refer to the first European visitors who could not speak the native language. *Haole* also describes a way of being. *The Molokai News* formerly headlined its police beat with "Report on Haole Activity," then explained that "perpetrators of crime are acting *haole*."

3. This is a pedagogical tool that I learned from my graduate school mentor, Dr. Jenny L. Nelson, at Ohio University. Jenny created this class with Dr. Karin Sandell.

Works Cited

Alexander, E. 1994. "Memory, Community, Voice." *Callaloo* 17 (2): 408–421.

Bourdieu, P. 1993. "Structures, Habitus, Practices." In *Social Theory: The Multicultural and Classic Readings*, edited by C. Lemert. Boulder, CO: Westview Press.

Deleuze, G., and F. Guattari. 1980. *A Thousand Plateaus: Capitalism and Schizophrenia*. Minneapolis, MN: University of Minnesota Press.

Freire, P. 1993. *Pedagogy of the Oppressed*. New York: Continuum.

Hamlet, J. D. 1999. "Giving the Sistuhs Their Due: The Lived Experiences of African-American Women in Academia." In *Nature of a Sistuh: Black Women's Lived Experiences in the Contemporary Culture*, edited by T. McDonald and T. Ford-Ahmed. Durham, NC: Carolina Academic Press.

hooks, b. 1990. *Yearning: Race, Gender, and Cultural Politics*. Boston, MA: South End Press.

hooks, b. 1994. *Teaching to Transgress: Education as the Practice of Freedom*. New York: Routledge.

Katagiri, D. 1988. *Returning to Silence: Zen Practice in Daily Life*. Boston: Shambhala.

Kincaid, J. 2000. *A Small Place*. New York: Farrar, Straus & Giroux.

Leeds-Hurwitz, W. 1998. Personal communication with author, February 20, 1998.

Matsuda, M. J. 1996. *Where Is Your Body? And Other Essays on Race, Gender and the Law*. Boston: Beacon Press.

Memmi, A. 1965. *The Colonizer and the Colonized*. Boston: Beacon Press.

Pope, J., and J. Joseph. 1997. "Student Harassment of Female Faculty of African Descent in the Academy." In *Black Women in the Academy: Promises and Perils*, edited by L. Benjamin. Gainesville, FL: University Press of Florida.

Rains, F. V. 1999. "Dancing on the Sharp Edge of the Sword: Women Faculty of Color in White Academe." In *Everyday Knowledge and Uncommon Truths: Women of the Academy*, edited by L. K. Christian-Smith and K. S. Kellor. Boulder, CO: Westview Press.

Rich, A. 1979. *On Lies, Secrets, and Silence: Selected Prose, 1966–1978*. London: W.W. Norton and Company.

Said, E. 1998. "Edward Said: The Voice of a Palestinian in Exile." *Third Text* 3 (4): 39–50.

Slaying the Dragon. 1988. Directed by D. Gee. Distributed by National Asian American Tele-communication Association. Videocassette.

Spalding, P. 1984. *Moloka'i.* Honolulu, HI: Westwind Press.

Trinh, T. M. 1989. *Woman, Native, Other: Writing Postcoloniality and Feminism.* Bloomington, IN: Indiana University Press.

Voss, K. 1999. Personal communcation with the author, May 1999.

Who Killed Vincent Chin? 1988. Directed by C. Choy and R. Tajima. Distributed by Filmakers Library. Videocassette.

Wiggins, G., and J. McTighe. 1998. *Understanding by Design.* Alexandria, VA: Association for Supervision and Curriculum Development.

CHAPTER ELEVEN

Contradictions in the Classroom: Reflections of an Okanogan-Colville Professor

DELORES BLACK-CONNOR CLEARY

Abstract

TEACHING IN A classroom of predominantly White students has been both rewarding and challenging. It has been rewarding because over my past six years of teaching former students have keep in contact with me and at least appear to have gained from taking my courses. It has been challenging because, although some students seem to respond well to my pedagogy and teaching style, others are intentionally provocative and call my professorial authority into question. These challenges emerge, in part, because of the underlying tribal values that guide my teaching as well as my conceptions of students. I see myself as a learner as well as a teacher, and I encourage students to question what I, and others, teach them.

I am hesitant to put myself forward or to recount narratives of my experiences as an exemplar for others. In this instance, I am overcoming this reluctance because there is value in collecting various accounts in order to establish commonalities and differences regarding how a teacher from one culture/ethnic group responds to a problem as opposed to how a teacher from a different group responds to similar problems. Ideally, each perspective enriches the other. What I have achieved has not been accomplished by me but has been given to me. As a result of the tribal environment in which I was raised, I am not only a fiercely independent person but also have strong ties to a group both individually and collectively. My behavior has been heavily influenced by the group, particularly by the elders within the community. At the same time, such persons have neither interfered with my independence nor constrained my choices. Although this seems convoluted, it is really fairly simple and, in any event, talking about myself seems silly. When autobiographical information, or any information, is conveyed, it no longer belongs to the speaker. However, I take full responsibility for what is said.

I was born and raised on the Colville Indian reservation in eastern Washington state. Non-Indian people sometimes do not recognize me as Indian. I do not exhibit the stereotypical physical attributes associated with the Western idea of what Indians look like. For example, I do not look like the guy on the nickel (of course, this is true of many of the native peoples found at these latitudes). My style of dress, after the first week of classes, is somewhat informal, so that there are those who say that I look and dress more like a student than a faculty member. I dress very formally the first week of class in order to help establish my professorial authority, then begin to dress somewhat informally. This casual attire seems to make students much more comfortable in approaching me, and because they are less intimidated they are less reluctant to share their problems, concerns and questions with me.

Teaching is where my heart is, although my experiences in academia at times have been difficult. When it comes to students, I have a caring ethic. I believe that caring about students and studentlearning validates not only my own experience but their learning experiences as well. It is through this caring ethic that students become empowered, and their learning experiences become transformative and emancipatory. Although I do not reach every student, the responses from the students that I reach have helped me realize that culturally responsive teaching[1] can be effective not only for non-traditional students but also for many traditional students.

As with most Indian students, I was not encouraged by public school personnel to attend college. The high school I attended did not present college as an option for most of the Indian students—that choice was reserved for non-Indians. As a consequence, I never considered pursuing a degree in higher education and actually returned to school quite by accident. I then received an associate of arts degree and went on to receive a bachelor of science and bachelor of arts in sociology at a small regional university. Again, quite by accident, I went on to attend graduate school at Washington State University, where I earned a master's degree and doctorate in sociology. When coupled with my worldview, the circumstances under which I went to school and continued to pursue my education and learning have greatly influenced my relationships with colleagues, administrators, and students. I have a unique relationship with my colleagues; a relationship that may be uncommon for minority faculty. I received my undergraduate degree from the university at which I now teach. Most of my colleagues were my professors when I was an undergraduate. Many of these colleagues are now retiring, and it may be the case that the present dynamics of the department may soon change. This is important, because I work in a department whose attitude toward me is very paternalistic. This carries benefits but it also carries costs. On the one hand, many of my colleagues are quite helpful in providing protection and counsel as I interface with others in the system. On the other hand, I do not feel as if I have control over my own career, and I fear that I am not seen as a full-fledged member of the faculty.

Other aspects of my personal life have helped me to relate to students in a positive way. I have two children that are the same age as many of my college students; therefore, I tend to treat many of my students as if they were my children. Although that may sound somewhat maternalistic, what it means is that I often find myself spending considerable time listening and giving advice on both academic and personal issues to students, mentoring these students, keeping them on task, and offering them encouragement. This has been crucial for some students, who have told me on several occasions (even after they have graduated) that they appreciate everything that I have done for them and that they would not have graduated without my reassurance and support.

I am now a tenured faculty member at Central Washington University, the small regional university where I have been teaching for the last six years. The university is located in a rural area and has branch campuses in five urban areas. Twelve percent of the student body comes from a variety of racial and ethnic groups, but many of these students attend one of the branch campuses. When the branch campus enrollment is excluded, the share of the minority student population who attends classes on the main campus hovers around 4 percent. I teach on the main campus in a department of three women and six men. The two most recent hires in our department have been minorities. The most recent member of the department is a male colleague who has a Dominican background. The remaining faculty members in the department are non-minority. The student population from which we draw comes, almost exclusively, from small homogenous towns. The political climate of these small towns tends to be ultra-conservative, and there is a substantial contingent in this population who supports Slade Gordon. Gordon has been identified in Indian Country as the "greatest Indian fighter alive." The faculty and administration in my university are also predominantly White. Minority professors on the main campus are clustered in the assistant professor rank. The upper echelon of the university administration is composed exclusively of members of the dominant group.

Central Washington University is located in one of what are considered the Indian states. This has had a significant impact not only on how Indians are viewed in general but also on how Indians are viewed by many students. The heated controversy surrounding Indian rights within the state has escalated the intensity of the debate concerning Indian sovereignty, it has led to increased stereotyping, and it has promoted the demonization of Indian people within this state. This demonization includes assertions that Indians are ignorant and dirty and that we lack the drive to succeed. Our students are not immune from incorporating this view as part of their belief systems. I have some students in my classes who have embraced many of the denigrating stereotypes that have been presented to them by policymakers and by newspapers and other media. Some of these students, then, see me as biased, particularly when I am discussing any topic related to American Indians.

This university is on a quarter system and I teach 35 credit hours per year. The only two lower-division courses that I teach are American Society, a basic survey course that deals with the intersection of race, class, and gender within institutions in the United States, and Ethnic Awareness, the required introductory course in our Ethnic Studies minor program. The other courses that I teach are upper-division elective courses that take two paths: Social Control and Inequality. Because this is a regional university, our class size is limited. Most classes are limited to forty-five students, but enrollments in many of my courses exceed that number.

Academics within the social sciences often have the view that academia is different from the non-academic world. This is especially true when issues of ethnic, gender, and class exploitation are addressed. Those outside the system assume that earning a Ph.D. gives one license to play with the big boys. It is thought that the ivory tower is concerned more with credentials and scholarly accomplishments than with ethnic and cultural background. Unfortunately, and inexcusably, racism is alive and well even in the upper echelons of education. My experience is consistent with the findings of other minority academics, who indicate that racism is a persistent presence in higher education (Reyes and Halcon 1988). Higher education is structured by race, class, and gender and further legitimizes social practices, reinforces power relationships, and creates conditions that shape human interaction and thus the classroom experience (Bonilla-Silva 1997). Higher education is controlled by Whites, and my students often lack knowledge of the histories and cultures of minority peoples. The few students who have been exposed to information about minority people have received that information from a dominant perspective. This is particularly the case when the subject is tribal peoples. One consequence of this state of affairs is that most of my students have preconceived negative notions about Indian people.

Social statuses are inseparable determinants of social inequality. It is the interaction of race, class, and gender that complicates the issues of power and status in the classroom. In my classroom it is apparent that these statuses are interlocking dimensions of the social structure and that such statuses impact all people. It is often very difficult to get students to recognize that race, class, and gender are embedded in the social system and that an individual's group membership is related to inequality. My students commonly rely on individual factors to explain behavior rather than on institutional expectations. Students always know someone who does not fit within the parameters of my empirical evidence. Often in my American Society class, the first issue that I have to deal with is the embeddedness of race, class, and gender. Students have a difficult time recognizing that the rules are directed toward people on the basis of these statuses. In addition, students rarely understand and appreciate that social interaction is shaped by the objective and subjective meanings assigned to these statuses or that such statuses are social constructs. Because race is a salient issue in American society, we often interpret class differences as based on race. Students tend to ignore the subjective meanings associated with class and base their perception of race and gender on what they see as objective measures. This is best illustrated by what a White middle-class male student wrote in his paper:

> I just don't see how you can say that if you are a minority woman and if you are poor that you have three strikes against you. There are laws against discriminating against minorities and woman it is not how it used to be and anyway how can anyone discriminate against poor people when they choose not to work. Most minorities are poor anyway so they are protected by legislation. Anyway, look at you it doesn't seem like you were affected by being a poor Indian woman—you are a professor.

This student's response is similar to many other responses I have had early in the American Society course. As an American Indian woman professor, I am often reminded by such responses of how individuals are uniquely racialized, classed, and gendered differently and, as such, experience and interpret these categories differently.

Race, class, and gender not only have independent additive effects but also such statuses interact, overlap, and combine (Anderson and Hill Collins 1995; Omi and Wyant 1994). The racial phenomena present in the classroom are the foreseeable outcomes of the racial structure of society; they are expressed both overtly and covertly in the interactions I have with my White students. White students are accustomed to controlling both the outcome of their racial interactions and the manner in which they approach issues of race. This results in an apparent contradiction in my relationship with students. I have found that students who take my classes go through a process. Some students become very uncomfortable when they discover that I am an American Indian; such students tend to consider dropping the class to avoid any interaction. This is particularly noticeable in my classes that deal with inequality issues. Recently, a female student came to me on the third day of class and wanted to drop the class. She said that she did not think that she would get an objective picture of the status of Indians in the United States because she believed that, although I might try to present an objective view, there was no way that I could since I was Indian—just as she could not be objective about marriage because she had been a victim of domestic violence. I often encourage students to stay in the course, and they often do. The next step in the process that students go through is one of anger about the misinformation given to them in high school. Students complain that they did not know this material and ask how could they have been so misled. As the course continues, the next step can take one of two forms. One form is tremendous guilt. Students commonly feel very uncomfortable in their own skin. I had a student who watched the film *Incident at Oglala* in my Punishment and Corrections class. She came out of class in tears and said "I feel terrible because I am White; how could I not have known this?" The other reaction is anger directed, primarily, at me. Recently, in a Minority Groups class, after discussing the American Indian experience, a female student came up and asked me "Why don't you Indians just want to be participants in American Society and quit whining about the past? Then maybe you would not have to lecture about how hard they have it and we can get on with the course." I think this is an important step in the process of coming to understand issues of inequality. I make it very clear to those students that this is part of what is to be expected and that the feeling will pass and that they will, ultimately, have a clearer understanding of how inequality manifests itself in American society. Most often students respond very well to me after I offer them insights to help them understand what they are feeling.

Student resistance to the research and theories that contradict their sense of the social order is common (Moore 1997; Lee 1993; Davis 1992). Often, such students will refuse to engage the content of the course. While focusing on the section of my Criminology course that discusses issues of race and crime, one student asked: "Are all we going to talk about is minorities? This is supposed to be a class about crime!" It is important to realize that minority-group perceptions of the law are discussed under this course design for only one week. Students simply dismiss theory, research, or ideas that contradict their view of the world. In my American society class, two White males persistently questioned every statistic, theory, and idea that I presented. Both students argued that I was tolerating immoral behavior and just making excuses for "those people." Further, just as Davis (1992) and Hartung (1991) found, my students often take a blame-the-victim approach. These same two male students asked me when were we going to make "those people" take responsibility for themselves and conform to dominant society. The two males interpreted my presentation of the course material as an attack on White middle-class males.

Although overt racism is rarely exhibited (because of the perceived rewards and punishments), covert racist behavior (including the symbolic covert racism that results from the lack of internalization) is promoted by the incongruence that results when the course material and its implications are juxtaposed against a student's value system. Commonly, it is covert racism that provides the impetus for a student to challenge the authority of the course material as presented and/or for that student to then be disruptive and distract the other students. One particular student in my American Society class would specifically attack the information about the effects of institutional racism. This behavior required my devoting extra time to material that should have been relatively quick and easy. An important component of my teaching philosophy is the establishing and nurturing of a learning community, so when this particular student became disruptive to the learning of others I asked him to come into my office. While I was reluctant to discourage his participation, I believed it was imperative that his participation be constrained. My remedy for him was that he could respond in a journal to the issues that I was discussing and that I would personally respond to those issues. Although this took additional time, which would not have been required of other faculty, it was an effective method for diffusing covertly racist behavior with its inevitable impact on other students.

Evaluation of my teaching by both colleagues and students is another problematic area—a result, in part, of my teaching style. This style creates an apparent contradiction in the classroom. My approach to teaching is student-centered and non-competitive, and I have high expectations for every student. I see myself as a learner as well as a teacher. I commonly use pedagogical techniques that lead to student success. A technique I often use is to insist on participation later in the quarter rather than earlier in the quarter. This is consistent with a standard American Indian approach to learning, which is that a student listens, watches, and, when ready, participates. Much of what I do pedagogically is derived from my own cultural experience, and I have found such methods to be very effective for most students.

My pedagogical approach is based upon aspects of my own tribal values.[2] My own tribal values influence the way I approach my students as individuals and the way I approach teaching. In many ways, my pedagogical approach is simply culturally responsive teaching. One way I approach my students is as a learner. I learn as much from my students as my students learn from me. Each of my students comes to class with different experiences. Those different experiences give rise to different intellectual, physical, social, and cultural needs. To meet those needs, I often develop the sociological content of my courses by listening to the concerns that my students express during various classroom activities. This is one aspect that makes me an effective teacher, because I see students as having an interconnected self. When students are resistant to what I am trying to teach, I encourage them to help me understand their resistance. I believe my practices of emotional support, cajoling, and coaching students complement my academic demands. In essence, I care about students as whole beings. I respect them and have high expectations for them, and I often use strategies to help them fulfill those expectations. For example, I allow them to redo assignments, papers, and exams until they reach those expectations.

Although there are other subtle ways that my Indian values influence my teaching, the two most direct influences involve the concepts of competence and collaboration. In many American Indian communities, people are not put on the spot; instead they are likely to watch until they can perform (Cleary and Peacock 1988). I have found this an effective method for my students. In some of my classes, I give my students the opportunity to give a presentation. Although I present this assignment as a requirement, I will allow students to substitute some other graded instrument. Many of the male students in my class do not have a problem with presentations, but often the females, particularly the returning students, do not want to give a presentation. My practice is to ask all students to come talk to me about the presentation. At that time, I tell each student that if, at the end of the class, they still feel that they cannot give a presentation, they can do something else to replace this assignment. I have never had a student who, at the end of class, could not do the presentation. I believe this is due to the practice they get in the collaborative group projects we have in class. In many American Indian cultures, it is inappropriate to compete to be better than someone else (Locust 1988; Dumont 1972; Havinghurst 1970). I establish a non-competitive learning environment in my classroom through the use of cooperative group work. I have found that my students respond positively to the cooperative learning activities I use in each of my courses.

Other faculty sometimes assess my teaching practices as less rigorous than more traditional methods of teaching. A colleague visited my classroom for the purpose of providing a peer review. In our subsequent meeting to discuss what he observed, this colleague judged that the class interaction was disorganized and I just let students talk without raising their hands and that some of the students appeared not to be paying attention. I explained that the students are encouraged to discuss points with each other through several different modes of interaction and that I do not require them to raise their hands. They often write notes to me and each other during lectures and discussion. In addition, I do not limit my role to that of simply a lecturer. The colleague interpreted my remarks as defensive and refused to continue our discussion of teaching. During my second year teaching, a non-Indian woman was also on the faculty. She had lived and learned in the Lakota community for a number of years and had developed a different perspective. This White woman professor also came to my class to conduct a peer evaluation. Because she took the time and effort to grasp my student-centered teaching style, she was able to make some very constructive criticisms, which helped me to structure an even more effective course.

I structure my courses so that most of my students are successful. I often use a method of contract grading,[3] portfolio assessment,[4] and rubric assessment (depending on the class and number of students in the class). In preparing contracts, I am keenly aware of particular objectives I want students to meet, what content I want them to learn, the experiences I want them to have, and the quantity and quality of the work I want them to produce. I also support my students in their acquisition of feelings of self-determination and in establishing ownership of their own learning. I require several written projects in my courses. Students are allowed to rewrite as often as necessary in order to achieve their own goals. The contradictions in the way my courses are evaluated by colleagues and by students can be attributed to my nontraditional pedagogical style. Consistent with previous research (Boice 1993), I have found that those members of the faculty who see my courses as less rigorous than other courses tend to explain away positive student evaluations by saying "Well, you know they like her and her classes are not very hard." My courses are in great demand, but often students who have not taken any of my courses mistakenly believe that I am an "easy mark." It is not until they take the course and learn to assume the responsibility for their own knowledge acquisition that they begin to discover the empowerment that education can provide. One particular student sums it up well:

> When I first took your course I took it because I heard that it was an easy course and
> you essentially got to do what you wanted. What I discovered is that I could learn
> and that learning could be fun and did not have to be a drag. I was really uncomfort-
> able with learning about racism and got very angry in the beginning, but as you
> taught us to take responsibility for our own learning process, I began to see that I
> could change it and apply it to other aspects of my life.

I am one of two Indian women in a tenure-track position on this university's main campus. We are each at the bottom of the ranks in the division of
labor. Even in the academic world, which is often seen as different from the
world outside of academia, there are glass ceilings and glass walls. The
courses that I am asked to teach and the program that I am asked to direct
require more work and are not part of the roster of required courses. When
the director of our ethnic studies program took a position at another university (we only offer an ethnic studies minor), I was the first person that the sociology faculty asked to run the program. The ethnic studies department at
our university is housed within the sociology department. I am continually
asked to teach the classes that deal with minority issues, and I have been expected to advise more students than any other colleague in the sociology department. This has consequences for my workload, which, in turn, has
consequences for my relationships with students.

I don't mean to imply that every student thinks that I am wonderful and
that I reach them all. On occasion, there are different standards of performance and evaluation by both faculty and students. Typically, evaluations are
based on student expectations, which may vary according to perceived power
and prestige. When anonymous student evaluations have been requested,
there have been occurrences of both covert and overt racism toward me.
Typically, such racism happens when the key content of a course has been
oppression or if an evaluation has been requested after a section in a course
in which I have discussed race, class, and/or gender. There are several clear
examples of such occurrences that relate to the intersection of race and class.
These anonymous written student evaluations[5] reflect the backlash surrounding issues of race and class (Baker and Copp 1997). During my first
year here, I taught a social problems class in which we discussed the issue of
using Native American names for sports teams and mascots. In one of my
course evaluations, a student wrote: "You should go back to the reservation
where you belong, you cannot teach students about anything with your ignorant, savage ways." In a criminology course in which I discussed issues of class
and crime, race and crime, and gender and crime using several personal experiences, another student wrote: "You should not let some lower class person
teach college." This student reaction was a result of the expectations some

students have of faculty behavior. In general, as long as I behave according to how students expect me to behave, I get fairly good evaluations, but when student expectations do not mesh with student perceptions of a faculty's behavior, then the student is more likely to give lower evaluations. Students tend to believe that professors are of the upper class, and when that belief is called into question, it can undermine my professorial authority. I have found this to be particularly true when teaching courses that challenge students' belief systems.

My experience has been that *when* I elicit feedback from students determines the content of their responses: Early in the semester feedback tends to be negative, while later in the semester feedback is often more positive. Early in the course I encourage my students to identify how they believe professors should act. I allow a great deal of freedom in my courses, and students are encouraged to say what they think. Most students do exercise this prerogative, in part because I establish a norm of mutual respect and tolerance for the broad range of human cultures and ideas, including ethnic and racial differences. This stance assures that students know that their intellectual explanations are grounded within a safe environment. Early in the course students often tell me that by reporting on the empirical information regarding different racial groups I am just skewing statistics and overreacting, being offensive, and blaming White people for all of the problems in society. Usually attitudes change by the end of the quarter—although not always. On occasion, because our department assigns a minority faculty member to teach courses dealing with inequality (and no one else in the department has an interest in such courses), student anger is promoted. Perhaps if students were able to enroll in an inequality course taught by a non-minority person they would be able to see that the course material is much the same—regardless of the ethnicity or race of the faculty person.

My credentials are on occasion challenged—by both colleagues and students. In part, this may be a result of my pedagogy. This does not happen overtly but covertly. When it happens, it is ignored by those who do not experience it directly or denied by those who contribute to it. Students often refer to me as "Miss Cleary." Those same students refer to all my colleagues, both men and women, as "Doctor _____." Some of this may be a result of my approachability, but much of it is attributable to the fact that they do not expect me, as an Indian woman, to have a doctorate, and many are quite surprised that I do.

My colleagues are also covert in the challenge to my credentials, which is really just a matter of their perception that I am a token. When I was hired, I was what this university calls an "opportunity hire." Now six years later, I have some colleagues who refer to me as the "opportunity hire"—implying that I do not have the credentials to have been hired as a regular hire. So my experience as a member of my department is unlike the experience of any other member. My experience is supported by the findings of Calasanti, Witt, and Witt (1998) who discuss the fact that the experiences of individuals in the same occupation and even in the same organization differ according to various social statuses. I suspect that I will always be known as the "little Indian girl" who is the "opportunity hire." According to Steele (1997), a feature of tokenism is that when negative stereotypes exist about a particular group, then members of that group often fear being reduced to the stereotype. This aspect of tokenism not only impacts on my ability to interact with students but also it seems as if I always have to be on guard much more than other faculty. If we attend a function that serves alcohol and I have a drink, I have to be careful, or faculty find it reason to reinforce their stereotypes and share those stereotypes with students. On one particular occasion, I was drinking alcohol at the department Christmas party and a fellow faculty member told a student that they had to watch me and make sure that I did not drink too much because "you know how Indians are, it's a genetic thing." Although meant as a joke, I feel that such remarks (in this case, a warning, really) certainly contribute to the undermining of my credentials and abilities and to the perpetuation of a stereotype. Often humor is used to identify, define, and reproduce statuses in the social structure. This may be done without an intent to harm, but it is, nonetheless, a perpetuation of racism.

A consequence of tokenism is typecasting. I genuinely care about students and want to mentor them. The minority students either seek me out or they are told to request me as an advisor. For example, one student mentioned to a faculty member that he was Native American, and instead of asking the student what his/her interests were the faculty member replied "Oh we have a Native American; you should go see her." This workload affects my interactions with students because the more students I have, the harder I work and the less time I have available to devote to each student. The less time I have to devote to each student, the more other faculty see me as not available to students. It becomes a catch-22. I am evaluated on the basis of how much I interact with students, it takes time to interact with each student, the more students I have the less time I have to devote to each student, the student complains to other faculty that I don't have as much time to give them as they would like, so I am criticized for being unavailable to students. In addition, other faculty and university requirements interfere with the time I have available to students. I am the minority representative on several search committees (there are so few in the pool to draw from and, after all, I fill two categories).

As is common with many minority faculty, I am called upon to be the expert on all Indian issues. Because this unreasonable expectation persists, I then feel pressure to learn about all aspects of Indian/non-Indian relationships. This takes additional time away from teaching and interacting with students. I have also noticed the one-minority-per-pot syndrome (Reyes and Halcon 1988) cropping up repeatedly in several search committees. When faculty searches are conducted, the covert racism is apparent. This phenomenon supports McComb (1989), who found that not only do White faculty believe that the entrance of minority personnel in academia affects departments but that this "invasion" will impact negatively on the academic integrity of the United States.

My interactions with students both inside and outside the classroom are also affected by my research interests. There is an assumption that my research and teaching interests deal with my experiences as a member of a minority group. While to some extent this is true, my research time is limited because of the courses I teach. There is not enough time in the day to teach and advise the number of students that I am expected to advise, serve on the committees on which I am expected to serve, keep up to date on course content, conduct research on minority issues, and do the other research in which I am interested. I am then evaluated on the basis of the courses that I teach and the service I do (which is primarily connected to the Indian community).

I have already addressed some of the ways that I deal with the covert racism that occurs in the interaction in the classroom and broader department level. I have found several other things to be very effective in improving my pedagogical methods. I learned very early in my teaching career that if I was going to teach about the experiences of all groups, I had to recognize that I grew up in an area that was Indian and White but had no other racial or ethnic groups and, as a result, I too have preconceived notions. Once I came to this conclusion, I began to clarify my own attitudes toward various groups. I admit to my students that I am as biased as they are. I do try to point out to them that every professor they meet is expounding their own views, even if such views are grounded in the literature, and what I am trying to do is bring balance to a system that has been unbalanced.

Even though I have had experience as an Indian woman, I do not have experience as an African American woman or an Asian American woman or a Hispanic woman. Therefore, I judge that it is important for me to include several guest speakers who can speak from personal experience and to select authors for students to read from those groups. These various mechanisms, among others, affect the interactions I have with students in the classroom. I have had some students who participated in the entire class, hated every minute of it, challenged everything that I said, and gave me terrible anonymous evaluations. But I have also had students in my class who made a significant change in ten weeks and came to understand their contributions to the perpetuation of inequality. These students began to step out of their own social milieu, to be critical of the world around them, and to question their preconceived notions of how the world is. This is why I continue to teach. I teach because I really, genuinely like and care for students. I am pleased when I get through to just one student and make a difference in that student's life since that person, in turn, affects another person's life. The most satisfying experience that I have had as a teacher was the contact that I had with a student who graduated from our department three years ago and recently sent me an e-mail.

> I don't know if you remember me but I took your American society class. I just wanted you to know that although while I took the class I hated it and thought that you were just another one of the whining bleeding heart liberals who misinterpreted data for your own gain and made excuses for your own people's poverty and other social problems. I have to e-mail you and tell you that although I did not realize it until I was out of school for about a year and began to look at the world around me that I learned so much in your class and am a better person for it.

It is because of the students who have kept in contact with me over the years, who send me information to use in my classes, who have just kept me current on what they are doing, or who have proudly demonstrated that they have had a positive impact on others that I keep teaching through what sometimes can seem like the darkest hour. But, as my student's e-mail suggests, sometimes the most stubborn students are affected, even though belatedly, by something said in class.

Delores Black-Connor Cleary is an Associate Professor at Central Washington University. She is an Okanogan-Colville born and raised on the Colville Confederated Tribes Reservation in northeast Washington state. She has taught at Central Washington University for five years in the areas of social inequality and social control. She is also the director of the Ethnic Studies program. She teaches social stratification courses, race and ethnicity courses, and social control courses. Her research interests include Native American issues, poverty, militarization of the police, and social psychology. She received a grant from the Institute of Public Media Arts to create an interdisciplinary year-long course on "isms" that included the use of autobiography and video. She has also received Indian Education (Title IX/JOM) grants for the Ellensburg School District, and she serves as chair of the Indian education parent committee.

Notes

1. Culturally responsive teaching has risen as a result of the interest in multicultural education. I would argue that culturally responsive teaching is a more effective pedagogy not only for minority students but also for students from the dominant group. For more information about culturally responsive teaching see *Culturally Responsive Teaching* by Geneva Gay (2000).

2. It is important to recognize that there is great diversity within Native America and therefore there is not one set of values. For a discussion of American Indian values see *Voices of Native America*, edited by Dr. Hap Gilliland (1997).

3. In a contract graded course, I lay out several options students can use to meet the objectives of the course, and students then construct their own course requirements to meet those objectives.

4. In those classes where I have students produce a portfolio, students are required to submit several written assignments, course responses, essay exams, and their own self-assessment. Students are also given a pre-essay question to answer and retake the same essay question at the end of the quarter.

5. Evaluation forms that are used at this university are given anonymously by someone other than the faculty person teaching the class. They are later summarized and returned to the department, where the secretary types up all of the comments and returns the summarized quantitative scores and qualitative statements to the faculty member.

Works Cited

Anderson, M., and P. Hill Collins. 1995. *Race, Class, and Gender: An Anthology*. 2nd ed. Belmont, CA: Wadsworth Publishing.

Baker, P., and M. Copp. 1997. "Gender Matters Most: The Interactions of Gendered Expectations, Feminist Course Content and Pregnancy in Student Course Evaluations." *Teaching Sociology* 25 (1): 29–43.

Boice, R. 1993. "New Faculty Involvement for Women and Minorities." *Research in Higher Education* 34 (3): 328.

Bonilla-Silva, E. 1997. "Rethinking Racism: Toward a Structural Interpretation." *American Sociological Review* 62 (3): 465–480.

Calasanti, T. M., S. Witt, and J. Witt. 1998. "A Critical Evaluation of the Experiences of Women and Minority Faculty: Some Implications for Occupational Research." *Current Research of Occupations and Professions* 10: 239–258.

Cleary, L., and T. Peacock. 1988. *Collected Wisdom: American Indian Education*. New York: Allyn & Bacon.

Davis, N. J. 1992. "Teaching about Inequality: Student Resistance, Paralysis, and Rage." *Teaching Sociology* 20 (3): 232–238.

Dumont, R. V. 1972. "Learning English and How to Be Silent: Studies in Sioux and Cherokee Classrooms." In *Function of Language in the Classroom*, edited by C. Cazden, V. John and D. Hymes. New York: Teachers College Press.

Gay, G. 2000. *Culturally Responsive Teaching*. New York: Teachers College, Columbia University.

Gilliland, H., ed. 1997. *"Voices of Native America: Native American Ideas, Ideals, Values, and Guides for Living as Expressed by American Indians, Past and Present, Famous and Unknown, and a Few Others: Including a Fable for Americans.* Dubuque, IA: Kendall/HuntPub.

Hartung, B. 1991. "Unstratifying Stratification: Teaching Race, Gender, and Class." *Teaching Sociology* 19: 66–69.

Havinghurst, R. J. 1970. *National Study of American Indian Education.* Washington DC: Office of Education.

Lee, J. 1993. "Teaching Gender Politics." *Teaching Sociology* 21 (2): 26–32.

Locust, C. 1988. "Wounding the Spirit: Discrimination and Traditional Indian Belief Systems." *Harvard Educational Review* 58 (3).

McComb, H. 1989. "The Dynamics and Impact of Minority Processes on Higher Education, the Curriculum, and Black Women." *Sex Roles* 21: 127–144.

Moore, M. 1997. "Biased and Political Student Perceptions of Females Teaching About Gender." *College Student Journal* 31 (4): 434–444.

Omi, M., and H. Wyant. 1994. *Racial Formation in the United States.* New York: Routledge.

Reyes, M. L., and J. J. Halcon. 1988. "Racism in Academia: The Old Wolf Revisited." *Harvard Educational Review* 58 (3): 299–314.

Steele, C. 1997. "A Threat in the Air: How Stereotypes Shape Intellectual Identity and Performance." *The American Psychologist* 52 (6): 613.

CHAPTER TWELVE

Pushing Beyond the Stereotypes and Fostering Collaboration: One Sistuh's Approach to Teaching Media Production

ZEINABU IRENE DAVIS

Abstract

AS AN AFRICAN American independent filmmaker and woman professor, I have been teaching media production at predominantly White campuses for over a decade. Teaching media production presupposes a model that is hierarchical. This model is not always the best for my students, and it is not the pattern for my own media work. I try to convey to students a collaborative approach that includes an analysis of stereotypes and the creation of alternative media images. This chapter focuses on my teaching experiences and the techniques I use to impart this perspective and my abilities to survive academia as an artist and professor.

I am an independent filmmaker who happens to teach in the university setting. I have been making films for the past eighteen years, working on dramas, documentaries, and experimental projects that primarily focus on the lives of African American women. I have been teaching in higher education for over a decade. In this chapter, I will detail how I approach the teaching of media theory and production through a methodology that emphasizes constant analyses of stereotypes and the production of media images from the perspective of a person who is engaged in making alternative media. Since I teach technical information, much of my instruction needs to take a hands-on approach that allows me to break down hierarchical notions of power within media production and to offer a model to students that emphasizes collaboration.

Personal History

Since my field is fairly new and my position still relatively unusual, it is necessary for me to provide some background on my personal history and the development of Black independent film in the United States. I was born in the early 1960s and am the child of working-class parents who raised me in Philadelphia, Pennsylvania. Neither of my parents completed college degrees, but they instilled a strong value for education within the family. My father and I were very close, and though he worked as a bakery laborer, he was an amateur photographer and former sailor who loved learning about new places and people. As I came of age in the 1960s and 1970s, my parents felt that I would receive a better education in Catholic schools, which I attended from first through twelfth grades. I was fortunate to attend college prep programs during the summer months in high school and became familiar with Ivy League institutions. I attended Brown University, and in 1979, I became the first on my father's side of the family to graduate from college. I was influenced to become a filmmaker by my college experiences, which included working at a public television station and the ABC affiliate in Providence, Rhode Island. However, studying abroad in Kenya, East Africa, was the single most important event that transformed my life and pushed me to become a filmmaker.[1]

In order to achieve my goal as a film director, it was essential that I attend a graduate program. Opportunities for young minority people to apprentice on major film productions are extremely limited now and were nearly non-existent in the early 1980s. I chose to attend UCLA's film program because it was a state school and the tuition was cheaper than it would be at a private institution such as New York University.[2] UCLA was also the base of an established a group of filmmakers known as the members of the LA Rebellion. Although the LA Rebellion filmmakers are thought to be primarily African American, in truth, it was a group of students of various races, ethnicities, and class backgrounds who were dedicated to fostering social change with their filmmaking. (Other filmmakers in this group include Montezuma Esparza, Gregory Nava, and key members of Visual Communications, an Asian Pacific Media Arts Center in Los Angeles.)

Graduate school was quite difficult for me. I was the only African American woman in my class, and for most of the time I was in school, there were not more than five African American graduate students at any given moment. Many times I turned to the LA Rebellion filmmakers for guidance and support. In particular, filmmakers such as Charles Burnett and Julie Dash provided mentorship and taught me how to create an atmosphere on a film set so that everyone who was working felt like they were truly a part of the project. By contrast, many times on Hollywood productions, the director gets to know the actors but not the production crew members who work so hard to make the director look good. This approach sometimes creates a rift between the cast and crew or the director and the rest of the crew. My filmmaking approach is to make the experience feel more like a family gathered together to make that most African of African American dishes, the stew called gumbo. The more help you have with "specialists" who prepare different aspects of the gumbo and pull it all together, the better it is.

During my time at UCLA, I was extremely fortunate to find a friend and then husband in Marc Arthur Chéry, with whom I have collaborated on several film projects (*Compensation, Mother of the River,* and *A Powerful Thang*). Marc writes the screenplays, I write the grants and direct. Being an independent filmmaker means that my films are primarily funded through my own means. Usually I cobble together funding from a portion of my salary as a professor and a variety of other sources—public and private grants, in-kind services from local businesses and artisans, use of equipment from the university and schemes such as T-shirt sales, bake sales, fund-raising letter campaigns, and so forth. Although I primarily work on my films full time in the summer, it generally takes several years to complete a project since the process of fund-raising is so time consuming.

Black Film History

African Americans began making films independently as early as 1911–1913 with the production of a short ten-minute film called *The Railroad Porter* by William Foster of Chicago. Early African American filmmakers include the Johnson Brothers with the Lincoln Motion Picture Company, actor/director Spencer Williams, and the most famous of them all, Oscar Micheaux, who wrote, produced, and directed more than forty films. Unfortunately, most of these films and much of this film history has been lost or not adequately documented. Black women also made movies, but their work is even more difficult to uncover. Women such as Madame C. J. Walker and Zora Neale Hurston made films as a part of their businesses or fieldwork, but there were other Black women filmmakers who we are just now beginning to uncover.[3]

Black women did not begin to develop a large body of work in filmmaking until after the 1960s. In fact, most of the twenty-five feature films done by Black women filmmakers were made after 1980. Most of these feature films have not had much national distribution, despite performing well on the festival circuit and garnering good reviews. Along with White and other women filmmakers, regardless of genre, most Black women filmmakers only make one film. To date, of the Black women who make dramatic feature films, none has yet been able to release a follow-up feature. Therefore it is pretty reasonable to state that Black women filmmakers currently working in the field can be seen as pioneers.

Being among this group of women is both exciting and frustrating. Knowing both the work and the films of fellow Black women filmmakers allows me to be an advocate and spread the word among students and the larger public. I give lectures on Black women's filmmaking for universities, public libraries, schools, and other community groups. I know that by example I have encouraged my students and others to become filmmakers or be actively involved in media production. My frustrations come with the acknowledgment that Black women's films are not accepted by the mainstream and that they are frequently labeled "too experimental or uncommercial" to actually be allowed the opportunity to reach audiences. Like other alternative media artists, Black filmmakers are implicitly expected to be producers, directors, and distributors of their works. This juggling act works for some people, but the cost both economically and emotionally is high. Energy is spent on promoting a film when it could be placed in developing new projects and making more films.

Artistic Philosophy

It would be more financially advantageous to me to make commercial, mainstream cinema. However, this would mean working on projects that continue to maintain the status quo and do not expand the vision of who we are as Americans. Certainly mass media has come very far from the limited notions of African American women as the mammy, the emasculating bitch, the tragic mulatto, and the asexual sidekick. Yet the current marketplace continues to construct images of African American women as welfare queens or bitches and 'hos. As an African American woman, I feel a strong affinity for and sense of responsibility in depicting broader images of women of African descent. At the core of nearly all my films is the expression of the lives of women of African descent, women whose lives are rarely portrayed in popular media—voodoo practitioners, slave women and girls, female jazz instrumentalists, politically radical women, and middle-class single mothers. I have been persistent and lucky enough to consistently produce award-winning works, including *Compensation* (1999), *Mother of the River* (1995), *A Powerful Thang* (1992), *A Period Piece* (1991), *Cycles* (1989), *Trumpetistically Clora Bryant* (1989), *Crocodile Conspiracy* (1986), and *Recreating Black Women's Media Im-*

age (1983).[4] Through my work, I attempt to alter and diversify the terrain of mass media in this country, thereby expanding visions and horizons. My focus is decidedly on women's experiences, whether the aesthetic concerns revolve around various cultural and social issues such as racism, AIDS, or problems within the Deaf community.

Through viewing my films, one can see a concern and love for literature and folklore, the centering of women at the core of the narrative, attention to detail in the production design that highlights an African diaspora aesthetic, and, finally, a gentle touch of humor. Although my work comes from a distinct personal and cultural perspective, the human experiences and emotional tones rendered in my films and videos reach a broad-based audience. I am motivated to continue my work by my ongoing anger with the stupidity of gender and racial stereotypes that Hollywood still inculcates. I am often inspired by my contact with audiences, who tell me what they like and do not like about my films and what they would like to see on film.

Through the influence of my worldwise father, my college experience, and the time I spent living in Kenya, I became very interested in the idea of pan-Africanism, which globally connects people of African descent through culture and experience. For years, it was generally taught that the enslaved Africans who were brought to the Americas did not retain any of their traditions because they were from various languages and culture groups, which prohibited them from communicating with each other. Another theory states that the institution of slavery eradicated African culture. Neither theory is true. As a result of slavery, African cultures in the Americas have absorbed influences from various European and Native American cultures, mixing and retaining elements from all. Since cinema history in the United States so often begins with racist ideologies, which were promoted most virulently in *Birth of a Nation* (1915), it is fitting that Black filmmakers should create our own cinema history, a history that explores and challenges how this syncretism of African American culture has taken place.

These experiences have taught me to be open to whole new communities of people and ways of communicating. They have further instilled in me a desire to use film and video more visually as an art form, because spoken words often get in the way of reaching others, especially those who are Deaf or speak a different language. Cinema can and does cross borders.

My Teaching Career

After I completed my M.F.A. degree, my husband and I moved to a small private college, Antioch College, in Yellow Springs, Ohio. A place widely known for students with liberal politics and a work-study curriculum,

Antioch was an ideal place to start my teaching career. A wonderful educator, Bob Devine, heavily mentored me as a teacher, and public funding for my filmmaking pursuits was available there. My students at Antioch College were a freewheeling bunch; they were as likely to make experimental abstract pieces about the beauty of raw meat as they were likely to make a socially conscious documentary about mineworkers in nearby Appalachia. However, Yellow Springs is a very small town of 5,000 people with very few young African American couples—we craved urban life and interaction with a larger, more diverse Black community.

One of the things I disliked the most about Yellow Springs was the lack of privacy faculty had. Due to the close-knit nature of the town and the school, a professor was always considered to be accessible to the students. I once had a student come in the supermarket with a camera at midnight asking me how to load it with film just as I was trying to get my premenstrual chocolate and potato chip groove on. I don't think my race or gender had anything to do with why this student approached me; he would have cornered whoever he saw. The point is that by the nature of the discipline, students feel that you are always on call as a media instructor. One of the ways I feel I have succeeded as an artist and professor is that I make sure that there is an emotional distance between my life as an artist and my life as a professor. I could not effectively achieve this at Antioch College.

After two years, we moved to Northwestern University, a Big Ten research university located just north of Chicago in the suburb of Evanston. I taught there for eight years and earned tenure during my time there. Northwestern University was generally less bureaucratic and had more equipment and facilities compared to the public university where I now teach. The students at my former institution were fairly homogeneous, despite some racial diversity. They all seemed to go to the same high schools and college prep programs. Very few of them were actually from Chicago. These students were very bright and articulate; however, they frequently harbored a grand sense of entitlement that was sometimes very difficult to take. There were times when it seemed that students wanted me to teach them how to make films and then actually make the films for them too. This was often an unstated tension that developed between myself and certain kinds of students. I always imagined that these students were children from Chicago's upper-crust North Shore, the kind of pampered children who were taken care of by a Black nanny in their youth—was I seen as an extension of this childhood experience?

I wanted to teach at a public university so that I could influence a broader range of students across different class and ethnic backgrounds.

UCSD meets this desire in some ways—the class backgrounds of the students are somewhat more varied than I am used to, but the population of students of color on campus is quite low and no different than what I have experienced in private institutions. The numbers of African American and Latino students are quite miniscule; in fact in an African cinema class of sixty students in Spring 2000, I had only three African Americans, all of them men. On the other hand, the Asian American populations are quite diverse—they include Chinese, Japanese, Vietnamese, Indian, Thai, Hmong, Laotian, Samoan, and Filipino. The minority population of the entire University of California system was decimated by the results of Proposition 209, which effectively wiped out affirmation action programs.[5]

The UCSD Experience

For the last two years, I have been teaching at a large public research institution, the University of California, San Diego. In the summer of 2000, I was promoted to the rank of full professor. I am one of three African American women in my field who has achieved this status. Although the school is located in the San Diego area, it is actually in La Jolla, a very exclusive area. The campus is beautifully landscaped and sits on a bluff overlooking the Pacific Ocean, but at the same time, public transportation to the university is quite limited, thereby keeping many local students without cars (who are often people of color) effectively barred from campus.

At UCSD, I teach in the communication department. The department is an amalgamation of interdisciplinary approaches. We are linguists, social scientists, political economists, and media makers. I am the only permanent African American faculty member; we sometimes employ another African American woman as an adjunct to teach public relations. There are two other women of color as faculty; one is from India and teaches the political economy of communication, and the other is a Latina in the area of human information processing whose research focuses on bilingual education. I primarily teach production or methods courses and usually teach one film theory/history course per year. We are on the quarter system in which classes last ten weeks, so there are three quarters in the course of the regular academic year that move very quickly. Sometimes courses are designed so that students begin a project in one quarter and then finish it in the next. In my department, the faculty teaches two quarters per year and usually two courses per quarter. However, we frequently have group and independent studies and internship students, so it can feel like you are teaching five classes.

Currently our department is quite burdened with over 800 majors and only twenty-one faculty. Our students do not major in production, but certainly there is a heavy demand for production courses and there are currently only three faculty who teach those courses. Class size depends on the course, but in general the production courses have to be small because of the limitations of the equipment. The advanced production courses usually have about twenty students, while the history/theory courses have much larger enrollments of sixty and above; it is not uncommon to have undergraduate courses with enrollments of 200. I have taught courses on documentary video production, sound design, film/video, non-linear or computer-based editing, film theory, and history courses such as African and pan-African cinema. In the production courses, I generally have one or two Black students, perhaps three or four Latino students, and about five or six Asian American students of various ethnicities. My larger theory and history courses, such as African Cinema, have generally had two or three Black students, a few Latinos, and at least ten to fifteen Asian American students out of a class of sixty students.

Most of my students are White, evenly distributed between male and female students. Many of them come from the Bay Area or Los Angeles; very few are actually from San Diego. These students are generally from solid middle-class backgrounds, although some students are wealthier than others. Many of the students work full-time jobs, although it is not usually because they need the money to stay in school. More often than not, it is usually to pursue the California lifestyle of buying and maintaining a car along with expensive automobile insurance. This situation sometimes saddens me. These students are so busy just going to classes and working that they do not get to enjoy or partake in other activities that college life has to offer such as attending presentations by guest speakers or engaging in campus politics or community life in San Diego.

I work with graduate students on both the M.F.A. and Ph.D. levels. I "moonlight" as an advisor to M.F.A. students in the visual arts department (my department does not grant this degree) and sit on the committees of several Ph.D. candidates, most of whom are incorporating some media production in their thesis. Most of my students at this level have been Black and/or women. These are generally my most time-consuming student relationships, but more often than not they are the most rewarding relationships. Nearly all of my former graduate students are now in academia and are doing quite well. I am happy at the thought that their graduate degree road was a little easier than mine was because I was there.

Teaching "Tech"

As a practicing filmmaker and university professor, I am often very different than many of my White male colleagues, who are generally more technically oriented than I am. Several male colleagues have been technical people in the film industry—cameramen or sound recordists usually. I classify my technical area of expertise as a director, but when I work on other peoples' productions I frequently record sound. However, my attitude toward media production is to be a jack-of-all-trades and a master of none. I need to know enough so that when I hire crew people I know what they can and cannot do for my own productions, but I do not feel that I have to be an expert on the latest camera or sound techniques.

Perhaps my male colleagues' propensity to be "techs" reveals a social pattern related to gender roles. According to the history of technology, prestige is conferred to those who know how to play with the "toys"; holistic and more generalist approaches that are used by women are frequently dismissed and not considered to be legitimate. Yet the experiences of my friends in the media industry often remind me that the contemporary directors who are constantly working are the ones who have a more generalist approach. Anyone can learn technique or how to play with the toys. The question remains: Do you know what to do with the toys once you get them?

My generalist approach allows for students to explore a variety of paths. I stress storytelling skills, basic writing and communication and an ability to collaborate with others. I encourage those who get excited by a particular field to become experts or specialists. Similarly, I encounter many students who consider filmmaking and videomaking to be a means to a lucrative career and lifestyle. Many of them want to work in Hollywood. I encourage those students to follow those dreams as well. I relate my personal experiences of working in the industry and let them know that I am happier being an independent filmmaker.

Production courses are limited to small enrollments because of equipment limitations. Undergraduate students usually are not permitted to make projects on their own until they reach senior status and even then only under unusual circumstances. Therefore, most students in the production courses must work in groups. In order for the groups to work well, there must be a certain degree of cooperation, respect, and, most important, a spirit of collaboration. Fostering collaboration is not the easiest way to teach production. Most teachers let the students figure out groups on their own. Since I cannot and do not want to micromanage student projects, I do not determine groups for the final projects done outside class time. However, when the students are in the beginning stages of learning the equipment in the classroom, I do determine who is in the groups and how they handle the equipment among themselves.

I am very careful to make sure that all of the students actually handle the equipment, particularly the cameras, and that each of them takes turns being the director, the camera person, the sound person and so on. I sometimes have to force the women and minority students to take the lead and pick up the equipment, but once I create an atmosphere where they know that they have to do this, they usually participate eagerly. This sometimes slows the process of doing the projects, and we sometimes don't get as far as I would like with technical skills during the class periods, but what this work does foster is more important than learning what a piece of equipment can do. Many people can read a manual and learn how to operate a camera. Yet few people can communicate to a group of people as a crew and get their vision captured on a piece of celluloid or videotape. I am teaching the students to work with each other, to practice their communication skills, to develop their relationships with each other, and to be patient with the process of creativity. For me, these are essential values that a good liberal arts education can impart.

My challenges in the classroom seem to be at the extremes—students who are know-it-alls or technophobes. Since I work and teach in a medium that is very popular, students often come to the classroom very cocky and think that since they have seen films all their lives they already know how to make them. These students, who are often (but not always) White male students, feel that as their professor I am standing in their way. I'm just an obstacle between them and the "toys," the equipment. Some of these students deliberately try not to take core production classes from me because they feel that they will not get enough of the technical information that they crave. They would rather take courses from the more technically oriented (read White male) instructors.

These types of students can be very disruptive in the classroom. They act bored during lectures or ask questions about technical topics that are much farther along in the course. Depending on the personality, there are several ways to deal with this type of student. If it is just one student, I usually try to take the student aside and see what the student really knows and what their background is. If they don't have the familiarity with the equipment that they say they do, then we discuss who their favorite director is. Usually they say someone who has been making films for a long time or someone who went to film school. I point out that there is no such thing as an "overnight" filmmaker—it takes many years of study and many production experiences to be a good director, producer, and so forth. If there are several students who come to class with this attitude, then I try to enlist them as informal teaching assistants. I pair them up with the other extreme of my students—those who are terrified of using the equipment. Frequently these groups of students are female and minority students. When these "technophobes" are self-identified or recognized by the teacher assistant, I try to speak with them outside the class and make sure that they are comfortable with the equipment. This is sometimes a fine line to walk, as the students may sometimes become too needy and dependent and want hand-holding through the entire filmmaking process. This often requires a great deal of diplomacy and reassuring the students that they can't really break the equipment by merely touching it. I tell them it is okay to make mistakes—that is why they are in school.

Media Literacy and a Worldview

In most all of my media courses, both production and theory, I teach media literacy—how to be critical and understand how the media works. I spend an entire class session or more on the discussion of stereotypes and popular images of Americans in mainstream media. I am very careful to explain to the students that we all have both positive and negative stereotypes ingrained in our psyches and that my classroom is a place to explore and address how we have come to some of these opinions and visions of others and ourselves. This is often a very tense experience for students, since they don't want to be labeled or thought of as racist, sexist, or just plain stupid. Sometimes students volunteer images and information freely and sometimes I have to coax them. But once they get into the process of analyzing and exploring these images, they usually cannot stop talking. Occasionally when some of the images are painful to discuss I will also bring in my own prejudices and stereotypes that I harbor about certain people. This often makes me feel very vulnerable, but my attitude is that I can't ask students to do something that I would not do myself. More often than not, my honesty is appreciated and not taken advantage of.

Another asset that I bring to the campus as a woman of color teaching is that I firmly believe in promulgating a global worldview. We are not just Black, White, Native, Asian, or Latino—we are also world citizens, and as such we are obligated to try to learn about others on the international scene and seek to understand multiple lives and experiences. Since it was so important in my own development, I actively and openly promote study-abroad experiences in all my classes.

When I teach a course on film history, students do not see just the Hollywood or American "classics" in my classroom. Students may see the classics in an excerpted form, but I take the opportunity to expose them to another cinema entirely that illustrates the technique or formal convention that I am trying to convey. Most media courses have a discussion of color and lighting.

Most cinema history courses in the United States overemphasize American cinema and will show you examples of color film from *The Wizard of Oz* (1939)or *Meet Me in St. Louis* (1945). My course on the same topic reveals that the use of color is very different among the national cinemas of the world. It is my obligation to take the opportunity to discuss the use of color from other cultures; I like to use examples from West African filmmakers such as Djibril Diop Mambety (*Hyenas* [1992]) and Chinese directors such as Zhang Yimou (*Red Sorghum* [1989]).

My own filmmaking is influenced by and borrows from world cinema, particularly filmmakers from Africa and the African diaspora. Many African filmmakers must communicate through their visuals rather than through dialogue, since there are so many languages that may be spoken in just one country. Master filmmakers such as Safi Faye, Souleymane Cisse, and Djibril Diop Mambety employ strong visuals rather than the spoken word to advance the plot, and thus this technique is important to me. My notion of pan-Africanism and its influence on my work is accepted by most of my students who appreciate the exposure to cultures much different than their own. Many students have commented that seeing the work of African filmmakers and my own filmmaking makes theory and technique more practical and con-crete to them. They are exposed to new ways of thinking about cinema, and some of them go on to take other world cinema courses and actively seek out foreign film.

Perception and Establishing Authority

Since I am fairly young and am still frequently mistaken as a graduate stu-dent, one of the most powerful ways that I have found to establish authority is to wear a blazer or suitcoat. I also tend to wear pants on teaching days, since I never know if I will need to hold the camera in my lap and cradle it with my legs or get down on the floor to demonstrate the proper procedures in changing the bulb of an expensive lighting instrument. After twelve years of Catholic school, the idea of a uniform has been ingrained in me. My cur-rent "uniform" consists of a brightly colored blazer; an African-print tunic, silk blouse, or T-shirt (depending on what I'm teaching and if there is a fac-ulty meeting); black jeans; and black fitness shoes. For most of my teaching career, I wore my hair in dredlocks—it never created a problem for anyone on campus. In fact, it may have made me seem more "cool" to some students. Currently my hair is in a short Afro, which seems to be the dominant style among Black women professors at my school. In general, I think that my looks make me appear approachable to students. My office hours are usually filled to the brim with students of all types wanting to get into the film industry or film school, visiting foreign students interested in studying American film, gay and lesbian students, and older, returning students who are just looking for a friendly face. In particular, I enjoy teaching my audio production course because I make the students do listening exercises and I sometimes get to hear new music that I may not have been exposed to. Teaching is a mutually beneficial experience—I learn from my students as much as they learn from me.

It is also important that I develop a good relationship with the people who are running the equipment room where the students go to check out the gear to make their projects. Again, this relationship solidifies my approach of collaboration. I frequently check with the equipment managers to make sure that my students are maintaining the equipment properly and to get suggestions from them on what new equipment we might obtain to improve the curriculum. Since I am not a technical expert, it is helpful for me to enlist the assistance of the equipment room staff as much as possible and to treat them with respect. I invite them to my class when appropriate and spend time with them to learn about the functions of the new gear that we have recently acquired. I think that forging these relationships helps me as a woman and as a person of color in the field. Since I try to extend the students' education beyond the classroom, these relationships make me move beyond being a solitary, perhaps "exotic," figure in the students' understanding of media. If the students can perceive me as part of a team that includes men, women, and people of color, perhaps this mix will make an impact on them. Perhaps they will demand this diversity when they go out into the workforce.

In my field, it is also important to keep your credibility established by constantly working and having your films/videos exhibited. When I first started teaching, I was more reticent about telling my students about my filmmaking activities and screenings because I thought it would sound like I was bragging. However, my student evaluations kept suggesting that I show more of my own work in the classroom. Now on the first day of class I openly tell my students that I am a working filmmaker. In addition to screening excerpts of my films and videos, I also let them know where my work is playing. Frequently my students have family or friends in the areas where I am screening, and sometimes this helps to develop audiences for my work. I also find that I have gained authority in the classroom by word of mouth and media exposure. When I was interviewed on CNN about my film being at the Sundance Film Festival in January 2000, both current and former students e-mailed and called me from across the country to offer congratulations and support. Word of mouth spread about my media appearances across campus, so for a few moments in the eyes of my students I became a "rock star."

My teaching and my work frequently go hand in hand. When I am fortunate enough to have the funding to mount a production, I almost always involve my students in as many ways as possible. In the pre-production period of a film, this might involve researching the topic, pre-interviewing subjects, and helping to gather price quotes to establish a budget. During production, I try to choose professional crew members who are willing to mentor apprentices, usually women and/or minority students who might not have the opportunity to intern on a production otherwise. At the same time, teaching works for me because I have to keep up with the changes in equipment. In order to keep pace with the industry, schools frequently have to purchase new equipment, and I have to learn it to be able to relay this information to students. If I worked only as a filmmaker on my own projects, I probably would not keep up with technological advances, primarily because I could not afford the equipment.

Self-Evaluation and Student Evaluation

It is important to be self-critical as a teacher and not become complacent with your teaching. The longer I stay a professor, the more difficult staying on top of the field becomes. In my field this is exacerbated by the constant technological changes that are taking place each year with the introduction of digital video, new film stocks, computer-based editing software that is constantly being updated, and so on. I can also see that since you have to go through so many hoops to get tenure and promotion/merit increases, after awhile you don't have enough strength to keep up anymore. You've done the work that you needed to get tenure, a promotion, or merit, and that should be enough. As I am asked to evaluate tenure files for candidates at other schools, it is clear that many people do just enough to get by. Yet when I get the files of women of color who are being considered for promotion and tenure, it is clear that they have taken their work extremely seriously and that their files are considerably thicker than those of many of their colleagues.

When I first started teaching, I would read the course evaluations as soon as I got them. I naïvely believed that the students would give me constructive criticism that could help me improve the class. Sometimes I got this type of criticism, but more often I did not. Overall, my student evaluations are positive; I have a reputation for being a "hard but fair" teacher. However, the student evaluations can be extremely debilitating because they are often laced with subtle or blatant racist commentary. Unfortunately, the anonymity of the student evaluations allows, and in some instances even encourages, students to make racist and sexist comments. In the spring of 2000, I received two evaluations that were obviously meant to hurt me. One student remarked that "Davis' lips are so big she has to carry her Chapstick in a water bottle." The same student went on to say that the "class would have been more interesting if the bitch would have lectured with a bone in her nose and a plate in her lip." Another student complained of having to attend an optional off-campus screening in San Diego: "If you make me go to the Malcolm X Library one more time, I'll take you to the David Duke Library."

Rather than just quietly accept these comments, I chose to make these evaluations public. In the past, I have shared sexist student commentary with my friends, my chair, and other members of my department, but these comments have pushed me farther. This is not an easy choice—I hate rehashing these comments, but I feel that it is important that other faculty and the administration know that this is going on. My colleagues in the department have been supportive; my chair is figuring out ways to make the student evaluation process more responsible and accountable. My experience has shown and allowed others to understand that hatred is something that afflicts many of us as women and as people of color on campus. Other women colleagues from various parts of the campus have been reaching out to me. The outcome of this incident is still unfolding as of this writing, and its long-term impact is in the making. Perhaps I need more time to develop emotional distance to write about it; it has been a challenge not to internalize this hatred. Recently I have found that I have been particularly leery of being around certain White male students at night or alone in my office during office hours. This experience has been quite an emotional roller coaster that I don't wish on others.

Environment and Success

I have been fortunate to be in supportive environments as a teacher. When I have had problems in the classroom I have discussed those matters with the chair of my department and, in some instances, the dean. What has helped me most is that I do have the ability to listen well and ask questions. As far as the tenure process was concerned, I spoke to many colleagues early on and frequently enough so that I was clear about what was expected from me to obtain tenure. Clarity about what qualified for tenure was particularly important in my case, since I generally do not publish as part of my research. It was crucial to know that my films would count toward tenure, and I got this agreement in writing from the dean as soon as I began my position.

At the time I received tenure at Northwestern University in 1996, five of the six faculty teaching production were women. In some ways, this situation probably fostered an environment in which the students treated me with respect. As women faculty, we shared teaching methods, teaching materials, and watched out for each other when we encountered "problem" students. As faculty, we encouraged each other to visit our respective classrooms. I learned a great deal from watching my colleagues teach and applied what worked or didn't work from them to my own teaching style.

For most of my university teaching career, I have been the sole African American or one of two African Americans in my department. I have always understood that I am of value to the department and the school in general because of my race and gender. Believe me, my face has been used in recruiting bulletins and admissions brochures enough times, so I know my appearance and presence is used to make the school look good. Having said that, then the university must balance the "promotion" of my image. I need travel money to go to conferences where I can be seen as an ambassador of my school, and I may need a little more time and research money than other colleagues because of the nature of my field. I always try to create an atmosphere such that the administration knows about my screenings and appearances in the community so that they too will become invested in these outreach efforts.

A few issues that concern me with the position and status of women of color faculty is the paternalistic attitudes of some of our male colleagues who perceive us as their protégés by helping us get through the process of tenure and promotion. After successfully receiving tenure, a number of women colleagues report that they are still considered "junior" by their peers. These are difficult relationships to negotiate, but it is best to address the concerns immediately rather than have them build up and then explode later. The other issue a minority faculty member constantly faces is learning and deciding to say "no" to the endless committee assignments the administration will place on you because of your identity. These were particularly hard for me when I first started, since I felt I had to do everything, but as I brought it to the attention of my chair and the dean, the volume of these requests seemed to reduce.

Summary

As a pioneer Black women filmmaker, the university has provided me with the means to establish and maintain a film career. My filmmaking and teaching have always been a symbiotic relationship, although at times one can overwhelm and subsume the other. Teaching is an extension of my filmmaking and a means by which I am able to influence others to consider alternative media images. I have survived and thrived in the academic setting because I have learned when to set the boundaries and to continue and maintain ties with my various communities. To be a good teacher requires creativity, resourcefulness, patience, and time. Luckily for me, those are some of the same qualities that make a good independent filmmaker.

Zeinabu irene Davis is a professor in the Department of Communication at the University of California, San Diego. She is an independent filmmaker whose works include the award-winning feature dramatic film *Compensation* and the short dramas *Mother of the River* and *A Powerful Thang.* Davis primarily teaches media production courses but also teaches and writes and lectures on African cinema, pan-African film, and women's film.

Notes

1. For a more complete discussion on how I became a filmmaker, please see my article, "Woman with a Mission: Zeinabu irene Davis on Independent Filmmaking" (1991) and Gwendolyn Audrey Foster's book, *Women Filmmakers of the African and Asian Diaspora* (1997).

2. Tuition fees at most graduate film programs do not include the costs of producing the projects that the students need to complete to obtain their degree. Projects can range in costs from a few hundred to many thousands of dollars. It is not uncommon for master's degree students to graduate with loans in excess of $40,000 and above.

3. An African American woman Ph.D. candidate at Northwestern University, Yvonne Welbon, has uncovered a great deal of information about these women. See her website at (www.sistersincinema.com) for more information.

4. My films and videos are available from California Newsreel (www.newsreel.org), Women Make Movies (www.wmm.org), and Third World Newsreel (www.twn.org).

5. The University of California is a system of nine campuses spread across the state; Berkeley and Los Angeles are among the largest of the campuses with more than 30,000 students on each campus. The low enrollment of minority students due to the backlash of Proposition 209 has affected all of the campuses, not just San Diego.

Works Cited

Birth of a Nation. 1915. Directed by D. W. Griffith. Distributed by Kino Video. Videocassette.

Davis, Z. i. 1991. "Woman with a Mission: Zeinabu irene Davis on Independent Filmmaking." *VOICES of the African Diaspora* 7 (3): 37–40.

Foster, G. A. 1997. *Women Filmmakers of the African and Asian Diaspora: Decolonizing the Gaze, Locating Subjectivity.* Carbondale, IL: Southern Illinois University Press.

Hyenas. 1992. Directed by D. D. Mambety. Distributed by KinoVideo. Videocassette.

Meet Me in St. Louis. 1945. Directed by V. Minnelli. Distributed by Warner Studios. Videocassette.

Red Sorghum. 1989. Directed by Y. Zhang. Distributed by New Yorker Films. Videocassette.

The Wizard of Oz. 1939. Directed by V. Fleming and R. Thorpe. Distributed by Warner Studios. Videocassette.

CHAPTER THIRTEEN

"Results Matter":
When the Other Teacher Teaches
English in the Bluegrass State[1]

LOU-ANN CROUTHER

Abstract

BEING A MIDDLE-AGED African American woman who teaches English in Kentucky is engaging and challenging. After sixteen years at Western Kentucky University in Bowling Green, I have a number of insights that may help Other Teachers, and other members of higher education institutions see that the particular experiences of Other Teachers need to be acknowledged and added to the variables taken into consideration for hiring, promotion, and tenure. I also believe this information will be helpful for novice Other Teachers, who are still too few in number and have much to offer the colleges and universities of the United States of America. During this process, I will discuss and analyze class, gender, race, and ethnicity issues that have a bearing on my teaching and/or on perceptions others have of me. I will also discuss and analyze professorial authority, power in the classroom, and student resistance.

For this essay, I will use some ideas prompted by one of my favorite writers, Zora Neale Hurston, to frame my comments and provide a refrain for this chapter. Hurston lived from 1891 to 1960, and may be best known as a Harlem Renaissance writer. Her essay entitled "How It Feels to Be Colored Me" is a lighthearted, humorous, satirical, and ironic work that promotes the connections among people of all races. It is an essay I return to often, and my students like it, as well. Hurston discusses how it feels to be colored at various times during her life and in various situations. She finds it hard to believe some people would choose not to be in her company. She ends the piece by implying we are all much the same, whether brown, white, red, or yellow. One part of the essay keeps me grounded and may provide solace for other Other Teachers. Hurston exults:

> But I am not tragically colored. There is no great sorrow dammed up in my soul, nor lurking behind my eyes. I do not mind at all. I do not belong to the sobbing school of Negrohood who hold that nature somehow has given them a lowdown dirty deal and whose feelings are all hurt about it. Even in the helter-skelter skirmish that is my life, I have seen that the world is to the strong regardless of a little pigmentation more or less. No, I do not weep at the world—I am too busy sharpening my oyster knife. (Hurston 1996, 1009)

Hurston's allusion is to Shakespeare's *The Merry Wives of Windsor*: "Why, then the world's mine oyster, / Which I with sword will open." As Other Teachers, we, too, should keep our oyster knives sharp! Before I describe the ways my perceived otherness influences my professional life, I will begin by briefly presenting biographical information, my work history, the context of my teaching, and some pertinent information about my school and the history of the Comonwealth of Kentucky. Although I was born in the South (Little Rock, Arkansas), many of my students erroneously assume I am a northerner since I was educated in Ohio and Indiana, and I have been told I do not sound like I am "from around here." I also grew up in large cities (St. Louis, Missouri; Columbus and Cleveland, Ohio), so my experiences are quite different from those of many of my students who are from rural areas. I must also mention that due to my parents' foresight, I spent my junior year of college at Dijon Université in Dijon, France, and the changes that made in my personal growth and my use of the French language are immeasurable. One of the benefits of that year is that I have an affinity for our international students. Early in the semester I privately let my international students know that I have had a similar experience and offer them my assistance, just as I offer to assist all my students who choose to learn more about campus and community services.

Both of my parents have master's degrees, and I am a third-generation college graduate on both sides of my family. My parents made a conscious decision to give me the ability to live in the predominantly White world, so they exposed me to a variety of people, activities, and places during my formative years, for this is also their world. Therefore, I can adjust to a variety of settings. I was taught to do well at my job but to realize that it is a job, just one part of my life. They were honest about the obstacles and challenges I would face as an African American woman, and they continue to be my greatest source of encouragement.

I have also benefited from the privileges ascribed to a single, heterosexual, able-bodied, native-English–speaking, middle-class, doctorate-holding, African American woman. I am thankful for these privileges and understand that African American women often are not valued highly in our society. I do not usually think of myself as being a member of a group of people considered Other, yet I realize some who see me that way might like to remind me often of my otherness. The fact that I am also an easygoing person who does not look for conflicts has, perhaps, made my professional path a bit smoother than it might have been. I will discuss this subject at length later in this chapter.

My first job after I earned my doctorate was as an assistant professor of English and director of drama at Benedict College, an historically Black college in Columbia, South Carolina. The one-and-a-half years I taught there were full of challenges and accomplishments. The drama position required that I be at school many afternoons and nights when programs were held in our state-of-the-art theater. I taught reading—a new subject for me—as well as introductory, intermediate, and advanced composition and world literature courses. Looking back, I remember being excited about my position, and I eagerly worked from 8 AM to 5 PM. I taught five courses one semester and four courses the next semester. Often, I felt somewhat like Helga Crane in Nella Larsen's novel *Quicksand* (1986). Helga is a single, African American professor at an historically Black college that was much more regimented than Benedict College. I shared, however, her sense of history and pride about being a part of an educational tradition. The thrill of teaching at an historically Black institution was even more fulfilling since both of my parents attended Lincoln University in Missouri, an historically Black college. I had grown up hearing their stories, knowing their friends, and reading their yearbooks from their years at Lincoln.

As a new instructor, I was called upon to use a variety of teaching methods and perform the required committee and university obligations. I learned much about dealing with students from various backgrounds and abilities, and graded large volumes of papers I assigned because I wanted my students to write as often as possible. (I quickly learned to be more conservative about assignments.) While at Benedict, I began to practice and modify my teaching philosophy and worked hard at being a good teacher. The most important thing I learned was how to be a teacher. I had been a student for so long I thought I knew a great deal about life on the other side of the desk. Of course, there was much more to learn. A knowledge of the hierarchy of a large organization was also vital to my survival at Benedict College, and that knowledge has also been useful to me at Western Kentucky University. The most important teaching concept I learned was to expect the best from both my students and myself.

As I mentioned, I have been at Western Kentucky University, or Western, for sixteen years. During that time, I have been the only African American professor in the Department of English. In the spring semester of 2000, of our thirty-three full-time faculty, approximately 55 percent were female and 45 percent were male. Of our twenty part-time faculty, approximately 80 percent were female and 20 percent were male. Each semester I teach four classes, and I usually teach some variety of our three required general-education courses: Freshman English, Introduction to Literature, and Junior English. The freshman and junior courses are basic and advanced composition courses, respectively, and average about twenty-two students each; the literature survey class can have from twenty-five to thirty students. I also teach two writing-elective courses from time to time that average about twenty-two students each: Informal Essay and Intermediate Composition. I teach a junior-level African American literature course every semester. It is an English elective, but it is required for African American Studies minors. There are usually about twenty-five students enrolled in that class each semester. In this chapter, I will refer to these courses individually by title, and I will also group the writing courses together and the literature courses together.

I have received and continue to receive positive institutional support from all levels of the administration at Western Kentucky University. I have no horror stories about tenure and promotion, and for that I am thankful. I attribute this fact primarily to the mentoring of my first department head, who came to Western in the fall of 1984, as I did. He supported and guided me throughout the six years prior to my successful tenure process and suggested that I write more before I successfully applied for promotion to associate professor. While interim department head for one year before my third department head arrived, this same colleague also helped me prepare a professional plan to help me work toward promotion to full professor. My second department head was also supportive and encouraged me to write an article similar to this chapter that discusses the teaching of African American literature at a predominantly White university. My present and third department head is also encouraging and supportive, and I have shared my present professional goals with her. All three department heads have written positive yearly evaluations and continue to offer their assistance.

Past and present college deans and academic vice presidents also remain willing to assist with my professional development. I have not had unreasonable class scheduling or class size concerns, and I teach when I choose to: I have two courses daily in the mornings or early afternoons. I was the English department's Willson Wood Professor during the 1999–2000 school year, an honor that provided released time, a stipend, and a research assistant. I received a faculty fellowship for research during the summer of 2000, and I was on sabbatical leave during the spring of 2001. I am grateful for the continuing support of all of my colleagues at Western Kentucky University.

Western is a regional (and aspires to be a national) state-supported university of about 15,000 students; at least two-thirds of them are first-generation college students. Most of our students are education, biological sciences, and communications majors. Of its 521 full-time faculty, 51 are minority and 203 are women (Office of Institutional Research 1999). The Western community is aggressively working to increase and retain diverse faculty members. Kentucky's history, however, may be thwarting its attempts. The Kentucky Legislature did not ratify the Thirteenth Amendment until 1970. Ku Klux Klan actions, lynchings, and the forcible eviction of African Americans from some locations in the Commonwealth persisted into the twentieth century. It easy to see the issues with which Kentucky's African Americans and members of other minority or marginalized races and ethnicities must contend. Other issues that may make Kentucky unappealing to some are its conservative voting record and its conservative religious views. A Ten Commandments monument, which has been in storage, may be reposted on the state house grounds, and some public schools may post the Ten Commandments as an historical document (Gerth 2000).

Of particular distaste to me, a non-Kentucky native, is the state song, "My Old Kentucky Home, Good-Night!," written by Stephen Collins Foster (1826–1864) in 1853. It is commonly said that the line about "darkies being gay" was changed in the 1960s and was replaced with "the folks" or "the people" are gay. Of course, many are sometimes brought to tears when this song is sung before the Kentucky Derby each May, a horse race in which the first jockeys were African American men. The word changes do little to change the song's nostalgic sentiments for antebellum days when "darkies" knew their place. And that "place" was not in a state university teaching English!

Historically, the Commonwealth has made sporadic attempts to improve the educational opportunities statewide, but these efforts have met with mixed results. On a more positive note, it is appropriate that this chapter required me to take a closer look at education in Kentucky as an Other Teacher during the tenth anniversary of the Kentucky Education Reform Act of 1990. In 1988, the state supreme court declared the public school system "inadequate and unconstitutional" (Kentucky Department of Education

2000). All segments of the state population have been working to ensure that every school is academically proficient by 2014.

To return to the refrain provided by Zora Neale Hurston's essay, I would suggest that Other Teachers read a number of the works about the challenges faced by women and minorities.[2] With this knowledge, we can use our oyster knives to our advantage. I will now move on to the subjects of professorial authority, power in the classroom, and student resistance. Valerie Ann Moore's (1996) aptly titled article "Inappropriate Challenges to Professorial Authority" and Lucila Vargas's (1999) article, "When the 'Other' Is the Teacher," will serve as guides for an analysis of some of my experiences.

Valerie Ann Moore defines "inappropriate challenges as behaviors suggesting incompetence based solely on certain professors' social characteristics, especially gender and race." These challenges require these professors to "justify their teaching methods, defend their knowledge, and prove their grasp of the material." In essence, these professors "must prove themselves each time they walk into their classrooms" (1996, 202). Just as in the greater society, people of color and White women on campus "often find it difficult to be recognized as authority figures." Moore also cites Angela Simeone (1987), who asserts that as female professors complete terminal degrees and/or grow older, they are perceived as being more authoritative.[3]

Vargas mentions that many "middle-class White undergraduates have never been in social situations led by a woman of color. When sorting out how to behave in the Other Teacher's classroom, these students have no experience to draw upon" (1999, 377). Therefore, these students should learn how to behave in such situations. And, as one of Vargas's respondents notes, since the world is multicultural, it would be in these students' best interest to know how to deal with the diverse members of the real world. I trust many of my students are learning this lesson in a state where about 7.3 percent of the citizens are African American, and less than 1 percent are members of other races (University of Louisville 1999). I must add that I sometimes have difficulty getting my students to engage in discussions, as do some of my colleagues. I do believe that in literature classes, especially, some of my students' concerns about what they think I think about a work frames and dampens their comments. They, perhaps, assume I share the worldview of the generic, media-produced, African American woman, particularly if they know few African Americans personally.

Moore's and Vargas's concerns are not foreign to my teaching experiences at Western. When I began teaching here, I was told I looked too young to be an assistant professor, and this may have been one of the reasons why students would ask about my credentials and teaching experience. The easy familiarity some White students immediately assume with Other Teachers, especially about personal subjects, is just one way the usual "boundaries between faculty and students" (Vargas 1999) can be eroded when an Other Teacher is the professor. I would answer my students' questions civilly, wondering what they might find that the departmental search committee and university administrators who interviewed me might have overlooked. Now that I have been here over a decade, my work record has reduced the number of times and the ways these kinds of questions are asked. Now I feel the questions express more genuine interest in my particular path in the profession. I now also have visibly gray hairs I choose not to color, I have always dressed professionally, and I discuss my educational history and experiences early in my courses, all steps Moore recommends.

Another way I have found to deal with issues that could challenge my authority in the classroom is by giving my "Second-Week Sheets speech." After class enrollment settles down after the drop/add date, usually the second week of classes, I have students introduce themselves to the class, and I begin the process by introducing myself. In addition to some brief biographical and educational information, I also mention my research interests and hobbies. During that same week, I have to work myself up to deliver information I do not include in my "course policies" because I want to spend time talking with my students about these subjects. They are subjects I knew about when I went to college, but these are different times, and I do not expect my students to have the same assumptions about university protocol as I did. I grew up knowing I was going to college, and I knew a little about college protocol before I got to campus. I would never have talked back to a professor or called a professor at home, things some of my students feel comfortable doing. Western Kentucky University, like many schools, has a Freshman Seminar class that helps freshmen learn about and become acclimated to college services and expectations, and I often remind my students of the importance of the information they learn in that class.

My "Second-Week Sheets" include information as basic as being quiet before and after the bell rings, sitting so I can see their faces, and not doing other work in class. I also remind my students that I dismiss them, not the bell. My students also learn that they are responsible for keeping up with their absences (I take attendance every day) and grades. I tell my students that everything counts in their assignments, such as spelling, content, grammar—an astounding necessity, I think, in an English class. Then I spend a good deal of time discussing the importance of respecting others. I also suggest that my students leave their attitudes at home.

I tell my students not to come to my office in an uproar about their grades. I suggest they see me after they have calmed down, when I will be happy to discuss their work and make corrections, if necessary. My students learn that they should not let me know when they take their graded papers to another professor, of any discipline, and that professor suggests they should have received a better grade. I call this "shopping a paper around." This tactic, I suggest, will make me think they should drop my class and take the course with the professor who gave them the better grade. I tell my students I will call them "Ms. _____" or "Mr. _____" and a first name of their choosing.

Finally, I tell my students to call me "Dr. Crouther" or "Professor Crouther" because I have an earned doctorate in English, and those two titles are appropriate. If they have thought about it, they may think they are only being disrespectful to me by calling me by another title. But I tell them they are disrespecting generations of family and friends who made sacrifices in order for me to be their professor, and I will not permit that. (One of my intermediate composition students wrote these sentences on a student evaluation: "I do not think Dr. Crouther should emphasize on her name 'Dr.' Crouther, because she somewhat offended me. It made me feel like I was beneath her." Clearly that is not my intent when I ask to be respected for my accomplishments. I wonder if this student has this reaction to all educators with a doctorate degree.) I ask if there are questions about any of the information, and then we proceed with the day's work.

Perhaps now it is clear why I must "work myself up" to give my second-week sheets speech. I have found that my classes go better if I tell my students these things at the beginning of the semester instead of thinking they understand what I expect. At about this time, I also tell my students to speak up and ask questions in class. We have no time to consider whether or not a classmate thinks they are cool or not because they do or do not participate in class activities. We have a job to do that requires that they understand their assignments. I suggest they ask me questions instead of their classmates, because I made the assignment, I will be grading the assignment, and I know the objectives of the assignment. No questions are "dumb," and I will repeat and restate concepts as many times as is necessary. I urge my students to have no questions about anything we are doing when they leave class each day. I also suggest that they speak up in class at least once each week.

Valerie Ann Moore ends her article about professorial authority with many options, which include not taking the challenges personally, dealing with them as they arise, and letting students look up information they might dispute for themselves (1996, 205). She also suggests ways the climate across campus can improve with cultural diversity training, more exposure to diverse faculty, and more administrative support (1996, 207). Now that I have been at Western sixteen years, students do not challenge my authority in the classroom often.

Much has been written about power in the classroom, my next topic, so I will make one crucial comment that will help Other Teachers keep their oyster knives sharp. Mary O'Hair and Joseph Blase's article "Power and Politics in the Classroom: Implications for Teacher Education" is helpful for novice teachers and those who train them. The section of special value to Other Teachers is called "Self-Protection" (1992, 13). In these paragraphs, the authors encourage teachers to "use power to protect themselves from students and their parents." I would also add colleagues, administrators, and the general university and community populations to those two groups—and any individual or group that might take issue with classroom and/or office proceedings. Although the article is not tailored to higher education teachers, I would suggest that Other Teachers, especially, keep a written record of what I call "incidents" with students and others that includes dates, times, the issue, and how, if, and when the matter was/is going to be resolved. The department head or chair may not need to see all of them, but I think that a paper trail is useful. Valerie Ann Moore reinforces this point by saying White female and minority teachers are forced to "waste time and expend energy in meeting or preemptively countering" (1996, 205) these kinds of challenges.

During my sixteen years at Western Kentucky University, I have had only four incidents that overtly challenged my authority and power. I have been fortunate. These confrontations arose because of the concerns of two White women and two White men. Three were handled in my office; only the most recent one required that I notify my department head. The student, who had misunderstood a course policy, had written a letter. I responded to the letter, and I gave the department head copies of both letters. My department head thought the student might have been preparing to bring charges against me, but that did not happen. This was a rare occurrence for me, but it reinforced the importance of a paper trail, which has been stressed by others since I began teaching.

Student resistance is the next subject I will illustrate.[4] E.-K. Daufin highlights the initial resistance I have also observed about my grading standards in all of my classes. She maintains that many students are more concerned about getting an "A" than they are about learning. "When the obstacle between them and a 4.00 happens to be a woman of color, there may be murder in their eyes. Many professors know that no matter how warm their personalities or lively their teaching styles, the honeymoon is over when students receive their first grades" (1995, 35). I had a related incident with an older student who was a member of an honors sophomore literature course I taught not long ago. She came to my office before the semester began to tell me she had a perfect grade-point average and wanted to maintain it. I was offended by her presumption that she wanted to guarantee herself an "A" in my course, too. Of course, I mentioned no such possibility. After she handed in some papers, it was clear that she was not doing "A" work. Naturally, she came in to talk with me about her work after she thought her perfect gradepoint average was threatened. Letters were exchanged in this case, too, but the student finally earned an "A" in the class, so that problem was eliminated.

I think some of the murder Daufin saw in her students' eyes is also due to the fact that writing, which she also teaches, is a personal and subjective skill. Those two factors add to the displeasure some may feel when they find out they might need to work harder to get the grade they desire. Some of my students remark on my course evaluations that I grade too hard and assign too much work. "She graded her papers not on content, but as if it were a grammar course." Some of my literature students also think I should not grade grammar mistakes since they are not enrolled in grammar classes. "I think the grade assignment is too harsh. Not all of us are English majors and sometimes too much was expected out of the class, overall, it was an effective class." "Her grading methods are harsh. I think she is a good teacher." Writing deficiencies are the most important academic problems some of my students have with the material they are assigned. I offer to work with them one on one, Western has a writing center students can attend, and there are a variety of on-line exercises and tutorials available. I tell all my students they can improve their writing skills with practice and time. Some choose to do the work required to get the results they desire; others do not.

Other issues of student resistance arise in literature classes, especially in my junior-level African-American Literature course. One comment on a course evaluation expresses this issue: "The class seems to have one objective, exposing racism. As a White student I felt it was being thrown in my face on a very regular basis. I'm not saying there [sic] things didn't happened [sic] and were horribly wrong, but I didn't think all energy of this class would be focused on them." My perceptions of that semester's class differs from this student's assessment, but the comments and feelings described are dealt with in a number of articles that discuss White students' defensiveness in classes that deal with gender, race, and oppression.[5] Another student said this about the same course:

You've opened up new doors for me in literature and writing. Thank you for your enthusiasm, help, and fulfilling answers to all of my questions. I plan to continue reading more in my book and more of my favorite authors. The current events that we discuss have also been enlightening. You seem to cover every angle without getting hung up, like most professors, on the critics' explanations of literary works. You allow us to express our views about the works and not totally your and other critics' views. Thanks for a great class. I'm so glad I took this class.

In my sophomore introduction to literature courses, I try to gently suggest to several resisting students, who are there because they must be, that they be open to works by writers of varied times and cultures. I sometimes have to work to get some of my students to look beyond the morals of the characters (many of my students come from conservative families) to see what the author would like for us to learn about ourselves and others from the text. I tell all my students they can say or write just about anything about a text as long as the text supports their critical assessments. Some students find this approach refreshing; some just want to know what I want them to tell me about the work. I offer suggestions, but they must choose their topics and organize their evidence as they see fit. I want all my students to think for themselves. I tell them I usually do not want to see their class notes in their assignments. I want to see what they think.

My attempts to persuade my students to broaden their horizons are difficult to gauge, and perhaps the best results will be evident long after they leave my classroom. Some might assume I will be a credible source when we discuss African American literature, but that is not necessarily the case. An occasional student will imply I am too close to African American literature to be objective about it; some will swallow whatever I say about the literature since I am an African American. I often ask my students in both literature classes if the race and gender of an author matter, and sometimes interesting discussion follows. Melanie Moore (1997) has shown that the gender of the messenger does matter in her sociology of the family classes. A male colleague who said much the same things as she did was well received by her students while she, often, was not. I often wonder if my students find my comments about writers such as Chaucer, Shakespeare, and other traditional White writers biased as well, or if they think I spout the "party line" about our "classical" writers yet become more fanatical about the literature of African Americans. This is a legitimate concern, because I do not swallow the "party line" about any writer. I measure him or her by reading the text, reading criticism, and filtering that through the lens of my experiences as a twentieth- and twenty-first-century African American woman.

Because I was reared by a teacher (and a social worker) and spent a good deal of time with teachers, I grew up knowing teachers were gifted people. I also grew up thinking I would probably be a teacher one day. I valued educators and the opportunities they offered their students. I knew education would be the key to my success, and I enjoyed learning. I also admired and respected teachers and did not question their authority or power in the classroom. Even in graduate school, I never challenged my professors. I might interpret the literature in an unusual way, but I was awed by the professors at Indiana University. This does not mean I did not question the information and opinions of my professors, I just did not resist their power in their classrooms or offices. I focused on the end result (I wanted my undergraduate and graduate degrees) and followed the requests of my professors. I knew college was more than the thirteenth grade and that much would be required of me. I also believed, and still do, that being a college student is a privilege, not a right, and I saw a college education as one way to make a better life for myself and my family.

I still believe these same things. I also believe that offering our students a liberal arts education is one way to continue to provide opportunities for all of the citizens of the United States of America so they will contribute to the continued improvement of our society. In a theoretically classless and casteless society such as ours, education offers hope for a better tomorrow. My belief in many of the ideals of the Declaration of Independence and the Constitution as well as my coming of age in the 1960s make me an optimist.

I would imagine that many of my students do not share my beliefs about these topics. Many in our society seem to show little respect for teachers. Some of my students are more concerned about their beginning salaries than they are about stretching their minds. Many students are not fond of writing or literature, so they are not happy about being in my general-education classes. Unfortunately, some of my colleagues think only English professors should care about a student's writing skills, and my department is sometimes blamed when a student in another major writes poorly. My students are writing more during their elementary and secondary years as a result of the Kentucky Education Reform Act; it is difficult to say whether many of them are better writers by the time they take college English classes. I understand that my students and I may view higher education and our roles in that process differently. I continue to do my best, and I expect the best from them. If the need arises for adjustments, I will talk with a student privately.

I feel I must address one more topic bell hooks (1994) presents in *Teaching to Transgress* before I conclude this chapter: the feelings some of my African American students have toward classes taught by African American professors. Perhaps this phenomenon also applies to other students who are members of the same race and/or ethnic group as their Other Teachers. Some of my African American students may want to coast and not be held to the class rules since I am a "sister" and understand "our racist society." (With the exception of my African-American Literature class, which is about 50 percent African American and 50 percent White, most of my classes have only two or three African American students.) This point of view is not evident as much now, maybe because some students believe I am a hard grader.

If this issue arises, it is usually apparent in my African-American Literature class. Some of those students think they will get at least a "B" in the class just because they are African American and come to class regularly. These students may exhibit negative attitudes or become openly hostile in class when they find they are required to be active readers, writers, and participants in the class. When these few students also find they are in class with White students who may know more about African American literature than they do, they privately express their frustrations about their ignorance of their own literature. In private settings, I tell my African American students of the coasting mentality that we have no time to commiserate about our society's ills; it is my job to prepare them to do what they can to be the best persons they can be. The college training they receive from my courses and others will assist them as they fight against injustice. I expect great things from all of my students, and they should know I will give them my best efforts.

So what can I offer Other Teachers from a state that is struggling to eradicate its educational deficiencies? What can I offer others reading this work who choose to make their schools' faculties more diverse? As Other Teachers, we can do what we have always done and persevere despite the hardships we face, and pray that the Other Teachers who follow us will have an easier road to travel. We can support each other on campus and across campuses. We can encourage our schools to share ideas about diverse faculties. We can use the methods already mentioned in this chapter and others in this book. We can continue to hold our country of employment to the promises offered in the Declaration of Independence and the Constitution. We can also find hope in the changing racial makeup of this country. We can try to have the additional duties of nurturing minority students and being showcased, for example, counted when we come up for tenure and promotion. We can maintain strong religious ties. We can call upon our ancestors who helped us get to the places we inhabit now. We can maintain strong ties with our families and friends. We can keep our sense of humor. We also need to do what we like to do and take vacations regularly so we can come back to our jobs refreshed. I know the challenges may never stop, but I believe we will be respected more as we get older and become more established in our professions.

I encourage Other Teachers to reflect Zora Neale Hurston's zest for life's possibilities. Celebrate the fact that you are an Other Teacher! Maintain your high standards and know that your schools are better because you bring your distinct personal and professional characteristics to your profession. The results of our lives and our contributions matter. Let us keep our oyster knives sharp!

Lou-Ann Crouther is an Associate Professor of English at Western Kentucky University in Bowling Green. She teaches introductory and advanced composition and literature courses, including African American literature. Her research interests include African American women's literature and other women's literature. She is also working on a collection of poetry. As the Willson Wood Professor of English during the 1999–2000 school year, she continued her research on little-known African American women writers for a manuscript in progress.

Author's Note

I wish to thank my mentor and colleague Albert J. Petersen Jr. for his editorial comments and suggestions.

Notes

1. This is the partial title of the *Tenth Anniversary Report on Education Reform in Kentucky*, written by the Office of Communications of the Kentucky Department of Education.

2. Three articles have been helpful to me in this area, even though they do not specifically deal with teaching composition and/or African American literature. Magda Lewis's (1990) article deals with the feminist classroom. Melanie Moore (1997) considers students' reactions to her sociology of the family course content as a function of their reaction to the messenger—a White woman. Nancy Davis (1992), like Lewis and Moore, also teaches about inequalities in her classes.

3. Robert J. Menges and William H. Exum's (1983) work mentions a wealth of variables, including scholarship and support networks. Angela Simeone's (1987) work examines gender-specific challenges to women educators, and finds the college atmosphere still daunting after more than 150 years. Racism is tackled by Maria de la Luz Reyes and John J. Halcon (1988) in a work whose primary subject is Chicanos in higher education, but all Other Teachers will benefit from the article. Victor Villanueva's (1993) book offers his experiences and those of students of color in his classrooms. E.-K. Daufin's (1995) and Aretha Butler Pigford's (1988) articles offer two views from African American women educators.

4. These articles and book chapters explain the defensiveness of White students in classes that deal with teaching privileged students about gender, race, and class oppression (Bohmer and Briggs 1991); teaching race, gender, and class (Hartung 1991); and teaching about women to male-identified students (Turkel 1986). A chapter by Leslie G. Roman (1993) analyzes White defensiveness, postmodernism, and anti-racist pedagogy. Bruce A. Jacobs's (1999) book helps my African-American Literature students deal with issues of resistance; it would also be of value to Other Teachers.

5. Menges and Exum (1983) and Reyes and Halcon (1988) are essential reading for those who care about the burdens of Other Teachers. The barriers mentioned in Menges and Exum are addressed by Gainen and Boice (1993), who offer guidance for those who would like to sustain diverse academic communities.

Works Cited

Bohmer, S., and J. L. Briggs. 1991. "Teaching Privileged Students About Gender, Race, and Class Oppression." *Teaching Sociology* 19: 154–163.

Daufin, E.-K. 1995. "Confessions of a Womanist Professor." *Black Issues in Higher Education*, March 9, 1995, 34–35.

Davis, N. J. 1992. "Teaching about Inequality: Student Resistance, Paralysis, and Rage." *Teaching Sociology* 20 (3): 232–238.

Gainen, J., and R. Boice, eds. 1993. *Building a Diverse Faculty*. San Francisco: Jossey-Bass Publishers.

Gerth, J. 2000. "ACLU Sues to Block Commandments Monument." *The Courier Journal* (Louisville), July 11, 2000, A1, A5.

Hartung, B. 1991. "Unstratifying Stratification: Teaching Race, Gender, and Class." *Teaching Sociology* 19: 66–69.

hooks, b. 1994. *Teaching to Transgress: Education as the Practice of Freedom.* New York: Routledge.

Hurston, Z. N. [1928] 1996. "How It Feels to Be Colored Me." In *The Norton Anthology of African American Literature,* edited by H. L. Gates and N. Y. McKay. New York: W.W. Norton.

Jacobs, B. A. 1999. *Race Matters: Navigating the Minefield between Black and White Americans.* New York: Arcade.

Kentucky Department of Education. *The 10th Anniversary Report on Education Reform in Kentucky. Results Matter: A Decade of Difference in Kentucky's Public Schools.* Office of Communications of the Kentucky Department of Education [cited June 20, 2000. Available from www.kde.state.ky.us/comm/commrel/10th_anniversary.

Larsen, N. [1928] 1986. "Passing." In *Quicksand and Passing,* edited by D. E. McDowell. Durham, NC: Duke University Press.

Lewis, M. 1990. "Interrupting Patriarchy: Politics, Resistance, and Transformation in the Feminist Classroom." *Harvard Educational Review* 60 (4): 467–488.

Menges, R. J., and W. H. Exum. 1983. "Barriers to the Progress of Women and Minority Faculty." *Journal of Higher Education* 54 (2): 123–144.

Moore, M. 1997. "Student Resistance to Course Content: Reactions to the Gender of the Messenger." *Teaching Sociology* 25: 128–133.

Moore, V. A. 1996. "Inappropriate Challenges to Professorial Authority." *Teaching Sociology* 24: 202–206.

O'Hair, M., and J. Blase. 1992. "Power and Politics in the Classroom: Implications for Teacher Education." *Action in Teacher Education* 14 (1): 10–17.

Office of Institutional Research. 2000. *Common Data Set: 1999–2000 Final* [World Wide Web]. Western Kentucky University 1999 [cited June 28, 2000]. Available from Http://www.wku.edu/Dept/Support/AcadAffairs/instres/.

Pigford, A. B. 1988. "Being a Black Faculty Member on a White Campus: My Reality." *Black Issues in Higher Education,* November 24, 1988, 76.

Reyes, M. L., and J. J. Halcon. 1988. "Racism in Academia: The Old Wolf Revisited." *Harvard Educational Review* 58 (3): 299–314.

Roman, L. G. 1993. "White Is a Color!: White Defensiveness, Postmodernism, and Anti-racist Pedagogy." In *Race, Identity and Representation in Education,* edited by C. McCarthy and W. Crichlow. New York: Routledge.

Simeone, A. 1987. *Academic Women: Working Towards Equality.* South Hadley, MA: Bergen & Garvey.

Turkel, K. D. 1986. "Teaching about Women to Male-identified Students." *Teaching Sociology* 14: 188–190.

University of Louisville. 2000. *Population Projections* (1999) [World Wide Web]. Kentucky Population Research 1999 [cited July 10, 2000]. Available from http://cbpa.louisville.edu/ksdc.

Vargas, L. 1999. "When the 'Other' Is the Teacher: Implications of Teacher Diversity in Higher Education." *The Urban Review* 31 (4): 359–383.

Villanueva, V. 1993. *Bootstraps: From an Academic of Color.* Urbana, IL: National Council of Teachers of English.

✥ CHAPTER FOURTEEN

Guess Who's Coming to Class: Teaching through the Politics of Race, Class, and Gender

ANNE B. ONYEKWULUJE

Abstract

IN WRITING A feminist Black female critique, I focus on the freeing of my soul, for "my soul is my own" (Etter-Lewis 1993). I use standpoint theory (Allen 1998; Buzzanell 1994; Hill Collins 1997; Hartsock 1997; Hennessy 1993; Longino 1993) to explore how developing and locating my Black female self at a predominantly White university is potentially both liberatory and oppressive. Finally, I address the ways the predominantly White classroom and university can set inclusive standards and create a new sociological community based on equality and equity for all selves and souls. The transforming of White academe into a sociological community based on equality and equity for all is a daunting task.

> The claim to personhood; the claim to share justly in the products of our labor, not to be used merely as an instrument, a role, a womb, a pair of hands or a back or a set of fingers; to participate fully in the decisions of our workplace, our community; to speak for ourselves, in our own right.
>
> Adrienne Rich (1976, xxviii)

In the predominantly White world of higher learning, Black faculty and students are few and far between. As an undergraduate, I selected sociology as a discipline for understanding this exclusion and oppression. Influenced by the works of cultural feminist writers bell hooks and Ann duCille, I decided in graduate school to use my sociological training and imagination to be inclusive and to teach from a cultural critical feminist perspective. In this political narrative essay, I use the works of bell hooks (1981; 1992; 1994; 1995),

Patricia Hill Collins (1991; 1996; 1997; 1998), and Ann duCille (1994) to discuss obstacles I face as a Black female professor "teaching through the politics of race, class, and gender." I use this expression to mean a constructed, contested, and oppressive teaching practice. Teaching how race, class, and gender operate as systems of social control becomes highly political. My challenge is to teach students to see race, class, and gender as socially constructed distinctions that support patriarchal forms of domination. This positive goal is workable if students participate in the inclusive thinking that challenges such structural arrangements. Unfortunately, some students do not like to participate in the analytical conversation that interrogates their stereotypical images and meanings. Surprisingly, for some, I add fuel to fire because, as a Black female professor teaching in a predominantly White campus, I stand before them representing social justice, change, and inclusiveness.

Teaching through this politics implies contradictions problematic to Black female professors. To illustrate, I want to include race, class, and gender in my teaching to draw attention to how these social dividers affect society. However, these same stereotypical categories are also used to oppress females like myself. It is hard to teach what oppresses you. I employ a feminist Black female critique as an interpretive framework to formulate a need for transformational change in the predominantly White world of bourgeois academe. In duCille's way of thinking, the "Black feminist female critique" is an intellectual approach to the study of the experiences of Black females, Blacks in general, and other members from socially disadvantaged backgrounds. As bell hooks would say, Black feminist thinking goes against the whole feminist idea that "women share a common plight."

Throughout the essay I focus on predominantly White classrooms as a site for creating sociology dependent upon the developments in the intellectual, cultural, and political powers of Black females like myself. I use the term "female" instead of "woman" because "female" makes it easier to omit the issues of identity and judgment associated with womanness. It is befitting for the reader to begin with a person's perception of the self as female or male and then proceed. From this perspective, a woman's identity is not judged. I also use the term "Black" to name my race because the notion of being Black seems to have shaped my personality more so than being labeled as an African American.

I applaud bell hooks and other cultural feminist writers for making their work so encouraging and empowering and for moving me beyond the "outsider within" (Hill Collins 1991; duCille 1994) frame of reference so that I too could be free to teach students to be free in their creativity. I salute

C. Wright Mills (1959) for his sociological insight. Mills's "sociological imagination" enables me to understand stereotypical remarks made about me as part of the difficulties other Black female professors face (Allen 1998; Daufin 1995; Pigford 1988). Thanks to many, I can handle the efforts made by some students to cast doubt verbally and in writing on my credibility—although the complexities involved in teaching unenlightened students can be overwhelming.

The project: A sociology for higher learning that claims personhood for the soul of the Black female professor. It must involve a commitment to the energy, the resources, and the imagination required to make the Black female's teaching through the politics of race, class, and gender a thing of the past. In discussing the project, I follow through its implications for research. In short, I posit that a public critique of academe can be healthy in building social relations and ending oppression.

Historic Stations

From its inception, higher learning in the United States was exclusionary and segregated by race, class, and gender. The process of integrating Black students and Black professors has been marked by what some have regarded as a dramatic increase in the numbers of Blacks in higher education. Krenzin contends:

> In the wake of Federal mandates to increase integration in institutions of education receiving government funds, there has been an extensive effort to increase the number of black faculty in predominantly white universities. The reasons for the Federal mandate, and for universities to seek to increase minority faculty representation even without that mandate, seem obvious. Black role models for both black and white students are long overdue. The manifestation of black competence, evidenced by the black professor, provides the "proof" still sought by a number of students (and faculty) that blacks have the intellectual capacity to compete with whites. (1995, 116)

The changes that have promoted desegregation, however, have precipitated a backlash. Brown describes a current backlash resulting from "social hostilities birthed by the rage and paranoia of White males who fear a loss of their historic station; these legal battles involving African-American access to higher education have resulted in giant steps backward on equal opportunity" (1996, 74). Collision's research found that the ethos of academic departments plays a crucial role in attracting minority faculty and students:

> Departments that value scholars of color are those that have a diverse group of faculty and that are preparing students of color to be professors. At Emory, four of the

12 professors in the education department are black and 40 percent of the doctoral students are minority. (1999, 26)

As I understand it, the act of competing in predominantly White universities is now supposed to be a "color-blind," "gender-blind," and "equitable" operation. The process of developing the intellectual, cultural, and political powers of us all should reflect this change in consciousness, and this new critical consciousness should be manifested in the classroom. However, according to Brown, "There are no standards which acknowledge integration or inclusion of all into America's ivy-covered towers" (1996, 75). Because I am Black and female and thought of as marginal by some students, I feel compelled to critique this condition.

Are there noticeable double standards that block development in the intellectual, cultural, and political power of Black females like myself? Of course. According to Brown (1996, 74–75), double standards may be the reason why the disparity between the numbers of faculty of Black and White descent entering the higher learning workforce is widening. This statement does not mythologize race as "pure," but it does suggest that being Black limits opportunities. I care about, depend upon, and want my university to inspire me intellectually, culturally, and politically to be the best I can be so that I can inspire my students to be the best they can be. This inspiration cannot come from oppression. Theoretically, one cannot teach through politics, but one must teach the politics of race, class, and gender that oppress. The soul must be free to teach, grow, and learn. One's soul must have the authority to gain knowledge, transform historic stations, and change. How can a Black female professor overcome the race, class, and gender constructs that can all too easily become attached to her very soul to transform herself into an unmarginalized person? How can White students surpass the historical stations that block their progress? How can I tear down the historical stations in each of my classrooms? Answers to these questions must be found in order for social change to occur.

In writing a feminist Black female critique, I focus on the freeing of my soul, for "my soul is my own" (Etter-Lewis 1993). I use standpoint theory (Allen 1998; Buzzanell 1994; Hill Collins 1997; Hartsock 1997; Hennessy 1993; Longino 1993) to explore how developing and locating my Black female self at a predominantly White university is potentially liberatory and oppressive simultaneously. Black female self is a new sense of self-worth; it is similar to bell hooks's notion of "decolonizing our minds." It is bringing to life the experiences and goals of Black females: It is empowerment.

Finally, I address the ways the predominantly White classroom and university can set inclusive standards and create a new sociological community based on equality and equity for all selves and souls. The sociological community is an arena where living social beings can be put to practice to create social change. It can be an intimate place in which different worldviews and value systems can coexist.[1] The transforming of White academe into a sociological community based on equality and equity for all is a daunting task. According to Abercrumbie, "Black faculty, staff, and students at predominantly White institutions have made sacrifices and fought discrimination in order to help other black people get an education" (1999, 112). This essay is not about Blacks getting an education. From a feminist Black female perspective, the process of educating all students must first begin with making students, faculty, staff, and administrators accountable for ending any negative experiences associated with the increasing significance of race, class, and gender found in my classroom. This accountability will come with critical consciousness, a change of consciousness in academe, and the unity and enhancement of my experiences per se. Building on bell hooks's idea of critical consciousness, I define critical consciousness to mean immediate learned attention to inclusions in order to build equality and equity within the predominantly White world of academe. It means consciously doing away with exploitation and domination. According to hooks, "To have a nondominating context, one has to have a lived practice of interaction. And this practice has to be conscious, rather than some sentimental notion that 'you are born into the world with the will to do good towards one another.' In reality, this nonexploitative way to be with one another has to be practiced; resistance to the possibility of domination has to be learned" (hooks 1994, 241).

On the Threshold

The politics of race, class, and gender add to the daily reminder that you are the Other and are marginalized in White academe. For me, teaching at a predominantly White institution is a self-transforming, liminal experience. My uncertainties about teaching at a White institution are expressed here in the context of an autobiographical account of my triumphs and tragedies. I commence my story with childhood memories that appear to be significant antecedents to my work as a Black female occupying a faculty position in the Department of Sociology at Western State University, a predominantly White comprehensive university. I perceive my past as a process that brought me to my present self. Journey with me as I tell my story of teaching through the politics of race, class, and gender. Visualize with me as I struggle to locate myself in the larger web of the predominantly White world of higher education. Listen as I describe the complexities of race, class, and gender that pervade daily life in my White classroom.

Remembering Childhood

In the late sixties, I entered second grade excited by the idea that Blacks and Whites could be schooled together for the first time. From that moment, I knew I was on a journey to find my place in the predominantly White world of bourgeois education and schooling. Living in poor and working-class Black culture did not prepare me for my journey into formal education. Nor did my early socialization prepare me to view teaching as a political process. For the first eighteen years of my life, I did not talk about or ask questions about race, class, or gender. In those days, I only processed the world around me, a world largely free of racial identities. In retrospect, my White teachers (during the formative years of schooling) gave me confidence in my abilities, though not in my identities.

My parents dared not and could not communicate to me, or to my four siblings, the effects of race, class, or gender on our subjective and objective selves. We knew enough to be proud Black folks. Best of all, they did not socialize us to believe we were disadvantaged by our sex, race, or class. Frankly, we did not know we were poor until a few Whites in our small rural southern community described in meaningless gestures over the years our lack of the finer things in life (e.g., car, television, and phone). The absence of these things was supposed to reflect our poverty. God, love, two parents, siblings, extended family, food on the table, clean clothes, health, and a roof over our heads made us feel the richness of humanity. These are the privileges I know about and can write of and the ones that I identify as particularly relevant to my autobiography at this point in my life. I interpret these privileges as the building blocks that transformed me into the self I am today. Those privileges of youth, along with my present privileges (a husband, four children, good health, extended formal education, and employed status), sustain me for the teaching challenges I face as a Black female professor on a predominantly White campus.

During those early years, I felt confident, but I was oftentimes confused by my childhood dreams, fears, and aspirations. The ugly spell segregation still had over Blacks in those days kept me fearful about my outcomes in life. I spent those early years anticipating the moment when I would find my place. By the time I entered the university, I knew I wanted to teach to integrate the Other. I never knew I would be viewed as that other. How naïve! I had selected sociology as my discipline in undergraduate and graduate school in order to understand marginalization, exclusion, and oppression. I felt this knowledge would prepare me to make my own contribution toward social justice. It saddens me to know that my undergraduate and graduate training failed to prepare me for the political nature of university teaching. Should I not have been impassioned with the desire to educate all persons about the value of difference and creativity? Would a historically Black university care enough to have prepared me for the challenges I face? Nonetheless, I wanted to be an integrative source and I wanted to help make White institutions integrative. So for the first steps of my journey, I chose two historically predominantly White institutions for my undergraduate and graduate education.

College: A Place about Life

I learned fast that the inequalities I would face in the real world would come from being Black, female, and employed. The overprotection my family provided and the caring my White male and female teachers offered would not last. It was in graduate school that I first realized I would use my sociological training and imagination to teach sociology from a cultural critical feminist perspective, one in which no group or individual would be seen as "The Other." Gaining the knowledge to take on this perspective freed my soul. I believed and felt that the soul must be free to teach, grow, and learn. I psyched my mind into believing one's soul must have the authority to gain knowledge, transform, and change. For the first time I knew I would teach college students their histories and cultures. I longed to have an influence over their souls and personalities, not their otherness. I worked hard in graduate school to learn how to combine theory with practice. Mine would be the pedagogical strategy that would teach all students, particularly Whites, to strive for a dialectical exchange of ideas, thoughts, and visions that would help shape or reshape their consciousness. I was transforming myself and believed others could do so if they really wanted to. I had studied and critiqued the literature on race, class, gender, and sexuality and found I was an example of the stereotypical construction of race, class, and gender discussed in the literature and data. With a new Ph.D. (a bourgeois credential), I felt ready to rearrange the true meaning of race, gender, and class through my teaching and research. I was ready to empower my teaching self with rich nourishment from my substantive areas of study. Added to my life experience, my studies in race, class, and diversity education gave me direction to include gender in all the courses I would grow to love to teach.

But, Why Question My Teaching Self?

My teaching self was constantly confronted with many unanswered questions. Why journey to teach at a predominantly White institution? Will

White students like me? Will they see me as an authority figure? Will they like my teaching method and style? Will uninterested White students appreciate the subject matter? Will White students think I am too Black? Will Black students think I am too White? Why dichotomize students, or myself, in this way? Will it cost too much of my time and energy to teach White students? Will it be worth the effort? Will my main goal to teach my undergraduate and graduate students to establish trust and a listening respect for each other be achieved?

After five years of teaching, I have learned that the answers to the above questions can only come with time. However, the resistance of some students and faculty to my teaching has devastated my journeying self a few times too many. Is my teaching self in danger? Do I see myself out there on the edge? Perhaps, but I chose to teach at such an institution so that I could challenge students to be open and free to end domination and to grow intellectually, socially, and culturally in preparation for an increasingly diverse world. I felt this large body of students was being robbed of the knowledge necessary for cultural growth and knowledge. I came to realize I have no choice but to come, enter, and re-enter the classroom and teach one day at a time. I was, and am, committed to this endeavor.

Acknowledging and seeing the world differently are vital for human survival. I have spent the last five years teaching an almost totally White student body knowledge about how our social world is constructed. My classes in race relations, cultural studies, social institutions, and social inequality are designed to employ instructional methods that demasculinize and demystify race, class, and gender. I hope my methods leave students with an understanding that race, class, and gender are simultaneous and intersecting systems of meanings that are embedded in the experiences of all people. The main focus of my teaching has been to get students to see how the intersecting meanings of race, class, and gender also shape systems of privilege and inequality. Reconstructing knowledge is a rewarding task that gives me the opportunity to bring diversity into the classroom.

I am a first-generation college graduate. In 1995, at 38, I was the first Black born in the United States of America to receive a doctoral degree in sociology at The University of Nebraska-Lincoln, historically a predominantly White institution. In 1996, I was the first Black female sociologist to be hired in a tenure-track position in a department of sociology at a predominantly White, border-state, regional institution of higher learning. Echoing Allen, "my 'only' status" has not changed during my years at Western State University (Allen 1998, 578). My evaluations show that students in general do want change. They want new consciousness. Most, however, are not ready to tackle the old order within the academy. Below are some opinions from students in my race relations course that describe how they believe changes are in order:

> This course is something that needs to be taught. Learning sociology from a black woman was especially nice because we were able to see a view in life that's not always weighed to the fullest. Mrs. O. is a very intelligent woman who definitely did her job well.

*   *   *

> Everyone states that through education, we can break down racism and stereotypes. If education is the key, this class needs to be part of the general education requirements. A lot has been learned about people from all ethnic backgrounds.

*   *   *

> I would like to say that I have enjoyed this course so much that I decided to make it my major! This has by far been my best class of the semester. I think I liked it so much because it was one of the few classes I could learn something from and then apply it to my surroundings.

*   *   *

> I liked that I got to hear a different point of view about race relations in America. I learned much about how much discrimination goes on and the subtle ways in which it is done.

*   *   *

> This is the first class I have enjoyed in a long time. I think the teacher was excellent, she showed no biases to any diversity or minority. She showed us how maybe all races should react to one another. Dr. "O" does a wonderful job.

The above excerpts show students describing their developmental needs to learn about diversity. My courses give students a chance to transcend and become motivated by different kinds of goals that may not specifically be laid out at predominantly White institutions. Students need challenging experiences and visions to help them decide who they want to be and how they want their world to be. Further, students need to be taught by caring professors committed to their developmental growth, be it intellectual, emotional, or cultural.

This group of caring professors should include Black female professors as role models. The notion of needing role models is affirmed by the remarks made by one student:

> I have learned so very much from you and I will never forget what you have taught me forever and for that I am eternally grateful! You were put on this earth (I be-

lieve) to change students lives and please know that you have accomplished this with me. You are inspiring, dedicated, and intelligent and I have never had a professor like you. You are a role model for African American women as well as everyone else. I admire you and I hope to have another class with you.

For the sake of my soul and my students alike, I must engage in radical political thought to bring about social justice and change. I must fight to become a role model for all students within the walls of White academe. Here is a sample of some of the responses from my students about respect and the atmosphere of my classroom:

> I believe I have learned more from this class than I have from any other here. It's always a delight to be here. I loved the atmosphere of the classroom. I usually never speak in other classes only when I have questions, and I have never felt scared to voice my opinion. I have learned a lot from the class debates. The semester went by too quickly!

*   *   *

> This is a great course in that it is much needed and should be required for all majors, I liked the extra reading material and the class discussions. It's not surprising that students can indeed get more from a class with a format that allows for participatory discussions. I have changed my attitude about a lot of things b/c of this course. In addition, I was happy that you had us move around and mix on the first day. Otherwise, I would not have met some great people.

Some of my students feel comfortable expressing themselves and being open to understanding that many people from different backgrounds play major roles in all American culture. Students get much needed knowledge when they take courses that offer race, class, and gender as issues affecting society. Again, I teach students to think critically about the politics of race, class, and gender barriers that can keep one from taking the necessary steps toward knowledge, transformation, and change.

Coming, Entering, Re-entering the Classroom as Students Resist

Even though many of my students are growing, I cannot begin to address the large number of students who daily take part in patriarchal ideological thinking that prevents their emotional and intellectual growth. I have had approximately 1,000 undergraduate students who came to my classroom because they needed to fill some general education or writing or ethnic requirement component. I find many are not passionately interested in the theory and practice of knowing what goes on beyond a patriarchal world. Many students do not feel comfortable moving out of their usual world and into a location that accepts and values difference. I have often wondered, based upon the gender composition of my department (eight White males, one White female, and one Black female), whether those White students who have only White male professors teaching them will be willing to cross boundaries into thinking critically about oppression in the world. Unfortunately, in my observations, I must continue to keep some students guessing about who is coming to class. I gladly welcome students who need to fill a requirement into my classes. It is a chance, as bell hooks says "to create a culture where those who could occupy the colonizing location have the freedom to self-interrogate, challenge, and change while the vast majority of the colonized lack such freedom is merely to keep in place existing structures of domination" (hooks 1994, 5-6). Some do consciously elect to keep in place existing attitudes about power.

Again, here are responses from some students in my Social Institutions, Race Relations, and Introduction to Sociology classes about me and my teaching:

> I feel that this teacher is unfair. She goes back on her word all the time, and as an education major I know not to do that to students. I also feel that she picks her favorites, especially those individuals that are of her own race.

*   *   *

> This teacher has a very narrow-minded, one sided point of view. She appears to be against anything resembling a white male.

*   *   *

> Her opinions seemed to be very prejudiced and stereotypical, only standing up for people who were in the minority or who were just like her. I would not recommend this professor to other students or have positive things to say about her teaching style. Her integrity and judgement were extremely poor and disappointing.

*   *   *

> I have really disliked this class because this professor has a bad attitude. She told our class she didn't have to do anything but die and it really upset me. She doesn't listen to what we have to say. Just because she is the professor everything is right. Wrong! She doesn't have our grades recorded and if I receive a bad grade I *will* be at the Head of the Departments office with my parents and other officials after grades are distributed.

*   *   *

> I love the class, but too much focus is placed on minority issues.

The attitudes exemplified by the above remarks can make teaching race, class, and gender courses difficult. These attitudes and opinions can function as obstacles to diversity education and development at White institutions.

Comments such as these cause me to question my methods. The political problem appears to be that previously held White male standpoints based on White males' lives, their history, interests, perspectives, and power did not invite the rest of us to interrogate our standpoints (hooks 1994). Almost all predominantly White institutions uphold the White male consciousness that so many students adopt as their own. Some folks and their students in academe simply took on a general way of thinking about those unlike themselves, thus excluding many as classmates, students, and as employable members in their predominantly White institutions. The same kind of domination can keep many Black female professors from becoming oppositional enough to invent themselves in ways that are "liberatory," especially in their classrooms. bell hooks says that

> if we fail to interrogate our standpoints, we may unwittingly undermine and betray allegiances to those who are less privileged. That vigilance is particularly needed at a time when there are so many material rewards offered us by mainstream white culture when we participate in the commodification of blackness in ways that betray radical commitment to social justice, to ending racism. (1995, 170–171)

I cannot give up cultural feminist thinking because it helps create new meaning and knowledge for my students' intellectual growth. However, honoring a cultural feminist perspective in which the Other is absent is, simultaneously, potentially liberatory and potentially oppressive. Knowing you are breaking ground for the less privileged is powerful, but the race, class, and gender stereotypes add to the daily reminder you are indeed the Other, at least in the minds of some students, faculty, and staff. The politics in those stereotypes can lead to social attitudes, prejudice, more stereotypes, discrimination, and a lack of mentoring and role modeling. bell hooks explains:

> Stereotypes, however inaccurate, are one form of representation. Like fictions, they are created to serve as substitutions, standing in for what is real. They are there to tell it like it is but to invite and encourage pretense. They are a fantasy, a projection onto the Other that makes them less threatening. Stereotypes abound when there is distance. They are an invention, a pretense that one knows when the steps that would make real knowing possible cannot be taken or are not allowed. (1995, 38)

How can disciplines, departments, and universities be reshaped? Most important, who should be held responsible for students' negative perceptions about race, class, and gender? Will the Black female professor ever be able to come to class not defined and labeled by race, class, or gender stereotypes? Some feel they must exert their power and authority over the Black female professor; to them my presence challenges the norm. For instance, I have had some students use the politics of race and gender to challenge me on my teaching methods and grading. As indicated in some of the student teaching evaluations that I quoted above, I have been challenged on integrity issues and have been accused of hating White males, of favoring my own race, and of having a bad attitude. I also painfully remember the one White female (at least she said she was White) student who tried to challenge my authority. I draw special attention to this situation because it is the first time on this journey that I felt that the effort to transform unenlightened White students was not worth the hurt, pain, and stress one may encounter when teaching becomes highly political. I remember her jumping up and shouting that she had spoken to the department head about my teaching and that he too had agreed with her complaints. I asked her to leave my class because she was interrupting learning. She refused. I left instead. In my conversation with the department's head, he reminded me how important it is to handle students with care in trying to calm them. Why was this nontraditional student upset in the first place? Why had I continued to allow her to interrupt my classes prior to this episode? I do have the authority to ask students to discuss the readings in class before their peers. This student felt it was my responsibility to discuss the reading; after all, I was the professor. Believing and trusting in my standpoint, I had the student permanently removed from my class.

Feminist Standpoint Theory

I often use feminist standpoint theory to question social realities that deny the kind of power and authority that I need in my classroom to offer interested students a new vision in order to learn and grow critically and creatively. According to Hennessy, "Theorizing discourse as ideology implies that the feminist standpoint is a critical practice, an act of reading that intervenes in and rearranges the construction of meanings and the social relations they support" (1993, 27). Essentially, feminist standpoint theory is useful because it provides insight for detecting patterns and behaviors that constitute social reality (Hennessy 1993). Standpoint theory challenges females to examine their perspectives about reality. Because I have established over the years a standpoint that empowers my teaching self, I was able to question this student's reality. Did she not like me because I was Black, of strained Black middle-class status, a female with authority and a terminal degree? Had I not had a standpoint I would not have had the power and authority to have the student removed from my classroom. However, such classroom episodes make the liminal teaching journey tedious and unproductive.

When I started teaching was I totally ignorant of the challenges that lay ahead of me? Or was I totally embedded in the concerns for students' growth and development? Progressive causes that resist ideological meanings that oppress or keep one marginalized or make students question the credibility of some professors but not others must never be undermined. I concur with Patricia Hill Collins's reading of standpoint theory "as an interpretive framework dedicated to explicating how knowledge remains central to maintaining and changing unjust systems of power" (1997, 375). Take for instance this White male's point of view:

> Anne, I'm in your soc 362 class this summer. After hearing you speak for an entire week I had to e-mail you to tell you of your powerful influence over people. My dad has been an administrator for over twenty years and I talked to him about you over the phone last night. I told my father about how powerful and sincere you were when you spoke in front of the class. For the first time I found myself not mentioning race. I never once said the black lady is my teacher for summer school. I actually told my father you didn't even need to be a teacher. He responded by asking why should she not be a teacher. I explained to him how you captured peoples attention when you spoke, and how sincere you were when explaining something to students. I told him you needed to be heard by all not just forty students. I guess the compliment I am trying to give is you make other people want to become better. I found myself for the first time today wanting to learn about different races and different backgrounds. My whole life has been black and white, but you've opened another door. Thanks!

My journey into teaching will continue because I know as a parent and an educator that students need to be taught by caring professors committed to their developmental growth, be it intellectually, emotionally, or culturally. The power of standpoint will carry me along the journey and will help me locate myself in the political climates created by some White institutions.

Locating My Journeying Self

I struggle to locate myself in the larger web of my predominantly White institution where Black faculty and students are few in number. While the state's Black population is nearly 8 percent, the most current data from the Kentucky Council on Postsecondary Education show that in the fall of 1998, the rate of resident graduate enrollment for Blacks was only 2.7 percent. The employment rate in 1997–1998 of Blacks in executive, administrative, and managerial positions in academe was 3.3 percent. Out of the 540 faculty that the university currently employs, there are 32 Black professors. Although there has been some progress in the last few years, we need more students and faculty to represent the growing diverse population we are starting to serve on this campus and within this conservative rural community. Progress is being made in this regard. On May 7, 1998, a draft of the University's Strategic Plan was issued to the University's Board of Regents. The draft outlined the need to "increase diversity of student body by 10 percent, as reflected in racial, ethnic, and international student population data."

Additionally, the plan called for an increase in the diversity of faculty by 10 percent based on race, ethnicity, and gender. I see myself on this campus located in a powerless role. At the same time, I feel responsible for helping to make the academy conscious of itself. I am situated in institutional contexts I did not make, but I am working to be part of the institution's remaking by providing diversity education to White students. As duCille points out:

> How do we negotiate an intellectually charged space for experience in a way that is not totalizing and essentializing—a space that acknowledges the constructedness of and the differences within our lived experiences while at the same time attending to the inclining, rather than the declining, significance of race, class, culture, and gender? (1994, 607)

I know race, class, and gender are crucial issues on my campus, but I do not see myself in my classroom, department, or on campus as an "outsider within" the academy (Allen 1998; Hill Collins 1991; duCille 1994). I do, however, see myself as powerless. I was once asked by a young colleague if I felt marginalized. I remember specifically answering the colleague that "only my presence but not me as a person" felt marginalized. As duCille says, "we are always already other" (1994, 612). Again, my standpoint sustains me daily. I claim my soul. I have tried from the very beginning of my liminal teaching journey to claim my personhood (Rich 1976; Smith 1987) irrespective of how students from rural parts of the state may see me. As stated previously, I use my sociological training and imagination to teach from a cultural feminist perspective in which no group or individual is seen as the Other. My presence may be marginalized, but my soul is not. Since graduate school, my challenge has been to help destabilize mainstream thinking in academe and to invite all to think and act freely in my classrooms. I acknowledge that there will be tension in my classroom, but I want my students to know that to think and act freely comes from respecting the human soul. The spell of White academe cannot and should not be allowed to keep the human soul in bondage. How can unenlightened White students and I unite our consciousness and make the classrooms enjoyable for wisdom and knowledge? Simply, it is a call for a sociology of academe.

The Project: A New Sociology in Academe

Sociology is a systematically developed consciousness of society and its social relations. This consciousness can be either good or evil. Sociology is an analysis of collective experiences. Sociology allows one to ask questions and seek answers about society. Academe is a fraction of society with its own set of social relations and its own unanswered questions. What seems to be missing in society as well as in the academy is an honoring of collective experiences. Students, professors, staff, and administrators are not working together on a shared political project to end oppression and create equality and equity for all. There are no political forces in place to end the politics associated with teaching race, class, and gender for inclusion in predominantly White institutions of higher learning. My experience at Western State University suggests that many students still support historic positions, and some refuse to let them go. The old consciousness of academe still ignores and excludes the presence and experiences of some of its members.

Under a new sociology of community, the presence and experiences of difference can be recognized and valued within academe. Incoming students can be required to complete diversity orientation workshops to assist them with their developmental needs regarding diversity. Social relations can be nurtured and developed. Specifically, Black females like myself can be located as valuable members of academe's total community without reference to race or sex. Students can grow to accept the right for individuals to hold complete power or agency over their own personhoods and diversities. For these changes to occur, a different sociology must be in place at predominantly White institutions. I would hope today that the old White male history, interests, perspectives, and power are not the view of the world that predominantly White institutions want their students to learn. I am convinced that a new sociology within academe can allow cultural diversity and attitudes that are "liberatory" for Black females to teach on the White campus and in the White classroom. But how can we unite our consciousness and make the academy conscious of itself?

This new sociology is designed to raise, and then unite, the consciousness of unenlightened professors, heads, deans, staff, administrators, members of boards of regents, and students in predominantly White institutions of higher learning. All related spouses, children, parents, grandparents, grandchildren, and legal guardians will be invited to take part in this new sociology to make teaching through the politics of race, class, and gender an insult of the past. Collective selves must be able to communicate their collective experiences across all boundaries with the potential for understanding each other irrespective of race, class, and gender. As bell hooks notes, "Liberation takes place only in a context where we are able to imagine subjectivities that are diverse, constantly changing, and always operating in states of cultural contingency" (1995, 248). Social disorganization occurs in academe and its classrooms when collective selves are divided. A sense of belonging is so important, and a sociological community is so necessary for students' growth and development.

A new sociological community is a call to revisit our intended intellectual work, develop a critique of domination, and to challenge patriarchal ideology so that the Black female's professorship matters in the classroom. bell hooks argues that

> recognition allows a certain kind of negotiation that seems to disrupt the possibility of domination. If a person makes a unilateral decision that does not account for me, then I feel exploited by that decision because my needs haven't been considered. But if that person is willing to pause, then at that moment of pause there is an opportunity for mutual recognition....This doesn't necessarily mean the person will change what they intended to do, but it means that (at least temporarily) I am not rendered an object by their carrying forth with their objective. (hooks 1994, 241)

bell hooks argues for the recognition of the roles of the Black female professor and the power of Black females, but not as objects. I do believe this arrangement is possible through practice in an intimate sociological community; a community in which all members can freely grow and feel that they are valued and respected in the discipline, the department, and the academy. Smith says that "in proposing remedies, we have in general, as in other fields of intellectual work, drawn on women's experience as the primary source to correct the situation" (1987, 61). Can Black female professors raise the consciousness of White faculty and students?

Such feminist theorists as Smith (1987) and Hartsock (1997) say that new knowledge can be found in understanding power relations. One wonders if some of this new knowledge cannot be gained from the experiences of Black female professors who are located in predominantly White institutions of higher education like myself. And whether this new knowledge might not be a source to correct teaching through the politics of race, class, and gender in the White classroom.

In Closing

I have used some of my student evaluations to share stories of frustration, struggle, and achievement in teaching. The excerpts presented call for a more diverse curriculum and a platform from which to challenge the unenlightened to use the new sociology to critically think about a more open community on predominantly White campuses and classrooms. Specifically, research is needed about the development of sociological explanations for the politics of race, class, and gender at predominantly White institutions of higher learning. This essay is a cry for research and a wake-up call to the rest of academe for long discussions about gender, class, and race. If sociology and its liberatory principles are practiced at White institutions, then students will be less consumed with concern about who is coming to class.

To all my readers, if teaching through the politics of race, class, and gender is your task, or part of your life experience in academe, I ask that you not let the internal and external barriers to the teaching self destroy your soul. Your soul is your own.

Anne B. Onyekwuluje is Assistant Professor in the sociology department at Western Kentucky University. She received her Ph.D. in 1995 from the University of Nebraska-Lincoln. She specializes in education, race, class, and gender inequality. Onyekwuluje wrote her dissertation on adolescents, parents, teachers, and administrators defining multiculturalism and diversity. She has written on African Americans' perceptions and fear of crime. Her latest two publications look at diversity and its impact on adolescents and schools. Her current project is about grant opportunities for strategies on diversity development for adolescents.

Author's Note

I wish to thank Jane Olmsted and Joan Krenzin for their comments and suggestions. I am also grateful to Wilma King, Osi Onyekwuluje, and Paul Wozniak for their helpful review in making this narrative essay workable. I would also like to thank my two sons, Kanayo (8) and Kené (6), for their helpful typing.

Note

1. See bell hooks's book *Outlaw Culture Resisting Representation* for a discussion of the beloved community (1994, 234-237).

Works Cited

Abercrumbie, P. E. 1999. "Preparing to Cross the River." *Black Issues in Higher Education* 16 (22): 112.

Allen, B. J. 1998. "Black Womanhood and Feminist Standpoints." *Management Communication Quarterly* 11 (4): 575-586.

Brown, M. C. 1996. "One, Two, Three. . . Red Light." *Black Issues in Higher Education* 13: 74-75.

Buzzanell, P. M. 1994. "Gaining a Voice: Feminist Organizational Communication Theorizing." *Management Communication Quarterly* 7 (4): 339-383.

Collision, M. 1999. "Achieving Career Satisfaction in the Academy." *Black Issues in Higher Education* 16 (20): 26-28.

Daufin, E.-K. 1995. Confessions of a Womanist Professor. *Black Issues in Higher Education*, March 9, 1995, 34-35.

duCille, A. 1994. "The Occult of True Black Womanhood: Critical Demeanor and Black Feminist Studies." *Signs: Journal of Women in Culture and Society* 19 (3): 537-629.

Etter-Lewis G. 1993. *My Soul Is My Own: Oral Narratives of African American Women in the Professions*. New York: Routledge.

Hartsock, N. C. M. 1997. "Comment on Hekman's 'Truth and Method: Feminist Standpoint Theory Revisited: Truth or Justice?'." *Signs: Journal of Women in Culture and Society* 2 (2): 367-374.

Hennessy, R. 1993. "Women's Lives/Feminist Knowledge: Feminist Standpoint as Ideology Critique." *Hypatia* 8 (1): 14-34.

Hill Collins, P. 1991. *Black Feminist Thought: Knowledge Consciousness and the Politics of Empowerment*. New York: Routledge.

———. 1996. "Toward a New Vision: Race, Class, and Gender as Categories of Analysis and Connection." In *The Meaning of Difference: American Constructions of Race, Sex, Gender, and Social Class*, edited by K. E. Rosenblum and T.-M. C. Travis. New York: McGraw Hill.

———. 1997. "Comment on Hekman's "Truth and Method: Feminist Standpoint Theory Revisited": Where's the Power?" *Signs: Journal of Women in Culture and Society* 22 (2): 375-381.

———. 1998. "Controlling Images and Black Women's Oppression." In *Seeing Ourselves*, edited by J. J. Macionis and N. V. Benokraitis. Upper Saddle River, NJ: Prentice Hall.

hooks, b. 1981. *Ain't I a Woman: Black Women and Feminism*. Boston: South End Press.

———. 1992. *Black Looks: Race and Representation*. Boston: South End Press.

———. 1994. *Outlaw Culture Resisting Representation*. New York: Routledge.

———. 1995. *Killing Rage*. New York: Henry Holt.

Krenzin, J. 1995. "Factors Influencing the Retention of Black Faculty on Predominantly White Campuses." *Research in Race and Ethnic Relations* 8: 115-138.

Longino, H. E. 1993. "Feminist Standpoint Theory and the Problems of Knowledge." *Signs: Journal of Women in Culture and Society* 19 (1): 201–212.

Mills, C. W. 1959. *The Sociological Imagination*. New York: Oxford University Press.

Pigford, A. B. 1988. Being a Black Faculty Member on a White Campus: My Reality. *Black Issues in Higher Education*, November 24, 1988, 76.

Rich, A. 1976. *Of Woman Born*. Tenth anniversary ed. New York: W.W. Norton.

Smith, O. E. 1987. *The Everyday World as Problematic: A Feminist Sociology*. Boston: Northeastern University Press.

CHAPTER FIFTEEN

A U.S.-Born Latina Professor: Cultural Stranger in My Own Classroom

DIANA I. RIOS

Abstract

I APPLY CONCEPTS used in intercultural communication research—that of the cultural stranger and the cultural Other—to describe my experiences in three separate public universities in the United States. I use the approach of autobiography of work to guide and frame this essay. My observations contain critical insights and evaluations about Latina professors and White student interaction in the classroom, which may range from dealing with "average" students to dealing with KKK members. I also share strategies for teaching excellence and inspiring optimism among women of color teaching in predominantly White classrooms.

The number of women faculty members teaching on college campuses across the nation has grown dramatically during the last four decades. Social movements; increased consciousness about ethnicity, race, and gender; and more inclusive hiring policies in higher education have contributed to increased diversity in colleges and universities. Still, the number of women of color who are part of the college teaching force has remained small. What this means for undergraduate and graduate students is that having a non-White faculty member lecturing to them and evaluating their oral and written performance has remained unusual. What the uniqueness of color, in particular, means for a Chicana (Mexican American), or a U.S.-born and -raised Latina is that she is still a cultural stranger on her own campus, in her own department, and in her own classroom (Medina and Luna 2000).

This critical essay will discuss how Latinas can be perceived and judged negatively by students in the predominantly White college classroom. I will use the conceptual approach of "cultural stranger" and "cultural other" that is more typically used in intercultural communication research on foreigners and host countries to describe the ethnocentric perceptions that U.S. students may have of the Latina-heritage professor. I will touch on related concepts of prejudice, ethnic/racial/cultural bias, and negative attribution. Biased expectations can include negative prejudgments about ethnicity/race, personal character, gender, and social class.

I will draw from eight years of professional experience teaching at three predominantly White campuses. These campuses are major universities in their respective states—the University of Texas at Austin, where I was a doctoral student; the University of New Mexico, Albuquerque, where I held my first job; and the University of Connecticut in Storrs, where I currently teach. I hold joint appointments in the Department of Communication Sciences and the Puerto Rican and Latino Studies Institute (PRLS). I serve as an Associate Director of PRLS.

The University of Texas (UT) is a huge university in the capital city of Texas. The campus sprawls across many acres of land. People of color attending the university are in the minority. Chicana/os and African Americans are more likely to be found in east Austin and south Austin working-class and working poor neighborhoods. During the late 1980s to the early 1990s, undergraduates and graduate students of color made their presence known to the university community and public through meetings, visits, events, and particularly during the "Racism Hearings" held by UT officials to document and understand racist incidents on campus.

The main campus of the University of New Mexico (UNM) is in Albuquerque. It is located in a rough, urban setting. Students of color, primarily of Spanish-speaking heritage, were significant but still in the minority when I taught there. Again, most of the people of color could be found in neighborhoods, not attending the university. Faculty of color are numeric minorities on both campuses.

The University of Connecticut (UConn) is enveloped by lush ruralness. New England gentility is a special brand, dripping with privilege. UConn has less diversity than UT or UNM. Ethnic minorities tend to live in big cities such as Hartford (thirty to forty minutes away) and attend community colleges. Faculty and students of color at UConn are numerical minorities. Like the other campuses, UConn faculty and students of color and their White allies are very vocal on campus with regard to diversity issues.

I draw from personal and scholarly sources to compose this essay. My resources include personal archive materials such as teaching evaluations, personal diaries, memos, and newsclippings. Given the nature of an "autobiography of work," I will use a first-person narrative style and heavily employ description. This essay contains advice primarily aimed at novice women of color who teach in majority White institutions. There is also advice to colleagues and administrators who wish to know what they can do to support women of color on their campuses.

Latina Academics as Cultural Strangers

The concept of the cultural stranger and related concepts in cross-cultural encounters is appropriate for my narrative about teaching in majority European American institutions. Gudykunst (1998) discusses cultural strangers as individuals who differ in cultural background to the extent that those who encounter this individual find the encounter disconcerting in various degrees because of cultural distinctions. The many facets of difference, either real or perceived, between Latinas and members of the majority in higher education produce an intercultural encounter laden with all the challenges and difficulties that typify intercultural interactions. A Latina's skin tone and color, hair texture, distinctive physical features, non-verbal style, verbal accentuation, cultural style, and behavior patterns do not match majority White characteristics. She is the cultural Other for the majority of her students.

Gudykunst explains that cultural strangeness provokes various reactions in intercultural encounters. Some may find the cultural stranger to be interesting or curious, while others may find the "stranger" to be dangerous to the order of their socio-cultural world. He suggests that because the United States is a land with a long history of cultural strangers, it has a normative tendency to find cultural strangeness interesting. Though this may indeed hold some truth, compared to less heterogeneous societies, the presence of ethnocentrism and overt and covert racism still places women of color such as Latinas in the role of cultural stranger in the United States.

I contend that the day when Latinas and all people of color do not have to be concerned about racial profiling (or "driving while Black or Brown"), real-estate redlining, unequal bank lending practices, exclusive hiring, unequal distribution of educational resources in primary and secondary education will be the day when we cease to be cultural and ethnic strangers in our own land. Latinas encounter overt and covert negative reactions to their presence in higher education that can be plainly called racist (Reyes and Halcon 1988). In the recent times of "enlightened racism" (the term belongs to Jhally and Lewis 1992), I would say that prejudiced and biased individuals may also exhibit sexist behaviors as proxies for racism in a given situation.

As cultural strangers, Latinas experience reactions in the classroom and at various campus sites that include prejudice, social stereotyping, and negative attribution. The much-quoted Allport has defined prejudice as "an antipathy based on faulty and inflexible generalization. It may be felt or expressed. It may be directed toward a group as whole, or toward an individual because he is a member of that group" (1954, 7). Ting-Toomey further states that "individuals can hold prejudices against others based on their skin color, foreign accent or local dialect, cultural or religious practice, and the like" (1999, 164).

Social stereotypes are a result of inflexible impressions, images, or "pictures in our heads" that we have of others. It is a result of oversimplified thinking about and categorizing of outgroups—those different from ourselves. Stereotypes are not inherently bad. However, narrow, rigid, inaccurate, or negative stereotyping of cultural strangers is indeed destructive in cross-cultural interactions (see Gudykunst 1998, 89–94). Ting-Toomey describes how, in the process of attribution, a perceiver tries to make sense of other people's behaviors and attribute meanings or causes to people's behaviors in the effort to manage a complex environment and add predictability and a sense of closure (Ting-Toomey 1999, 152).

There are different types of attribution. In the process of perceiving the Other, the Other is subject to scrutiny for perceived individual or environmentally based dispositions. So the perceiver weighs information that can be attributed to the individual themselves (e.g., being Chicana, *Boricua*,[1] Cubana) and factors outside the individual (e.g., icy weather conditions, crowded hallways, old video equipment). For example, students seeing their Mexican American or Puerto Rican instructor come in ten minutes late for a class will be faced with weighing the individual-based information and the environmental data they have. Will majority students intuitively think the instructor is lazy or had too long a siesta, given her culture and ethnicity? Or will they attribute her lateness to external conditions such as icy sidewalks or crowded hallways? When the video and audio equipment fail in the classroom during the viewing of a video, is it because the instructor herself (as a woman, as a person of Latino heritage) was incapable of understanding and working with the technology, or is the technology at the public university overused?

A fundamental attribution error is committed when the perceiver overestimates the influence of negative dispositional factors in explaining a stranger's negative performance and underestimates situational factors. For example, if students attribute a Latina instructor's lateness to her being of Latino heritage and culture "because Hispanics can't keep time" and underestimates icy sidewalks or crowded hallways, they have committed a fundamental attribution error.

Early in my teaching life I found the appropriateness of these and other concepts to explain the behaviors of students to be ironic. I was teaching several overenrolled courses in intercultural communication,[2] and the classroom, group, and individual interactions I had were shocking to me. As many academic teacher-scholars can attest, it is a surrealistic feeling to conduct research on ethnic and racial groups, prepare lectures for a class on the nature of prejudice, and have various manifestations of prejudice or stereotyping appear before one's eyes. In my early experiences, I concluded that I was either going to go insane and begin obsessing about yellow wallpaper[3] or a Dalí oil on canvas, or I needed to seek coping mechanisms (see section below) in order to increase success in the majority classroom.

Women of Color Gaining Teaching Experience

I found that it was hard for women and women of color to get teaching experience in graduate schools. I thought that ambition, my academic track record as a doctoral student, and my academic pedigree from the University of Michigan, Ann Arbor and the University of California at Berkeley would be enough evidence for a decision maker to let me experience a classroom at the University of Texas at Austin. Evidence indicated that I and other women like me were not considered to be important contributors to the teaching pool. We could only guess that negative traits were attributed to us or that we were typed as weaker or somehow lesser because of our gender and color.

I discussed my situation at length with decision makers at the Center for Mexican American Studies (CMAS), which invested in my teaching by funding me for three semesters. The Center demonstrated to me and other women of color over the years that we were valuable teaching assets. I felt professionally validated. The positive traits that I knew I possessed were attributed to me. I was typed as intelligent and worthy. CMAS granted me a unique privilege that, as I was painfully aware, many other women of color at UT campuses and across the United States would not have. Not all campus units such as CMAS were as developed and well funded for research and teaching. Also, research and teaching units such as CMAS are rare on U.S. campuses.

"It takes a few years to make a good teacher," my father told me calmly on the trip from the Oakland International Airport to our home in Contra Costa County. As a beginning professor, I would go "home" sometimes to visit my family in the San Francisco Bay Area. I would look forward to staring out on what was left of the view of San Pablo Bay from the bedroom of my teenage years. The pines grow enormously over the years. My father is a veteran educator and teacher trainer with years of experience in high schools, junior colleges, and universities. I knew that he knew what he was talking about, but I was little consoled because my evaluation scores from undergraduate students would go up and down, and I wanted them to stay up. I wanted excellence and perfection in myself, as I had expected and achieved in university studies. Perhaps I could take a little brain chip out of my father. Maybe he could loan me a little bit of experience in a small vial and then I could give some back when I got more experience.

The fact was that I was a novice teacher and professor with a great deal to learn about teaching and the politics of teaching. I was privileged to have a role model like my father, a man of color who taught during the contexts of countrywide school desegregation, civil rights movements, and beyond. Cultural politics in and out of the classroom reached extreme heights while he was in academia. I would ask, and he would recommend multicultural education books and excitedly tell me about the latest technique he was using with his education students. Personal experience was something I needed to get on my own. Currently, having had more years of teaching, I can still say that one never stops learning about new teaching techniques that keep student interest and promote learning. As a woman of color I know from personal experience that one never stops learning about how to better negotiate the cultural tides of politics in the White academy.

There is nothing like experience. What would have eased my journey toward more consistent, higher student evaluation scores and more effective teaching, in the eyes of the students, would have been teacher training and teaching mentorship in my field of communication. Research I institutions often neglect instructional training among their graduate students and faculty. Such institutions place a high priority on developing new research and theories. I am glad to see that many schools are currently paying more attention to instructional training. I have a passion for research, but I would have also enjoyed on-the-job training in classrooms with a supervising faculty member in the field of communication.

Ideally, teaching mentorship in communication should include practical information about grade and classroom management across types of courses. What is also helpful is information about the types of students to expect and the array of reactions and behaviors one can expect. In short, it helps to know about the sunny and murky sides of students and how to best manage these factors.

New Area of Specialty

A true challenge that I experienced in teaching at UNM was that I had been trained in mass communication research with a specialization in Latino audiences and ethnic/racial groups but I would be teaching primarily in another specialty. I saw a job at UNM, which was building a new program in intercultural communication, as an interesting one, one that I could grow into over time. According to the departmental vision, the small quiet department was going to become the best in the country. I liked that kind of vision, and I wanted to be part of it through effective teaching and research. My big task was to learn a new area for undergraduate instruction. Let me point out that intercultural communication is a different specialty than mass communication, even if one has sociological and anthropological supporting studies in ethnic and racial groups.

My undergraduate teaching evaluations started off low and went up and down as I was learning to teach large numbers of different kinds of undergraduates. UNM had a strong teaching mission and admitted students from expensive area prep schools as well as those who were from poorer schools and were the first in their families to go to college. The more privileged students tended to be White, though there were also working-class White students struggling with their families to survive. The less privileged students were more than likely to be Brown, Black, or Red. European American students were the majority in my large undergraduate classes. I needed to find ways to reach all these students, who had varying levels of college expectations and preparation. Working on ways to reach a variety of students in my new area of teaching was exhausting. Even though there is an overlap in intercultural and mass communication, these two sub-fields are vastly different. I currently have expertise in selected areas in intercultural communication, but gaining that expertise has taken several years.

I took solace in my small Latino graduate seminars where I could share my trained specialty. The comfort I receive from teaching a seminar in my specialty was compounded with the comfort of sharing a space with students of Spanish-speaking heritage. The seminar attracted upper-level undergraduates and some master's students who tended to be Chicana/os, Hispana/os, Latina/os or "Mexicanos."

Classroom Workshops and Visitations

As a new professor, I had some valuable experience to build on from graduate student days. I had a vague idea about what worked and what did not and how to proceed as a tenure-track professor. I, like many before me, learned about undergraduate teaching through trial and error during my first tenure-track job. I attended teaching workshops, talks, and presentations about teaching techniques. Blue-ribboned teaching veterans passed on their knowledge to us fledglings. I would have like to be injected with teaching knowledge *and* experience.

A faculty member visited my classroom once and was kind. She gave some general feedback that was helpful to me. I spoke to nice colleagues who shared with me the way they designed assignments. Once, an administrator (who I refer to as El Patrón because of his style) visited during the last fifteen minutes of my Latino graduate seminar. University and departmental support for teaching, however profound or fleeting, is important for a new assistant professor. It is especially important for women of color, who may not have had teaching experience during graduate school.

It is also important for colleagues not to use strategies that could undermine the professional authority of their new untenured women faculty of color. During two separate semesters at UNM, faculty and graduate students were to trade visits, in order to give each other feedback about the undergraduate courses they were teaching. One semester an overzealous graduate student, who was the patrón's student, was intent on doing her job as a teaching critic. Her observation and feedback was of no help, since she appeared to think that she had the authority of the patrón, though she certainly did not. I was reluctant to provide feedback to someone who would not take it seriously. I also felt angry that this student was given the authority to file a report on me, though she was unfamiliar with my area of teaching, had a great deal less research and teaching experience than I, and had never taken a course with me. Another White graduate student visitor was cheerfully helpful. We shared the approach that "we were all in the teaching business together and let us help one another." We were able to share friendly ideas with one another about our students and, overall, our interaction was enjoyable. Despite our positive exchanges, though, the student was not a seasoned university instructor.

My recommendation is not to appoint graduate student "experts." The university or college has a responsibility to provide high-level professional teaching support and evaluation from colleagues that will improve teaching and support authority in the classroom. Effective teaching is a component that is examined in one's tenure review and therefore deserves appropriate attention. It is tempting for departments, whose senior faculty are busy, to look toward graduate students to assist. However, placing a student at the same level as a faculty member challenges the professional identities that faculty are cultivating. Because women of color must grapple with cultural and racial issues in perception among students in the majority classroom, there is more of a risk that a graduate student, placed in the role of peer evaluator, might do more harm than good.

Latina Faculty Isolation

While at UNM, I was in the southwestern part of the United States, where there are a great many people of Mexican heritage. I could count on authentic food and affordable trips to Mexico, but I was culturally isolated. I was the only Ph.D.-holding tenure-track faculty of color in a department emphasizing a specialty in intercultural communication. I felt this irony to be overwhelming. I was sad to be the only woman of color in the department besides my friends the secretaries. The secretaries became some of my best friends and we would have lunch off the hacienda or go out for dinner and a movie. They would console me and share insights about the practical workings of the university. They did not have easy lives at work, and I cherish the time they set aside to try to make things easier for me.

What I found to be quite sad living in the southwest as a Brown woman professor was that my professional identity could be dismissed. I experienced sexism and racism from individuals who could be either Brown or White. One White male professional at UNM, with whom I had heated discussions in my office regarding topics in my trained specialty, could not accept that I was the expert. Did he see a lower class Mexicana chamber maid who did not make the bed right in his room with her head bowed and a timid "Sí, señor" coming from her lips? I always looked people in the eyes. This person demonstrated that when he interacted with me he saw the Other. Unfortunately, he communicated this perspective to his students who, in turn, did not see me as a "real" professor. I saw a strange rerun of displays of sexism, racism and plain collegial disrespect while at UConn with other colleagues and then, later, with some students. These incidents made me lose respect for certain colleagues and their students and made me feel socio-cultural isolation in the academy as a Latina woman and faculty member.

Professional Authority and Culture Wars

As I review my old intercultural communication materials, I cannot help but wince at those materials whose content was extremely challenging to students in the majority classroom. Using these materials in the majority classroom proved to be difficult in varying degrees. The materials containing the most commentary about U.S. racism or racial/ethnic inequities and conflict provoked the most severe reactions from students who worked to subvert my professional authority. Some of these materials were Thomas Kochman's *Black and White Styles in Conflict* (1981) and Spike Lee's movies *Do the Right Thing* (1989) and *Jungle Fever* (1991).

Spike Lee's films showed strong images of cultural misunderstanding, bigotry, and hatred. Robert Young's *The Ballad of Gregorio Cortez* (1983) and Robert Redford's *The Milagro Beanfield War* (1988) were quite a bit less offensive to students, though they did contain Anglo-Mexicano[4] and Anglo-Hispano[5] conflicts. *Milagro* evoked emotion regarding Anglo-Hispano conflicts with regard to land development and water rights across students since these are historically sensitive issues in the southwest. The film *Mr. Baseball* (1992) was the least offensive. By contrast to all the films described above, majority students and others found *Mr. Baseball*, a comedy starring Tom Selleck, proved the least provoking. Students enjoyed the comedic situations in which the *gaijin*, a foreigner in Japan, found himself.

I believe that the comedic tone and the foreign setting of *Mr. Baseball* allowed the video to be the most palatable. Also, in this video, the European American man Jack Elliott is the key character that audiences are brought to understand, pity, and identify with. Because this man is the victim of cultural misunderstandings, European American audiences are allowed vindication throughout the film, despite the ballplayer's demonstrated ethnocentrism and cross-cultural gaffes. *Milagro* does have comedic situations, but it deals with more substantial cultural conflicts. *Ballad* is a serious film about Mexican/European/American misunderstandings on the border. There are White good guys and bad guys, but it is clear that our hero is a misunderstood Brown man, and most of the bad guys are the White men in the posse that chases him.

What I discovered was that the professional authority of women of color is threatened when she examines Whiteness. I have noticed that many European American students tend to become angry, dissatisfied with the class, and resentful of the instructor when Whiteness is examined and typical White behaviors are placed under the magnifying glass (as they are in Spike Lee's films). A "culture war" is declared (Nieto 2000). Thomas Kochman's saving grace in my undergraduate intercultural courses was that he was European American (though some students assumed he was Black). Otherwise, the students' claims that "you can't say that about White people" and "that's just *not* true" would have turned into more vicious commentary, which, over the years, I have seen from students.

To the accompanying video *Do the Right Thing*, many undergraduate students were apparently pushed to their core. Many students could barely take turns, talking over each other during discussion. The video I placed on reserve for them in the university video library was stolen, forcing several to reluctantly rent the video for another viewing as they were writing their essays about Black and White communication styles. Since I assigned a video and a book that many students found difficult to grapple with, they dismissed the material as invalid and dismissed concepts I presented during my lectures.

I cannot say that the material undermined my professional authority. The material opened Pandora's box, and out flooded White rage with me as the targeted Other at the head of the class. Several students decided to reject my academic authority as part of their rejection of investigating Whiteness and White-Black interactions. Given the tone of students' voices, word choices, and non-verbal communication, I could tell that several students were very uncomfortable, to say the least.

The students that I described at UNM had no affiliation with neo-Nazi movements or the Ku Klux Klan. They were average students, in my estimation. That is, all except two obvious European American male skinheads who would interrupt me in mid-sentence with negative comments about my lecture or the required materials we were using. When I would followup on their comments, assuming at first that they did not learn proper manners as children, they would reveal that they had not examined the materials closely enough to form thoughtful observations. The comments were knee-jerk reactions that were difficult for me to decipher. One of these students used terms such as "tribalism," which I soon found to be linked to White supremacist and reactionary ideas about multiculturalism (see ideas espoused by Schlesinger 1995). Student outbursts by extremists and by mainstream students chipped away at the learning atmosphere and the morale of students who were in the class to really learn.

What was going on in these troubled, angry students' minds, I could only guess. But their behaviors indicated that they were attributing to me traits to make me lesser in their minds. Their comments to me had overtones of disdain. Students would sigh, snort, squirm, roll their eyes, move their heads back and forth, grimace, or just stand up and walk out of the room without explanation. Rejecting the instructor was a step in their rejection of the loathed materials the instructor had made them watch.

Students' frustration with class materials or with their grades can bring their innermost prejudices to the surface. All those things "bad" about people of your ethnic heritage and gender can be attributed to you and then spill out of their mouths. Biased students' simply good, mediocre, and poor performance can be completely attributed to the teaching performance, nationality, and gender of the instructor. In futile attempts to restore their preconceived order of Latina subordination, I witnessed too many troubled majority students launch attacks to undercut the Brown woman authority above them.

At the end of two separate semesters, one young European American man cursed at my closed office door with gender slurs and other verbal insults that cannot be printed. He attributed many negative characteristics to me. Another older-than-average European American man angrily told me in the hallway that he had been discriminated against and threatened that he would "let it go" this time. Both these students at UNM were angry that they had not received A's. These students made clear that the gendered and ethnic expectations they had about me—that I would give them A's because their "higher" position in society as White men demanded it—had not been fulfilled. Apparently, in their minds, I was lower than they in characteristics of perceived social class, gender, and race/ethnicity. They attributed to me an inherent deficiency based on my personal characteristics.

Above I describe comments outside my office and in the hallway. I was shocked to see some of these comment types written in my end-of-semester student evaluations. I could direct hallway students down the hall to the departmental office. Regarding student evaluations, I tried to focus on constructive feedback and asked advice from friendly allies. So what is a woman faculty of color to do with students who push the envelope of freedom of speech and freedom of expression in the classroom? The classroom is a place where young minds exercise their ideas and should be able to healthily debate concepts and theories. They should be able to propose new interpretations. They should be able to voice their very own interpretations.

Because I believe in free student expression, it was difficult for me to silence the voices that I heard in the classroom. It was difficult for me to have to make the decision that students had crossed over the line of healthy debates and healthy challenges. Of course, when I witnessed students crossing over the line on several occasions I became quite disgusted and disillusioned with the ideal of healthy challenges in my large intercultural communication classrooms. Deep down inside I wanted La Llorona to spirit the "bad" students away and dump them in the nearest arroyo, or better yet the Rio Grande. ("La Llorona" translates to "the weeping woman." She is a legend in parts of Mexico and in U.S. regions with Mexican heritage concentrations. She is a lost female soul who weeps and cries out in the night in search of her lost children. She favors areas where there are streams, rivers, and lakes.)

My experiences at UNM, however distasteful they were, prepared me for any negative outbursts students in New England might concoct. When I was rudely, repeatedly interrupted and contradicted during my guest lecturing in a cross-cultural communication class at the University of Connecticut,[6] I handled two European American male students more curtly and proceeded with my train of thought rather than allow the students to derail me. One of the students took the cue to adjust his behavior while the other continued to interrupt.

Immediately after my visit, I telephoned the Office of the Dean of Students. I explained that the instructor was new and was at a loss as to how to handle situations with this student, and so I myself was taking action. The staff person with whom I spoke shed light on strategies to handle a case such as the one I faced in the event that it ever happened again. He emphasized that students are expected to follow a code of conduct and that they are all introduced to their manual when they enter the university. Students whom I perceive as disruptive to the class and who interfere with the learning process of other students can be asked to leave for a specified period of days or on a permanent basis. In extreme cases instructors can use the telephones that are available in the newer classrooms to call the campus police for assistance.

The student at UConn received a phone call and a formal letter in the mail from the Office of the Dean of Students, which, I was told later, he took very seriously; his overall behavior in the classroom improved with the ethnic minority instructor regularly teaching the cross-cultural communication class. I was satisfied that I did not have to think about La Llorona coming all the way over to New England. She would have enjoyed all our rivers, but she had to be content with the Southwest for now.

In this incident at UConn, the support from the dean's office was important in the reassertion of professional authority to the UConn student. My curt response in the class was appropriate, but the phone call and the letter from the dean's office was crucial. My actions and decision to consult with the dean of students strongly stated to the student that that women of color faculty will not be Others for his venting of racial or gender-based aggression and prejudice. Women of color should hold all students accountable for their behavior and call the proper authorities for advice or support if necessary. Women of color on the receiving end of aggression from students should not ignore or excuse the aggression as lack of manners or simple immaturity.

University staff and faculty who hear about or witness such incidents should take positive action to support the faculty member, since too many incidents go unreported or are swept under the rug. Typically faculty of color share these stories among themselves and do not share them even with White allies because faculty of color do not have confidence that their interpretation of events will be believed. Overall, there is no cure for students' perceptions of Latinas as cultural strangers or as the Other. But the exhibition of negative feelings about her ancestry and gender are not to be tolerated.

Coping Mechanisms

Derman-Sparks and Phillips say that "teaching about racism makes enormous demands on the instructor's personal as well as professional resources. We are dealing with highly charged material that personally affects us, our families, our children, and our friends and that invokes intense emotional responses in us as well as in our students" (1997, 146). Let me extend this observation and say that the mere presence of women of color in the classroom is an act itself that "interrupts" (a term used by Lewis 1990) the established norms of European American male structures. The content of a course need not be about race, ethnicity, culture, gender theory, or politics. Negotiating the reactions to my presence in the majority classrooms has consistently placed emotional and professional burdens on me, and I have found it necessary to seek constructive coping mechanisms.

A graduate student I will call Sofia informed me of a Chicana Latina group that she and other Chicanas had recently formed at UNM. The group, called Las Comadres, provided cultural respite for all the Chicanas on campus who were negotiating the reactions to their presence in the classroom as instructors, students, or staff. In Spanish, comadre literally means "co-mother." It is a term that typically refers to a close friend or relative who is part of a Latino family's fictive kinship or blood relative network. It is not a term to be used loosely, and one is honored to be referred to as comadre or compadre (the masculine form). Chicana graduate students and faculty at UNM were many miles away from families, and so students like Sofia saw it fitting to establish an interpersonal network of women who would be comadres to each other.

The times that I took part in a gathering of Las Comadres made me feel connected and joyous. We were not cultural Others when we were together. We ate home made foods with authentic ingredients, code-switched with ease, and confided in one another about relationships and campus politics. A parallel group composed of Chicana faculty would have provided a more powerful place for me to relax and vent. Most important, a parallel group would have been a place where I could have sought advice about teaching and research. Unfortunately, we Chicana faculty were scattered across campus, isolated in our own departments or comfortably set in long-established cliques.

At the University of Texas, I participated in two Latina Chicana support groups specifically designed by and lead by a Chicana psychologist. I recall that the Chicana psychologist was in high demand in private practice because she was so effective and well credentialed. A special, temporary grant had to be gained in order to keep the group in existence. Professionally led groups or informal groups of *comadres* can be very useful for Chicanas and Latinas who need cultural connections with women who share similar challenges in higher education. Universities should invest in professionally led groups and should encourage the formation of informal groups of women of color. It supports the retention efforts of institutions of higher education to have a space where women academics can leave the role of Other behind.

Mentoring Students as a Coping Mechanism

Teaching Latino research seminars and mentoring undergraduate and master's degree students were wonderful mechanisms for coping with the intercultural shocks of covert and overt ethnic and gender bias. I was not treated as the Other under these circumstances. These students sought my seminars and my individual guidance because of my specialties in communication research. I invested a great deal of time in undergraduate students who were the first in their families to go to college. I noticed that I spent more time with them than an average faculty member would, because I understood how high the stakes were for these students of color. I felt it my duty to support them in earning their baccalaureate degrees and sending them off to graduate school in law, psychology, public policy, and communication studies. The undergraduates who called themselves Chicana/os, Hispana/os, Latina/os, Navajo, or Pueblo were a priority in my teaching mind (there were few African Americans or Asian Americans at UNM). These would be the leaders of their communities. Chances were that many of my students would not want to leave the Southwest, given the cultural and spiritual significance of the region that many thought of as "Aztlán." (Aztlán is an ancient Aztec name for lands populated by indigenous peoples. To Chicana/o thinkers, Aztlán represents far more than a geographic location; it represents an entire socio-political worldview.) European American women and men also sought me out, and I mentored them with similar care. Students representing a rainbow of colors still call me in Connecticut for a hello, a word of advice regarding a career move, or a letter of reference.

The communication seminars I taught at UNM were small and allowed personal interaction with each advanced undergraduate and master's degree student. I could be more myself in these seminars. I did not expect nor did I experience cultural or gender-based conflicts. We could discuss several issues at length regarding ethnicity, race, gender, and communication. Students could select their very own topics for in-depth research, and I would show them how to structure their first social science review of literature. Often all students were Spanish speaking, and when that was the case we could use culture-based terms with facility and without explanation. The master's degree students tended to select me to direct their theses, which were natural outcomes of the reviews of literature they completed for the seminar.

Research projects at my graduate school institution, UNM, and UConn have allowed me to mentor and work side by side excellent students of all colors and sexual orientations. These have been projects that strike a chord in myself and in the students themselves. Some of these projects are: "Women Respond to the Film *Like Water for Chocolate*," "Mexican/Spanish Heritage Audiences and the Mass Media," "Latina/os and the Internet," "Women Audiences at the Movies (World War II)," "Interethnic Relationships," and "Latino and African American Communication."

Overall, my mentoring of others has proven to be an excellent coping mechanism. My students and I hold mutual respect for one another. I am eager for them to achieve the most that they are capable of doing. Upon reflection, I could say that perhaps I spent too much time mentoring at UNM. Perhaps I could have created more time boundaries between myself and the students that I found myself invested in. The ideal at UNM would have been that the students of color had a large number of faculty, of all colors, of all gender preferences, to dedicate more time to them. However, the success I saw in the students, and still see, affirms to me that I could not have conducted myself in any other way at the time. I still believe that it is of utmost importance to educate, mentor, and support students of color. My advice to European American colleagues and administrators is to take the mentoring mission upon themselves as well. There are too few faculty of color to go around.

Validation and Privilege

Ethnic centers and institutes have played a role in my "coping" with the White academy by giving me validation and support. But I can also see that I have been greatly privileged by my affiliation and activities with these units. These are all opportunities that not all women of color have had. At UNM, my research was partially supported by grants from the Southwest Hispanic Research Institute. At UConn, my position as an Associate Director at PRLS has indicated UConn's continued confidence in my demonstrated abilities in research, administration, and teaching. Research support has also facilitated my projects at UConn.

Other privileges that I often neglect to acknowledge have to do with having an able body. Also, I am bilingual and bicultural, using U.S. standard English and standard Latin American Spanish. My ease with language and my bicultural and middle-class experiences have often allowed me to move in and out of Anglo and Latino cultural realms.

Concluding Observations

In this essay, I used the cultural stranger and other related concepts to shed light on the experiences of a Latina faculty member in majority institutions. Because I used the approach of an autobiography of work, it was necessary for me to use personal examples from my life on three campuses, two in the Southwest and one in New England. Though I hesitated in presenting any of the above information for public reading, I expect that the information will help prepare women of color faculty who are beginning their careers in academia as well as give insights to women who are currently in the midst of their teaching careers. Despite socio-cultural hurdles, it is very possible for women of color to have excellent teaching experiences and become superb instructors. Teaching can be so rewarding and inspirational.

Given that the colors of our future (Chideya 1999) are so diverse, it behooves small teaching colleges and large research universities to nurture and support instruction among their graduates and faculty of color. I am glad to see diversity education efforts implemented by colleges and universities across the country. In support of humane and positive campus environments for all people, European Americans and students, faculty, and administrators of color are currently working on policies and programs in expectation of the future.

Diana I. Rios is Assistant Professor in the Department of Communication Sciences and the Puerto Rican and Latino Studies Institute, University of Connecticut. She is also Associate Director of Puerto Rican and Latino Studies. She conducts survey and field research on Chicana/o Latina/o audience use of English- and Spanish-language television, newspapers, radio, and cinema. Her most recent projects include Latino audiences, Latino and African American communication, and the memories of women of color of Golden Age cinema stars. She teaches and publishes in interdisciplinary areas of mass communication.

Notes

1. *Boricua* is another term for Puerto Rican.
2. Courses were supposed to be smaller with enrollments of twenty. Departmental pressures increased enrollments in undergraduate upper division intercultural communication courses to forty, fifty, and seventy-five, until it became obvious that effective intercultural communication teaching was better in courses with fewer students.
3. "The Yellow Wallpaper" is a short story by Charlotte Perkins (1989) that describes a woman's slow descent into insanity. Her husband and other male authorities are patronizing and controlling. Symptoms of her emotional retreat are revealed in her obsession with the patterns and the color of her room's yellow wallpaper.
4. I and other scholars use the term "Mexicano" or "Mexicana" to describe someone from Mexico.
5. The term "Hispano" is often used among New Mexicans of Latino heritage to describe themselves.
6. Based on my previous experiences, I declined to teach any undergraduate intercultural or cross-cultural communication courses.

Works Cited

Allport, G. 1954. *The Nature of Prejudice*. Cambridge, MA: Addison-Wesley.

The Ballad of Gregorio Cortez. 1983. Directed by R. M. Young. Distributed by New Line Home Video. Videocassette.

Chideya, F. 1999. *The Color of Our Future*. New York: William Morrow and Company.

Derman-Sparks, L., and C. B. Phillips. 1997. *Teaching/Learning Anti-Racism: A Developmental Approach*. New York: Teachers College Press.

Do the Right Thing. 1989. Directed by S. Lee. Distributed by Universal Studios. Videocassette.

Gilman, C. P. 1989. "The Yellow Wallpaper." In *The Yellow Wallpaper and Other Writings by Charlotte Perkins Gilman*. New York: Bantam.

Gudykunst, W. 1998. *Bridging Differences: Effective Intergroup Communication*. 3rd ed. Thousand Oaks, CA: Sage.

Jhally, S., and J. Lewis. 1992. *Enlightened Racism: The Cosby Show, Audiences, and the Myth of the American Dream*. Boulder, CO: Westview Press.

Jungle Fever. 1991. Directed by S. Lee. Distributed by Universal Studios. Videocassette.

Kochman, T. 1981. *Black and White Styles in Conflict*. Chicago: University of Chicago Press.

Lewis, M. 1990. "Interrupting Patriarchy: Politics, Resistance, and Transformation in the Feminist Classroom." *Harvard Educational Review* 60 (4): 467–488.

Medina, C., and G. Luna. 2000. "Narratives from Latina Professors in Higher Education." *Anthropolgy and Education Quarterly* 31 (1): 47–66.

The Milagro Beanfield War. 1988. Directed by R. Redford. Distributed by Universal Studios. Videocassette.

Mr. Baseball. 1992. Directed by F. Schepisi. Distributed by Universal Studios. Videocassette.

Nieto, S. 2000. *Affirming Diversity: The Sociopolitical Context of Multicultural Education*. New York: Longman.

Reyes, M. L., and J. J. Halcon. 1988. "Racism in Academia: The Old Wolf Revisited." *Harvard Educational Review* 58 (3): 299–314.

Schlesinger, A. M. 1995. "The Disuniting of America: Reflections on a Multicultural Society." In *Campus Wars*, edited by J. Arthur and A. Shapiro. Boulder, CO: Westview.

Ting-Toomey, S. 1999. *Communicating Across Cultures*. New York: Guilford.

CHAPTER SIXTEEN

Yellow Lotus in White Lily Pond: An Asian American Woman Teaching in Utah

PRITI KUMAR

Abstract

IN THIS CHAPTER, I trace my experiences from my early years in India to my professional maturity in the United States in order to address issues of professorial authority, classroom resistance, and my own transformative learning. Since teaching is shaped by many complex personal beginnings, I employ a life history narrative to reflect on my story. Who and where I am is the key to understanding what my experiences have been. I have crossed many borders, built numerous bridges, negotiated power sharing, and survived in the White academy, mostly because of inner strengths gained through my unique experience as the Other. Margins/borders and centers intermingle in my life to create the motif of this autobiographical narrative.

> Living in the Borderlands means you fight hard to resist the gold–elixir beckoning from the bottle. (Anzaldúa 1987, 194)

My story is the story of border crossings. I must share my past journeys with my readers in order to make connections with my life as the Other Teacher in the White academy. My beginnings, my travels, and my cultural strengths are intertwined with my pedagogical choices and classroom strategies. As a first-generation immigrant, I feel close to Gloria Anzaldúa's imaginary travelers in *Borderlands/La Frontera: The New Mestiza,* who accept their duality and who are destined to crossing borders forever. Like them, I too live and breathe in two realities, assume dual personalities, and orbit between middle and margins. I hope my readers will be able to glean the real issues from these autobiographical anecdotes.

Young Adulthood, Middle Passage, and Mature Years

Imagine the fear and apprehension in the heart of a 13-year-old girl sitting in a crowded women's compartment of Indian railways. About fifty women and children were packed like bees in a beehive in a car made to seat thirty people. Some were standing, some were pushing others to make more space for themselves, and some were sitting on their tin trunks. Among this assortment of mothers, sisters, and daughters, I was an oddity. I, who was traveling alone without an adult escort (which is rare in India), became the center of the inquisitive gazes of others. I tried to ignore their piercing eyes upon me as much as I could by looking down so that I would not have to answer their questions. This was my first trip to the big city of Allahabad, where I was to continue my education, since my little town had no girls' school beyond eighth grade. I had insisted on taking this trip alone because I was aware that having my brother or someone else to escort me meant two train tickets—a luxury of added expenses I should not ask of my parents. This first border crossing was so traumatic that I can still feel the jitters of it. Questions such as "What if I do not make my train connections?" or "What if I lose my luggage?" buzzed in my head. I sat on my little suitcase the entire time for security.

I did make this first trip alone safely, and with each following trip over the next six years while I completed my high school and then my B.A. degree in 1955, the journey became more and more enjoyable and secure. Now, I too would lunge for the first available break in seating space and wriggle my body between strangers to make enough room to sit. I would also meet the inquiring eyes with defiant disregard, open my cheap romance book and, depending on my financial situation, buy spicy *pakuaras* (vegetable fritters) or roasted peanuts from the passing vendors and start munching. I had learned to cross the borders, to negotiate unfamiliar situations, and develop my inner self-reliance. Like Anzaldúa, I had carved my own reality for myself. "By creating a new mythos—that is a change in the way we perceive reality, the way we see ourselves and the way we behave—la Mestiza creates a new consciousness" (Anzaldúa 1987, 80). This ability became a great asset for me in my adult life. Even though at times I was confused, scared, and homesick, I was happy and grateful for this opportunity to continue my education and for having an uncompromising and courageous mother, who visualized the value of female education in spite of financial hardships. She convinced my grandfather, the patriarch of our family, to permit me to leave home to complete my education. This break from my loving family and these early experiences in India are the basis of my independent nature, an independence that is still uncommon in a deeply patriarchal society such as India.

After teaching in various universities in India from 1961 to 1969, I followed my husband when he came to the United States for an advanced degree, reliving that first emotional train journey as I took my first trans-Atlantic flight alone with my two young children. As an adult, I was trying to be calm and confident, but my face must have mirrored my inner fears and apprehensions because my 9-year-old son looked at me and said, "Don't worry Ma, I'm with you," and held his 4-year-old sister's hand tightly. With a jolt I realized that I was transforming into my 13-year-old self. I caught hold of my fears and smiled at my children to reassure them, even though my mind was buzzing with mundane and pragmatic questions such as, "Will I make my connecting flight at London?" With only 10 British pounds in my purse I was terrified of any emergency expenses before reaching my destination. Again, I did make this journey safely, fully realizing the enormity of the act of physical border crossings.

Only now, after spending thirty years in the United States, do I feel able to analyze and reflect on the complexities of my cultural negotiations. For me, immigration as an adult was like a "gradual renaissance" or like a "living reincarnation" (an oxymoron we immigrants are forced to live with). We humans cannot shed our past like snakes shed their old skins. Rather, we are like snails; we carry our "homes," our cultural norms, with us wherever we go. Like snails, we can take refuge in our shells when we feel threatened or challenged or when we encounter unfamiliar and cruel acts of discrimination and devaluation. I vividly remember the times during those early years when I was penetrated by the curious "White gaze" because I was wearing a sari, had a *bindi* (red dot) on my forehead, was many shades darker in skin color, or spoke in an accent too foreign. I felt like an imposter trying to understand the Western winds while my heart and soul were still drenched in the Eastern rain. Sometimes I would return to my new apartment in Kent, Ohio, and cook dal with my Indian spices in order to pacify my hunger for "home." I had to wear Western clothes for work, but I continued to change into my sari and kick off my shoes as soon as I entered my home. Gradually, I started to feel comfortable and was able to celebrate my new home. Only after blending our two cultures do we immigrants feel secure enough to analyze our internal and external transformations.

I never wished to get rid of my past or my birth culture, but I was also eager to assimilate and acculturate in my adopted country and its culture. In order to survive in my new environment, I was keen to remodel, recreate, and re-envision my roles as educator, mother, and wife. My journey depicts my ongoing, ever-present transformations. My ability to adjust and negotiate was

necessary and helped me become the person I am today. I know how to survive in many circumstances and live in multiple cultures, partly

> because I am a Mestiza
> I continually walk out of one culture into another,
> because I am in cultures all the time. (Anderson and Hill Collins 1995, 77)

After my full-time teaching job in India, I had to face the disappointment
of finding only a part-time teaching position in Kent, Ohio. For my family to
survive and pay the bills, I had to find another job. I crossed the professional
border of educated teacher in India to become a "worker," first in a fast-food
restaurant and then in a little grocery store. For a pure vegetarian like me,
handling and selling meat was a major border to cross. Working in a service
or minimum wage job was such a demotion in status for my middle-class Indian mindset that I remember not mentioning my fast-food work to my extended family in India. Between 1970 and 1974, we crisscrossed the country
from Kent, Ohio, to Ogden, Utah, to Boise, Idaho, and then back to Ogden.
During this time, I had several jobs and lost some of my preconceived notions
of Indian, middle–class work ethics. I also gained useful insights into the
minds and lives of Mestizas like us and their ever-changing, ever-challenging
roles. My family and I can identify with Gloria Anzaldúa's *La Mestiza*. I am
the woman who

> learns to juggle, had a plural personality, operated in a pluralistic mode—nothing is
> thrust out, the good, the bad, the ugly, nothing is rejected, nothing is abandoned.
> Not only does she sustain contradiction, she turns the ambivalence into something
> else....It is where the possibility of uniting all that is separate occurs. (Anderson and
> Hill Collins 1995, 79)

My marginalization and duality became much more pronounced for me
when in 1974 I decided to go back to graduate school so that I could enter
the U.S. higher education job market. I had my admission papers in hand and
my apprehensions in my heart when I started my classes at the University of
Utah. I was worried about the sixty-mile commute and about juggling my
home duties and schoolwork with my children's schedules, but I was confident about my ability to meet the level of academic rigor. I had been a good
student in India, a recipient of two gold medals from Allahabad University.
Ironically, surviving in the White academy proved to be my hardest cultural
crossing. I changed my area of study from linguistics to comparative literature
after one quarter, assuming that my master's degree in Hindi literature with a
special emphasis on Sanskrit Literature would be an asset for me. How wrong

and how naïve I was. To this day, I cannot discuss or even write about my humiliation in the White academy without shedding some tears.

Picture a sari-draped, middle-aged, brown-skinned petite woman sitting among all White, all young, mostly male students and gathering enough inner strength to point out the similarities between *The Song of Roland* and the classic eleventh-century Hindi epic, *Alha-Udal*. The curious, almost demeaning looks and the dead silence of my classmates and the White male professor still roar in my heart. In all of my comparative literature classes, my professors ignored my knowledge and expertise of Hindi and Sanskrit languages and literature. I felt that others also devalued my ancient Indian culture and my history. I felt that my age, my skin color, and my accent pushed me to accept my marginal existence and also forced me to develop survival skills in this unfriendly and somewhat hostile environment.

These experiences have transformed me and my teaching strategies. After experiencing firsthand the devastating effects of uncaring and exclusionary approaches of the White male professors at the University of Utah, I vowed never to be like them. No theorist could have taught me the value of inclusivity better than the bitter experiences I had to endure as the Other Student. My pedagogy shifted and changed forever. I understood that La Mestiza:

> constantly has to shift out the habitual formations; from convergent thinking, analytical reassigning that tends to use rationality to move toward the single goal (a Western model), to divergent thinking, characterized by movement away from set patterns and goals toward a more whole perspective, one that includes rather than excludes. (Anderson and Hill Collins 1995, 79)

To validate the cultural heritage of all my students, one of the writing assignments for my English composition classes requires my students to answer the question "Who am I?" I ask them to trace their cultural inheritances, explore and analyze their multiple inner strengths, and celebrate their differences. My hope is that the students will acknowledge their uniqueness even though most of them consider themselves part of the "melting pot" of mainstream America. Most students find this a very challenging but rewarding assignment and realize that we all are La Mestiza in some form or other.

The narrative of my middle passage is important and is interrelated to larger social and cultural issues. Lisa Lowe argues that all personal stories are closely connected with "real" lives and their larger social environment (1996, 156). My life history is a reflection of this concept. In retrospect, I cherish the bitter and hard lessons I learned at the University of Utah; they have shaped and transformed my teaching ability. These experiences have given me many gifts—such as sensitivity to the needs of my students and the recognition of the importance of emotional nurturing and caring. Perhaps these hard times sowed the seeds of my desire to transform my course curricula by addressing multicultural issues.

Now, in my mature years, I have a clearer sense of my Otherness. I know that my dual perceptions, my numerous border crossings, and my pluralistic existences are crucial factors that impact on my classroom authority and my students' reactions. The visual image of a teacher affects her students before the contents of her character and the substance of her expertise get a chance to manifest themselves. I am painfully aware of my Otherness in my mostly White classrooms. Ironically, a friend who is also a first-generation immigrant—from England—never has to apologize for her English accent. But I, who learned English in India because this friend's ancestors colonized my country, still have to carry the burden of a "less privileged" accent, even in this free and diverse society. I can recount many incidents in and out of the White academy where people have asked me "How did you learn English?" or "Where are you from?" because I am the Other in their perception.

Surviving in the Cold White Lily Pond

I have been teaching at Weber State University for twenty-four years. Our campus is located in Utah, which is a predominantly Mormon state. It is characterized primarily as a commuter undergraduate university. This teaching-learning institution has approximately 15,000 students. In 1999 racial/ethnic minorities constituted 6.2 percent of our student body. Out of 408 faculty members, 47 (8.7 percent) are racial/ethnic minorities. Over 70 percent of the freshman who took the ACT in 1999 declared themselves to be part of Utah's dominant religious group, the Church of Jesus Christ Latter-Day Saints.

When I joined the faculty ranks in 1976, Weber State University was a much different place than it is now. There were very few women faculty of color and no cohesive support system for new faculty. I joined the English department as an adjunct faculty member with no benefits, no professional mentor, and no voice to bring about any changes. In 1981, I was hired as an instructor on a full-time contract with no possibility of tenure. I have what they call de facto tenure since I have been there for so long. My primary responsibility was to teach English composition classes, which were (and still are) in high demand. My employers had no desire or inclination to tap the other resources and expertise I brought with me. For them, Asian or Indian literature was non-existent, unknown, and irrelevant. No one even inquired about my previous teaching expertise in India. My department and the administration never realized the bargain they were getting in hiring me! I could have been the resident expert in Hindi and Sanskrit languages. I do take responsibility for allowing them to exploit me intellectually and professionally; jeopardizing my family's financial welfare was not an option, and my meek Asian background and my personality prevented me from being a vocal adversary in those early years. Nonetheless, I still get very angry at the way my administration treated me and continues to degrade and exploit other women faculty of color.

I urge novice Other Teachers to do what I could not or would not do. Get involved in the politics of the academy and take some calculated risks. It pays to be a squeaky wheel. A recent article by Ruth Y. Hsu provides an accurate analysis of the nature of the academy. I agree with her assertion that "Our reluctance to face the political nature of the academy allows for the continued marginalization of minorities in both our status and our ability to change academic culture" (2000, 194). In spite of compelling socio-ideological conditions that control the economic resources of the academy, we faculty of color must learn the intricacies of campus politics. As Hsu further proposes, "If we wish to see significant changes, minority faculty members and administrators must gain more control over the budgetary process and the administration of the university, including the selection and appointments of the deans, program directors and presidents and chancellors and development of strong faculty unions and senate committed to diversifying and liberating the institutions" (2000, 193).

As a first-generation Asian immigrant woman, I did not recognize, or estimate, my own power, and thus failed to use it constructively. I hope Other Teachers will learn from my experiences and force their department chairs, deans, and administrators to value and reward the contribution that women of color make to the White academy. Women faculty of color need to seek mentors and connect with other senior faculty members on their campus. I did this, but belatedly. After ten years, I became involved with women's studies, with Asian studies, and with diversity issues on campus. There I found support to develop courses on Asian and non-Asian literature, the first addition to the canon in my department.

Classroom Survival and Strategies

For the first few quarters at Weber State University, I taught classes wearing my native sari, which accentuated my Otherness even more. Later, as I switched to Western attire, I began to contemplate my survival in Utah, which is a predominantly Mormon state. It was obvious to everyone that I was the "alien" with brown skin and a "weird" accent. I used to start my first class by describing my educational background, as if to justify my authority and worthiness as an English teacher. I do not do that anymore. My longevity has given me more authority and confidence. I know my past has also played an important role in establishing my authority.

The journeys of my young adulthood, the lessons of my middle years, and the security of my mature years have made me the best teacher I can be. All contributed to my survival in the White academy. Raw determination can sometimes accomplish seemingly impossible tasks, but another crucial factor in my survival has been the support of other women faculty, both White and women of color.

The academic year 1989–1990 was a transformative year for me. I got involved in two of my favorite issues: women's studies and the debate on multiculturalism. A core group of women faculty worked together to propose a women's studies minor. We formed a reading group and a working group that met regularly and provided a supportive environment to all of us. This gave me fresh air to breathe and new ideas to develop. Another fortunate event was meeting a newly hired professor in the English department whose vision and teaching strategies corresponded with my interest in introducing multicultural approaches into our composition and literature classes. This colleague and I have worked together ever since and have presented papers, written articles, and received grants for course development and revisions. I strongly feel that finding my niche among supportive colleagues has been crucial for my classroom success. My suggestions to novice Other Teachers would be to seek out other like-minded women faculty on their campus. The support, guidance, and encouragement I received from my colleagues (both White women and women of color) transformed me into a multiculturalist and an expert in Asian and non-Western literature in my department and on my campus. "Like an ear of corn—female seed bearing organ—the Mestiza is tenacious, tightly wrapped in husks of her culture. Like kernels she clings to the cob; with thick stalks and strong brace roots she holds tight to the earth—she will survive the crossroads" (Anzaldúa 1987, 81).

Teaching Strategies

The pedagogy I used in India was what Freire calls the "banking" method, where the professor is the pundit at the podium and the students are the recipients of her wisdom (1998). Reading feminist theories convinced me to transform my pedagogy. Like Shiela Ming Hwang, I felt that feminist pedagogy suits me because it "involves asking many open-ended questions without settling on a 'correct' reading of a text, thereby allowing students to voice their own thoughts; inviting students to doubt their instructor's interpretations begins the process of student empowerment" (2000, 155). This approach can be risky for an Other Teacher, but it can be liberating too. I find this open-discussion format very challenging but rewarding.

In my composition and literature classes, along with small-group work, class discussions and presentations, I have two written exercises that set the tone of my classroom approach. For the first exercise, I ask students to write about a time when they felt like an outsider, a minority, or an oddity. Then I ask them to reflect on, and write about, their feelings of powerlessness to control the reactions of others toward them. This exercise transcends the classroom. After completing the exercise, most students are able to realize the following: We can all be powerless at some time or another; we are not always responsible for this condition; being powerless in one situation is not being helpless in all situations; and awareness of our limits does not preclude the possibility of change. As an Other teacher, I extend this notion of power when we discuss multicultural writings.

The second exercise is about making choices. First, I ask students to name three countries other than the United States where they would like to live in the event that they could not live in the United States. I also ask them to give a reason for each of their choices. Then I ask them to write about the three countries where they would least like to live. Finally, I ask them to reflect on what their choices reflect about their own values. This exercise generates lively discussion in class. When we select places where we would or would not like to live, we uncover our prejudices and biased perceptions about others. The exercise reveals to students the preconceived notions behind their preferences. Since I emphasize diversity issues in my classes, this exercise is a perfect precursor to course readings.

Another useful strategy I employ in my classes is journal-writing. I call it a reading and talking journal. Students must respond to and critique a reading, while expressing their own views on the issues at hand. Here they can talk to me and ask me questions not only about the readings but also about any matter related to the class. This private dialogue provides a safe place for students to express their pleasures or apprehensions. I read their journals carefully and respond to their inquiries in writing. I find journal-writing to be a way to maintain classroom authority and defuse disruptive outbursts in the class. The possibilities are limitless. Novice teachers can modify and employ it in their classes.

The last useful instrument I will discuss is the "self-evaluation and reflection" assignment that I give to all my classes at the end of the semester. I give this evaluation in addition to, but separate from, my departmental course evaluations. I do not grade this evaluation, but students earn a number of points for doing it. For this evaluation, I ask students to respond, in a narrative form, to four sets of questions. One set is about the advice that they would give to another student who plans to take my class (e.g., deadlines and other class expectations, most useful attitudes in class, and the benefits of the course). Another set is about the textbook, and another is about the ways in which specific class activities helped them enhance their cultural awareness. The last set is optional, and students earn no points for completing it. It has to do with their perceptions of me and my performance. It asks them to reflect on their first impressions of me as their teacher and then to compare it with their perceptions at the end of the semester. This tool constantly keeps me on my toes. My students are very candid and provide excellent feedback that helps me reshape the class in the future.

Power and Evaluations

Mostly in my composition classes, my class evaluations over the years have mixed comments about me that reflect students' own apprehensions and preconceived notions about my ethnicity. On the one hand, I am rated quite highly on interpersonal communication and understanding. To quote them, I am "very accessible, always willing to help, to explain and reach out," but I am also "hard to understand, unclear about what is expected of the class, too demanding, and a teacher who makes them do a lot of busy work." Over the years, after reading these comments, reviewing and rewriting my class expectations, and giving detailed descriptions of each assignment in my composition classes, I find that these remarks continue to occur. It seems to me that some students put on their own blinders after seeing my brown skin and hearing my "foreign" accent.

To better understand students' perceptions and for my own self-study, I have started to ask very pointed questions in my end-of-semester "reflections" assignment. I ask students to compare their perceptions from the first day of class with their perceptions at the end of the semester. Sometimes students frankly admit their prejudices after hearing me for the first time and share their apprehensions with others. By the end of the semester, however, some of these students almost forget that I have an "accent," and some are honest enough to tell me that they were ashamed to have been so judgmental or prejudiced. One student said:

> To give my honest opinion I was a little biased. I honestly didn't understand how a woman with such strong accent could teach English. I can truthfully say I am ashamed of some of the racial opinions I had of you as being my teacher. I never re-

alized I was prejudiced—I mean I don't dislike or discriminate against others, just often judge people by their appearances. I think after spending the semester with you all my judgments are disproved. In no way do I find you unqualified for your job....The only thing I am resentful of is my own poor judgment.

Another student from the same class expressed her doubts like this:

When I first walked into class I was wondering why I do have an English teacher who has not grown up to speak English as a primary language? I was questioning myself after class if I want to stay in the class and have a teacher that could not speak English like I do, (What I mean is you had an accent)....Now I like your accent and I have gotten used to it so now to me it is no big deal but the beginning of class I had a hard time getting used to it. I am not resentful for staying in the class. I think it is great that you are teaching and I think and know you know a lot and feel you have gained a lot of great experience over the years.

Even though many students commented on my accent, nearly all of them were very reassuring and even complimentary about my teaching by the time they were about to finish the semester. Among many more examples that support my analysis, I quote the comments of two more students:

After I got to know you better, I accepted you just fine. You are really smart and funny. You make things so clear and give us other's points of view to look at. You have been one of the best teachers and you are a kind good woman....I am really comfortable with your accent, color, race and gender.

* * *

After spending the semester in your class I came to appreciate what you have accomplished. Your teaching methods are sound, and you have more knowledge about English than I will ever hope to have. I have learned more from your class than I did in High or the 1010 class.

It is intriguing and interesting, but not surprising, to note that I am perceived very differently in my literature classes, which focus on non-Western writers (Indian Women Writers, Asian Women Writers, and Global Perspectives on Literature). In these classes my professorial authority is seldom challenged or questioned. The students are also more mature and self motivated because these classes are not required. Even though I use videos, guest lecturers, and small-group discussions in all my classes, these pedagogical strategies seem to produce more favorable responses in my literature classes than in my composition classes. It seems to me that in general the students' perceptions and motivations are more crucial for classroom success than teachers' practices and pedagogies.

When I ask students in my literature classes to reflect on the same questions as in my composition classes, I hear dramatically different answers. One recent response from my Indian Women Writers class sums up these students' general reactions to me quite clearly:

> My first reaction to seeing you (a woman of color with an accent) I was excited because since it was a class on women from India and you obviously being an Indian woman I know you could give insights and details that we would not be able to get from someone who has studied India or even visited India many times.
>
> I don't think your accent, color, race or gender has had any effect on me. It is inspiring to see a woman get far in life and be recognized for her achievements. Your race and gender just makes these achievements even more amazing because this culture has a way of discouraging those of another race. I am definitely not resentful of your authority because like I said above it is inspiring to see a woman achieve so many things.

Another student shared her insightful reflections more placidly:

> When I took this class, I knew that I was to be learning of Indian women writers, obviously, so I was not at all surprised when we came to class and you were there to greet us. Rather, I was reassured; I mean, what better person would there be to teach us about Indian Woman writers than an Indian Woman writer? Who else could tell us the mythology and the gods and goddesses of Hinduism so well? Someone who experiences and lives in the culture every day would be my answer.

Here, not only is my authority established by my national origin but my duality is also accepted as an asset by this student. She pays me a great compliment when later in her reflection she mentions that "the class was a great success and I don't think there is another professor who could have made it so, regardless of color or religion....Perhaps you and this class have affected me more than I know."

These samples are very good for my ego, but they also reconfirm my pedagogical goals, especially the ones I formed during my graduate experiences about never undervaluing and thus undermining my students' knowledge base. I had promised myself that, unlike my professor at the University of Utah, I would always try to reach my students on a personal level even though I might be unfamiliar with their religious or literary backgrounds. Here is yet another example of how a student confirmed my beliefs in teaching global literature:

> I am so grateful that I took this class. It has really opened my eyes to see the world differently. I found your extensive background and knowledge of India so interesting and fascinating. It has added a valuable dynamic and dimension to the class. I know

this class would not have had the same impact on me if it had been taught by a White male teacher.

In the final analysis, I feel that my various border crossings, my pluralistic perspectives, and my gender and race have made a positive impact on me and, I think, on my students. What I learned from my life experiences made me a better interpreter of the multiple journeys we all are bound to take from time to time. I am a more sensitive and more passionate person because of my bittersweet life experiences. I am really grateful and flattered when my students feel emotionally nurtured and sustained by my classroom behaviors and interactions, as evidenced by this student's comment:

> I consider you a great teacher and influence, but even more importantly I am glad to call you a friend. Someone said, "the greatest compliment is to be called a friend." I truly believe it. I knew that you sincerely cared about us in your class.

Sure, I have my color, race, gender, and accent with me wherever I go, but I also share my love of teaching and learning with my students. My students' resistance is mostly temporary and students are able to take with them my love, concern, and caring for them in their hearts when they leave my classes. I call this a success and want to celebrate that along with all the hurdles we women faculty of color have to surpass. At the same time I must not forget my border crossings and must remember that:

> To survive the Borderlands
> You must live *sin fronteras*
> By a crossroads. (Anzaldúa 1987, 195)

Conclusion

Asian cultures encourage humility as a virtue, especially in women. Women are encouraged to be on the periphery rather than to tell their own narratives. Perhaps this explains why autobiographical writing is only a recent phenomenon among Asian American women writers. I carried this cultural concept in my heart, never realizing that my story is worth telling. Self-study using a life history empowered me to tell my story without the apologies that my Asian cultures expect. Goodson (1992) asserts that studying teacher's lives provides valuable insights and assists educational reform and restructuring. This reflection and analysis of my classroom experiences helped me to put my teaching experiences as a woman of color in proper perspective.

I have purposefully avoided recommending specific solutions to the problematic issues that I address in this essay because I feel that generalizing the treatment of Other can be dangerous. Each situation requires its own so-lutions, and I hope readers will find solutions of their own. The complex is-sues of race, national origin, gender, class, and ethnicity have many layers and require constant negotiation and multiple solutions.

Priti Kumar has taught at Weber State University in Ogden, Utah, since 1976. She teaches English writing and literature classes in the English De-partment. She also teaches courses on world literature and Asian women writers. She has a master's degree in Hindi literature with a special emphasis on Sanskrit literature from Allahabad University, India. She completed her second master's degree in comparative literature at the University of Utah. Her research on multicultural education has been published in scholarly journals.

Works Cited

Anderson, M., and P. Hill Collins. 1995. *Race, Class, and Gender: An Anthology.* Belmont, CA: Wadsworth Publishing.

Anzaldúa, G. 1987. *Borderlands/La Frontera: The New Mestiza.* San Francisco: Aunt Lute Books.

Freire, P. 1998. *Teachers as Cultural Workers: Letters to Those Who Dare Teach.* Boulder, CO: Westview Press.

Goodson, I. F. 1992. *Studying Teachers' Lives.* London: Routledge.

Hsu, R. Y. 2000. "'Where's Oz Toto?'": Idealism and the Politics of Gender and Race in Academe." In *Power, Race, and Gender in Academe,* edited by S. Lim and M. Herrera-Sobek. New York: Modern Language Association.

Hwang, S. M. 2000. "At the Limits of My Feminism: Race, Gender, Class and the Execution of a Feminist Pedagogy." In *Power, Race, and Gender in Academe,* edited by S. Lim and M. Herrera-Sobek. New York: Modern Language Association.

Lowe, L. 1996. *Immigrant Acts.* Durham, NC: Duke University Press.

CHAPTER SEVENTEEN

Marginality as an Asset: Toward a Counter-Hegemonic Pedagogy for Diversity

RYUKO KUBOTA

Abstract

AS A JAPANESE woman jointly appointed by education and Asian studies departments as a second-language teacher trainer, and as a Japanese language instructor, my teaching experiences have been both positive and negative, depending on students' interests, their perception of my credibility, and instructional arrangements. This chapter analyzes these experiences by drawing on Pierre Bourdieu's concept of capital. My cultural and linguistic capital has been valued by students learning Japanese language, whereas it has not been by students preparing to become Spanish and French teachers. This chapter suggests a counter-hegemonic pedagogy that appropriates marginality as a strategy to advocate for diversity.

My teaching experiences in North American institutions of higher education in the past twelve years have been both fulfilling and challenging. The dual nature of this experience seems to have resulted from the different degrees to which students appreciate the value of my cultural and linguistic background, a background different from that of mainstream White professors. Drawing on concepts of power and capital, in this chapter I explore why my experiences have been both positive and negative and suggest that the marginality of women faculty of color be transformed into a strategy for advocating diversity.

Before describing my teaching experiences, I will briefly present my personal history. I was born in 1957 in Japan and received my education there through college. After obtaining my undergraduate degree, I taught English as a foreign language in Japanese public schools for five years. English is a second language for me, and it was not a language I used for daily purposes until I came to the United States to live for one year as a school intern in my mid-20s. Two years later, I came back to America as a graduate student. Second-language teaching has always been my career. Since 1988, I have been teaching Japanese as a foreign language in the United States as well as in Canada, where I received my doctorate degree in education. After teaching at a small private graduate school in California for three years, I moved to a large research university in North Carolina in 1995. I currently teach Japanese and prepare kindergarten to twelfth grade (K–12) teachers of foreign languages and English as a second language. The teaching experiences I describe in this chapter took place in this public university.

Situated in the southeastern United States, the university enrolls African American students as the largest minority student body. Although there is a growing number of other minority students, the proportion of Asian students is much smaller than in California or Ontario, where I previously taught. The number of Asian faculty is also smaller compared to where I taught before. At this university in North Carolina, the students I teach have mainly been Whites.

Many minority faculty across the country have split appointments (Johnsrud and Des Jarlais 1994; Johnsrud and Sadao 1998). I, too, currently hold a joint appointment in the School of Education and in the Curriculum in Asian Studies in the College of Arts and Sciences. My position was created for initiating teacher preparation for K–12 Japanese as a foreign language. In the School of Education, I team-taught Methods of Teaching Second Languages (the methods course, hereafter) for the first three years. This course aimed to prepare K–12 teachers of foreign languages. The class mainly enrolled Spanish language majors, but there were a few French, German, and Latin majors. The students were mostly undergraduate seniors, but there were a few master's students. After three years, there was a major change in the program. I discontinued teaching this course and developed a new course titled Language Minority Students. This new course is one of the requirements for obtaining a K–12 teaching license in English as a second language. The course enrolls undergraduates, master's students, and practicing teachers. In the Curriculum in Asian Studies, I have taught Advanced Japanese language courses (third-year level) to mostly undergraduate students and Structures of Japanese, a course designed for K–12 pre-service teachers of Japanese as a foreign language. Since the latter course usually attracts Japanese native speakers and enrolls a very small number of students, I will focus on the former—that is, the Japanese language course—in this chapter.

Excluding native Japanese-speaking students from the focus of my reflective analysis does not mean that teaching students from Japan has posed no problem for me. I have had some Japanese students who treated me in disrespectful ways. When I was teaching at a private institution in California, a female Japanese graduate student came to my office to seek advice. During the conversation, she called me Kubota-*san* (Ms. Kubota), using -*san* instead of -*sensei* (which literally means "teacher"), a title customarily used for teachers. Having never been called Kubota-*san* by my Japanese students over ten years of my prior teaching experience, I was taken aback. As discussed later, this incident demonstrates that power is relational rather than absolute. Given the fact that some Japanese ideology legitimates the superiority of native speakers of English and the White race (Kubota 1998a), it is possible that, to this student, a Japanese woman faculty appeared less legitimate as a professor than White faculty on the same campus.

The level of success in my teaching of different courses in North Carolina has been quite different—while students in the Japanese courses and the Language Minority Students course were generally satisfied with my instruction, many students in the methods course, particularly in the first two years, did not appreciate my teaching. As other women professors of color have found (Amin 1999; Ng 1995; Thomas 1999; Vargas 1999), I also found that my credibility as an instructor was harshly challenged by these students. The next section will describe these positive and negative experiences in more detail.

Positive and Negative Experiences

My teaching experience in the Japanese language courses has been successful, judging from my interaction with the students both in and outside the class as well as from the course evaluations. The class typically attracts undergraduate students who have previously taken Japanese courses for two years, as well as a few students who have learned Japanese by other means. Every year, there are a few students who have visited or lived in Japan. Although the majority of the students are White, there are usually a few students with Asian or other ethnic backgrounds. As for gender balance, there are usually slightly more males than women. Some of the students are Asian Studies majors for whom advanced (third-year or above) study in an Asian language is required. However, for non-Asian Studies majors, these courses are optional. Therefore, the students are highly motivated, trying to fulfill their intellectual interests or pursue their future careers. Both in and outside the classroom, I speak Japanese with students and encourage them to use only Japanese when they talk to me. When students are unable to express themselves in Japanese,

I allow them to use English, while I still try to respond only in Japanese using simple vocabulary and sentences. In my teaching experience, Japanese language classes have rarely posed difficulties.[1]

Contrary to this positive experience, my three years of teaching the methods course in the School of Education were quite difficult. This course enrolled students who were becoming Spanish, French, German, or Latin teachers. The course aimed to develop the knowledge and skills necessary for teaching a second language and included topics such as teaching methodologies and techniques, second-language acquisition theories, classroom management, and so on. The majority of the students were seniors and the rest were master's students. The seniors were mostly in-state students, whereas the master's students tended to come from other states. The class enrolled predominantly White Anglo female students. During the three years I taught the methods course, only two African American women and one White man enrolled in the class. The students I had difficulties with were mainly undergraduate White women.

I taught this course with a White woman colleague, a specialist in Spanish language pedagogy, who had taught the class for over ten years. She was also proficient in other languages. In this team-teaching arrangement, decisions about the content, text, and evaluation methods were made mainly by my colleague, though I provided some input. The course was split into two halves of the semester, and each of us taught one half. During the first year, I observed my colleague's teaching during the first half and took over in the second half. Class observations helped me understand the process of instruction in this particular context and maintain instructional continuity. However, my colleague and I obviously did not share commonality in terms of age, race, culture, and language background, which influenced not only how we physically looked but also how we interacted with students and made instructional decisions. My privilege as a middle-class woman with an able body did not help me earn the same respect that my colleague did. The effort to keep instructional continuity might have inadvertently accentuated a difference in teaching style and a perceived level of teaching competence. In the final course evaluation, some students actually initiated comparisons between the two instructors and judged me to be the "less competent instructor."

For three years, my course evaluations were below average. They also contained negative written comments, particularly during the first two years. Several female undergraduate students were confrontational and often challenged my grading. They also showed disrespectful attitudes explicitly, such as by talking to me in a rude manner, whispering to each other in class right after I made a certain comment, refusing to listen to my suggestions during one-on-one conferencing, and so on. In the third year, the class atmosphere improved, but the numerical course evaluation still fell significantly below average.

One of the largest complaints voiced by the students was that I did not speak Spanish or French. My colleague and I tried to convince the students that regardless of the language taught, the fundamental approach to teaching a second language is the same and that whether or not the professor speaks a particular language does not affect his/her ability as a teacher trainer. To me, this was indeed the case. When my students gave a teaching demonstration in Spanish, French, German, or Latin in front of their peers, I was able to point out strengths and weaknesses in their teaching. The fact that I had taken basic Spanish, French, and German courses when I was in college might have also helped to some extent. Nonetheless, many of the undergraduate Spanish majors, in particular, were unsatisfied with my limited Spanish language proficiency and questioned my credibility as a teacher educator.[2] One wrote, "I do not feel that our French and Spanish lessons can be fairly graded by someone who is not proficient in either language."

Elsewhere, I have critiqued the one-size-fits-all approach to second-language teaching that tends to disregard minority perspectives and needs arising from such situations as teaching students with exceptionalities and teaching less commonly taught languages (Kubota 1998b). The emphasis on the universality of teaching methodologies contradicts, to some extent, what I critiqued. However, it was only the most practical concept that could convince the students of my credibility. In this particular setting, I struggled against a discourse that privileges a White teacher with a native or native-like command of English and Spanish. I needed to coopt an aspect of the one-size-fits-all discourse to counter a discourse that undermined my authority. This demonstrates multiple and often contradictory subjectivities produced by discourses and a struggle to strategically position oneself in competing discourses (Weedon 1999).

Another complaint made by some students had to do with my proficiency in English. Students wrote in their course evaluations that my English proficiency was a "barrier" and a "limiting factor" in understanding and answering students' questions. One student wrote, "explanations were sometimes slow and thus failed to keep our attention." The perceived limitation of my English language skills was also equated with "little or no interpersonal skills." Such criticisms demonstrate an unfortunate irony; these students were preparing themselves to become second-language teachers charged with advocating linguistic and cultural diversity in the schools.

Other complaints were that the grading was arbitrary and that, during the first year, I was unable to explain clearly the procedures for the teaching practicum that was supposed to follow the methods course. Given the fact that I did not have autonomy over grading methods and that anyone who is new to a system may not have a complete understanding of how the system works, these complaints seem quite harsh and unreasonable.

However, not all students were negative about my teaching. Some students recognized my competence, commitment, and caring personality and expressed appreciation for my teaching. These students viewed the complaining students as immature and disrespectful. One student wrote, "Sometimes, other students in class would become feisty and frustrated due to Dr. Kubota's non-native English....If I were to evaluate the classroom mentality, I would have graded it a very poor." Another student commented by referring to Japanese language lessons I presented as examples: "The fact that you were Japanese was helpful to me—seeing how teaching methods of foreign languages are universal."

One of the strategies I began to use in order to confront these challenges was to communicate explicitly to the students on the first day of class that I am different from White professors. I would ask whether the students had ever had an instructor from Asia with an accent. Then I would stress the fact that I have a different cultural and linguistic background compared to my teaching partner or other White professors and that being in my class is a great opportunity for them to learn firsthand intercultural communication as they interact with me. It is difficult to judge whether this strategy directly influenced the improvement of the class atmosphere in the third year, but I no longer had unpleasant moments like the ones I previously experienced.

In 1998, there was a major change in the teacher-preparation program that made me discontinue teaching the methods course. Now, I was to design a different course titled Language Minority Students, which has become a course I teach every year. The course explores issues of culture, multicultural education, second language acquisition, bilingual education, literacy, federal and state policies for students with limited English proficiency, and so on. This course enrolls undergraduate and graduate students preparing to become schoolteachers as well as teachers who are already teaching, most at elementary schools. The students are predominantly White women.

Learning from the strategy developed in the methods class, I take a significant amount of time on the first day of class to introduce myself and communicate that learning to interact with me helps students understand intercultural communication and cultural diversity, things that these students will inevitably experience in their profession. I emphasize the fact that I have a different cultural and linguistic background that influences my teaching style. I mention that I am a second-language speaker and that students need to accommodate my communication needs and styles. I stress that it is important for them to take advantage of this opportunity to develop skills to work with people from different backgrounds. Perhaps because these students are already interested in learning about different cultures and communicating with non-native speakers of English, I have rarely had problematic moments. I have also received good course evaluations. Students wrote such comments as the instructor was "interested, engaged, enthusiastic, concerned, well-versed, and competent" and "This was the best course (including all undergraduate and graduate courses) that I have ever taken!"

My teaching experiences have been both positive and negative. How can this discrepancy be explained? In the following section, I will attempt an analysis by drawing on concepts of power and capital.

Power and Capital

That I had two such opposite experiences demonstrates how the authority of the instructor is perceived differently in different contexts. More specifically, students' perceptions of my legitimacy as a teacher varied due to different kinds of interplay among my background and expertise, students' academic interests, their willingness to negotiate my cultural and linguistic knowledge and skills, and the particular instructional context. My experiences demonstrate that the perceived authority, prestige, and power of an instructor are not constant or absolute; rather, they are relative and unstable, implicated in power relations that exist in a particular situation. Here, the notion of capital as power theorized by Bourdieu is useful.

Following Marxism, Pierre Bourdieu defines capital as "accumulated labor" in materialized and embodied forms (1986, 241). The distribution and availability of capital influences a chance for success in a particular social arena. Bourdieu posits that there are various forms of capital, such as economic capital (money and property rights), cultural capital (dispositions of the mind and body, cultural goods, and educational credentials), social capital (resources linked to social networks of connections), symbolic capital (prestige, reputation, and fame), and so on (Bourdieu 1986; 1991) and that an unequal distribution of capital produces and reproduces social stratification, domination and subordination. What Bourdieu regards as important is cultural capital, which includes not only cultural goods but also a variety of resources, including such things as "verbal facility, general cultural awareness, aesthetic preferences, information about the school system, and educational credentials" (Swartz 1997, 75). Cultural capital is produced, transmitted, and accumulated in educational institutions such as schools and universities. In the American context, for example, valued cultural capital, which is usually that of middle-class White American families, is legitimated and reproduced through teaching and learning. Cultural goods as well as knowledge, skills, and dispositions inherited and accumulated by middle-class White Americans obviously have a high value in the mainstream society and function as power.

It is important to note, however, that power and the value of capital are not absolute but relational. The perceived value of capital changes depending on what the participants of social interactions are interested in investing in. Likewise, in order for power to exist, the participants need to recognize its value. In cross-cultural contexts, such as in my experience, participants from different cultures bring their own cultural capital to the cross-cultural inter-action, but the perceived value of the capital is different depending on a par-ticular social context, or *field.* Thompson (1991), in his introduction to Bourdieu's work, defines *field* as "a structured space of positions in which the positions and their interrelations are determined by the distribution of differ-ent kinds of resources or 'capital'" (14). This indicates that capital "only re-ceives its value from that ascribed to it by field operations" (Grenfell and James 1998, 25). The relational nature of capital and power echoes Michel Foucault's notion of power. Power, for Foucault, is neither possessed by someone or some institution nor is it imposed top down; rather, it exists eve-rywhere. There is a "multiplicity of force relations," and the states of power are always "local and unstable" (Foucault 1978, 93). Thus, power is "exer-cised from innumerable points, in the interplay of nonegalitarian and mobile relations" (94).

To put these theories in context, the students in my Advanced Japanese language class, who were investing in learning Japanese language and culture, perceived a positive value in the cultural and linguistic capital that I, as a na-tive of Japan, brought to the instructional field. In this particular field, despite the fact that it was situated in an American institution where White middle-class race, culture, and English are usually valued, my cultural and linguistic capital functioned as symbolic capital and power that allowed me to exercise my authority as a professor. This authority also enabled me to reinforce the language policy in the classroom. The Japanese-only policy was unproblem-atically accepted by students, which further allowed me to use my native lan-guage as legitimate linguistic capital.

Similarly, in the Language Minority Students class, my cultural and lin-guistic capital was valued and legitimated. Although the instructional con-tent was very different from the Japanese-language class, the students in this class were interested in learning about issues related to second language acquisition and cultural diversity. These issues are directly relevant to my own experience as a second-language speaker and as a person from a different culture making it in American academia. In this sense, my cultural and linguistic capital, considered to be hybrid, attracted my students' interest. However, unlike the Japanese-language courses, in which my cultural and linguistic capital was almost automatically valued, I felt that convincing the students of its positive value would require some effort on my part. Had I not set a stage on which I presented myself as a culturally and linguistically different instructor and emphasized the importance of intercultural communication, I might not have had a positive experience in this course. Nevertheless, in both cases, the value of my cultural capital was recognized and converted into symbolic capital and power. Students perceived me as a legitimate and competent instructor.

Conversely, some students in the methods course identified very little of value in my hybrid cultural and linguistic capital. They were interested in learning how to teach Spanish or French, and to them, only an instructor with Spanish-English or French-English bilingual proficiency and with a thorough knowledge of the system could help them pursue their interest. They identified no intersection between what they were investing in and my cultural and linguistic capital. To them, the cultural and linguistic capital that I brought to the instructional field was irrelevant or illegitimate. Thus, they highlighted and criticized a perceived *lack* in my cultural and linguistic capital. Of course, what I experienced with these students may not be explained solely in terms of capital. What if I were an American-born Asian instructor with a native-level Spanish-English bilingual proficiency? Would my students find no problem with my English and Spanish? Unfortunately, a study conducted by Rubin (1992) suggests a negative answer even there. Rubin found that a group of American undergraduate students who listened to a recorded lecture in standard American English while being presented with a picture of an Asian woman to indicate who the instructor was, perceived more accent and performed more poorly on listening comprehension than a group who listened to the same recorded lecture with a picture of Caucasian woman as the instructor. Here, racial prejudice needs to be taken into account. Then, what about gender? What if I had been a Japanese male? That students might not have been as hostile was indicated to me by a Japanese male professor of communication studies who once taught in an American university. After listening to my struggle, he commented, "I never had a problem like that. Maybe there is something wrong with the way you teach." Thus, issues of race and gender cannot be ignored as factors interacting with language and culture.

Unlike many Spanish majors in the methods class, other students in the course did recognize the value of my cultural and linguistic capital. They appreciated my using Japanese to give examples of how to teach a second language. My cultural and linguistic capital was viewed not as lacking but as offering new perspectives. They were also interested in learning about different cultures and languages including my cultural and linguistic heritage. In fact, during my three years of teaching this course, two students—one specializing in French and another specializing in Latin—were accepted into the Japan Exchange and Teaching Program, and they taught English in public schools in Japan.

In sum, in different instructional fields, the value of my hybrid cultural and linguistic capital was perceived differently. This fluctuation of value reflects and constitutes the dynamic relations of power between the students and me. My cultural and linguistic capital was recognized in the Japanese class, where students' learning goals matched the cultural and linguistic expertise that I brought to the instructional field. Also, the Language Minority Students class recognized my cultural and linguistic heritage and my cross-cultural experiences as relevant to what they were learning, identifying them as a legitimate capital. In these two cases, my cultural and linguistic capital also functioned as symbolic capital in these instructional fields and allowed my exercise of power as an instructor. In contrast, some of the students in the methods class denied the value of my cultural and linguistic capital. Occasionally, they resisted working with me or challenged my legitimacy as an instructor. In this situation, effective teaching and learning severely suffered from this perceived illegitimacy of my power.

These instances demonstrate that instructional fields are indeed sites of struggle for power. Compared to faculty who have a higher social status in terms of race, gender, class, and language, minority faculty (including myself) tend to be confronted with more intense struggles for power. Nonetheless, it is important to note again that power is not exercised unidirectionally and that the relations of power can be contested and transformed from within (Foucault 1978). This opens up a possibility for counter-hegemonic pedagogy in our classrooms.

Counter-Hegemonic Pedagogy That Affirms Diversity

Like many women teachers of color, I have had challenging and sometimes painful experiences in teaching that relate directly to my position as a woman of color. As these experiences illustrate, one cannot assume that the power relation between the teacher and students is universally alike. The unique challenges confronted by women teachers of color require different teaching strategies. Amin (1999), for instance, argues that in the context of teaching English as a second language, White native English-speaking teachers who tell students honestly "I don't know the answer to the question, but I will find out," humanize their image. However, this response may not work for a woman professor of color, because it could reinforce the image of her as an incompetent teacher. A strategy to overcome this image could be to spend an enormous amount of time preparing for classes and anticipating all possible questions. This is a strategy to compensate for our marginality. However, another strategy is to appropriate this marginality and to turn it into a tool for advocating racial, ethnic, and linguistic diversity.

As I mentioned earlier, in order to overcome the challenge I faced, I began to use my cultural and linguistic background as a tool for raising students' awareness that they must acquire the knowledge, skills, and attitudes needed to successfully negotiate in our culturally and linguistically diverse society. In the beginning of a course, I disclose my cultural and linguistic background in as detailed a manner as possible. I even mention some of the painful experiences I have had in interacting with students in the past. This strategy appears to accentuate the problematic of the Otherness and marginality, but the important point is to appropriate this Otherness to our advantage in order to promote diversity.

Diversity has become a buzzword in various aspects of higher education. In teaching, professors who are sympathetic to multicultural education strive to include diverse perspectives and ensure that students with diverse backgrounds express their voices. However, multicultural education tends to focus on a simplistic celebration of differences rather than encourage critical inquiry into the unequal relations of power that construct and perpetuate these differences (Kincheloe and Steinberg 1997; McLaren 1995). Contrasted with this superficial approach to multiculturalism is critical multicultural education, which envisions social justice and social transformation for democracy through both affirming and interrogating differences (Kincheloe and Steinberg 1997). Social justice and transformation cannot be accomplished without dialogue across differences. In our diverse society where cross-cultural and cross-linguistic contact in schools, universities, and workplaces is increasingly becoming the norm rather than the exception (Cummins and Cameron 1994), the ability to accommodate, communicate, and collaborate across racial, ethnic, and linguistic boundaries is absolutely essential.

This ability, however, cannot be developed through imposition or coercion. It has to be developed through a mutual learning process that occurs between the dominant and the marginalized. In various social settings such as schools, universities, and workplaces, it is usually the marginalized or the

Other who is forced to accommodate the dominant linguistic and cultural norm. For example, Lippi-Green (1997), critiquing discrimination based on English accents, argues that when members of a dominant language group interact with people with non-standard accents, they often feel that it is legitimate to reject their role as a listener and quickly blame the other for any communication difficulty. However, both the listener and the speaker ought to share the responsibility for communication in order to create more egalitarian communicative relationships. This shared responsibility echoes the notion of mutual accommodation advocated by Nieto (2000; 1999) in the context of critical multicultural education in schools. Paralleling Lippi-Green, Nieto argues that in a truly democratic society, accommodation is a two-way process, allowing negotiation among all participants in social interactions.

The notion of mutual accommodation and negotiation rightly applies to the relation between women professors of color and their students. As do minority students in schools and universities, women teachers of color often find themselves accommodating the dominant cultural, linguistic, and pedagogical norm in their struggle for recognition of power and authority in instructional settings. However, it should not always be the woman teacher of color who accommodates; her students too must learn to alter their expectations and appreciate differences. In order to promote equality and social justice, we, as educators, must first value our own cultural and linguistic capital and communicate its value to our students. We need to appropriate our marginalized hybrid cultural capital for advocating diversity. Disclosing one's ethnic and cultural experiences to set a stage for advocacy is one way. Another way might be to appropriate one's own ethnic communication style and require that the audience shift in its paradigms in order to understand different experiences and cultural values. These strategies transform our experiential knowledge coming from marginality into a privileged location (hooks 1994). This centralization of marginality is, in bell hooks's term, "counter-hegemonic cultural practice," which draws a "definite distinction between that marginality which is imposed by oppressive structure and that marginality one chooses as site of resistance, as location of radical openness and possibility" (hooks 1990, 22).

Communicating the value of our own cultural capital opens up a possibility for promoting critical multiculturalism on campus and in wider society. By giving a positive value to our own uniqueness and using it strategically to advocate diversity in our teaching, we not only empower ourselves but also provide our students with precious opportunities to critically understand and negotiate differences. Yet, diversity and social justice cannot be promoted solely by the efforts of women teachers of color. The counter-hegemonic pedagogy becomes truly effective when it is supported by other colleagues and administrators. All educators must recognize the multiple relations of power in instructional settings, understand the challenges that women faculty of color face, and take responsibility to confront various forms of social injustice. It is necessary for women faculty of color, their colleagues, and administrators to make a social and educational commitment to treasure everyone's cultural and linguistic capital.

Ryuko Kubota, Assistant Professor at the University of North Carolina at Chapel Hill, came to North America as a graduate student from Japan. She has received her MAT degree in Teaching English as a Second Languages (ESL) from the School for International Training and her Ph.D. degree in second language education from the University of Toronto. In the past eleven years, she has been involved in teaching Japanese and foreign language/ESL teacher training at predominantly White campuses. Her research interests include critical pedagogy, multicultural education, and culture in second-language teaching. Her articles have appeared in numerous academic journals.

Notes

1. One difficult experience was teaching a graduate course for preparing Japanese-language teachers at a private institution. Again, the difficulty seemed to stem from unequal relations of power. There was a sense at the institution that the field of Teaching English as a Second Language (TESL) was more advanced than the field of teaching foreign languages. This was perhaps influenced by the fact that the foreign language faculty at this institution mainly consisted of non-native English-speaking professors from abroad. On a few occasions, I heard TESL professors describe their foreign language colleagues as traditional and authoritarian. The students in my course were taking classes from these TESL professors and might have been influenced by this attitude.

2. There could be several reasons why the majority of complaining students were in-state undergraduate Spanish language majors. The reasons include a lack of maturity, less previous contact with Asian people compared to out-of-state students, and the fact that the other instructor was a Spanish specialist. Also, a sense of elitism that exists in foreign language education might have been strong among these students, fueled by defensiveness against the perceived low status of Spanish in this country (see Ortega 1999).

Works Cited

Amin, N. 1999. "Minority Women Teachers of ESL: Negotiating White English." In *Non-Native Educators in English Language Teaching*, edited by G. Braine. Mahwah, NJ: Lawrence Erlbaum Associates.

Bourdieu, P. 1986. "The Forms of Capital." In *Handbook of Theory and Research for the Sociology of Education*, edited by J. G. Richardson. New York: Greenwood Press.

———. 1991. *Language and Symbolic Power*. Translated by G. Raymond and M. Adamson. Cambridge, MA: Harvard University Press.

Cummins, J., and L. Cameron. 1994. "The ESL Student IS the Mainstream: The Marginalization of Diversity in Current Canadian Educational Debates." *English Quarterly* 26 (3): 30–33.

Foucault, M. 1978. *The History of Sexuality, Volume I: An Introduction*. New York: Vintage Books.

Grenfell, M., and D. James. 1998. *Bourdieu and Education: Acts of Practical Theory*. Bristol, PA: Falmer Press.

hooks, b. 1990. *Yearning: Race, Gender, and Cultural Politics*. Boston, MA: South End Press.

———. 1994. *Teaching to Transgress: Education as the Practice of Freedom*. New York: Routledge.

Johnsrud, L. K., and D. C. Des Jarlais. 1994. "Barriers to Tenure for Women and Minorities." *The Review of Higher Education* 17 (4): 335–353.

Johnsrud, L. K., and K. C. Sadao. 1998. "The Common Experience of 'Otherness': Ethnic and Racial Minority Faculty." *The Review of Higher Education* 21 (4): 315–342.

Kincheloe, J. L., and S. R. Steinberg. 1997. *Changing Multiculturalism*. Buckingham: Open University Press.

Kubota, R. 1998a. "Ideologies of English in Japan." *World Englishes* 17: 295–306.

———. 1998b. "Voices from the Margin: Second and Foreign Language Teaching Approaches from Minority Perspectives." *Canadian Modern Language Review* 54 (3): 394–412.

Lippi-Green, R. 1997. *English with an Accent; Language, Ideology, and Discrimination in the United States*. New York and London: Routledge.

McLaren, P. L. 1995. "White Terror and Oppositional Agency: Toward a Critical Multiculturalism." In *Multicultural Education: Critical Pedagogy, and the Politics of Difference*, edited by C. E. Sleeter and P. L. McLaren. Albany, NY: State University of New York Press.

Ng, R. 1995. "Teaching Against the Grain: Contradictions and Possibilities." In *Anti-racism, Feminism, and Critical Approaches to Education*, edited by R. Ng, P. Staton and J. Scane. Westport, CT: Bergin & Garvey.

Nieto, S. 1999. *The Light in Their Eyes: Creating Multicultural Learning Communities*. New York: Teachers College Press.

———. 2000. *Affirming Diversity: The Sociopolitical Context of Multicultural Education*. New York: Longman.

Ortega, L. 1999. "Rethinking Foreign Language Education: Political Dimensions of the Profession." In *Foreign Language Teaching and Language Minority Education*, edited by K. A. Davis. Honolulu, HI: Second Language Teaching & Curriculum Center, University of Hawai'i.

Rubin, D. L. 1992. "Nonlanguage Factors Affecting Undergraduates' Judgments of Non-Native English-speaking Teaching Assistants." *Research in Higher Education* 33 (4): 511–531.

Swartz, D. 1997. *Culture and Power: The Sociology of Pierre Bourdieu*. Chicago and London: The University of Chicago Press.

Thomas, J. 1999. "Voices from the Periphery: Non-Native Teachers and Issues of Credibility." In *Non-native Educators in English Language Teaching*, edited by G. Braine. Mahwah, NJ: Lawrence Erlbaum Associates.

Thompson, J. B. 1991. "Editor's Introduction." In *Language and Symbolic Power*. Cambridge, MA: Harvard University Press.

Vargas, L. 1999. "When the 'Other' Is the Teacher: Implications of Teacher Diversity in Higher Education." *The Urban Review* 31 (4): 359–383.

Weedon, C. 1999. *Feminism, Theory and the Politics of Difference*. Oxford, MA: Blackwell.

CHAPTER EIGHTEEN

We Do Not Want You to Be Human, We Want You to Be Right: Dilemmas of Legitimacy in Environments of Privilege

FREDI AVALOS-C'DEBACA

Abstract

IN MANY INSTITUTIONS of higher learning, the responsibility of teaching courses that center on race, class, gender, and ethnicity are often relegated to women professors of color. Chicanas who are committed to a liberatory pedagogical practice may face an even greater challenge. In addition to racial and gender stereotypes, students may also find it difficult to legitimate teachers who want to establish a co-intentional model of learning that is less hierarchical and authoritarian. This autoethnographic essay records shifts in student consciousness in relation to the communicative choices of the instructor in a course in Intercultural Communication. The essay provides an analysis of the communicative dialectic between an approachable and credible style that liberatory pedagogues must constantly negotiate.

As an adjunct faculty member at a California State University campus, I teach courses that focus on the politics of gender, race, class, and ethnicity. For this reason, I am deeply committed to liberatory pedagogical theory and practice. Liberatory pedagogical practice "is positioned as that which attends to teaching/learning intended to disrupt particular historical situated systems of oppression" (Lather 1992, 121). It encourages students to move away from passive modes of learning and to engage in a critical examination of all forms of received knowledge. Consequently, these courses have always been the spaces where I have experienced the most disturbing, challenging, and rewarding moments of my teaching career. Students have often exhibited a great deal of resistance to both the content of the course and my pedagogical approach, which encourages them to understand the power of their own agency.

My pedagogical strategy has been informed by Paulo Freire. Freire's early work was aimed at developing and implementing pedagogical techniques designed not only to teach literacy but also to raise the "consciousness" of the impoverished and politically disempowered populations he served in Latin America. His project was primarily one of de-colonization. Freire argued that pedagogy that seeks to "instill" knowledge by "explaining to the people their own action" is useless (Freire 1997, 35); instead, the oppressed must transform reality not by intellectual reflection but through a particular mode of directed dialogue between the oppressed and their teachers that leads to praxis. This is because "liberating education consists of acts of cognition, not transfers of information" (Freire 1997, 64). Thus, knowledge is co-constructed through a never-ending process of communication and *action.* Critical pedagogy must be a "pedagogy of people engaged in the fight for their *own* liberation" [emphasis mine].

I have continually grappled with the application of these critical pedagogical practices (developed first for highly motivated adults who were actively engaged in a struggle for their physical survival) to students who are very young, experientially limited, and economically privileged. In other words, very few of my students walk into my classroom intellectually and emotionally motivated to engage actively in understanding their position of privilege. In addition, they often find it difficult to legitimate instructors who want to establish a co-intentional model of learning that is less hierarchical and authoritarian. One student expressed it this way: "We do not want you to be more human, we want you to be right." Students seem to share a cultural expectation that in the social world, right answers exist and that good teachers will provide them. Barbara Hillyer Davis explains an internal conflict that I share: "Since we want students to struggle with questions that do not have right answers, we are ourselves struggling against that deeply acculturated expectation" (1985, 252).

This autoethnographic essay explores my experience as a Chicana teaching courses in communication. It documents my struggle to develop a curriculum that attempts to negotiate my political and moral call for the implementation of a critical education with the realities of my students' social positionalities and the limitations imposed by the institution where this education actually takes place. Although my experiences and my perceptions are my own, I hope that this work will provide some insight into the particular challenges of professors who have faced, and continue to face, the interlocking effects of gender, race, class, and ethnicity in their classrooms. I used the following questions to initially guide this study: How do privileged students receive/reject dissonant information from a female Other in a position of authority? What pedagogical verbal and nonverbal strategies are more/less useful in helping them deconstruct their own privileged position? And, What explains the lower levels of student resistance that I experienced teaching my most recent course in Intercultural Communication in the fall of 1999? I explore these questions by contrasting my six years of teaching a wide variety of communication classes with the quality of classroom interaction I experienced teaching this particular course. Although I use this course as a focal point in the essay, many of the strategies that I employed are a synthesis of pedagogical practices that I use in all my courses. Indeed, this ethnographical work has allowed me to bring my collective teaching experience into a clearer focus.

Over the course of the semester, I collected and analyzed participant-observation materials (field notes), interviews with former and current students, written assignments, and informal and formal written evaluations from students. Drawing on several types of data has allowed me to gain a deeper and clearer understanding of the students' and my own positionality as an instructor.

The Campus

The campus where I teach is only ten years old. Both the campus and the student population are small when compared to other more established Cal State campuses. Students are required to enter the university with at least a 2.8 grade point average. Over the course of the four years I have worked there as a lecturer, many students have told me that the university was their "second or third choice." Students who either do not want to leave or cannot leave the San Diego area or have been rejected from San Diego State University (considered a flagship campus) turn to San Marcos for their education. However, most students I have talked to upon arrival are pleased to discover that the campus at this stage of its development can provide an excellent and more personal educational experience. At present, it can be compared to a small liberal arts college where, as one student expressed it, "professors know your name." Perhaps for this reason, the campus is a very friendly place. People greet strangers in the hallways, elevator, and cafeteria. Open space and the constant noise of construction equipment and work crews surround the university. This serves as a continual reminder to both students and faculty that it is a university still "under construction." The campus has a sense of expectation and restlessness that I have not experienced at more established institutions. Although the campus is located in a very diverse community, the majority of students are White and middle class. There is a sizable population of Asian Americans and Latinos and a very small number of African American students. In the four years that I have taught here, I have only had three African American students. The class population of my Intercultural Communication class reflected the demographics of the larger campus.

Personal History

My entry into the academic field came relatively late in life. Although I had been politically conscious during my teens and early twenties, I spent nearly seventeen years in a traditional corporate environment. My father was a union organizer, and I grew up in a highly charged political environment. In my late teens, I (unsuccessfully) led an attempt to organize workers in a warehouse where I was employed. Over time, my passion for politics waned. I married at the age of 19 and slowly moved up the corporate ladder, first in banking and later in real estate development. I had every intention of returning to this profession upon completion of my B.A. in communication. However, soon it became clear to me that I was well suited for a career in the academy. While completing my M.A. in communication I became a teaching associate and was immediately given my own classroom. From the moment I nervously faced my first class in Theories of Oral Communication, I knew that I had a passion for teaching. Now, despite the low pay and lack of employment security as an adjunct instructor, I cannot imagine doing anything else with my life. However, I have been rewarded by excellent teaching evaluations, an award for excellence in teaching, and a profound sense of personal satisfaction that I had never previously known. I now teach courses in Media and Society, Interpersonal Communication, Persuasion, Oral Communication, Group Communication, and Intercultural Communication. I have been helped along the way by a loving husband, a family, and a network of supportive friends and colleagues. Throughout my academic career, I have also received the support of mentors to whom, even today, I continue to turn for advice and support. However, it is my strong spiritual grounding that inspires, motivates, and sustains me on a daily basis.

Over the course of the last ten years, I have reclaimed my political self. I identify most strongly with the term Chicana. For me, "Chicanisma" is both a political identity and a quest for the political power necessary for Latinas/Mexicanas to transform existing systems of power through direct political action. As a Chicana and a feminist, I reject feminism that ignores differences in power relationships among women and those that tend to "subsume all differences into a male/female dichotomy" (Maher 1987, 98). I share the feeling of the Black feminist statement written by the Combahee River Collective that a "general statement of my politics should be an active commitment to struggling against the racial, sexual, heterosexual, and class oppression" and that it is a "synthesis of these oppressions which creates the conditions of our lives"(1983, 210).

My research has led me to the jungles of Chiapas, Mexico, where I explored the Zapatista National Liberation Army's use of new media as a tool for political and cultural emancipation. My interest in this area has continued. My recent work has examined the ways non-governmental organizations use new media as a means to elicit Third World solidarity in the United States. Currently, I am finishing my Ph.D. in cultural studies. It was in the field of cultural studies that I was introduced to tenets of liberatory pedagogy.

A Modified Liberatory Pedagogical Practice:
Overview of My Pedagogical Practice

I began my teaching career with very little training and no basis in pedagogical theory of any kind. However, even before I began to explore liberatory and feminist critical pedagogical practice, I had felt it was important for me as a teacher to encourage students to develop critical thinking skills that would allow them to challenge mainstream modes of thought. I have always encouraged students to look for what is not readily visible and to try and seek out the missing or downplayed elements of any form of received knowledge. For this reason, when I first discovered the literature, my interest and engagement with liberatory pedagogical practice was immediate. What was less immediate was my ability to apply these highly abstract theories concretely in my classrooms. What I discovered was that the flattening of hierarchical structures that these theories promote do not always serve the best interest of the students, the instructor, or the learning process itself. Oftentimes, it was necessary for me to supplement or substitute liberatory pedagogical practices with traditional pedagogical methods (i.e., lectures and a kind of distant or impersonal authoritarianism that allowed me to stand firm on course requirements). Like John Schilb, I have tried to develop an "organizing mentality which does not try to get everything 'right' at once, but rather lets the complexities of the process guide the organizer as it proceeds" (1985, 254). Liberatory pedagogical theory serves as the primary tool that I use to help me negotiate this process.

I will provide a brief overview of some of the liberatory pedagogical, feminist, and communication theories that have helped me deal with the complexities of the teaching/learning process. As previously mentioned, I will use the interactions of one class experience as a point of contrast with other Intercultural Communication courses I have taught. However, I use similar strategies in all the upper- and lower-division communication courses I teach. Because communication skills lie at the heart of a participatory classroom, I believe that many of strategies discussed here are applicable to, or can be adapted to, most college classrooms and instructors invested in liberatory pedagogical practice.

Communication theory has helped me to link many abstract pedagogical theories to concrete practice in the classroom. David Lusted argues that pedagogy is "the transformation of consciousness that takes place in the intersection of three agencies—the teacher, the learner, and the knowledge they produce"(1992, 3). Thus, pedagogy itself is inherently about communicative interaction. Intertwined in this discussion will be how I was able, or not able, to successfully utilize these theories and my own political, ethical, and professional struggle to determine when they were or were not appropriate. Because I use a variety of pedagogical approaches, including what I describe as "mini-lectures," my pedagogical strategy cannot be seen purely as a "liberatory pedagogical practice" that depends on a more dialogical approach. For example, when discussing or introducing new or complex communication concepts, I feel it is my responsibility to provide some initial guidance before I open the topic to group discussion. My lectures typically take between 15 to 20 minutes in a class period that lasts 1 hour and 15 minutes. I have found that not only do students expect this type of support; it is often necessary to help them unpack difficult and highly esoteric concepts.

Also, students who walk into my classroom have very little experience with liberatory pedagogical practice. They have been socio-culturally conditioned by years of existing in an educational system that has legitimated some teaching practices (i.e., an authoritarian/dogmatic approach, highly structured or little classroom discussion, and a high power distance between teacher and students) while it delegitimates others (i.e., a non-absolutist approach and certain immediacy behaviors). For this reason, it is important that I am capable of displaying a range of communicative behaviors that include traditional pedagogical approaches (e.g., authoritative) and those that work to encourage a flattening of hierarchical relations between teacher and students. It is unrealistic to believe that student expectations formed in decades of exposure to traditional educational practices will disappear when entering spaces for alternative forms of learning/teaching. It is necessary that instructors learn to negotiate students' expectations of authority and certainty with their own commitment to co-construct an active learning environment with their students. Attempts to co-construct a classroom where a critical and participatory democracy can be realized must be seen as a multidimensional and complex process of negotiation (Hogelucht and Geist 1997). This process of a negotiated classroom order requires an ability to express certain degrees of authority, warmth, and approachability that open up the possibility for a liberatory pedagogical practice.

Liberatory Pedagogical Practice

Liberatory or critical pedagogical theory insists that critical pedagogical practice be guided by a deep commitment to social justice and change. The classroom itself becomes a site where this type of change can take place. Students who find themselves in spaces where critical pedagogy is practiced are not passive recipients of static information. They are co-creators of knowledge. Stated differently, they must become actively engaged in their own learning process. Ultimately, students must come to a "new awareness of selfhood and begin to look critically at the social situation in which they find themselves,…and take the initiative in acting to transform society" and the organizations upon which that society is built (Freire 1997, 50). Critical pedagogues, then, must attempt to learn from students by allowing them to describe their own social, cultural, intellectual, and moral positionality. In essence, there is a flattening of the hierarchy between teachers and students. An instructor must also be prepared to "transform her or his own understanding in response to the understandings of students" (Ellsworth 1992, 92). Stated differently, it is a learning environment in which teachers become students. It requires educational spaces where these learning conditions can be constructed and "consists of ground rules for classroom interaction….While the specific forms and means of social change and organization are open to debate, there must be agreement around the goals of dialogue" (1992, 106).

Ground Rules and First Impressions

For me, ground rules for democratic interaction and dialogue that lie at the heart of liberatory educational practice have become an important *starting* point in a semester-long process. Very early in my teaching career, I began to discuss the need for, and my expectation of, respectful communication on the first day of class. Over the years, I have refined the way I approach the discussion of communicative ground rules. As a result, students have consistently commented on the high level of comfort they have felt in expressing themselves in my classes.

It is on the first day of class that I begin to set the ground rules for interaction and my expectations for high-quality work. However, in courses in intercultural communication this process will eventually lead paradoxically to an ability to critique the constructed nature of knowledge and the type of "rational" discourse these very ground rules promote.

In the fall of 1999, for the first time since I began teaching this class, I took an entire week (rather than the one day I typically set aside) early in the semester to discuss critical thinking and argumentation skills. I labeled this section of the syllabus "Preparing for the Course." We applied basic argumentation skills and strategies to many intercultural situations. Students were asked to identify and deconstruct fallacious forms of reasoning and inductive, deductive, and causal reasoning. For example, I asked students to deal with their gender or ethnic stereotypes surrounding bad drivers and suggested that they were using a fallacious inductive form of reasoning that makes claims without enough evidence to make generalizable assertions. It was in this section that students were introduced to the concept of the dialectic as a basis for constructive classroom dialogue. This section became an invaluable teaching strategy. In the intercultural classroom, it establishes a *preliminary* foundation for the need to critically think through concepts and opinions. However, equally important to the success of the class is our ability to demonstrate respectful communicative behaviors and the opportunity to develop these skills.

I ask the students not to hide behind passive-aggressive behaviors (i.e., eye-rolling, working on other materials during class lectures or discussion, constant yawning, talking to classmates, and arriving late or not at all). I inform students that these behaviors are just as aggressive as a student telling me to "go to hell," and I will interpret them as such. Stated simply, their non-verbal behaviors are just as real as their verbal responses. I also tell them that these communicative ground rules are important in any classroom, but in an intercultural course, we will be going down some very difficult intellectual and emotional terrain and that it is imperative that we co-construct an environment of trust. When students see other students acting in disrespectful and aggressive ways, they begin to see the class as a hostile environment in which even the teacher is not afforded respect. I ask students to leave the class or not return if they do not think they are capable of acting respectfully. I am willing to take the risk of perhaps alienating some students at this point, because without respect for me and their classmates, a course in intercultural communication would be a disaster. (In the fall 1999 class, after the first week, four students did not return.) I tell students that "in this class, the only thing that anyone can do that is wrong is to act disrespectfully toward me or your colleagues." Later in two midterm evaluations students made note of my first day performance. Jay[1] wrote, "On the first day you scared me a little—I almost did not come back. But now I realize why you had to come on so strong. This classroom could have really gotten out-of-hand." Connie wrote, "When I first came into your classroom, I wanted to run out. I did not know if I would be able to live up to your expectations, but I have....You turned out not to be anything like I expected early in the semester." In my own experience, it is much easier to perform authority early in the semester and then to relax the approach in the weeks that follow. Indeed, it is difficult to gain control of the class if in the initial encounter students do not see the professor as credible. Paradoxically, without gaining their respect early in the class through a presentation of authority, it would be difficult, perhaps impossible, to get to a place that then allows me to relax some of these initial barriers. If students continue to see me as highly authoritarian, they will not be comfortable discussing some of the most important concepts of the course. Here it is important to note that on my formal teacher evaluations many students complimented me on what one student described as my "approachable and friendly style."

It seems that despite the fact that I may alienate or scare some students, my early presentation of ground rules also proved to have a positive effect on many students in this and in other classes. Also, it has been my experience that most students want to be challenged and that they respect certain displays of authority. Indeed, the feminist teacher must come to recognize her power "and must claim her authority if her students are to claim their own" (Culley 1985, 211). For this reason, I am very conscious of my physical presentation in the classroom. For example, for the first few weeks of the semester, I dress in a very traditional business attire. This is because an instructor's credibility level is often determined within one minute of the first face-to-face encounter (Richmond and McCroskey 1995).

Early in my teaching career, I began my class with a more approachable style. However, what I discovered was that an approachable style presented early in the semester was open to misinterpretation by students as a kind of weakness. Gender *and* ethnic role expectations may place Chicanas/Latinas in a negative double bind when trying to establish credibility in classroom interactions. One reason for this is that Chicanas/Latinas are often portrayed in mainstream media as members of an underclass who are subservient, passive, and highly emotional. For individuals who have not had an opportunity to develop relationships with this population, these images may be their only experience with Latinas. The presentation of authority may be a more critical teaching strategy for women of color than it is for White women and White men.

Many times, students ask me questions that reveal their ethnic stereotypes. For example, I have been asked on numerous occasions "Why do you speak English without an accent?" Or I have been told, "You cannot be Mexican-American; you speak so well!" Because of my light skin, students have actually attempted to argue with me about my identity as a Chicana. It seems that my identity as a member of a marginalized population makes it difficult for some students to accept me as an individual who possesses a certain degree of expertise and authority. One young woman who had been shopping for classes during the first week of the semester told me, "When I first saw you I thought to myself, 'this is not going to work,' but then I listened to you a while and I realized that you are really smart." It has become clear to me that both my ethnicity and my gender affect, at least initially, many students' perception of me as a credible instructor. I have heard other female colleagues of color make similar observations about their own experience.

Also, I often find it difficult to negotiate my personal commitment to the development of a "critical consciousness" through the use of liberatory pedagogical practices with students' preconceived notions of the credibility of female instructors. That is, a female instructor may still cause students a certain degree of conscious and unconscious cultural dissonance. According to Culley, Diamond, Edwards, Lennox, and Portuges, "In our culture, the role of nurturer and intellectual have been separated not just by gender, but by function: to try and recombine them is to create confusion" (1985, 13). Many students have told me that they do not have male teachers who care as much as women professors. It appears that some students have developed certain role expectations for male and female instructors. When these role expectations are violated, students often become angry. I have seen evidence of this in their reactions when I refuse to accept late papers, change their grades, or excuse them from class without a written excuse. I have asked them "Would you feel comfortable giving Dr. C. [a respected male professor known for his gruff manner] the same excuse?" Usually, when this question is posed, they are silent.

Also, due to these socio-cultural role expectations, students may often mistake or misread an approachable style as intimacy cues. This was the case with Gail, a student in my fall 1999 intercultural class, who had interpreted my approachable style as a license to not complete course assignments (she had joined the class after the second week and had not witnessed my earlier performance of authority). Gail was surprised to discover that I would not take her late work or excuse her from attending class without a written excuse. She said, "But you are so nice—like a friend." Students also often feel comfortable touching me or telling me highly personal details of their life. It has not been uncommon for younger students (17–21) in my lower-division classes who find themselves doing poorly to comment, "But you always are so nice to me. I did not know that I was doing so badly." For this reason, I tell the students throughout the course of the semester to remember not to "mistake my smile for a lack of fortitude." I must learn to negotiate the dialectic of approachability and the credible communication behaviors necessary to enforce standards; my work in this regard is what this chapter attempts to record.

Post-Structuralist Feminist Pedagogy

The critical thinking skills introduced early in the semester in all the courses I teach serve as a springboard for respectful and critically engaged classroom interaction. However, in a course in intercultural communication, the overarching goal of the semester is to help students deal more critically and realistically with gender, racial, ethnic, and socio-economic differences. Students are asked to come to terms with the limits of knowledge and the process of communication itself. Eventually they are asked to begin to deconstruct their notions of democracy, dialogue, and the assumption that rationalized, individual subjects are capable of agreeing on universalizable "fundamental moral principles" that lie at the foundation of much liberatory pedagogical practice (Ellsworth 1992, 108). The power differences and socio-political positionalities of the members of the class itself require a more complex understanding of cross-cultural communication. Even among a highly homogenized class, the notion that we can agree on a singular notion of truth through structured dialogue is highly problematic. In this light, communication across cultures can often be seen as more of a process of information-sharing than dialogue. Here I turn to a fundamental principle of another kind of liberatory pedagogy: post-structural feminist pedagogy.

Post-structural feminist pedagogy refuses to accept what many critical pedagogical theories propagate. That is, it rejects the Enlightenment notion that through rational discourse students' voices and their differences can become united both in their efforts to identify systems of oppression and in their efforts to transform them (Ellsworth 1992). In other words, it is the acceptance that all knowledge is partial, open-ended, and relational. Carmen Luke and Jennifer Gore describe this approach as an "indeterminacy that lies in its rejection of certainty promised by modernist discourse, a rejection of self-certain and singular subject, and a rejection of knowledges that promise answers which lead to closure" (1992, 7). However, it takes time and sensitivity to grasp these concepts.

Post-structural feminist pedagogy also opens up the opportunity for discussion of the inequalities that exist among the members of the class. We began an examination of how power differences are manifested in classroom interaction. Questions such as Who speaks more? And How do we consciously or unconsciously silence each other across our differences? I ask all students to do a personal inventory about how they take up or do not take up communicative space. I then place the students in groups. This is done in order not to publicly embarrass or put students on the spot. In the fall 1999 Intercultural Communication class, the exercise resulted in a meeting in my office with three female students, two White women and one Latina. They had come to tell me that the exercise had sparked an ongoing discussion about the topic among many members of the class. To me this was a hopeful sign. In a fifteen-week class, I do not think it is always possible to reverse decades of social and cultural conditioning, but I do believe that the questions the class engenders can lead to positive change over time.

About three weeks into the Intercultural Communication course, I introduce Stella Ting-Toomey's (1999) theory of mindfulness (e.g., the understanding that all knowledge is partial). I encourage students to "understand that the world is larger than their experience of it." This statement becomes a mantra that I and the students use throughout the semester. In the four years that I have been teaching this particular course, it is this fundamental concept that is the most difficult for my students to grasp when they deal with others who are different than themselves. In a highly individualist culture such as ours, it is not surprising that students have been encouraged to use themselves as the ultimate yardstick against which they measure others. If they "have not seen it" or if an issue "does not bother" them, it is often hard for them to accept that others see things differently.

Although I had always used these concepts in my classroom, in the fall 1999 course, for the first time, I was able to locate a textbook that reflected this approach. This may explain why I did not get the degree of resistance I have normally received when I have introduced this topic. The textbook may have served as a form of authority that I was not able to represent solely through lectures in other Intercultural Communication classes. In other words, it may have given legitimacy to my arguments. In the fall 1999 semester, I also noticed less resistance to the possibility that much of the mediated information we receive may be compromised by the fact that ownership of our media lies in the hands of only a few powerful corporations. Here too, for the first time I used an outside authority to support this issue. I introduced the topic by showing a video (*Crisis of the Cultural Environment: Media Democracy in the 21st Century*, distributed by Media Educational Forum) featuring George Gerber (an older White male) that provided a great deal of evidence for this position. Although it is not possible at this point to know if these teaching tools were significant mediating variables, there was a marked difference between the reaction of this class to these topics and the way these topics had been received previously in other Intercultural Communication courses I have taught. As a woman of color, it may be necessary for me when dealing with classrooms that are predominantly White to use evidence from scholars with whom they can feel a sense of connection. An outside authority may have allowed me to depersonalize this type of dissonant information. These pedagogical tools can serve to diffuse the stereotypes that have emerged from the "culture wars" backlash about "angry" people of color. Stated differently, it may have helped students not to view this information strictly as my personal ax to grind.

Another tenet of critical feminist pedagogical theory that impacts my teaching practice is the notion that difference can and should be reframed and embraced as a "force for creative energy....Only then does the necessity for interdependence become un-threatening" (Lorde 1984, 111). Early in a course in intercultural communication, I ask students to think about a time in their lives when they experienced some sort of intellectual, emotional, or spiritual growth. Inevitably, they will bring up instances that involved a certain degree of pain; for example, a death in the family or a professor who pushed them to achieve. I ask them to consider why real growth is seldom easy and encourage them to question a socialization process that has led many of them to see conflict as ultimately a negative force. I suggest that dealing with people and ideas that are different than their own can force them to develop a clearer understanding of their own beliefs and may lead them to a new understanding of the world. I ask students to reframe the conflicts that may occur in the classroom as an opportunity to learn from people who do not think the same way that they do. This exercise has helped me to diffuse a great deal of hostility and has opened up my ability to play the devil's advocate when discussing highly controversial issues. However, in order to do this, often I must take an analytic or distant approach. It is important for me not to sound as though I am chastising my students. According to Chan, "this analytical distance" allows her to maintain a less accusatory stance. But at the same time, this distance may rob students of color "of an important forum in which to express their confusion, hurt, and anger" (1989, 278).

My greatest challenge in putting this tenet into action in the classroom is encouraging members of minority groups to speak. Often, students of color seem reticent in classroom interaction. Here, I would like to point out that I do not expect students of color to serve as representatives for their culture or co-culture. In fact, some students of color have so strongly assimilated into the dominant culture that they have told me that they feel no attachment to their culture of origin. Nevertheless, I have found that many times students from marginalized populations do not speak because they do not feel comfortable sharing their experience in a predominantly White classroom. It is usually only after having met with students in my office on an individual basis, a mandatory requirement of the course, that students of color begin to open up. During those meetings, I have an opportunity to discuss with each student their impressions of the course. Students of color often tell me that they feel overpowered by the majority opinion or they express anger at what they perceive to be White students' inability to grasp a reality other than their own. One student expressed his frustration this way: "Why should I put my self out there? They do not get it. They do not want to get it. I am one of 150 Black students on this campus. It is not worth it." He chastised me for "trying to teach White students about things they do not want to know." In the fall 1999 course, a Latina asserted that "I am glad they have a place to learn about and come to terms with their own history. But it's their turn to feel angry and upset about it." Although in many cases, silence is a form of resistance, in others it is not. Chan suggests that students of color may be silent in the hope "that silence will spare them ridicule: 'If I do not say anything, maybe they won't notice that I am different'" (1989, 275). However, in courses that foreground social justice issues, "such a silence ultimately serves the racial or sexual status quo" (Spelman 1985, 243).

I take the opportunity to directly address the political consequences of silence in the section of the intercultural course devoted to language. I often ask students to read Audre Lorde's "The Transformation of Silence into Language and Action." This short essay is about silence and its inability to "save you" from social injustice (1984, 40). I ask them to form groups to discuss the essay and give them a list of questions to consider. For example, "When was the last time you did not speak out about an injustice that you believed had been done to you, and what was the outcome of that silence?" It is a powerful exercise. After this discussion, students will frequently repeat Lorde's oft-quoted statement, "Your silence will not save you" in classroom discussions and on their written responses to readings. After this exercise, the young Black male student did offer his opinion from time to time. In the fall 1999 class, two female students, one African American and one Salvadoran American, took the opportunity to speak about their own experiences with racism during a "public-forum" class that I had devoted entirely to students who wanted to share their personal intercultural experiences with the class. It is in the opening of opportunities like these that students are allowed to use "subjective experiences to…become a vocalized, hence tangible, element in the culture" of the classroom (Chan 1989, 276).

Although I have had some success in drawing students of color into the larger classroom discussion, it is an issue with which I continually struggle to find solutions. Like Chan, I believe that courses such as Intercultural Communication must first help non-White students to arrive at a some clarity about their own positionality as members of marginalized populations, and then "they must help White students come to terms with the fact they may unwittingly be what Kenneth Clark has called 'accessories to profound injustice" (1989, 277). Lastly, we must try to make the classroom an arena where these new possibilities for understanding can take place.

One thing is clear, however; only when students feel that they can speak their truth, without fear of serious ramifications from me or other students, can we begin to hear their voices. However, it must be noted that the co-construction of a safe classroom environment does not mean that students (or the instructor) are allowed to ignore their own participation in systems of oppression. This is why critical feminist pedagogy must be about both content and process (Schewsbury 1987). A major component of this process is the ability to understand that classrooms are emotional arenas. While many critical feminist scholars acknowledge and celebrate emotionality in the classroom, I have found very little literature that provides concrete examples of how to use emotionality as a creative force for learning. Here, I turn to theories of emotional intelligence (Goleman 1995).

Dealing with Emotions in the Classroom

Because sexism, racism, and White privilege are emotionally volatile topics, these issues must be presented in a manner designed to increase students' ability to understand and actively engage with the subject matter. This is especially important in classrooms where students are predominantly White and middle class. Both a nonverbal and verbal rhetorical sensitivity must be employed when asking students to confront their own positions of privilege. Linguistic choices are important when determining how to rhetorically frame disturbing concepts. However, it is in the realm of nonverbal communication that emotions are expressed and negotiated (Ting-Toomey 1999). It is in this affective domain that students come face to face with their deepest fears and desires. This is because racism is less a cognitive issue than it is an emotional one. In other words, you cannot simply explain racism or sexism away. Along with theory, there must be a place where both students and teachers can explore and analyze their collective emotional reactions to these issues.[2] Simply stated, these are issues of both the head and the heart. Emotions allow us to "loosen deep-seated, self interested investments in unjust relations" (Ellsworth 1992, 105). I watched myself continually shifting my communicative approach based on a moment-to-moment analysis of both the cognitive and emotional needs of my students. For this reason, as stated earlier, I often adopt an analytical distance to avoid the perception that I am trying to chastise my students. However, although this allows me to defuse students' hostility toward me and/or the arguments presented, this does not mean that my classrooms are devoid of emotionality. Indeed, when the deep-rooted belief systems of students are being challenged, analytical distance on my part does not prevent strong emotional reactions. Analytical distance itself is a way to deal with emotions. Teaching and learning in classrooms such as Intercultural Communication that deal with issues such as sexism, racism, and social injustice must involve pedagogical strategies designed to engage participants as whole people.

In my classroom, I have tried to develop a heightened sense of students' emotional reactions by paying close attention to their facial expressions, body positioning (whether it is tense or relaxed), and tone of voice (natural, sarcastic, quivering, or shrill). In the fall 1999 course, outside the classroom, I carefully analyzed conversations and written assignments to determine the general emotional climate of the class. These instruments also served as means to check my own in-class perceptions.

The development of emotional intelligence is also encouraged by helping students learn strategies for dealing with anger (i.e., identify their emotional response as it begins to emerge) (Adler and Towne 1996). I call this process "taking five steps back," which I have adapted from John Dewey's "reflective thinking agenda" as a means with which to analyze this early response (as cited in Caputo, Hazel, and McMahon 1997). I ask my students to learn to take these steps when they begin to feel angry or upset about some of the language that is employed in articles, films, and class discussions. I ask them to not allow anger to shut down their ability to analyze the main point of the work. First, I ask them to begin to monitor their physical emotional response (i.e., rapid heartbeat, sweaty palms, shaky hands, or a flow of adrenaline) as soon as it begins to happen. Then, I ask them to begin to ask themselves a series of questions about this response: Am I really in physical danger? Do I always respond this way to this particular person or topic and why? What am I really angry about? And finally, what if what the article or individual is saying is true? How would that change my reaction or opinion? Only after carefully analyzing the main argument(s) of the article/work should they make positive or negative judgments. It is important to note, however, that I do not ask them not to feel or get angry at all. Anger is an important emotion; it can serve as an important warning sign that something is wrong (Hochschild 1983). Anger can also provide the emotional impetus for personal transformation and social change (Culley et al. 1985). Anger that can be chanelled positively can become a means to increase knowledge through passion. In the classroom, it is only when anger becomes a default response to oral or written stimuli that may contain trigger words such as "racism," "White privilege," "feminism," "sexism," and "White male privilege," that it becomes a block to understanding the positions of others.

Throughout the fall 1999 semester, in classroom discussions, in written assignments, in conversations with me, and in the midterm evaluations students used the phrase "five steps back." For example, Ann wrote, "You really needed to 'take five steps back' when reading this article...I realized that it was not what George Lipsitz [the article was "The Possessive Investment in Whiteness"(1995)] was saying that made me mad—it was the way in which he was saying it." This sentiment was expressed several times in class. In this way, students were encouraged to go beyond the rhetorical choices of the author or film in order to uncover the fundamental message. To many students' surprise, they often found themselves in agreement with the points the works made despite their initial default reactions to it.

I took a great deal of time preparing the class for a bell hooks's video on media representation. In the video hooks uses the term "White male supremacist capitalistic patriarchy" to explain a system of hegemony that popular culture promotes. I was nervous about showing the video to the class because of the confrontational language it contained. Indeed, it would have been much easier not to show it. I would not have risked the negative reactions of the students. I decided that the answer was not about the concept itself; the challenge was in how to frame it in a way that would allow students to remain open to its message. After the video, James, a White male, said, "When you first started talking about the video, I thought—great, another angry Black woman. But, when I took the 'five steps back,' I realized that she is really being fair." Sabrina, a White female, said, "I do not think I would have gotten past the first five minutes of this video without getting mad. But, I was able to stay open. I think she could have been less in our faces, but I understand her points." This opened a space to help the class deconstruct their stereotypes about Black women in general. The ideas in this video became key concepts that students themselves applied throughout the course.

When I talked about this project with three other colleagues who are also women of color teaching related material in predominantly White universities, I found myself involved in very heated debates. I was accused of emotionally coddling students and of not being willing to tell them the "truth" as it "really was." One colleague and friend said, "You must say what it is. You cannot sugarcoat this. They need to hear it in these terms." While I strongly agree that students should be informed about the stark reality of past and present social injustice, this information will do nothing to change the state of race or gender relations if the students reject the message before they can allow themselves to begin to understand or engage with the arguments these theorists offer. They may *hear* the information, but they will not *listen.* To insist that students should be confronted with this information without taking into consideration the source of much of their resistance is unrealistic.

However, the level of burnout of many of my colleagues who have taught these courses for years can be severe. Teaching courses that ask students to risk stepping out of their own belief systems often meets with extreme anger and resistance. Embedded in this resistance are the unconscious stereotypes that some students hold of both women and minorities that continuously places our legitimacy as instructors in question. The sense of anger and frustration that I myself have often experienced has stymied my creative energy. When this has happened, my anger has become a form of internalized oppression. Antonia Darder contends that critical educators can "fall prey to fatalism—a condition that negates passion and destroys the possibility to dream—making them each day more vulnerable and less able to face the challenges before them" (1997, 27). Liberatory pedagogical practice, then, can be a form of liberation for students and teachers. It has allowed me to transcend "limitations in order to discover that beyond these situations, and in contradiction to them, lie *untested feasibilities* for personal, institutional, and socio-economic restructuring" (Darder 1997, 21). Ultimately, liberatory pedagogy holds the possibility of the liberation of self and freedom from internalized oppression for all who practice it. However, this can only be possible if students and teachers remain open to the other's positionality. It must become a transactional process of discovery. In other words, we must also be prepared to take our own "five steps back."

Many of my students come from socio-economic environments that insulated them from contact with many of the realities of social injustice. They are often very emotionally disturbed to discover the reality of systemic racism that had been invisible to them and their position of privilege as White individuals. In the fall of 1999, this was evidenced by three students who told me outside of the classroom that they had experienced anger and resistance from their families, friends, and romantic partners when discussing the content of the course with them. Dionne said, "My boyfriend really thinks that you are brainwashing us. He told me that I will get back to normal when this semester ends. I told him he was wrong." She asked me if her boyfriend could sit in during the next class so that she "could prove to him" that I was not "evil." In previous semesters, students have expressed similar experiences. For example, a young White male from the deep South, after spending a week with his family, spent over an hour in my office expressing his conflicting emotions. He feared that his family and friends would begin to distance themselves from him, and he was concerned about his growing feelings of disgust toward them. He, too, used the word "brainwashing" to describe the language his family used in their reaction to the course and his changing perspective.

In the fall of 1999, I decided to bring this issue to the entire class. I asked students if they were experiencing difficulty when trying to discuss the class and its content with friends and family. The response was overwhelming. I began to list the labels that were being ascribed to the students' new understanding of the world. Some of the terms I listed were communist, feminist, racist, traitor, gullible, and pawn. I allowed them to talk through their experiences. Many were afraid that they could no longer continue to be friends with many individuals in their social circle. I told them that it was not going to be easy to carry this knowledge and that I did not have any easy answers. I shared my own experiences dealing with racist friends and family. Indeed, there are no simple solutions in these circumstances. In essence, this course asks them to confront their deeply embedded beliefs about equality and democratic practice in the United States. I must recognize that I am asking them to take a tremendous risk. They have a great deal to lose as well as a great deal to gain from this knowledge.

No one is willing to have their fundamental belief system pulled out from under them without some degree of resistance. When dealing with these sorts of issues, instructors of privileged students must attempt to analyze the source of this resistance and use this knowledge to reframe the material in a way that will not cause high degrees of defensiveness. At the same time, instructors must remain sensitive to the levels of personal, social, and moral anxiety that this knowledge may cause students, particularly those who come from conservative political or religious backgrounds. I am continually humbled by the courage many students exhibit in their willingness to confront these issues by recognizing their own conscious and unconscious participation in structures of oppression.

I have also been challenged by students who, for whatever reason, and despite my best efforts to reach them, refuse to critically engage with the concepts of the course. Here it is important to note that disagreement with these concepts is a form of critical engagement; however, dismissing them without first attempting to understand them is not. Although I do not condone disruptive classroom behavior, hostility can and often does leak through (i.e., absences, poor work, and mean-spirited comments on reaction papers). Because of the emotional costs of dealing with these students, it is important that they do not become the focus of my efforts to reach the rest of the students. However, requesting a face-to-face meeting with these students can help.

I am a teacher who is strongly committed to social action and transformation. I do not shield my students from the harsh realities of racism, sexism, or hatred. But I do attempt to understand and respect my students' positionalities. One way that this can be demonstrated is to rhetorically frame social justice issues in a way that will allow them the ability to maintain a sense of self-esteem and develop an openness to understanding the lived reality of people who are different than themselves.

Conclusion

This autoethnographic essay focused on my experiences teaching an upper-division course in intercultural communication. I was able to use this work as a mechanism to carefully record and analyze how my six years of teaching enabled and constrained my ability to co-construct a liberatory educational classroom environment in the fall of 1999. What has emerged from this experience is a clearer understanding that many students enter the college classroom with stereotypes about certain gender and ethnic roles and notions of legitimate teaching styles (which are often in direct opposition to the tenets of liberatory and critical feminist pedagogical practice). However, these preconceptions can be mitigated through a presentation of both authority and approachability and through the ability to make appropriate linguistic choices. In my classroom, I was able to shift my communicative approach based on a moment-to-moment analysis of class attitudes and needs and the use of rhetorically sensitive language. It must be noted here that my presentation of authority and my verbal-rhetorical approach were designed to touch middle-class sensibilities. When I teach at colleges where the students are largely members of socio-culturally marginalized groups, I make different linguistic and performative choices.

I had experienced a great deal more resistance to the content of this course from White students in previous intercultural courses. In the past, although the experience was highly rewarding, I often found myself emotionally and intellectually exhausted from classroom interaction. Students often associated disturbing or culturally dissonant information with me as a person. Stated differently, they often attempted to "shoot the messenger" rather than deal directly with difficult information. They also had some difficulty interacting in a classroom where many of their notions of teacher credibility and legitimacy were being challenged. Although much of this resistance dissipated later in the course, I found the courses to be draining. As a result, I have often found myself walking into classrooms emotionally armed to deal with high levels of student resistance. In the fall of 1999, this did not happen. Students did exhibit some resistance to the content of the course but not at the levels I had previously experienced.

There are a number of reasons that this may be true. First, I have more teaching experience at upper-division levels, which allowed me to improve my ability to teach this course. For example, in the fall of 1999, I spent an entire week early in the semester setting the framework for critical analysis and mindful communication. This allowed students to identify flaws in agreements and to develop critical thinking skills. Most important, they were able to move on to develop a sense of the partiality of knowledge and truth. Second, this class was much smaller than other classes I have taught. This allowed me to establish closer relationships with students both in and outside the classroom. I was able to build a personal bond with each student very early in the semester. This increased the level of trust between us and may have helped to mitigate potential conscious or unconscious hostility that we may have directed at one another. Also, I was able to spend more time providing personalized written responses. The smaller classroom (twenty-five versus thirty-five students) allowed me more opportunities to experiment with different pedagogical strategies. For example, it allowed me to give my students more space for group discussion. Several students said that group work helped them to bond with their classmates. Personal relationships between students may reduce the tendency to feel threatened or verbally attack one another. Third, it was the most ethnically diverse classroom I had ever had. Although only one-third of the class was non-White, it may have helped students to understand the position of disenfranchised populations by allowing them to directly interact with these students, particularly during group discussions. Fourth, for the first time I used material (a textbook and videos) that served as a way for me to depersonalize dissonant information. Finally, I have physically aged over the six years that I have been teaching. As an older instructor, my age may also add to my credibility.

From a more general perspective, my light skin and the middle-class mode of communicating (which includes a particular style of dress) that I have developed also may make me less threatening to my students. Several of my colleagues have noted that this has given me an advantage in dealing with privileged White students. I know that my years growing up in a predominantly White neighborhood and working in a traditional corporate environment for nearly half of my life have affected both my language and my physical presentation. However, it is equally true that these adjustments have on occasion also made me less approachable to working-class students of color. What serves as a privilege in one context may make you suspect in another.

Adjunct faculty who choose to use liberatory pedagogical theory and practice do so at a greater risk than tenured or tenure-track faculty. First, the amount of preparation time that is necessary is tremendous. The salaries adjuncts receive for this extra effort does not compensate for the time and energy that is required for establishing, and teaching in, liberatory spaces. Also, my contract is negotiated from year to year (and in some institutions where I have taught the contract is from semester to semester). At the present time, I have no claim to permanent full-time employment or benefits outside the bounds of an annual contract. Adjuncts must also negotiate their need for employment (which is often based primarily on teaching evaluations from students) and their ethical commitment to offer more than just a surface exploration of issues such as sexism and racism, which may elicit negative responses from some students. For many of my colleagues who work in departments that are less supportive than mine, this reality can serve to stymie creativity. For example, when experimenting with new pedagogical strategies, you may often need more than just one semester to develop and refine them. However, if early on the method is met with a great deal of negativity from students, adjuncts may choose to abandon this course of action for a safer or more traditional mode of pedagogy. It is a tightrope that all adjunct professors continually must walk.

Instructors who are committed to the practice of liberatory and feminist pedagogy must also constantly interrogate the appropriateness of this model. Insisting on the use of only one pedagogical strategy that may be based on a misguided sense of idealism will do little to encourage students to learn to analyze, critique, or change existing systems of injustice that impede cross-cultural communication. Indeed, there may be times when a more authoritarian model of learning may be more appropriate.

One instance may be classrooms of over fifty students; in such classrooms it may be difficult or impossible to build the levels of trust necessary for the practice of critical pedagogy. In this circumstance, it would be unrealistic to believe that students would have the time necessary to "name their world" on a personal level. Generally speaking, large classrooms are not conducive to the creation of the safe spaces that are necessary to encourage full student participation. However, asking professors to teach courses that foreground issues such as race, class, or gender with forty or more students may indicate a lack of commitment on the part of administrators to the goals of the course.

When these courses are to be used primarily as a means for the administration and students to check off diversity requirements, a great harm is being done to all the parties involved. One result of this attitude is increased burnout and frustration on the part of instructors who are deeply committed to teaching excellence and who sincerely believe, as I do, that these courses have the potential to improve the quality of the lives of their students and their communities. Students have often told me that they have walked away from similar courses feeling even more confused, angry, and helpless to change structures of oppression. Ultimately, a quality education in these subjects can only occur if the institution has the means and the administrative will to support it.

Finally, women of color who are strongly committed to the practice of liberatory pedagogy may be challenged in ways that our White male and female colleagues are not. However, one way that these challenges can be effectively overcome is by a willingness to confront our own biases and stereotypes about White students that may or may not be based on personal and/or classroom experiences. We cannot ethically ask our students to confront what we ourselves are unwilling to confront. Indeed, no two classrooms are ever exactly the same. Each classroom must be seen as a unique opportunity for learning. We must learn from previous experience—but we cannot allow either positive or negative experiences to reduce our ability to remain open and flexible.

Fredi Avalos-C'deBaca has been teaching full-time since 1994. Currently, she is a lecturer at California State University, San Marcos, where she teaches lower- and upper-division courses including Media and Society, Intercultural Communication, Interpersonal Communication, and Theories of Oral Communication. She is currently completing her Ph.D. in cultural studies at Claremont Graduate University in Los Angeles, California. She has a master's degree in communication from San Diego State University and a B.A. in speech communication from the same university. Her teaching and research focus on issues of culture, communication, and organizational development. She has also done extensive research on the Zapatista National Liberation Army's use of new media as a means for political, cultural, and social emancipation.

Notes

1. All student names have been changed. It is important to note that I provided an opportunity for current and former students to respond to an early draft of this essay. Although over fifteen students picked up copies of the draft, only one student gave me feedback.

2. I am not suggesting that classroom discussion be turned into a form of academic therapy. Instructors must carefully balance classroom discussion so that personal experience is tied to the theories under review. A fundamental tenet of liberatory and feminist pedagogy is that personal experience is the place where theory becomes relevant. The ability to communicate both empathy and the "authority" necessary to keep the discussion on point is important.

Works Cited

Adler, R. B., and N. Towne. 1996. *Looking Out Looking In.* 8th ed. Fort Worth, TX: Harcourt Brace College Publishers.

Caputo, J. S., H. C. Hazel, and C. McMahon. 1997. *Interpersonal Communication: Using Reason to Make Relationships Work.* Dubuque, IA: Kendall/Hunt Publishing.

Chan, S. 1989. "On the Ethnic Studies Requirement: Part One: Pedagogical Implications." *Amerasian* 15: 267–280.

Combahee River Collective. 1983. "A Black Feminist Statement." In *This Bridge Called My Back: Writing by Radical Women of Color,* edited by C. Moraga and G. Anzaldua. New York: Kitchen Table: Women of Color Press.

Culley, M. 1985. "Anger and Authority in the Introductory Women's Study Classroom." In *Gendered Subjects: The Dynamics of Feminist Teaching,* edited by M. Culley and C. Portgues. Boston: Routledge and Kegan Paul.

Culley, M., A. Diamond, L. Edwards, S. Lennox, and C. Portuges. 1985. "The Politics of Nurturance." In *Gendered Subjects: The Dynamics of FeministTeaching,* edited by M. Culley and C. Portuges. Boston: Routledge & Kegan Paul.

Darder, A. 1997. "Teaching as an Act of Love: Reflections on Paulo Friere and his Contributions to Our Lives and to Our Work." In *Reclaiming Our Voice: Emancipatory Narratives on Critical Literacy, Praxis, and Pedagogy,* edited by J. Frederickson. Los Angeles, CA: Association for Bi-lingual Education.

Davis, B. H. 1985. "Teaching the Feminist Minority." In *Gendered Subjects: The Dynamics of Feminist Teaching,* edited by M. Culley and C. Portgues. Boston: Routledge & Kegan Paul.

Ellsworth, E. 1992. "Why Doesn't This Feel Empowering?: Working Through the Repressive Myths of Critical Pedagogy." In *Feminisms and Critical Pedagogy,* edited by C. Luke and J. Gore. New York: Routledge.

Freire, P. 1997. *Pedagogy of the Oppressed.* New York: Continuum.

Goleman, D. 1995. *Emotional Intelligence: Why It Can Matter More Than IQ.* New York: Bantam Books.

Hochschild, A. R. 1983. *The Managed Heart: Commercialization of Human Feeling.* Berkeley, CA: University of California Press.

Hogelucht, K. S., and P. Geist. 1997. "Discipline in the Classroom: Communication Strategies for Negotiating Order." *Western Journal of Communication* 61: 1–34.

Lather, P. 1992. "Post-critical Pedagogies: A Feminist Reading." In *Feminisms and Critical Pedagogy*, edited by C. Luke and J. Gore. New York: Routledge.

Lipsitz, G. 1995. "The Possessive Investment in Whiteness: A Radicalized Social Democracy and the 'White' Problem in American Studies." *American Quarterly* 47: 369–380.

Lorde, A. 1984. *Sister Outsider: Essays and Speeches*. Trumansburg, NY: Crossing Press.

Luke, C., and J. Gore. 1992. "Introduction." In *Feminisms and Critical Pedagogy*, edited by C. Luke and J. Gore. New York: Routledge.

Lusted, D. 1992. "Why Pedagogy?" *Screen* 27: 2–14.

Maher, F. A. 1987. "Toward a Richer Theory of Feminist Pedagogy: A Comparison of 'Liberation" and 'Gender' Models for Teaching and Learning." *Journal of Education* 167 (3): 91–100.

Richmond, V. P., and J. C. McCroskey. 1995. *Nonverbal Behavior in Interpersonal Relations*. Boston, Allyn & Bacon.

Schewsbury, C. M. 1987. "What Is Feminist Pedagogy?" *Women's Studies Quarterly* 15 (3 & 4): 6–14.

Schilb, J. 1985. "Pedagogy of the Oppressors?" In *Gendered Subjects: The Dynamics of Feminist Teaching*, edited by M. Culley and C. Portuges. Boston: Routlege & Kegan Paul.

Spelman, E. V. 1985. "Combating the Marginalization of Black Women in the Classroom." In *Gendered Subjects: The Dynamics of Feminist Teaching*, edited by M. Culley and C. Portuges. Boston: Routledge & Kegan Paul.

Ting-Toomey, S. 1999. *Communicating Across Cultures*. New York: Guilford.

CHAPTER NINETEEN

Opening a Dialogue: From a White Student's Perspective

KRISTINA CASTO

OSTENSIBLY, THIS BOOK is about how a group of women of color have succeeded as teachers in the predominantly White university. However, the subtext of the book is about the emotional and spiritual journey that has empowered some women faculty of color to challenge the power structure inherent in the classroom and in academe in general. The problems posed in this work are indicative of how power relations in mainstream society and culture in the United States are also embedded in the ivory tower. The solutions offered are indicative of how powerful a tool pedagogy can be in challenging those power relations.

As a White woman graduate student, an aspiring teacher, and a product of/participant in U.S. culture, I have found working on this book to be an invaluable learning experience. I was the research assistant for this project and, as such, I participated in the process of shaping the anthology. What I learned from this anthology is that teaching at the university level is not just about dealing with students and potential classroom resistance, and it is not just about facing racism and/or sexism in the classroom. It is about dealing with an entire community of colleagues, researchers, and students who are embedded in an institutional bureaucracy that, in many cases, has yet to deal with endemic problems of sexism and racism. What this book has provided me, and provides for its readers, is the insight of sixteen mentors who have lived the experience of the academic community and have succeeded as instructors. Obviously, nothing can replace experience, but aspiring teachers can begin to prepare for, or at least learn some strategies for, dealing with the potential problematics of the classroom. Furthermore, the different pedagogical practices and philosophies presented in this book provide an excellent

overview of strategies for those of us who view teaching and learning as a political practice and thus a potentially liberating experience.

While this book has been written for the benefit of women of color, I
have found in discussions with my graduate cohorts (both White women and
women of color) and from my experience as a graduate student and teaching
assistant that these pedagogical strategies and classroom management skills
can be helpful for White women and women of color alike. Witnessing the
intense struggle that many of the contributors to the anthology went through
in articulating their classroom experiences has made me more sensitive to the
intense emotionality and vulnerability that comes with the teaching experience, particularly to those who are perceived as Other. I have seen this same
struggle on a daily level at my institution. I have found that the problems,
strategies, and solutions presented in this book have opened the door for a
new dialogue among my colleagues and myself. Being a part of this work has
made me more aware of the necessity of building the support networks that
sustain so many teachers, and it has opened up a space for me to gather, and
give, support.

What emerged from my readings of the manuscripts is that Other teachers are not necessarily bounded by race or gender, they are bounded by a social and political system that positions them as something other than the
norm in U.S. society. Because of their position as Others these professors
have been forced to view teaching and learning as a personal endeavor that
bleeds into the social and political. Their understanding of how knowledge is
learned and internalized is concomitant with their understanding of how they
have been constructed by others. This means that each author has been
forced to deal with a dominant set of shared cultural assumptions, or constructions, that must be negotiated, accepted, or broken down in the classroom.

Depending on her particular life philosophy, her specific background, and
her personal pedagogy, each contributor has found strategies of negotiating,
accepting, or rejecting the cultural constructs of race and ethnicity that is su-
perimposed on her. Ultimately, as seen in this work, teachers who practice
liberatory pedagogy must find a balance between professorial authority and
the personal, equitable engagement that is such an integral part of the
teaching-learning experience. Some contributors have found that in some
cases negotiation over and/or acceptance of certain constructs have been
helpful in the classroom, particularly when their ethnic or racial identity is
perceived to give them authority over the topic of certain courses. Another
form of the acceptance of cultural constructs is the practice of acknowledging
that their identity, for one reason or another, makes them more accessible to

students, who regard them as mentors or mother figures. While potentially emotionally taxing, this accessibility can lead to a dialogue that is ultimately beneficial to the professor who is invested in liberatory pedagogy. In the anthology's essays we can see how some professors have appropriated the mentor, or "mother," identity while maintaining a certain amount of authority that is necessary in the classroom.

At the same time, many of the essays describe strategies for rejecting, or breaking down, the identity constructs that undermine the teaching-learning process and the authority of the professor. What is particularly well illustrated is how the teacher's deeply personal rejection of social assumptions can create havoc in the classroom, a space where the dominant societal assumptions of race, class, gender, and ethnicity are defined and instilled in many students. Asking some students to question a set of dominant societal assumptions can be an emotionally harrowing task. The sixteen mentors who have contributed to this book all have invaluable advice on toeing the line between critical learning and alienation that forms the borders of societal assumptions.

Despite the emotional turmoil that comes from dealing with embedded racism and the reconstruction of civility and dialogue in the classroom, each professor reiterates the ultimately fulfilling nature of teaching. It is this positive, but realistic, tone that has made the book an inspiration to me and will hopefully inspire others to pursue a career in teaching.

Kristina Casto is a second year master's student at the University of North Carolina at Chapel Hill. She is a recipient of the Park Fellowship at the School of Journalism and Mass Communication. Her areas of research and interest include the portrayal of juvenile delinquents and juvenile killers in the popular press and globalization and the media.

INDEX